Fourth Edition

FOCUS ON PSYCHOLOGY

A Guide to Mastering

PETER GRAY'S PSYCHOLOGY

Mary Trahan

Worth Publishers

Focus on Psychology

A Guide to Mastering Peter Gray's **Psychology**, Fourth Edition
by Mary Trahan

Copyright © 2002, 1999, 1994, 1991 by Worth Publishers, Inc.

Printed in the United States of America

ISBN: 0-7167-5163-1

Printing: 2   3   4   5
Year: 05   04   03

Worth Publishers
41 Madison Avenue
New York, NY 10010
www.worthpublishers.com

FOCUS ON PSYCHOLOGY

Contents

To the Student

Why This Guide Is Written As It Is

I have written this guide to help you master Peter Gray's *Psychology*. The guide is interactive—like a tutorial or like my own style of classroom teaching. I write something, and you write something back; often our back-and-forth writing amounts to a brief conversation about the ideas presented in Peter Gray's textbook. The guide is intended to do more than develop a knowledge base in your mind. It is my hope that you will not only only come to understand psychology better but will gain a deeper understanding of what it *means* to understand, and will see better how to achieve understanding in your other studies. Additionally, I hope you will develop an increased confidence in your own ability to think and to learn.

This study guide puts into practice some of the principles psychologists have discovered through investigations of learning and memory, namely, the importance of organization and elaboration. Organization repeatedly has been shown to facilitate the learning, retention, and use of information. It is not only the organization of the information on the page, but the organization of the information in the mind that matters. The former merely facilitates the latter. I have tried to produce a study guide that helps you to organize what you are putting into your memory. Elaboration involves *doing* something active and meaningful with the material you read, not just transferring it passively from the textbook page to your mind to the study guide page. We are engaging in elaboration when we draw parallels, summarize, produce examples, criticize, compare, ponder analogies, and apply general concepts to specific cases. Elaboration, in short, involves thinking. And thinking is not only the most effective way to learn, it is also the most interesting!

How to Use This Guide

This guide is not intended to be a supplement to your study of the textbook; nor is it simply a means of checking your understanding after you have finished studying. It is designed to be your guide in studying the text. Each chapter of the study guide has the following features:

1. An **introductory summary** gives you an overview or "map" of the chapter in the textbook and an initial acquaintance with some of its major ideas before you begin to read the chapter.

2. **Italicized instructions** advise you on how to proceed at each step in the study process—letting you know, for example, when to read the chapter thoroughly and when to skim it, when to go on to the next section and when to review first.

3. The **Integrated Study Workout** is the heart of the study guide. Divided into sections according to the major topics of the text chapter, the Workout contains a variety of questions as well as brief passages that help to put the questions in context. Often hints are provided that direct you to examine a relevant table or graph. The questions help you to identify what is most important in the textbook, to break sections down into manageable parts, and to probe the material for critical ideas.

    Preceding the Workout is a table that shows which study guide questions are related to each of the Focus Questions in the text. The Focus Questions are designed to help you concentrate on the purpose of each segment of the text. If your instructor has recommended that your exam preparation include or center on specified Focus Questions, the corresponding study guide material would make a particularly effective review.

4. Two **Self-Tests** will help you to assess your understanding. Each Self-Test contains fifteen multiple-choice questions and two essay questions.

5. **Answers** are provided for selected items from The Integrated Study Workout, generally those items that are objective or have very short answers. Answers for all multiple-choice questions, many accompanied by explanatory comments, and model answers to essay questions are also included, along with textbook page references.

Because of the organization of each study guide chapter and the instructions that guide you through them, I need say little more about how to use this study guide. However, I do wish to make two recommendations: One is that you read and implement the following section by the psychologist Richard O. Straub on organizing your time and studying more effectively. The second is that you avoid an all-or-none attitude in your studying. I hope you will make the time to complete each chapter of this guide, because doing so will maximize your learning. But please do not feel that you must answer every single question to make its use worthwhile. Doing three-fourths of the questions is better than doing none. Further, do not feel that you must write out all of your answers in complete sentences. The correct few words will usually help you most. Make sure your answers are clear, organized, and complete enough to be valuable to *you*. After all, this is your guide—only you will read it.

I wish you success in your studies and encourage you to write to me if you have any comments or suggestions.

Acknowledgments

Many thanks to Peter Gray for writing such a wonderful text and for somehow managing to improve it to a remarkable extent on each successive revision. It is a textbook that is truly worth studying, an exceptional accomplishment. I feel fortunate indeed that my chance to "teach on paper" came with Peter Gray's book. I also owe a debt of gratitude to all the staff at Worth Publishers, who have helped me to shape this study guide from its inception. Worth is a remarkable publisher, with an uncommon commitment to excellence and innovation. On this fourth edition, I particularly wish to thank Graig Donini, Eve Moeller, Stacey Alexander, and Betty Probert for their fine work and support.

To my colleagues and students over the years, who have taught me about psychology and about teaching, thanks. I am indebted to my teachers at Loyola University in New Orleans, where I began my study of psychology; to faculty and students at the University of Michigan, where, as a graduate student, I developed a love for psychology and a devotion to teaching; and especially to many students and colleagues at Randolph-Macon College for the rich variety of teaching experiences afforded me.

As always thanks to my friends. I know how blessed I am to have them.

How to Manage Your Time Efficiently and Study More Effectively

by Richard O. Straub

How effectively do you study? Good study habits make the job of being a college student much easier. Many students, who *could* succeed in college, fail or drop out because they have never learned to manage their time efficiently. Even the best students can usually benefit from an in-depth evaluation of their current study habits.

There are many ways to achieve academic success, of course, but your approach may not be the most effective or efficient. Are you sacrificing your social life or your physical or mental health in order to get A's on your exams? Good study habits result in better grades *and* more time for other activities.

Evaluate Your Current Study Habits

To improve your study habits, you must first have an accurate picture of how you currently spend your time. Begin by putting together a profile of your present living and studying habits. Answer the following questions by writing *yes* or *no* on each line.

_____ 1. Do you usually set up a schedule to budget your time for studying, recreation, and other activities?

_____ 2. Do you often put off studying until time pressures force you to cram?

_____ 3. Do other students seem to study less than you do, but get better grades?

_____ 4. Do you usually spend hours at a time studying one subject, rather than dividing that time between several subjects?

_____ 5. Do you often have trouble remembering what you have just read in a textbook?

_____ 6. Before reading a chapter in a textbook, do you skim through it and read the section headings?

_____ 7. Do you try to predict exam questions from your lecture notes and reading?

_____ 8. Do you usually attempt to paraphrase or summarize what you have just finished reading?

_____ 9. Do you find it difficult to concentrate very long when you study?

_____ 10. Do you often feel that you studied the wrong material for an exam?

Thousands of college students have participated in similar surveys. Students who are fully realizing their academic potential usually respond as follows: (1) yes, (2) no, (3) no, (4) no, (5) no, (6) yes, (7) yes, (8) yes, (9) no, (10) no.

Compare your responses to those of successful students. The greater the discrepancy, the more you could benefit from a program to improve your study habits. The questions are designed to identify areas of weakness. Once you have identified your weaknesses, you will be able to set specific goals for improvement and to implement a program for reaching them.

Manage Your Time

Do you often feel frustrated because there isn't enough time to do all the things you must and want to do? Take heart. Even the most productive and successful people feel this way at times. But they establish priorities for their activities, and they learn to budget time for each of them. There's much in the saying "If you want something done, ask a busy person to do it." A busy person knows how to get things done.

If you don't now have a system for budgeting your time, develop one. Not only will your academic accomplishments increase, but you will actually find more time in your schedule for other activities. And you won't have to feel guilty about "taking time off," because all your obligations will be covered.

Establish a Baseline

As a first step in preparing to budget your time, keep a diary for a few days to establish a summary, or baseline, of the time you spend in studying, socializing, working, and so on. If you are like many students, much of your "study" time is nonproductive; you may sit at your desk and leaf through a book, but the time is actually wasted. Or you may procrastinate. You are always getting ready to study, but you rarely do.

Besides revealing where you waste time, your diary will give you a realistic picture of how much time you need to allot for meals, commuting, and other fixed activities. In addition, careful records should indicate the times of the day when you are consistently most productive. A sample time-management diary is shown in Table 1.

Plan the Term

Having established and evaluated your baseline, you are ready to devise a more efficient schedule. Buy a calendar that covers the entire school term and has ample space for each day. Using the course outlines provided by your instructors, enter the dates of all exams, term paper deadlines, and other important academic obligations. If you have any long-range personal plans (concerts, weekend trips, etc.), enter the dates on the calendar as well. Keep your calendar up to date and refer to it often. I recommend carrying it with you at all times.

Develop a Weekly Calendar

Now that you have a general picture of the school term, develop a weekly schedule that includes all of your activities. Aim for a schedule that you can live with for the entire school term. A sample weekly schedule, incorporating the following guidelines, is shown in Table 2.

1. Enter your class times, work hours, and any other fixed obligations first. *Be thorough.* Using information from your time-management diary, allow plenty of time for such things as commuting, meals, laundry, and the like.

Table 1   *Sample Time-Management Diary*

Behavior	Monday Time Completed	Duration Hours: Minutes
Sleep	7:00	7:30
Dressing	7:25	:25
Breakfast	7:45	:20
Commute	8:20	:35
Coffee	9:00	:40
French	10:00	1:00
Socialize	10:15	:15
Video game	10:35	:20
Coffee	11:00	:25
Psychology	12:00	1:00
Lunch	12:25	:25
Study Lab	1:00	:35
Psych. Lab	4:00	3:00
Work	5:30	1:30
Commute	6:10	:40
Dinner	6:45	:35
TV	7:30	:45
Study Psych.	10:00	2:30
Socialize	11:30	1:30
Sleep		

Prepare a similar chart for each day of the week. When you finish an activity, note it on the chart and write down the time it was completed. Then determine its duration by subtracting the time the previous activity was finished from the newly entered time.

2. Set up a study schedule for each of your courses. The study habits survey and your time-management diary will help direct you. The following guidelines should also be useful.

(a) Establish regular study times for each course. The 4 hours needed to study one subject, for example, are most profitable when divided into shorter periods spaced over several days. If you cram your studying into one 4-hour block, what you attempt to learn in the third or fourth hour will interfere with what you studied in the first 2 hours. Newly acquired knowledge is like wet cement. It needs some time to "harden" to become memory.

(b) Alternate subjects. The type of interference just mentioned is greatest between similar topics. Set up a schedule in which you spend time on several *different* courses during each study session. Besides reducing the potential for interference, alternating subjects will help to prevent mental fatigue with one topic.

(c) Set weekly goals to determine the amount of study time you need to do well in each course. This will depend on, among other things, the difficulty of your courses and the effectiveness of your methods. Many

Table 2   *Sample Weekly Schedule*

Time	Mon.	Tues.	Wed.	Thurs.	Fri.	Sat.
7–8	Dress Eat	Dress Eat	Dress Eat	Dress Eat	Dress Eat	
8–9	Psych.	Study Psych.	Psych.	Study Psych.	Psych.	Dress Eat
9–10	Eng.	Study Eng.	Eng.	Study Eng.	Eng.	Study Eng.
10–11	Study French	Free	Study French	Open Study	Study French	Study Stats.
11–12	French	Study Psych. Lab	French	Open Study	French	Study Stats.
12–1	Lunch	Lunch	Lunch	Lunch	Lunch	Lunch
1–2	Stats.	Psych. Lab	Stats.	Study or Free	Stats.	Free
2–3	Bio.	Psych. Lab	Bio.	Free	Bio.	Free
3–4	Free	Psych.	Free	Free	Free	Free
4–5	Job	Job	Job	Job	Job	Free
5–6	Job	Job	Job	Job	Job	Free
6–7	Dinner	Dinner	Dinner	Dinner	Dinner	Dinner
7–8	Study Bio.	Study Bio.	Study Bio.	Study Bio.	Free	Free
8–9	Study Eng.	Study Stats.	Study Psych.	Open Study	Open Study	Free
9–10	Open Study	Open Study	Open Study	Open Study	Free	Free

This is a sample schedule for a student with a 16-credit load and a 10-hour-per-week part-time job. Using this chart as an illustration, make up a weekly schedule, following the guidelines outlined here.

professors recommend studying at least 1 to 2 hours for each hour in class. If your time-management diary indicates that you presently study less time than that, do not plan to jump immediately to a much higher level. Increase study time from your baseline by setting weekly goals [see (4)] that will gradually bring you up to the desired level. As an initial schedule, for example, you might set aside an amount of study time for each course that matches class time.

(d) Schedule for maximum effectiveness. Tailor your schedule to meet the demands of each course. For the course that emphasizes lecture notes, schedule time for a daily review soon after the class. This will give you a chance to revise your notes and clean up any hard-to-decipher shorthand while the material is still fresh in your mind. If you are evaluated for class participation (for example, in a language course), allow time for a review just *before* the class meets. Schedule study time for your most difficult (or least motivating) courses during hours when you are the most alert and distractions are fewest.

(e) Schedule open study time. Emergencies, additional obligations, and the like could throw off your

schedule. And you may simply need some extra time periodically for a project or for review in one of your courses. Schedule several hours each week for such purposes.

3. After you have budgeted time for studying, fill in slots for recreation, hobbies, relaxation, household errands, and the like.

4. Set specific goals. Before each study session, make a list of specific goals. The simple note "7–8 PM: study psychology" is too broad to ensure the most effective use of the time. Formulate your daily goals according to what you know you must accomplish during the term. If you have course outlines with advance assignments, set systematic daily goals that will allow you, for example, to cover fifteen chapters before the exam. And be realistic: Can you actually expect to cover a 78-page chapter in one session? Divide large tasks into smaller units; stop at the most logical resting points. When you complete a specific goal, take a 5- or 10-minute break before tackling the next goal.

5. Evaluate how successful or unsuccessful your studying has been on a daily or weekly basis. Did you reach most of your goals? If so, reward yourself immediately. You might even make a list of five to ten rewards to choose from. If you have trouble studying regularly, you may be able to motivate yourself by making such rewards contingent on completing specific goals.

6. Finally, until you have lived with your schedule for several weeks, don't hesitate to revise it. You may need to allow more time for chemistry, for example, and less for some other course. If you are trying to study regularly for the first time and are feeling burned out, you probably have set your initial goals too high. Don't let failure cause you to despair and abandon the program. Accept your limitations and revise your schedule so that you are studying only 15 to 20 minutes more each evening than you are used to. The point is to *identify a regular schedule with which you can achieve some success.* Time management, like any skill, must be practiced to become effective.

Taking Lecture Notes

Are your class notes as useful as they might be? One way to determine their worth is to compare them with those taken by other good students. Are yours as thorough? Do they provide you with a comprehensible outline of each lecture? If not, then the following suggestions might increase the effectiveness of your notetaking.

1. Keep a separate notebook for each course. Use $8^1/_2 \times 11$-inch pages. Consider using a ring binder, which would allow you to revise and insert notes while still preserving lecture order.

2. Take notes in the format of a lecture outline. Use roman numerals for major points, letters for supporting arguments, and so on. Some instructors will make this easy by delivering organized lectures and, in some cases, by outlining their lectures on the board. If a lecture is disorganized, you will probably want to reorganize your notes soon after the class.

3. As you take notes in class, leave a wide margin on one side of each page. After the lecture, expand or clarify any shorthand notes while the material is fresh in your mind. Use this time to write important questions in the margin next to notes that answer them. This will facilitate later review and will allow you to anticipate similar exam questions.

Evaluate Your Exam Performance

How often have you received a grade on an exam that did not do justice to the effort you spent preparing for the exam? This is a common experience that can leave one feeling bewildered and abused. "What do I have to do to get an A?" "The test was unfair!" "I studied the wrong material!"

The chances of this happening are greatly reduced if you have an effective time-management schedule and use the study techniques described here. But it can happen to the best-prepared student and is most likely to occur on your first exam with a new professor.

Remember that there are two main reasons for studying. One is to learn for your own general academic development. Many people believe that such knowledge is all that really matters. Of course, it is possible, though unlikely, to be an expert on a topic without achieving commensurate grades, just as one can, occasionally, earn an excellent grade without truly mastering the course material. During a job interview or in the workplace, however, your A in Cobol won't mean much if you can't actually program a computer.

In order to keep career options open after you graduate, you must know the material and maintain competitive grades. In the short run, this means performing well on exams, which is the second main objective in studying.

Probably the single best piece of advice to keep in mind when studying for exams is to *try to predict exam questions.* This means ignoring the trivia and focusing on the important questions and their answers (with your instructor's emphasis in mind).

A second point is obvious. How well you do on exams is determined by your mastery of *both* lecture and textbook material. Many students (partly because of poor time management) concentrate too much on one at the expense of the other.

To evaluate how well you are learning lecture and textbook material, analyze the questions you missed on the first exam. If your instructor does not review exams during class, you can easily do it yourself. Divide the questions into two categories: those drawn primarily from lectures and those drawn primarily from the textbook. Determine the percentage of questions you missed in each category. If your errors are evenly distributed and you are satisfied with your grade, you have no problem. If you are weaker in one area, you will need to set future goals for increasing and/or improving your study of that area.

Similarly, note the percentage of test questions drawn from each category. Although exams in most courses cover *both* lecture notes and the textbook, the relative emphasis of each may vary from instructor to instructor. While your instructors may not be entirely consistent in making up future exams, you may be able to tailor your studying for each course by placing *additional* emphasis on the appropriate area.

Exam evaluation will also point out the types of questions your instructor prefers. Does the exam consist primarily of multiple-choice, true–false, or essay questions? You may also discover that an instructor is fond of wording questions in certain ways. For example, an instructor may rely heavily on questions that require you to draw an analogy between a theory or concept and a real-world example. Evaluate both your instructor's style and how well you do with each format. Use this information to guide your future exam preparation.

Important aids, not only in studying for exams but also in determining how well prepared you are, are the *Progress Tests* provided in this Study Guide. If these tests don't include all of the types of questions your instructor typically writes, make up your own practice exam questions. Spend extra time testing yourself with question formats that are most difficult for you. There is no better way to evaluate your preparation for an upcoming exam than by testing yourself under the conditions most likely to be in effect during the actual test.

A Few Practical Tips

Even the best intentions for studying sometimes fail. Some of these failures occur because students attempt to work under conditions that are simply not conducive to concentrated study. To help ensure the success of your time-management program, here are a few suggestions that should assist you in reducing the possibility of procrastination or distraction.

1. If you have set up a schedule for studying, make your roommate, family, and friends aware of this commitment, and ask them to honor your quiet study time. Close your door and post a "Do Not Disturb" sign.

2. Set up a place to study that minimizes potential distractions. Use a desk or table, not your bed or an extremely comfortable chair. Keep your desk and the walls around it free from clutter. If you need a place other than your room, find one that meets as many of the above requirements as possible—for example, in the library stacks.

3. Do nothing but study in this place. It should become associated with studying so that it "triggers" this activity, just as a mouth-watering aroma elicits an appetite.

4. Never study with the television on or with other distracting noises present. If you must have music in the background in order to mask outside noise, for example, play soft instrumental music. Don't pick vocal selections; your mind will be drawn to the lyrics.

5. Study by yourself. Other students can be distracting or can break the pace at which *your* learning is most efficient. In addition, there is always the possibility that group studying will become a social gathering. Reserve that for its own place in your schedule.

If you continue to have difficulty concentrating for very long, try the following suggestions.

6. Study your most difficult or most challenging subjects first, when you are most alert.

7. Start with relatively short periods of concentrated study, with breaks in between. If your attention starts to wander, get up immediately and take a break. It is better to study effectively for 15 minutes and then take a break than to fritter away 45 minutes out of an hour. Gradually increase the length of study periods, using your attention span as an indicator of successful pacing.

Some Closing Thoughts

I hope that these suggestions help make you more successful academically, and that they enhance the quality of your college life in general. Having the necessary skills makes any job a lot easier and more pleasant. Let me repeat my warning not to attempt to make too drastic a change in your life-style immediately. Good habits require time and self-discipline to develop. Once established, they can last a lifetime.

Chapter 1   The History and Scope of Psychology

READ *the introduction below before you read the chapter in the text.*

Psychology is defined as the science of behavior and the mind. Like all sciences, psychology attempts to answer questions through the systematic collection and logical analysis of objective, observable data.

Even before the official beginnings of psychology in the nineteenth century, developments in philosophy and science prepared the way for it. For example, Descartes' dualism, Hobbes's materialism, the thinking of British empiricists in philosophy, and the work of Charles Darwin and of pioneering physiologists helped to lay the groundwork for a science of psychology.

Once psychology was established as an area of scientific inquiry, it was shaped by the influences of several different perspectives. Each perspective has been based on a different notion of what psychology's focus should be, and how relevant questions can best be answered. Each has made a unique contribution.

For example, structuralism, an approach associated with Wilhelm Wundt and Edward Titchener, had the goal of identifying the basic elements, or structures, of the mind. William James was instead interested in the purposes and functions of the mind, which led to his approach being called functionalism. Gestalt psychology proposed that the mind cannot be understood as a collection of elements but must be seen in terms of organized wholes. Behaviorism, which focuses on learning, was founded by John B. Watson. He excluded the mind from study altogether because, unlike behavior, the mind cannot be observed directly. Another highly influential behaviorist was B. F. Skinner. Behaviorists widened the field of psychology's subject matter to include nonhuman behavior, commonly studying rats, pigeons, and other animals, in large part to draw conclusions about humans. Ethologists also studied animal behavior but emphasized animals' unlearned behavior in their natural habitats and regarded this as an end in itself.

Physiological psychologists sought to understand the physiological mechanisms underlying all behavior. Sigmund Freud's psychoanalysis developed around the concept of the unconscious mind and its influence on conscious thought and behavior. Humanistic psychology emphasized conscious awareness of oneself and self-control. It promoted positive self-concepts and self-actualization. In different ways, both cultural psychology and social psychology take account of the importance of the social context in which thought and behavior occur. Cognitive psychology, the dominant approach for the last several decades, explores the acquisition, organization, retrieval, and use of knowledge to guide behavior.

Psychology is an academic discipline related to the natural sciences, social sciences, and humanities. It is also a profession. Professional psychologists may work to add to our knowledge of mind and behavior or to apply that knowledge for practical ends. They are employed in settings that include colleges and universities, elementary and secondary schools, various clinical settings, business, and government.

LOOK *over the table of contents for this chapter in your textbook before you continue with your study.*

Notice that there are focus questions in the margins of the text for your use in studying the material. The following chart lists which Study Guide questions relate to which focus questions.

Focus Questions	Study Guide Questions
Introduction	
1	1–2
Before Psychology: Preparing the Intellectual Ground	
2–4	1–6
5–6	7
7	8

The Integrated Study Workout

Complete one section at a time.

Introduction (pages 1–4)

1. Psychology is the science of
    _____ (observable actions, of a
    person or animal) and _____ (an
    individual's sensations, perceptions, memories,
    motives, emotions, thoughts, and other subjective
    experiences).

2. The author presents these three ways of charac-
    terizing psychology:

    a.

    b.

    c.

Before Psychology: Preparing the Intellectual Ground   (pages 4–8)

*CONSIDER these questions before you go on. They are
designed to help you start thinking about this subject, not
to test your knowledge.*

Is it really possible for us to study behavior and the
mind scientifically?

Is psychology's development related to other academic areas, such as philosophy or biology, or is it an
isolated field of study?

How are the mind and the body related?

*READ this section of your text lightly. Then go back and
read thoroughly, completing the Workout as you proceed.*

Psychology, the science of behavior and the mind,
emerged in the second half of the nineteenth century.
The very idea of this new science would have been
unimaginable without earlier developments in philosophy. René Descartes, a French philosopher, was a
key figure in these developments.

1. Explain the doctrine of dualism accepted by the
    church in the seventeenth century.

2. How did Descartes' version of dualism make way
    for a science of behavior?

3. How would a strict adherence to Descartes'
    theory limit psychology?

Thomas Hobbes, a British contemporary of Descartes,
departed much further from the church's accepted
position on dualism. His views then helped to create
British empiricism.

4. What ideas were central to Thomas Hobbes's
    materialism?

5. According to the British empiricists such as Locke, Hume, and the Mills, what is the original basis of all knowledge and thought?

6. From the perspective of the empiricists, is a scientific psychology possible? Why or why not?

Progress in biological science during the nineteenth century helped to create an intellectual climate in which psychology could develop.

7. Physiology was one field of science in which knowledge was growing.

   a. How did physiology's new understanding of reflexes help to lay the foundation for a scientific psychology?

   b. Describe the view known as reflexology.

   c. What influences came from an increased understanding of localization of function?

8. What contribution did Darwin's theory of evolution make to the new science of psychology?

The Evolution of Psychology: A History of Alternative Perspectives (pages 8–24)

> CONSIDER these questions before you go on. They are designed to help you start thinking about this subject, not to test your knowledge.

Where and when did psychology get its start?

How much has psychology changed over the years?

Every discipline has its heroes and heroines—for example, Shakespeare in English literature and Marie Curie in physics. Who are some of the great figures of psychology's past.

> READ this section of your text lightly. Then go back and read thoroughly, completing the Workout as you proceed.

Although German scientists had already been doing psychological research for years, 1879 is usually cited as the date of psychology's birth. In that year Wilhelm Wundt started a laboratory at the University of Leipzig. He had already published psychology's first textbook as well as two volumes summarizing psychological research. Since psychology's founding, several competing schools of thought have developed. Each has conceived of psychology's goals, possibilities, and methods differently.

1. Fill in the chart on pages 4 and 5 to get an overview of the most important approaches in psychology. ("Major figures" should include those individuals who were most directly responsible for developing a given school of thought. "Significant influences or related approaches" may refer to persons, concepts, or schools of thought to the extent that each applies.)

Now that you have a firm foundation in the most important approaches to psychology, answer the following more specific questions.

2. An approach central to Wundt's work involved measuring the speed of mental processes.

   a. Why did Wundt want to do this?

   b. Describe a basic reaction-time study.

Approaches to psychology	Major figure(s)	Significant influence(s) or related approaches	Major goal(s) or concept(s)	Primary method(s)	Impact on psychology	Limitations
Structuralism						
Functionalism						
Gestalt psychology						
Behaviorism						
Ethology						
Physiological psychology						

Approaches to psychology	Major figure(s)	Significant influence(s) or related approaches	Major goal(s) or concept(s)	Primary method(s)	Impact on psychology	Limitations
Psychoanalysis						
Humanistic psychology						
Cultural psychology						
Social psychology						
Cognitive psychology						

    c. Which of Wundt's ideas are fundamental to today's cognitive psychology?

3. Why did Titchener's method of introspection fail scientifically?

4. How did James's use of introspection differ from that of Titchener's?

5. How does the *phi phenomenon* illustrate the Gestalt psychologists' major point? How was this same essential point applied to problem solving?

6. What were four principles of Watson's behaviorism?

7. What did Skinner's version of behaviorism have in common with Watson's? How did it differ from Watson's?

8. How and why did behaviorism and ethology interact initially? by the 1960s?

9. How did Karl Lashley view complex behavior?

10. Today, psychological psychology is often called _____ .

11. What observations led Freud to his psychoanalytic approach? Explain Freud's most fundamental concept.

12. Explain humanistic psychology's concept of an actualizing tendency.

13. What did Wundt think about the role of culture in psychology? What was the focus of Vygotsky's research?

14. How is social psychology different from cultural psychology?

15. How did Jean Piaget and Noam Chomsky contribute to the emergence of cognitive psychology?

16. A primary analogy for the mind used in cognitive psychology is a(n) _____ .

Psychology as a Discipline and a Profession
(pages 24–26)

> CONSIDER these questions before you go on. They are designed to help you start thinking about this subject, not to test your knowledge.

Is psychology considered a natural science? a social science? or one of the humanities?

What kind of work do psychologists do, and where do they do it?

> READ this section of your text lightly. Then go back and read thoroughly, completing the Workout as you proceed.

Colleges and universities are generally made up of departments representing specific academic disciplines. Often, we speak of disciplines as falling into one of three divisions—natural sciences, social sciences, and humanities.

1. How does psychology fit into this way of categorizing the disciplines? Explain your answer.

The many influences in psychology's past have helped to make psychology a very diverse field today. That diversity is evident not only in the content of academic psychology but also in the many professional endeavors of psychologists.

2. List four types of settings in which psychologists work, and indicate the kind of activity they might carry out in each.

   a.

   b.

   c.

   d.

> Be sure to READ the Concluding Thoughts at the end of the chapter. Note important points in your Workout. Then consolidate your learning by answering the focus questions in the margins of the text.

> After you have studied the chapter thoroughly, CHECK your understanding with the Self-Test that follows.

Self-Test 1

Multiple-Choice Questions

1. Darwin felt that natural selection:
   a. could not help us to explain evolution.
   b. could help us to understand anatomy but not behavior.
   c. could be applied to plants and nonhuman animals but not to humans.
   d. gradually formed the present anatomy and behavior of living things.

2. Descartes' theory of human action is a version of dualism because it includes both:
   a. mind and behavior.
   b. mind and spirit.
   c. body and soul.
   d. philosophy and science.

3. The British empiricists believed that thought ultimately derives from:
   a. logical analysis.
   b. the brain's innately determined physiology.
   c. free will.
   d. sensory experience.

4. Which important advance in nineteenth-century physiology helped to prepare the way for scientific psychology?
   a. new understanding of the neurological basis of reflexes
   b. rejection of the idea that specific parts of the brain have specific functions
   c. discovery of the basic arrangement of the nervous system
   d. discovery of an anatomical basis for the distinction between the conscious mind and the unconscious mind

5. As defined in the chapter, psychology is the science of:
   a. behavior.   c. the mind.
   b. the brain.   d. behavior and the mind.

6. The person usually credited with the founding of scientific psychology is:
   a. William James.
   b. James Watson.
   c. Wilhelm Wundt.
   d. Edward Titchener.

7. The structuralists wanted to understand the structure of:
   a. the brain and spinal cord.
   b. reflex behaviors.
   c. learned rather than instinctive behaviors.
   d. the mind.

8. The consensus today concerning the method of introspection is that:
   a. it was successful because it was systematic and objective.
   b. it was successful because it forced subjects to break down conscious experience into basic elements.
   c. it was unsuccessful because it depended on the private conscious experience of the person introspecting.
   d. it was unsuccessful because it was performed by untrained individuals.

9. The functionalists believed that, in order to understand the human mind, one must first understand its:
   a. elementary parts and processes.
   b. purposes.
   c. physiology.
   d. counterpart in lower species.

10. A contemporary psychologist says, "A square cannot simply be reduced to a set of four lines." What historical influence on this person's thinking is evident?
    a. functionalism
    b. structuralism
    c. psychoanalysis
    d. Gestalt psychology

11. The studies of children's intellectual development conducted by Swiss psychologist Jean Piaget contributed to the rise of:
    a. cultural psychology.
    b. cognitive psychology.
    c. behavioral neuroscience.
    d. S-R psychology.

12. Behaviorism's name stems from the central belief that:
    a. studying the mind is useful only as a way of explaining behavior.
    b. studying behavior is the only way to unlock the secrets of the mind.
    c. behavior is psychology's only proper object of study because it alone is observable.
    d. behavior can be understood only in its pure state, isolated from environmental influences.

13. A psychologist is studying the defensive behavior of ground-nesting birds by observing them in their natural environment. Which perspective does this person most likely represent?
    a. ethology
    b. behaviorism
    c. physiological psychology
    d. structuralism

14. According to Freud's psychoanalytic theory, which of the following is true of the conscious mind?
    a. It represents only a small portion of the mind.
    b. It has complete and direct access to the unconscious mind.
    c. It is unaffected by the unconscious mind.
    d. It must never become aware of disturbing memories if the patient is to recover.

15. Which of the following psychological perspectives has placed the least emphasis on animal research?
    a. ethology
    b. behaviorism
    c. structuralism
    d. physiological psychology

Essay Questions

16. Discuss the commonalities, differences, and interrelations of behaviorism and ethology.

17. Explain and contrast the basic theoretical tenets of structuralism and Gestalt psychology. Be sure to make clear why followers of these two schools of thought would tend to disagree, even about the very questions to be asked by psychology.

After you have assessed your understanding on the basis of Self-Test 1 and have tried to strengthen your preparation in any areas of weakness, GO ON to Self-Test 2.

Self-Test 2

Multiple-Choice Questions

1. Wundt used the results of reaction-time tasks to break down complex mental processes into their component parts. In which of the following approaches would this method fit?
   a. cognitive
   b. psychoanalytic
   c. physiological
   d. none of the above

2. Reflexology, the notion that all behavior involves reflex action, was key to the development of:
   a. psychoanalysis.   c. behaviorism.
   b. structuralism.   d. functionalism.

3. Darwin's emphasis on the survival value of behavior was a major influence on:
   a. psychoanalysis.
   b. social psychology.
   c. cognitive psychology.
   d. functionalism.

4. For psychologists 1879 has historical significance because it was the year that the:
   a. first psychological research was done.
   b. first laboratory of psychology was opened at a university.
   c. first book on structuralism was published.
   d. psychologist Wilhelm Wundt was born.

5. According to Descartes' version of dualism:
   a. even some complex behaviors can occur without any involvement of the soul.
   b. the body has exclusive control over behavior, while the soul has exclusive control over thought.
   c. all behavior involves interaction with the soul.
   d. the body fully controls both behavior and thought.

6. One of the founders of structuralism was:
   a. Kurt Lewin.   c. Edward Titchener.
   b. Edward Thorndike.   d. Noam Chomsky.

7. William James's approach to psychology was based on the notion that _____ are the most important aspects of human consciousness and action.
   a. elementary sensory experiences
   b. buried memories
   c. purposes and goals
   d. cultural differences

8. Which early psychological approach focused on the special nature of organized wholes?
   a. structuralism
   b. Gestalt psychology
   c. cognitive psychology
   d. psychoanalysis

9. Which method of investigation does cognitive psychology generally employ?
   a. observing and describing actual behavior in natural settings
   b. introspection
   c. inferences about mental processes based on observable behavior in controlled situations
   d. interviews

10. The behaviorists were primarily influenced by _____ , whereas the ethologists were primarily influenced by _____ .
   a. the British empiricists; Darwin
   b. Darwin; the British empiricists
   c. the British empiricists; Descartes
   d. Darwin; the structuralists

11. The person sitting next to you on the plane tells you that her work involves stimulating a small area of a cat's brain to learn if there are any effects on its eating. You could correctly say, "Oh, you're a(n) _____ ."
   a. behaviorist
   b. physiological psychologist
   c. ethologist
   d. cognitive psychologist

12. The term *psychoanalysis* refers to:
   a. Freud's method of treating individuals with psychological problems.
   b. Freud's theory of the mind.
   c. an approach to psychology that emphasizes the mind's use of rational analysis.
   d. both a and b.

13. Arthur is a graduate student who has studied the history and customs of Japan and the United States in order to understand differences in the people of these nations. He is most likely studying _____ psychology.
   a. humanistic   c. social
   b. cultural   d. psychoanalytic

14. Cognitive psychology often uses a _____ analogy, likening the mind to _____ .
   a. computer; a program
   b. computer; computer hardware
   c. mechanical; a hydraulics system
   d. communications; a switchboard

15. Which of the following is true of the early behaviorists?
   a. They believed that there is no basic difference between the principles of animal and human behavior and often studied animals.
   b. They believed that there is little basic difference between the principles of animal and human behavior but restricted their study to humans.
   c. They believed that there are fundamental differences between the principles of animal behavior and the principles of human behavior and so restricted themselves to studying humans.
   d. They believed that there are fundamental differences between the principles of animal behavior and the principles of human behavior and were more interested in studying animal behavior.

Essay Questions

16. What is the proper subject matter of psychology according to the behaviorist? according to the cognitive psychologist? Be sure your answer specifies the role of behavior in each approach.

17. Discuss the ways that Descartes and the British empiricists helped to prepare the way for a scientific psychology. Also point out any limits that their philosophies set on such a science.

Answers

Introduction

1. behavior; the mind

The Evolution of Psychology: A History of Alternative Perspectives

10. behavioral neuroscience

16. computer program

Self-Test 1

1. **d.** (p. 8)
2. **c.** (p. 4)
3. **d.** (p. 6)
4. **a.** (p. 6)
5. **d.** (p. 3)
6. **c.** Psychological research had been conducted in Germany prior to the founding of Wundt's laboratory at the University of Leipzig. But the founding of that laboratory represented an official acceptance of psychology by the academic establishment and provided a firm basis for the growth of the field. Wundt also wrote the first textbook in psychology. (p. 9)
7. **d.** (p. 10)
8. **c.** Introspection is inherently unsuitable as a form of scientific evidence because it is private. What one person experiences cannot be directly experienced by another person and thus does not permit the public verification that science requires. (pp. 10–11)
9. **b.** This emphasis on purposes was related to

Darwinian influences on the functionalists. (p. 11)

10. **d.** Gestalt views on the special status of organized wholes are clearly implied by the statement. (p. 12)

11. **b.** (p. 22)

12. **c.** (p. 14)

13. **a.** (p. 16)

14. **a.** In Freud's thinking, the conscious mind represented only the proverbial "tip of the iceberg." According to Freud, the unconscious mind is purposely hidden from direct inspection by the conscious mind. Freud believed that the conscious mind could be powerfully affected by the forces of the unconscious and by the mind's attempts to modify those forces. He used various methods to bring the disturbing thoughts into consciousness so that patients could deal with them. (p. 18)

15. **c.** (p. 14)

16. Both behaviorists and ethologists concentrated on animal behavior and insisted on careful observation, but their methods, motivations, and points of view were quite different. Behaviorists were interested in learning, while ethologists were interested in complex behaviors that animals did not need to learn. The behaviorists were influenced by the British empiricists, who claimed that all knowledge comes through sensory experience and is thus learned. The ethologists, on the other hand, were most influenced by Darwin; they believed that adaptive behavior was powerfully shaped by evolutionary forces. The behaviorists were generally interested in animals because they provided a scientifically controllable way of studying learning, which, they thought, involved the same principles in both animals and humans. In contrast, the ethologists were interested in animal behavior for its own sake. The two schools began to interact more cooperatively after each learned lessons consistent with the other viewpoint. For example, by the 1960s, it was becoming clear to behaviorists that animal species differed in the types of responses they could learn. This forced them to acknowledge that learning must be examined in the context of a particular species' evolutionary history and survival needs. Ethologists, as they branched out to study mammals, were forced to acknowledge that these animals were much more affected by learning than the animals, such as birds and fish, that they had previously studied. (pp. 13–17)

17. The structuralist approach had as its goal the identification of the basic elements of the mind. Structuralists saw the mind as being made up of

basic structures combined to form more complex structures combined to form still more complex structures. They believed that the complex could be understood by separating the whole into its parts and seeing how the parts were put together. The Gestalt psychologists had a very different viewpoint about the nature of parts and wholes. They believed that a whole, whether a whole perception or a whole problem solution, had a special status. It could not be completely understood in terms of its parts. Some characteristics or qualities of the whole only emerge at the level of the whole, as in the *phi phenomenon*. The fundamental question for structuralists is: What are the parts that make up the complex whole? But the Gestalt psychologists would see this question as quite incomplete and potentially misleading. (pp. 10–11, 12–13)

Self-Test 2

1. **a.** (p. 10)
2. **c.** (p. 7)
3. **d.** (p. 8)
4. **b.** (p. 9)
5. **a.** (p. 4)
6. **c.** Titchener was a student of Wundt's, and his approach was heavily influenced by that of his mentor. (p. 10)
7. **c.** (p. 11)
8. **b.** (p. 12)
9. **c.** (p. 22)
10. **a.** (p. 16)
11. **b.** (p. 17)
12. **d.** (p. 18)
13. **b.** (p. 20)
14. **a.** Using the computer analogy, the brain would be comparable to the hardware of the machine, and the mind to a computer program. (p. 23)
15. **a.** (p. 14)
16. Behavior was the very thing that behaviorists wanted to understand. The mind, with all its perceptions, judgments, and motivations had been the traditional object of study in psychology. The behaviorists felt that this traditional work had

come to nothing because it was hopelessly tangled in unscientific speculation. The mind could not be seen or touched or measured. It was, in the behaviorist view, an elusive abstraction. Behaviorists demanded an objective, observable science of psychology and believed it could only be had if behavior—observable and even quantifiable—were the object of study. (Although some behaviorists refused even to consider mental constructs, *S-O-R* behaviorists such as Tolman admitted into their theories some mentalistic kinds of ideas.) For the cognitive psychologist, the mind is still the proper object of study. Its abstract and hidden nature does not exclude it from scientific study, just as the abstract and hidden nature of the atom does not prevent physicists from studying it. However, because the mind is not directly observable, as the behaviorists pointed out, the structures and processes of the mind must be inferred from observable behavior. (pp. 13–15, 22–24)

17. Descartes' dualism suggested the existence of a body and a soul, both of which affect behavior. According to the theory, the body can control even some complex behavior directly, without any involvement of the soul. Descartes argued that any human activity that is essentially like an activity an animal can perform does not require the soul, since animals were assumed to have no souls. Descartes thus offered a new view of the body as a mechanism that follows natural laws and can therefore be understood through science. However, the nonmaterial soul was believed by Descartes to be responsible for all thought. Unlike the body itself, the soul was not subject to natural law. Rather, it was thought to have free will. Because it was not operating under natural law, the soul, and the behaviors it willed the body to perform, could not be studied by science. The British empiricists contended that all behavior was based on physical mechanisms and that all knowledge, thought, and action could be traced back to the world of sensory experience and thus could be studied scientifically. (pp. 4–6)

Chapter 2   Methods of Psychology

> *READ the introduction below before you read the chapter in the text.*

Psychology employs scientific methods to answer questions about the mind and behavior. Scientific methods involve the systematic collection and analysis of objective, publicly observable data. The story of Clever Hans, a horse purported to have extensive knowledge of many subjects, such as history and arithmetic, illustrates the value of a scientific approach in drawing conclusions.

The scientific process involves the use of facts to develop theories. From theories, scientists derive hypotheses about what will happen under specific conditions. Then they test their hypotheses—producing more facts.

In order to produce and evaluate facts, hypotheses and theories, psychological researchers employ various strategies. These strategies can be categorized along three dimensions. One dimension is research design: Some studies involve controlled experimentation; others search for correlations between variables; and others simply describe behavior systematically. Another dimension is the setting: Some research is conducted in laboratories, but other studies are carried out in natural environments—in classrooms, public parks, city streets, or sports arenas, for example. The third dimension is the data-collection method: In some cases, the data may consist of information reported by the individuals being studied. Alternatively, the data may come from direct observations and measurements made by the researchers.

Statistical analysis is used to help psychologists understand the meaning of the data collected through research. Descriptive statistics summarize the data in useful ways. Inferential statistics indicate whether patterns in the data are reliable or repeatable, given that data are always somewhat affected by random variation.

Research must be designed with various precautions in place. For example, care must be taken in selecting research subjects and assigning them to groups. Even the way a variable is measured requires careful consideration. Some safeguards must be used to keep the researchers' expectations from affecting the data. Other safeguards must be used because the expectations of research subjects can produce misleading data.

Finally, a number of research guidelines exist for ethical purposes, to protect the rights and welfare of research subjects.

> *LOOK over the table of contents for this chapter in your textbook before you continue with your study.*

> *Notice that there are focus questions in the margins of the text for your use in studying the material. The following chart lists which Study Guide questions relate to which focus questions.*

Focus Questions	Study Guide Questions
Lessons from Clever Hans	
1–3	1–5
Types of Research Strategies	
4–7	1, 4–9
8	2, 10
9	3, 11–15
Statistical Methods in Psychology	
10–11	1–8
12–13	9–11
Minimizing Bias in Psychological Research	
14–15	1–2
16–17	3–6
18–20	7–10
Ethical Issues in Psychological Research	
21	1–5

The Integrated Study Workout

Complete one section at a time.

Lessons from Clever Hans   (pages 29–32)

CONSIDER these questions before you go on. They are designed to help you start thinking about this subject, not to test your knowledge.

What concepts and attitudes are essential for a scientific approach to knowledge?

Is skepticism important only for combatting deliberate attempts to deceive?

READ this section of your text lightly. Then go back and read thoroughly, completing the Workout as you proceed.

Psychology has been considered a science since its beginnings. Therefore, as scientists, psychologists must attempt to answer their research questions scientifically—i.e., through the systematic collection and analysis of objective, publicly observable data. The story of Clever Hans helps to teach us some important lessons about the scientific approach.

1. What was claimed for Clever Hans? Who made the claim?

2. Was the case of Clever Hans a deliberate hoax? Explain.

3. How did Oskar Pfungst uncover the truth about Clever Hans? What was his final conclusion about the basis for Hans's amazing performance?

4. Define these terms: *fact*, *theory*, and *hypothesis*. Make sure your answer explains how they are related.

5. What are the major lessons to be learned from the case of Clever Hans?

   a.

   b.

   c.

Types of Research Strategies
(pages 32–38)

CONSIDER these questions before you go on. They are designed to help you start thinking about this subject, not to test your knowledge.

If optimism was found to be correlated with career success, would it mean that optimism causes greater career success?

What makes an experiment an experiment?

What other methods besides experiments do psychologists use to study behavior and the mind?

How can psychologists study behavior in a natural setting?

READ this section of your text lightly. Then go back and read thoroughly, completing the Workout as you proceed.

You will understand psychological research better if you appreciate the variety of research strategies used. Below are listed three dimensions of research strategies—the research design, the research setting, and the method of data collection. Identify the different categories of each dimension below. (See Table 2.1)

1. The research design:

   a. _____ A procedure in which a researcher systematically varies one or more independent variables and notes any change in one or more dependent variables, while holding other variables constant.

   b. _____ A study in which a researcher observes or measures two or more variables to find relationships among them but does not manipulate any variables.

   c. _____ A study in which the goal is not the systematic investigation of relationships between variables but rather the description of behavior.

2. Research settings:

   a. _____ Subjects are studied in a specially designated area that allows better control of environmental conditions or facilitates data collection.

   b. _____ Subjects are studied in an environment not specially set up for purposes of research, such as a park, a restaurant, a kindergarten, or a living room.

3. Data-collection methods:

   a. _____ The people being studied rate or describe their own behavior or mental state in some way.

   b. _____ The researcher observes and records the behavior of interest.

4. Categorize each of the following situations along the three dimensions of the taxonomy.

   a. A developmental psychologist has randomly divided elderly residents of a nursing home into three groups, each of which receives a different type of treatment intended to enhance life satisfaction. At the end of the study, the psychologist asks the residents to rate their life satisfaction using a series of questions.

      Type of design? _____

      Type of setting? _____

      Type of data collection? _____

   b. A psychologist is interested in spatial skills as they relate to aviation safety. Subjects who are licensed pilots are brought in and tested on a special apparatus that simulates various emergencies. The apparatus records how quickly and appropriately the subjects maneuver the "aircraft" to avoid imminent danger. The psychologist wants to see whether performance on this apparatus is related to scores on a paper and pencil test of spatial ability.

      Type of design? _____

      Type of setting? _____

      Type of data collection? _____

   c. A clinical psychologist wants to better understand the means by which social support systems help terminally ill patients. The psychologist sits in on group support sessions and family visits of selected patients, carefully recording what happens.

      Type of design? _____

      Type of setting? _____

      Type of data collection? _____

Experiments allow researchers the greatest degree of control and permit strong conclusions about cause and effect.

5. How do the terms *independent variable* and *dependent variable* relate to the terms *cause* and *effect*?

6. In the following examples, indicate which are variables by writing *V* in the blank provided.

   _____ **a.** intelligence

   _____ **b.** height of adult males

   _____ **c.** number of days in a week

   _____ **d.** major in college

7. In the following situations, indicate independent variables with *IV* and dependent variables with *DV*.

   a. A researcher randomly assigns subjects to groups that differ in size (_____). All subjects are then asked to perform the same task. The researcher measures the average amount of work each person does (_____).

   b. Subjects report childhood memories that come to mind (_____) after being exposed to verbal, visual, or smell cues (_____) associated with common childhood experiences.

   c. Researchers observe how long subjects work on a word puzzle (_____) after being told that they are good or poor puzzle solvers (_____).

   d. Subjects are prescribed varying dosages of a drug (_____) designed to reduce symptoms of depression. After a month, they are rated by themselves, by family members, and by counselors on various dimensions related to depression (_____).

   e. Researchers calculate the average academic grades of children (_____) at 3 months, 6 months, 1 year, and 2 years after the death of a parent (_____).

8. What is the difference between a within-subject and a between-groups experiment?

Correlational studies can provide useful and interesting information when it is not possible to manipulate a variable directly. A psychologist cannot, for example, assign subjects to different genders or occupations.

9. Correlational studies do not permit us to draw cause-effect conclusions as experiments do.

   a. Why is this so?

   b. Consider Diana Baumrind's work on parental discipline styles. Why would cause-effect conclusions be inappropriate in this study?

Research can be conducted in a laboratory setting or in a field setting. Each has certain advantages and drawbacks.

10. What are the special merits and limitations of laboratory studies? of field studies?

11. What is a field experiment?

Psychologists can collect data in a number of different ways within two broad categories.

12. Two major ways of collecting self-report data are _____ and _____ .

13. Two major ways of collecting observational data are _____ and _____ .

14. Provide two concrete examples of each data-collection method mentioned above. (Use examples from the text, or, better still, make up your own examples.)

   a. self-report

b. observation

15. Compare the advantages and disadvantages of self-report methods, naturalistic observation, and tests.

Statistical Methods in Psychology
(pages 38–41)

> *CONSIDER these questions before you go on. They are designed to help you start thinking about this subject, not to test your knowledge.*

What does it mean when someone says two things are correlated?

Science has the reputation of being quantitative. How does psychology make use of math?

> *READ this section of your text lightly. Then go back and read thoroughly, completing the Workout as you proceed.*

Data are useful only to the extent that they can be summarized and interpreted. Statistical procedures are critical to that step in the research process.

1. Descriptive statistics help us to

   _____ a set of data.

The mean and median are measures of central tendency. They help to summarize the data by giving us one "typical" number that serves to represent the whole data set. (*Hint:* Look at Table 2.2, text p. 39.)

2. The mean of the numbers 4, 6, 9, 8, 3 is

   _____ .

3. The median of the numbers 8, 6, 5, 10, 12 is

   _____ .

Variability is the extent to which the scores in a set of data differ from one another. The standard deviation is a common measure of variability. (In a sense, the

measure of variability tells us how well the measure of central tendency represents the data set. For example, if all the scores in the set are fairly similar, the mean might represent them well. If there are widely differing scores, the mean would represent them less well.)

4. Which set below has the higher variability? (Circle a or b)

   a. 3 6 7 6 8 5

   b. 1 5 2 9 4 11

A correlation coefficient is a descriptive statistic that expresses the strength and direction of the relationship between two variables. (*Hint:* Look at Figure 2.3, text p. 39, for the items below.)

5. A correlation coefficient can vary between

   _____ and _____ .

6. The sign + or – indicates whether the relationship is positive or negative—in other words, the

   _____ of the relationship.

7. The absolute value of the coefficient indicates the

   _____ of the relationship. Lower

   numbers indicate _____ relation-

   ships, while higher numbers indicate

   _____ relationships. Numbers at or

   near zero indicate _____ correla-

   tion.

8. In the following scatter plot, what kind of correlation is indicated—negative or positive? weak, moderate, or strong?

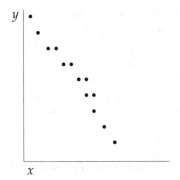

Data are always subject to a certain amount of random or chance variation. These random influences can keep us from seeing real, systematic patterns in the data, somewhat the way noise on a telephone line prevents us from hearing the speaker's voice clearly. They can also make it appear as if certain patterns exist when in reality they do not. Inferential statistics help us to decide when the patterns we see are real and repeatable, not just a product of chance.

9. Explain what it means to say that a given set of results is significant at the 5 percent level.

10. What elements are taken into account in determining statistical significance?

a.

b.

c.

11. Statistical significance is not the same as practical significance. Explain.

Minimizing Bias in Psychological Research
(pages 42–46)

> CONSIDER these questions before you go on. They are designed to help you start thinking about this subject, not to test your knowledge.

What are some issues you should examine in evaluating the believability of a psychological study?

Are scientists as objective as they ideally would like to be, or are they sometimes swayed by their own biases, like nonscientists?

> READ this section of your text lightly. Then go back and read thoroughly, completing the Workout as you proceed.

Considerable care is involved in designing sound research studies. There are several known sources of bias and error in research, and researchers must constantly guard against them.

1. Explain the difference between error and bias. Why is bias a much more serious problem?

2. How can a biased sample come about in an experiment? in a descriptive study?

The measurement procedure used by the researcher is an important factor in minimizing error and bias.

3. What does it mean to say a measure is reliable? What problem results from low reliability?

4. Define *validity*. What problem results from low validity?

5. Can a measurement be reliable and yet not be valid? Give an example to support your answer.

6. A measurement procedure has _____ validity if it seems to make sense on the surface. A measurement procedure has _____ validity to the extent that it correlates well with another, more direct index of the same characteristic.

Bias can also result from the wishes and expectations brought into the research situation by either observers or subjects.

7. How can an observer's expectations bias results? How can we avoid such observer-expectancy effects in experiments?

8. Explain the concept of a subject-expectancy effect. What is the best way to avoid this problem?

9. An experiment that guards against both observer- and subject-expectancy effects is called a(n) _____ experiment.

10. Which kind of expectancy effect produced the apparent phenomenon of facilitated communication?

Ethical Issues in Psychological Research
(pages 47–48)

> CONSIDER these questions before you go on. They are designed to help you start thinking about this subject, not to test your knowledge.

What are the most serious ethical challenges encountered in psychological research?

Do psychologists give serious attention to ethical issues involved in using animals as research subjects?

What kinds of ethical principles do psychologists observe?

> READ this section of your text lightly. Then go back and read thoroughly, completing the Workout as you proceed.

Those who conduct psychological research are obliged to observe ethical as well as scientific principles.

1. List the three major issues in research with human subjects.

   a. _____

   b. _____

   c. _____

2. How do researchers deal with these issues?

3. The use of deception in psychological research is particularly controversial.

   a. Why do some psychologists object to deception in research?

   b. How is the use of deception in psychological research justified by some?

4. What are the obligations of researchers who use animal subjects?

5. What are some steps the profession as a whole has taken to oversee ethical practices in psychological research?

a.

b.

> Be sure to READ the Concluding Thoughts at the end of the chapter. Note important points in your Workout. Then consolidate your learning by answering the focus questions in the margins of the text.

> After you have studied the chapter thoroughly, CHECK your understanding with the Self-Test that follows.

Self-Test 1

Multiple-Choice Questions

1. Which of the following is a lesson that should be learned from the case of Clever Hans?
   a. We must not be misled by science's claims of objectivity.
   b. Unless we take a skeptical approach to any situation, we may be led to believe what is simply not true.
   c. When an unusual and interesting claim is made, we should suspend our skepticism and look first for evidence that supports the claim.
   d. The intelligence of nonhuman species should not be underestimated out of human arrogance.

2. Which of the following is the mean of the numbers 2, 4, 4, 6, 9?
   a. 2   c. 5
   b. 4   d. 25

3. A procedure in which the researcher systematically varies one variable, holding all others constant, to see if another variable is affected, is called a(n):
   a. correlational study.
   b. observational study.
   c. experiment.
   d. double-blind study.

4. An experimenter wants to see whether caffeine has any effect on the ability to concentrate on a visual task. In this study, the caffeine would be the:
   a. independent variable.
   b. between-groups variable.
   c. dependent variable.
   d. within-subject variable.

5. Cause is to effect as _____ is to _____ .
   a. constant; variable
   b. dependent variable; independent variable
   c. independent variable; dependent variable
   d. experiment; correlational study

6. A psychologist tries to find out whether there is any relationship between the number of older siblings a child has and the size of the child's vocabulary at age 3. This is an example of a(n):
   a. experiment.
   b. correlational study.
   c. descriptive study.
   d. laboratory study.

7. A psychologist explores the behavior of children in their first competitive sports experience, recording the variety and frequency of various social behaviors. What type of research strategy is involved here?
   a. experimental
   b. correlational
   c. descriptive
   d. within-subject

8. The purpose of descriptive statistics is to:
   a. help us decide whether research conclusions based on the data are warranted.
   b. help us collect data more efficiently.
   c. help us summarize data in a meaningful way.
   d. do all of the above.

9. The chapter categorizes research strategies in terms of:
   a. research design, description, and data analysis.
   b. data collection, type of experiment, and statistical analysis.
   c. research design, setting, and data-collection method.
   d. observation, correlation, and setting.

10. Which of the following is the median of the numbers 25, 5, 15, 20, 30?
   a. 5
   b. 15
   c. 19
   d. 20

11. A psychologist uses test X to measure a person's creativity. The test is administered several times with widely varying results. Test X apparently lacks:
   a. observer expectancy.
   b. face validity.
   c. a double blind.
   d. reliability.

12. A result is termed "statistically significant" if it:
   a. is probably due to chance.
   b. cannot possibly be due to chance.
   c. has less than a 5 percent probability of being due to chance.
   d. is large enough to be of practical importance.

13. The host of a radio call-in show asks listeners to phone in their views on affirmative action—for, against, or not sure. The results are suspect because of:
   a. a sample that is probably biased.
   b. poor criterion validity.
   c. the fact that the study is merely descriptive.
   d. the between-groups nature of the experiment.

14. The value of a correlation coefficient varies between:
   a. 1.00 and 100.00.
   b. −10.00 and +10.00.
   c. 0.00 and 1.00.
   d. −1.00 and +1.00.

15. Clever Hans's abilities were apparently due to:
   a. placebo effects.
   b. low reliability.
   c. observer expectancy.
   d. a double-blind procedure.

Essay Questions

16. How do facts, theories, and hypotheses fit into psychology?

17. What are the three major ethical issues that must be considered in psychological research with human subjects? How do psychologists deal with these issues?

After you have assessed your understanding on the basis of Self-Test 1 and have tried to strengthen your preparation in any areas of weakness, GO ON to Self-Test 2.

Self-Test 2

Multiple-Choice Questions

1. Which of the following describes an independent variable?
   a. a variable not correlated with any other variables
   b. the variable the researcher observes and measures in an experiment
   c. the variable the researcher deliberately manipulates in an experiment
   d. a variable that is held constant in an experiment.

2. Which type(s) of research design permit(s) direct cause-and-effect conclusions?
   a. experiments
   b. correlational studies
   c. descriptive studies
   d. both experiments and correlational studies

3. A within-subject experiment is one in which:
   a. there is only a single subject.
   b. a given subject experiences all the different conditions of the experiment.
   c. the data are collected by self-report.
   d. the experimenter is interested only in the subjective experiences of the subject.

4. A psychologist varies the amount of practice time provided for different sets of subjects in a target-shooting task. The question is whether accuracy will be affected. The psychologist is conducting a:

   a. correlational study.
   b. between-groups experiment.
   c. within-subject experiment.
   d. descriptive study.

5. A psychologist asks people to complete a confidential questionnaire to determine whether physical fitness is related to self-esteem. The psychologist is conducting a(n) _____ study.

   a. experimental
   b. correlational
   c. double-blind
   d. descriptive

6. A psychologist visits a chemical plant to interview people engaged in a labor strike there. This would be:

   a. an experiment in which data collection is by self-report.
   b. a correlational study in which data collection is observational.
   c. a descriptive study in which data collection is observational.
   d. a field study in which data collection is by self-report.

7. A study examines the effect of different incentives ($5 and $50) on people's willingness to perform a mildly embarrassing task. In this study, _____ would be the independent variable and _____ would be the dependent variable.

   a. incentive; willingness to perform the task
   b. willingness to perform the task; incentive
   c. incentive; whether subjects receive $5 or $50
   d. willingness to perform the task; the number of people tested

8. We often use _____ as an indicator of the variability in a data set.

   a. the standard deviation
   b. central tendency
   c. a correlation coefficient
   d. the mean

9. A procedure that succeeds in measuring what it is intended to measure is said to be:

   a. unbiased.
   b. reliable.
   c. valid.
   d. correlated.

10. Which of the following correlation coefficients would indicate the strongest correlation between two variables?

    a. −0.80
    b. 0.00
    c. +0.50
    d. +0.75

11. Suppose a research result shows a difference between the two groups studied. Suppose further that inferential statistics show that the likelihood of the difference being due to chance is 30 percent. Is the result statistically significant by the usual standards?

    a. Yes.
    b. No.
    c. Well, yes and no—it's 70 percent significant.
    d. It's impossible to say based on the information provided.

12. In an experiment, which of the following factors is *not* taken into account in a test of statistical significance?

    a. the size of the observed difference between means
    b. the number of times the study has been repeated
    c. the number of subjects
    d. the variability of the data in each group

13. The more consistent the result of a measurement procedure when used on the same subject under the same conditions, the more _____ the measure is.

    a. reliable
    b. unbiased
    c. independent
    d. valid

14. Which of the following is the mean of the numbers 10, 20, 30, 40, 100?

    a. 10
    b. 30
    c. 40
    d. 55

15. If the results of an experiment are actually due to the beliefs of the subjects and not to a real effect of the independent variable, we say:

    a. the subjects are blind.
    b. the study involves a double blind.
    c. there is bias.
    d. there is a within-subject effect.

Essay Questions

16. Briefly describe the case of Clever Hans, and explain the lessons we should learn from it.

17. Explain the phenomena of observer-expectancy and subject-expectancy effects in research. What measures can be taken to guard against them?

Answers

Types of Research Strategies

1. **a.** experiment
   b. correlational study
   c. descriptive study
2. **a.** laboratory
   b. field
3. **a.** self-report
   b. observational
4. **a.** experiment; field; self-report
   b. correlational; laboratory; observational
   c. descriptive; field; observational
6. Items **a**, **b**, and **d** are variables, whereas **c** is a constant.

7. **a.** IV, DV
   b. DV, IV
   c. DV, IV
   d. IV, DV
   e. DV, IV
12. questionnaire; interview
13. naturalistic observation; test

Statistical Methods in Psychology

1. summarize
2. 6
3. 8
4. Set b has higher variability
5. −1.00 and +1.00
6. direction
7. strength; weaker; stronger; no
8. a strong negative correlation.

Minimizing Bias in Psychological Research

5. Yes. For example, eye color would be a reliable but not valid measure of honesty.
6. face; criterion
9. double-blind

Ethical Issues in Psychological Research

1. **a.** right to privacy
   b. possible discomfort or harm
   c. use of deception

Self-Test 1

1. **b.** (pp. 31–32)
2. **c.** (p. 39)
3. **c.** Only the experiment involves this much control. It is the control that allows conclusions about cause-and-effect relationships from experimental data. (p. 33)
4. **a.** (p. 33)
5. **c.** (pp. 33–34)
6. **b.** (p. 35)
7. **c.** (p. 36)
8. **c.** (p. 38)
9. **c.** (p. 32)

10. **d.** Remember, the median is the middle number when numbers are ranked from lowest to highest. The mean, on the other hand, is the arithmetic average. (p. 39)

11. **d.** (p. 43)

12. **c.** Scientists have established 5 percent as an arbitrary cutoff point. The rationale is that a 5 percent chance that a result could be due to random factors is a small enough chance to take a gamble on because we would be wrong only 5 percent of the time. (p. 41)

13. **a.** (pp. 42–43)

14. **d.** (p. 39)

15. **c.** (p. 44)

16. Psychology, like all scientific endeavors, seeks to explain its subject matter—in this case behavior and the mind—objectively. In other words, it relies on fact rather than pure opinion or speculation. A psychologist carrying out research in some area of inquiry would attempt to make sense of known facts (or observations), perhaps producing a theory that explains them. That theory would then be used to produce hypotheses, that is, predictions about what would be observed in particular circumstances. Then those predictions are systematically tested, and the facts or observations produced by the test may require further theorizing, predicting, and testing. (p. 31)

17. The three major ethical issues involved in psychological research are the right to privacy, the possibility of discomfort or harm to subjects, and deception. The first issue demands that information obtained from or about subjects be dealt with in a way that safeguards the individual's anonymity. Both the issues of privacy and harm or discomfort can be handled largely by obtaining informed consent from subjects and by letting them know they can quit the study at any point. Psychologists must also compare the potential risks to subjects with the potential scientific benefits for humankind before entering into the research. If risks can be avoided or minimized, there is an obligation to do that. Deception is probably the most controversial issue. Opponents say deception is never acceptable, but others counter that it is comparatively rare, generally benign, and often scientifically necessary. (p. 47)

Self-Test 2

1. **c.** (p. 33)

2. **a.** (p. 33)

3. **b.** (p. 34)

4. **b.** (p. 34)

5. **b.** (p. 35)

6. **d.** (p. 36)

7. **a.** (pp. 33–34)

8. **a.** (p. 39)

9. **c.** (p. 43)

10. **a.** To assess the strength of the relationship, look only at the absolute value of the coefficient, not the sign. The second strongest correlation coefficient among the alternatives would be d. Alternative b indicates the absence of any relationship between the two variables. (p. 39)

11. **b.** The arbitrary cutoff point to establish statistical significance is often 5 percent. Below the cutoff, the results are considered significant; above the cutoff, the results are considered not significant. In other words, if the results had only a 5 percent or lower probability of occurring by chance, then we are essentially "betting" that they *aren't* due only to chance. There is no such thing as a partially significant result. Further, if there really were a 30 percent chance that our results were due to random factors, it would be a very risky bet to proclaim that they really weren't. (p. 41)

12. **b.** (pp. 40–41)

13. **a.** (p. 43)

14. **c.** (p. 39)

15. **c.** (p. 46)

16. Clever Hans was a horse owned by a retired German schoolteacher named von Osten. Von Osten tried to prove his hypothesis that horses were as smart as people and simply needed to be educated to show that they were. After several years of training, Hans could apparently answer questions about math, geography, history, and other subjects by moving his head or tapping his hoof. Von Osten's claims were widely accepted, even by many scientists. However, a psychologist by the name of Oskar Pfungst discredited poor Hans in a series of careful experiments. When Hans was prevented from receiving subtle unintentional cues from his "teacher" or others in his admiring audiences, he was unable to answer the questions put to him. This case is a classic lesson in the value of skepticism in science. We must not accept something as true just because we would like it to be true or because on casual observation it appears to be true. We must test a claim and see whether it can be explained in some other fashion

than the one we favor. It is also a lesson about the importance of making observations under carefully controlled and systematically varied conditions. Further, the case of Clever Hans can serve as an illustration of observer-expectancy effects, a problem that results when a researcher inadvertently cues a subject as to what is expected from him or her. (pp. 29–32)

17. One difficulty that psychological researchers often face comes from the very fact that they and their subjects are intelligent, thinking creatures. The researcher on the one hand and the subject on the other may both be affected by expectations. The researcher may unwittingly pass on expectations to the subject, who may just as unwittingly (or deliberately) comply with those expectations. If that happens, the results of the study are not a reflection of nature as the researcher hoped they would be. Instead, they are just a reflection of the researcher's own beliefs. Likewise, the researcher's observations and judgments may be influenced by his or her own expectations. For example, if the researcher expects the subject to behave nonaggressively in a particular situation, behavior that is ambiguous or even slightly aggressive may be perceived as nonaggressive. These kinds of effects, which stem from what the observer believes or expects, are referred to as observer-expectancy effects. Subjects, too, may develop their own expectations. For example, a subject who knows she is receiving a drug intended to suppress appetite may experience appetite suppression for reasons due to the expectation, not to the drug. Blind and double-blind studies can be very useful in preventing expectancy effects. In blind studies, the observers are not given access to information that could fuel observer-expectancy effects. In other words, they are unaware of a given subject's treatment condition and thus have no basis to apply their expectations. In double-blind studies, both the observer *and* the subject are unaware of what treatment the subject is receiving. Thus double-blind studies protect against both observer- and subject-expectancy effects. (pp. 44–46)

Chapter 3

Genetic and Evolutionary Foundations of Behavior

READ the introduction below before you read the chapter in the text.

Chapter 3 focuses on the impact of genetics and evolutionary adaptation on behavior. Adaptation is a means of accommodating to changed circumstances. (Evolution is just one level on which adaptation occurs; another is learning, which will be considered in Chapter 4.)

Genes, the biological units of heredity, affect our anatomy and physiology and, through these, behavioral characteristics. They exert their influences by one, and only one, means—by governing the manufacture of the body's many different protein molecules. Genes always work in interaction with environmental influences. The chapter explains how genetic information is passed down from one generation to the next through sexual reproduction. Such concepts as genetic diversity, genetic relatedness, genotypes and phenotypes, and dominant and recessive genes are explained.

In some cases, a single gene can affect a particular aspect of behavior or cause genetic disorders that have behavioral consequences. For example, in humans, phenylketonuria (PKU) is a disorder that can result in severe mental retardation. Although it is caused by a recessive gene, the right diet—an environmental influence—can drastically reduce the damage done by the disease. This fact underscores the point that genes and environment work together.

Most differences among individuals stem from the combined effects of many genes in interaction with the environment. We call charasteristics stemming from combined genes polygenic characteristics. Polygenic characteristics vary in degree from one individual to another—that is, each individual will have more or less of the characteristic.

The mechanism by which evolutionary adaptation takes place is natural selection, a concept advanced by Charles Darwin. Darwin argued that inheritable changes that enhance the chances of survival and reproduction tend to be passed on to the next generation while inheritable changes that hinder survival or reproductive chances are lost. In current evolutionary thinking, Darwin's critical insights are combined with a modern understanding of genes.

People have long engaged in selective breeding—reproducing plants and animals in such a way that desirable traits are developed, enhanced, or continued. Evolution depends on natural selection, defined above, in which the demands of life in a particular environment determine what is a "desirable trait." Both environmental change and genetic variability contribute to evolution. It is important to recognize that evolution does not involve foresight, since many common misconceptions about evolution stem from this erroneous assumption. Although functionalism, which emphasizes the purposes of behavior, is well suited to an evolutionary viewpoint, not all characteristics that emerge through evolution should be assumed to be useful.

The chapter next explores the field of ethology. Ethology is the study of species-typical behaviors—behaviors so characteristic of a species that they can help to identify it. Ethologists prefer to examine behavior in its natural context and attempt to understand it from an evolutionary perspective. They have found that, in some species, relatively fixed patterns of behavior occur in response to particular stimuli. In other species, especially humans and other mammals, behaviors are much more flexible and less controlled by specific stimuli.

Ethologists have used deprivation experiments to uncover the environmental conditions necessary for the development of certain behavior patterns in individual animals. They have used two types of comparisons—homology and analogy—in trying to understand the evolutionary development and functions of behaviors.

Sociobiology involves an effort to understand the social systems of humans and other animals in evolutionary terms. One major focus of sociobiologists has been sexual behavior. Robert Trivers, for example, has suggested that the relative parental investments required of males and females of a given species will strongly affect the mating patterns seen in that species. Another focus of sociobiology has been aggression, both that involved in territorial defense and that involved in establishing social status within a living group. Sociobiologists have also offered hypotheses to explain helping behavior in animals. The most controversial ideas in sociobiology concern human behavior. Because of past abuses of evolutionary thinking, many people are skeptical or actively critical of work in this area. Sociobiologists have nevertheless pointed out certain tendencies in human behavior that may have arisen due to evolutionary factors. The chapter describes several fallacies in evolutionary thinking that we should try to eliminate from our thinking.

Look over the table of contents for this chapter in your textbook before you continue with your study.

Notice that there are focus questions in the margins of the text for your use in studying the material. The following chart lists which Study Guide questions relate to which focus questions.

Focus Questions	Study Guide Questions
Genes and the Inheritance of Behavioral Characteristics	
1–2	1–5
3–5	6–20
6–11	21–32
12–14	33–36
Natural Selection and Its Implications for Psychology	
15–18	1–8
19–22	9–15
Ethology: The Study of Species-Typical Behavior Patterns	
23–26	1–8
27	9–10
28–31	11–18
Sociobiology: The Comparative Study of Animals' Social Systems	
32–37	1–11
38–40	12–17
41	18–21
42–47	22–27

The Integrated Study Workout

Complete one section at a time.

Genes and the Inheritance of Behavioral Characteristics (pages 54–66)

CONSIDER these questions before you go on. They are designed to help you start thinking about this subject, not to test your knowledge.

How can a microscopic physical thing like a gene affect something psychological such as verbal ability?

How are genes passed down from parents to children?

How genetically similar are people who are biologically related?

Is it possible to counteract a genetic problem by environmental means?

What clues lead scientists to believe that differences among individuals on some specific trait are due to a single gene or to many genes?

READ this section of your text lightly. Then go back and read thoroughly, completing the Workout as you proceed.

Genes are the basic building blocks of heredity. If we want to understand the genetic contribution and evolutionary forces that shape behavior, we must understand how genes exert their effects and how they are transmitted from one generation to the next.

1. Do genes affect behavior directly? Explain.

2. Genes affect physical development by directing the synthesis of _____ molecules, of which there are about 70,000 kinds in the human body. Specifically, each gene provides the code that determines the sequence of _____ in a single type of protein. These proteins may be _____ or _____ . Physically, genes are segments of long molecules of _____ .

It is very important to understand that the effects of genes are always interwoven with the effects of the environment. Neither one alone can affect the biology or the behavior of an individual.

3. In the context of this chapter, what does *environment* mean?

4. How are genes thought to play a part in long-term behavioral changes resulting from experience?

5. Distinguish between a genotype and a phenotype.

It is useful to understand how genetic material is passed down from parents to offspring in sexual reproduction.

6. Strands of DNA are arranged in cells in structures called _____ .

7. How many pairs of chromosomes are in a normal human cell (except an egg or sperm cell)?

8. How do the sex chromosomes of males and females differ?

Cells can divide in two ways. One type of cell division is mitosis, the other, meiosis. An understanding of meiosis is important for understanding the hereditary transmission of genetic information and the way that genetic diversity comes about.

9. What is the purpose of mitosis? How is the genetic material in one resulting cell related to the genetic material in the other resulting cell?

10. Since the cells in all parts of your body (excluding egg and sperm cells) have the same gene content, how can the cells end up being so different from one another—cells in your stomach lining versus cells in your brain, for example?

11. Meiosis is the type of cell division that produces _____ or _____ cells. The process begins with _____ cells in the testes or ovaries. The DNA content of such a cell can be divided among the resulting cells in an infinite number of unique combinations because of the process of _____ prior to the first cell division as well as the _____ of chromosomes during the two cell divisions of meiosis. The number of chromosomes in each egg or sperm cell produced is _____ . Though they look alike for the most part, a person's egg or sperm cells are quite different because they contain different _____ .

In human sexual reproduction, the egg and sperm cells unite, combining their genetic information.

12. The union of an egg and a sperm produces a single new cell called a(n) _____ , which contains 23 _____ of chromosomes. The zygote then grows through the process of _____ .

13. Why is each zygote different from any other?

14. Explain the evolutionary advantage of reproducing sexually as opposed to asexually.

15. Identify the two types of twins, giving two names for each type. How are the twins genetically related in each type of twinning?

20. Explain the concept of percent relatedness. What is a person's percent relatedness to his or her biological mother? biological father? biological sibling?

We often talk about chromosomes in terms of pairs. In the case of humans, we usually say there are 23 pairs of chromosomes, not 46 chromosomes, although both are true. The pairing is emphasized because it has important consequences. It is not only the chromosomes that are paired but also the genes they carry. (*Hint:* Look at Figure 3.4 on text page 58.)

16. What is an allele?

Gregor Mendel is famous for his elegant studies of genetics in peas. Mendel's work, done in the nineteenth century, still offers a clear picture of certain hereditary patterns.

21. In one experiment, Mendel studied wrinkled-seed peas and round-seed peas. Explain Mendel's breeding procedure.

17. What does it mean to say someone is heterozygous at a particular locus? to say someone is homozygous at a particular locus?

22. Why did all of the F_1 generation have round seeds?

18. What does it mean to say an allele is dominant? to say an allele is recessive? Are all gene pairs either dominant or recessive? Explain.

23. Why did three-fourths of the F_2 generation have round seeds and the other one-fourth wrinkled seeds? (*Hint:* Look at Figure 3.5 on text page 60.)

Scott and Fuller revealed just such a pattern in the behavior of two dog breeds—cocker spaniels and basenjis. In other words, they showed that a particular behavioral trait was controlled by a single gene locus with one allele dominant over another. (*Hint:* See Figures 3.6 and 3.7 on text page 61.)

19. In each of the following cases, assume that there is an allele *M* which is dominant and an allele *m* which is recessive. Indicate which allele (*M* or *m*) will be expressed in the phenotype for each case.

 _____   a.   The individual is heterozygous.

 _____   b.   The individual is homozygous for *M*.

 _____   c.   The individual is homozygous for *m*.

24. How did purebred cocker and basenji puppies react when approached by a human who was a stranger to them?

25. When dogs of the two breeds were crossbred, how did the resulting (F_1) offspring behave in the same fear test?

26. When dogs of the F_1 generation were mated, what did the researchers observe with respect to the offspring's fearfulness? What conclusion was supported regarding the genetic basis of this type of behavior in cockers and basenjis.

27. Do these results indicate that fear in dogs is controlled by a single gene locus? that environment is irrelevant to the matter of fear in cockers and basenjis? Support your answer.

Some human disorders that affect behavior are also inherited in this basic single-gene fashion. Phenylketonuria (PKU) is an example of a disorder caused by a recessive gene.

28. What are the effects of PKU if it is left untreated?

29. What is the genetic basis of PKU? How does the genetic cause actually affect the body?

30. How can the effects of PKU be minimized through an environmental treatment?

31. How does the fact that genes are paired decrease the likelihood of developing certain genetic disorders?

Most single-gene disorders are produced by recessive genes, but a few are caused by dominant genes.

32. What is the evidence that at least one type of specific language impairment (SLI) results from a dominant gene? (*Hint:* See Figure 3.9 on text page 63.)

Some people have more friends than others. Some people sleep longer on average than others. Some people learn musical skills more easily than others. Most of the differences among individuals reflect the combined influences of many genes (in interaction with the environment, of course), not the effects of single genes.

33. Characteristics affected by many different genes are called _____ characteristics. When we measure differences among individuals in such traits, they will differ from one another in _____ rather than in type. In other words, individuals will not fall into distinct groups. Most often, the set of scores obtained for polygenic traits approximates a(n) _____ distribution. (*Hint:* Look at Figure 3.10 on text page 64.)

Selective breeding has been practiced for thousands of years to produce more desirable strains of plants and animals. Scientists have used selective breeding to produce strains of animals with specialized behavioral tendencies.

34. What is the basic approach followed in selective breeding?

Robert Tryon's work with "maze bright" and "maze dull" rats clearly pointed out that even complex behaviors, such as a rat's ability to learn a maze, can be genetically influenced.

35. How did Tryon produce the two strains of rats? How did he control for the possibility that the rats' "maze brightness" or "maze dullness" was due to what they learned from their mothers rather than to their genes?

36. Why is it important to note that Tryon tested his subjects only on their ability to learn a particular task?

Natural Selection and Its Implications for Psychology (pages 66–71)

CONSIDER *these questions before you go on. They are designed to help you start thinking about this subject, not to test your knowledge.*

Did Darwin know about genes when he developed his theory of evolution?

Since evolution is supposed to involve adaptation, how does nature "know" which traits will be adaptive in future generations?

Can individuals inherit traits that their parents have acquired through experience?

What are mutations, and what do they have to do with evolution?

How fast does evolution take place?

Does every characteristic that evolves in a species evolve for a particular purpose?

READ *this section of your text lightly. Then go back and read thoroughly, completing the Workout as you proceed.*

The publication of Charles Darwin's *The Origin of Species* in 1859 was a landmark event. It has had tremendous impact on the way we understand both

biological and psychological issues. Darwin used the familiar concept of selective breeding—which he termed *artificial selection*—as a point of reference. His major point was that nature, too, involves a kind of selective breeding. He called this *natural slection*.

1. Explain the concept of natural selection.

Darwin developed his theory without knowing anything about genes. Mendel's work, a first step toward understanding genes, was not yet known in the scientific world. Darwin knew only that *something* existed which was passed on from one generation to the next and which could change, forming the basis for evolutionary changes in a species.

2. List two sources of the genetic variability that is the foundation of evolution. Which is the ultimate source of genetic variation?

3. What is a mutation? Is it likely to be helpful or harmful? How does this fit in with natural selection?

4. Explain Lamarck's notion of the inheritance of acquired characteristics. Is this idea accepted today?

Evolutionary change is propelled by environmental change.

5. Specify some aspects of the environment that might change and thereby lead to evolutionary change?

6. Is evolutionary change always slow and steady? Support your answer.

7. Can complex genetic changes, such as those involved in brain organization, occur as rapidly as simpler changes, such as skin pigmentation? Why or why not?

People sometimes fall into intellectual traps in thinking about evolution. Several related misconceptions stem from the mistaken assumption that evolution involves foresight.

8. State three specific forms this fundamental misunderstanding can take.

   a.

   b.

   c.

Psychologists are of course interested in the effects of evolution on behavior.

9. Briefly explain how the process of natural selection can affect behavior.

10. How compatible is the functionalist approach in psychology with an evolutionary perspective on behavior?

Psychologists and biologists who take an evolutionary perspective distinguish between two kinds of explanations of behavior.

11. Define the terms below.

   a. ultimate explanation

   b. proximate explanation

12. Are ultimate and proximate explanations of behavior necessarily incompatible? Support your answer.

An explanation may be plausible, even elegant, and yet be incorrect. We must be careful to insist on scientific evidence in evaluating an explanation. We must also realize that not every characteristic results directly from natural selection. In other words, a characteristic doesn't necessarily exist because it is in itself useful.

13. Suppose a group of individuals leave their homeland and settle in a new area far away. These individuals happen to carry genes that produce descendants with bigger feet as compared with the feet of individuals who stayed behind. This difference is due just to chance and not to selection and is therefore an example of

_____ .

14. A specific characteristic may evolve not for its own adaptational benefits but as a mere _____ of an adaptive change. This characteristic could even be useless or harmful rather than helpful. Gould explained the _____ of the female spotted hyena in this way.

15. Such alternative explanations for characteristics are more likely to apply to one of the following. Which one? (Circle your answer.)

    a. Simple modifications of existing structures

    b. The basic existence and organization of structures

Ethology: The Study of Species-Typical Behavior Patterns (pages 71–80)

> *CONSIDER these questions before you go on. They are designed to help you start thinking about this subject, not to test your knowledge.*

Are there certain behaviors that seem to mark a dog as "doggy" or a fish as "fishy" or a person as "human"?

Do facial expressions mean the same thing across different cultures, or does each culture develop its own code?

> *READ this section of your text lightly. Then go back and read thoroughly, completing the Workout as you proceed.*

Ethology began in Europe in the 1930s as a branch of zoology. Ethologists focus on animal behavior as it occurs in natural settings. They attempt to understand species-typical behaviors, learn what environmental factors are required for them to develop in the young of a species, and identify the evolutionary origins of the behaviors.

1. Behavior patterns so characteristic of a species that they help to identify the species, such as dam building in beavers or speaking in humans, are called _____ behaviors.

In the case of the insects, fish, and birds studied by early ethologists, specific environmental stimuli may reliably produce the same response in all members of the species.

2. The stimulus that can elicit such a response is called a(n) _____ , and the response is called a(n) _____ . The relationship between the stimulus and response is essentially a(n) _____ , although the response is generally more complex and more context-sensitive than that term usually suggests.

Tinbergen uncovered several specific sign stimuli in studying the stickleback, a small fish.

3. In what biological context did the male stickleback attack other males? What was the sign stimulus for attack?

Human emotional expressions can be regarded as examples of species-typical behaviors. This idea was advanced by Darwin and has been supported by recent scientific research.

4. What kind of atlas did Paul Ekman and Wallace Friesen produce and how did they do it? (*Hint:* See Figure 3.14 on text page 72.)

5. Summarize Eibl-Eibesfeldt's evidence for the universality of the eyebrow flash. Does it necessarily follow that a universal nonverbal signal like the eyebrow flash is free of cultural influence?

The concept of species-typical behavior had to be modified when ethologists began to consider mammals as compared to fish or insects, for example.

6. Why are fixed action patterns and sign stimuli inappropriate in explaining the species-typical behaviors of mammals?

7. Explain the concept of biological preparedness, and relate it to either walking or talking in humans.

8. Why is it better to treat species-typical behavior as a relative concept rather than an absolute one?

A major interest of ethologists has been the environmental conditions necessary for species-typical behavior to develop in an individual's lifetime. The deprivation experiment has often been used to investigate this issue.

9. What is the logic behind deprivation experiments?

10. Contrast the findings in studies of fighting in rats and singing in white-crowned sparrows.

Ethologists cannot uncover the evolutionary course of behavior the way other scientists can uncover the evolutionary course of anatomy. Behavior leaves no fossil record, after all. An approach that *is* available to the ethologist is to systematically compare behaviors in present-day species.

11. It is important to distinguish two different classes of similarities ethologists use in their thinking. (*Hint:* See Figures 3.18 and 3.19 on text pages 76 and 77.)

    a. A(n) _____ is any similarity between species that exists because of convergent evolution.

    b. A(n) _____ is any similarity between species that exists because of their common ancestry.

    c. _____ has taken place when different species independently evolve a common characteristic because they have similar habitats or lifestyles.

12. In practice, how can ethologists distinguish between similarities based on homology and those based on analogy?

13. What kinds of questions can analogies and homologies help us to answer? (Answer separately for analogies and for homologies.)

14. Briefly summarize Darwin's work comparing different species of bees in order to understand the evolution of hive building.

Homologies have also been useful in understanding the evolution of smiling, laughing, and other behaviors.

15. Two kinds of human smiles can be differentiated: _____ and _____ .

16. What is the silent bared-teeth display seen in monkeys and apes? What is its apparent meaning? What kind of human smile is it thought to be related to?

17. What is the relaxed open-mouth display seen in monkeys and apes? What is its apparent meaning? How is it related to laughing and the happy smile in humans?

18. What is a vestigial characteristic? How can homology help us to understand a vestigial characteristic such as the human infant's grasp reflex? Can motives be vestigial in nature?

Sociobiology: The Comparative Study of Animals' Social Systems   (pages 81–93)

> *CONSIDER these questions before you go on. They are designed to help you start thinking about this subject, not to test your knowledge.*

Why do some species have long-term male-female sexual relationships while others do not?

Does fighting between animals of the same species make sense in evolutionary terms? Wouldn't it be costly to the species?

Why do some animals mark territories with their body scents?

Can human behavior be reasonably explained in evolutionary terms?

Are there some identifiable errors to watch out for in evolutionary arguments?

> *READ this section of your text lightly. Then go back and read thoroughly, completing the Workout as you proceed.*

In most species, especially very social species like ants, chimpanzees, or humans, a comprehensive understanding of behavior requires us to consider behavior in its social context.

1. Sociobiology is the study of

_____ in animals and generally

focuses on the _____ of species-

typical behaviors.

2. An approach often used in sociobiology is comparison by analogy. Briefly describe this approach.

Patterns of mating have been a major area of study in sociobiology. One way to classify different patterns of mating is according to the number of partners a male or female mates with over a particular period of time. Four classifications are commonly recognized.

3. In _____ , one male bonds with

more than one female. In _____ ,

one female bonds with more than one male. In

_____ , a male and a female bond

only with one another. In _____ ,

members of a group containing more than one

male and more than one female mate with one

another.

Sociobiologists are interested not only in why animals develop particular mating systems but in how mating systems affect other aspects of the animals' lives. Robert Trivers has related various patterns of courtship and mating behavior to a concept he calls parental investment.

4. Define *parental investment*.

5. What general principle relates parental investment to courtship and mating patterns in Trivers's theory?

6. Answer all three parts to this question about polygyny, the most common mating system in mammals. According to Trivers, why does high female parental investment lead to each of the following?

   a. polygyny

   b. large size of males

   c. high selectivity in the female's choice of a mate

7. Answer the following questions regarding polyandry, the most common mating system for some fish and birds.

   a. Why does polyandry make sense for egg-laying species?

   b. How do sex differences in the polyandrous species known as spotted sandpipers support Trivers's theory?

8. Answer the following questions regarding monogamy.

   a. What conditions should lead to equal parental investment and thus monogamy?

   b. How is equal parental investment related to sex differences in size and strength?

   c. In what kinds of species is monogamy common? Give specific examples.

9. What evolutionary reasons might underlie the fact that social monogamy is not always matched by sexual monogamy?

10. What evolutionary advantages might be conferred by polygynandry in chimpanzees and bonobos?

11. Contrast mating behavior in bonobos with that in chimpanzees.

Sociobiologists have also given a great deal of attention to the subject of aggression.

12. How do sociobiologists and ethologists define *aggression*?

An important form of aggression is territorial aggression.

13. Why do animals engage in territorial aggression?

14. What are two means by which animal species accomplish territorial defense without actual physical battle? Give some specific examples.

Animals that live in large groups have found various means to manage aggression within their ranks.

15. How and why are submissive signals used to limit aggression within a colony?

16. What is a dominance hierarchy, and how could it limit physical aggression?

In some species, dominance is not based entirely on individual fighting ability and dominance hierarchies are not rigid.

17. In chimpanzees and bonobos, what factors other than a male's own fighting ability may help to determine his dominance?

Animals of a given species may fight with one another even to the point of injury or death. But they may also help one another. Help sometimes takes the form of cooperation, and at other times appears to be altruistic.

18. Correctly identify each of the following.

   a. _____ occurs when an individual helps another at the expense of its own survival or reproductive capacity.

   b. _____ is any behavior that increases the survival or reproductive capacity of another individual.

   c. _____ involves an individual's helping another while at the same time helping itself.

19. How does kin selection theory explain the occurrence of altruistic behavior? What evidence supports this theory?

20. How does reciprocity theory explain the occurrence of altruistic behavior? Has behavior consistent with this theory been observed in the animal world?

21. In what sense are both theories attempting to redefine altruistic behavior as not really altruistic?

The most provocative area for sociobiological thinking has been human social behavior. Historical distortions of evolutionary thinking have prompted many people to be cautious about human sociobiology despite the fact that psychologists increasingly consider it a useful perspective. In considering human sociobiology, we must be aware of certain fallacies that can lead to such distorted thinking.

22. What is the naturalistic fallacy? Illustrate your answer with an example of such distorted thinking.

23. What is the deterministic fallacy? Illustrate your answer with an example of such distorted thinking.

After you have studied the chapter thoroughly, CHECK your understanding with the Self-Test that follows.

Cautions aside, sociobiologists have produced quite interesting hypotheses regarding human behavior—including the human preference for living in communities, nepotism, human mating patterns, and male violence.

24. Which ape species are we humans most like in terms of our tendency to live in communities? Why might humans be predisposed to live in communities?

25. Define *nepotism*. How widespread is it? How well does it fit with the kin selection theory of altruistic behavior?

26. Explore the evidence that humans evolved as a somewhat polygynous species.

27. Is there evidence to support the view that men are generally more violent than women? How could sociobiology help to explain sexual jealousy as a motive for male violence?

Be sure to READ the Concluding Thoughts at the end of the chapter. Note important points in your Workout. Then consolidate your learning by answering the focus questions in the margins of the text.

Self-Test 1

Multiple-Choice Questions

1. Genes that can occupy the same locus—and can thus pair with one another—are called:
   a. homozygous.   c. alleles.
   b. dizygotic.   d. dominant genes.

2. Suppose a person well-informed in the area of genetics refers to "genes for spatial ability." A correct interpretation of this phrase would be:
   a. "genes that directly control a person's ability to process spatial information and have no other function."
   b. "genes that produce a particular anatomy and physiology, which in turn affect a person's spatial ability."
   c. "genes that directly control cognitive ability in general and spatial ability in particular."
   d. that it's a joke since genes have no effect (direct or indirect) on psychological functioning.

3. Meiosis results in egg and sperm cells containing _____ the number of chromosomes contained in each of the body's other cells.
   a. exactly
   b. half
   c. twice
   d. four times

4. The value of sexual—as opposed to asexual—reproduction is the production of offspring that are:
   a. genetically diverse.
   b. genetically uniform.
   c. genetically similar to their parents.
   d. numerous.

5. Genes affect both physical development and behavior by directing the synthesis of:
   a. DNA.
   b. chromosomes.
   c. alleles.
   d. structural proteins and enzymes.

6. Suppose members of a particular species of geese exhibit an unlearned and very reliable series of movements to retrieve an egg that has rolled out of the nest. This behavior would be an example of a(n):

   a. sign stimulus.
   b. vestigial characteristic.
   c. altruistic behavior.
   d. fixed action pattern.

7. Any characteristic that varies in a continuous fashion in a population should be presumed:

   a. to be polygenic.
   b. to be based on a single gene.
   c. to involve whole chromosomes.
   d. not to be genetically influenced.

8. Tryon's attempt to selectively breed "maze bright" and "maze dull" rats:

   a. resulted in failure.
   b. showed that only very small differences could be produced, even over 20 generations.
   c. showed that large differences could be produced over several generations.
   d. proved that genes are more important than environment in determining intelligence.

9. In the process called *natural selection*:

   a. the breeding of certain domestic animals is controlled in order to produce desirable traits in future generations.
   b. inherited traits helpful in overcoming barriers to survival and reproduction are more likely to be passed down to offspring.
   c. genes that will be helpful in suiting offspring to future environments are selected for.
   d. nature "selects" the traits of the next generation by way of a random shuffle of genes.

10. If chance factors alone cause the gene pools in two populations of a species to differ, we refer to the situation as:

    a. genetic drift.   c. artificial selection.
    b. genetic deviance.   d. proximate change.

11. The very effective dietary treatment of phenylketonuria (PKU) is evidence that:

    a. the disease is not hereditary as was once believed.
    b. nutrition can change genetic makeup.
    c. environmental and genetic factors interact to determine physical and behavioral outcomes.
    d. the disease does not involve a dominant gene.

12. Deprivation experiments are designed to answer ethological questions about:

    a. whether a particular behavior is species-typical.
    b. the sign stimulus for a particular behavior.
    c. the evolutionary course of a particular behavior.
    d. the environmental conditions needed for an individual to develop a species-typical behavior.

13. Similarities between species that are due to convergent evolution are called:

    a. analogies.
    b. homologies.
    c. analogies in mammals and homologies in nonmammalian species.
    d. homologies in mammals and analogies in nonmammalian species.

14. The ability of premature human infants to support their weight with the grasp reflex is probably an example of:

    a. the inheritance of acquired characteristics.
    b. a vestigial characteristic.
    c. a correlate of structure.
    d. ritualization.

15. According to Robert Trivers, polygyny is related to _____ parental investment.

    a. high female/low male
    b. low female/high male
    c. equal male and female
    d. no particular pattern of

Essay Questions

16. Sociobiologists contend that certain behavioral tendencies in humans arise from our evolutionary history. Discuss two of these tendencies.

17. Does evolution involve foresight? Explain.

After you have assessed your understanding on the basis of Self-Test 1 and have tried to strengthen your preparation in any areas of weakness, GO ON to Self-Test 2.

Self-Test 2

Multiple-Choice Questions

1. Which of the following is true of polygenic effects?
   a. Most measurable differences between people can be explained in terms of single genes; that is, they are not polygenic.
   b. Without examining the genetic material itself, there is no way to determine whether a characteristic is polygenic in origin.
   c. Eye color is a classic example of a polygenic effect.
   d. The distribution of scores for a polygenic trait often approximates a normal distribution.

2. The normal human cell (other than egg or sperm cells) contains _____ pairs of chromosomes.
   a. 12   c. 23
   b. 22   d. 46

3. The process by which cells divide for the purpose of normal body growth is:
   a. mitosis.
   b. meiosis.
   c. crossing over.
   d. protein synthesis.

4. We can assume that _____ are genetically identical.
   a. identical twins
   b. fraternal twins
   c. both identical and fraternal twins
   d. no two people

5. A friend of yours has brown eyes and her mother has blue eyes. Assuming that blue is recessive and brown is dominant, you can conclude that your friend:
   a. is heterozygous for eye color.
   b. is homozygous for eye color.
   c. is monozygotic for eye color.
   d. is brown-eyed as far as phenotype is concerned, but you can infer nothing about her genotype.

6. When Mendel crossed purebred wrinkled-seed peas with purebred round-seed peas, he found that all of the F_1 generation had round seeds. When he bred the F_1 peas with one another, he found that:
   a. the F_2 peas all had round seeds.
   b. the F_2 peas all had wrinkled seeds.
   c. half the F_2 peas had round seeds and the other half had wrinkled seeds.
   d. three-fourths of the F_2 peas had round seeds and the other one-fourth had wrinkled seeds.

7. The primary job of genes is to direct the sequence of _____ that make up each type of protein molecule.
   a. DNA
   b. amino acids
   c. RNA
   d. enzymes

8. Which of the following is true of mutations?
   a. Mutations have little effect on the course of evolution because they are so rare.
   b. Mutations are errors in the replication process; as such, they inevitably lead to harmful changes in the structure of DNA.
   c. Although mutations usually have harmful consequences, they are sometimes helpful.
   d. Mutations are the new collections of genes that result from the normal reshuffling of genes in sexual reproduction.

9. Which of the following represents a question posed from a functionalist perspective?
   a. At what rate does evolution take place?
   b. Which species are most closely related to one another?
   c. What are the possible uses of the human voice?
   d. Why do dogs have such a keen sense of smell?

10. The human taste for sugar, which may have several negative health consequences, can be understood as a:
    a. vestigial characteristic.
    b. genetic side effect.
    c. species-typical behavior.
    d. result of nutritional deprivation.

11. Birds, some insects, and some mammals can fly. Similarities among these groups are not due to common ancestry and would thus represent:
    a. homologies.
    b. analogies.
    c. vestigial characteristics.
    d. fixed action patterns.

12. An *ultimate explanation* of behavior is an explanation of:
    a. the mechanism that actually produces the behavior.
    b. the immediate environmental conditions that bring on the behavior.
    c. the form a behavior will ultimately take upon further evolution.
    d. why a particular evolutionary development offered an adaptive advantage.

13. A species in which an individual female bonds with several males would be classified as:
    a. polygynandrous.   c. polygynous.
    b. polyandrous.   d. monogamous.

14. Which of the following is *not* a means of limiting fights between members of the same species?
    a. the tendency for animals to keep out of territories marked by others
    b. the establishment of dominance hierarchies
    c. the tendency for an intruder in another animal's territory to become less aggressive
    d. the adoption of a polygynous mating system

15. When we assume that human genetic biases toward certain behaviors cannot be countered by learning or culture, we are falling prey to the _____ fallacy.
    a. deterministic   c. naturalistic
    b. foresight   d. genetic dominance

Essay Questions

16. What is PKU? What causes the disorder? How does the example of PKU illustrate the importance of considering genetics and environment together?

17. How do sociobiologists explain animal behavior that appears to be altruistic?

Answers

Genes and the Inheritance of Behavioral Characteristics

2. protein; amino acids; structural proteins; enzymes; DNA

6. chromosomes

7. 23

11. egg; sperm; precursor; crossing over; random distribution; 23; genes

12. zygote; pairs; mitosis

19. **a.** *M*, **b.** *M*, **c.** *m*

33. polygenic; degree; normal

Natural Selection and Its Implications for Psychology

13. genetic drift

14. side effect; large clitoris

15. a

Ethology: The Study of Species-Typical Behavior Patterns

1. species-typical

2. sign stimulus; fixed action pattern; reflex

11. **a.** analogy, **b.** homology, **c.** convergent evolution

15. happy; greeting

Sociobiology: The Comparative Study of Animals' Social Systems

1. social systems; ultimate functions

3. polygyny; polyandry; monogamy; polygynandry

18. a. Altruism, **b.** Helping, **c.** Cooperation

Self-Test 1

1. **c.** (p. 58)

2. **b.** Genes have their effect only by controlling the manufacture of proteins. In that way, they affect an individual's anatomy and physiology. Their effects on behavior are due to the particular anatomy and physiology they create and are thus indirect. (p. 54)

3. **b.** There are 23 pairs of chromosomes in most of the body's cells, but only 23 chromosomes in an egg or sperm cell. When the egg and sperm combine to form the zygote, the full complement of 23 pairs of chromosomes is restored. (p. 56)

4. **a.** Sexual reproduction essentially "shuffles the genetic deck" to produce great diversity in offspring. Diversity offers an evolutionary advantage in that some of the many different types of individuals created may be capable of adapting more successfully to changing environmental conditions. (p. 58)

5. **d.** (p. 54)

6. **d.** (p. 71)

7. **a.** A polygenic characteristic can often be described in terms of a normal distribution. A single-gene kind of pattern is indicated by stepwise variation. (p. 64)

8. **c.** (pp. 64–65)

9. **b.** Remember that natural selection acts to produce offspring better suited to the current environment, not some future environment. Natural selection is driven by success or failure in that current environment. It cannot be affected by an unforeseen future. (p. 66)

10. **a.** (p. 70)

11. **c.** (p. 62)

12. **d.** (p. 75)

13. **a.** Convergent evolution refers to a situation in which similarities of environment or lifestyle lead to similar but independent evolutionary developments. The root of the similarity is not genetic relatedness. In this case, we have an analogy, not a homology. (p. 76)

14. **b.** It may help to remember that a vestige is a leftover trace of something from the past. (p. 80)

15. **a.** (p. 82)

16. Sociobiologists seek to find biases in human behavior that are understandable from an evolutionary perspective. One such bias is the tendency to live in communities. Whether humans live in smaller towns or larger cities, they tend to group together, with smaller groups, such as families, forming within the larger ones. Humans suffer loneliness when apart from human companionship and regard those who deliberately avoid such companionship as deviant. The tendency may have come about because humans were better able to preserve their safety, acquire food, rear children, and do other things that aid in survival of self and species as part of a group than alone.

Another tendency is toward nepotism, in which individuals help kin more than nonkin. In a number of societies, related individuals are more likely to share goods and land with one another than with nonkin. Kin tend to come to one another's aid more than nonkin, for example, in taking orphaned children within the family. Also, violence may be lower among related individuals than among unrelated individuals in similar living arrangements. The evolutionary explanation for this would be similar to that offered by the kin-selection theory of altruism. Individuals helping kin or sharing with kin are helping to perpetuate genes they share with those individuals. (*Note:* The chapter mentions other tendencies pointed out by sociobiologists that would work equally well in answer to this question.) (pp. 89–93)

17. One of the most common errors people make in thinking about evolutionary adaptation is to assume it involves foresight. Natural selection operates on the basis of the current environment, not on the basis of some future environment. This should be obvious given the way natural selection operates. Selection comes about only because individuals with genes helpful in overcoming obstacles to reproduction pass those genes on, whereas individuals with unhelpful or harmful genes will tend not to pass them on since they will have fewer or no offspring. Future environments can't sort individuals into those two categories—those who successfully reproduce and those who don't. Only the present environment can.

A second common error is the assumption that every trait has evolved for its adaptive value. Random factors can affect the direction in which a particular population evolves, as in genetic drift. Also, some traits evolve as nonadaptive side effects of adaptive changes. Finally, some structures that evolved for particular adaptive reasons can then be used for other nonadaptive purposes. For example, there is nothing particularly adaptive about solving crossword puzzles. The human brain can be used for that purpose but it certainly did not evolve for that purpose. (pp. 68–71)

Self-Test 2

1. **d.** (p. 64)

2. **c.** (p. 56)

3. **a.** (p. 56)

4. **a.** (p. 58)

5. **a.** Since your friend's mother has blue eyes and blue is recessive, you know her genotype; she has two blue-eye alleles. Since your friend received one of her genes for eye color from her mother, she must have one blue-eye allele. Since she's brown-eyed, the other allele must be a dominant brown-eye allele from her father. (p. 59)

6. **d.** The original purebred round-seed peas had only round-seed alleles to contribute to offspring, whereas purebred wrinkled-seed peas had only wrinkled-seed alleles. In the F_1 generation, all peas have one round-seed allele and one wrin-

kled-seed allele. Because the F_1 generation all had round seeds, we know that round-seed alleles are dominant. When F_1 peas are bred with one another, one-fourth of the peas will have two wrinkled-seed alleles, one-fourth will have two round-seed alleles, and the remaining peas will have one of each type of allele. But because round-seed alleles are dominant, all but the one-fourth with two wrinkled-seed alleles will be round-seeded. (pp. 59–60)

7. **b.** (p. 54)

8. **c.** As the text states, mutation is ultimately the basis of all genetic variation, because it alone introduces truly new genetic information. (p. 67)

9. **d.** The functionalist seeks to understand actual behaviors, not potential behaviors, and the ways they promoted survival and reproduction in the species. (p. 69)

10. **a.** (p. 80)

11. **b.** The case described is one resulting from convergent evolution. (p. 76)

12. **d.** (p. 69)

13. **b.** (p. 81)

14. **d.** (pp. 86–87)

15. **a.** (p. 90)

16. PKU stands for phenylketonuria, a genetic disorder produced by a single recessive gene. A person with PKU lacks an enzyme for handling phenylalanine, an amino acid found in milk and other protein foods. Without the enzyme, phenylalanine is turned into a toxic acid that severely damages the brain. But the disease can be treated environmentally—specifically, through diet. If the person does not take in phenylalanine, the acid is not produced and the brain is not damaged. Keeping phenylalanine out of the diet is especially important in infancy since brain development is critical then. It is also important when a woman with PKU is pregnant. (pp. 62–63)

17. Both kin-selection and reciprocity theories try to reframe behavior that is apparently selfless as behavior that is in some sense selfish. Kin-selection theory suggests that the gene promoting the "altruistic" act in an individual may be destroyed, but other copies of the same gene in the individual's kin will be saved as a result; in this case, it is the gene that is "selfish." In reciprocity theory, there is an expectation of the favor being returned at some future time. (p. 88)

Chapter 4　　　　　Basic Processes of Learning

READ *the introduction below before you read the chapter in the text.*

Learning involves adaptation to the environment that occurs within an individual's lifetime. It is a set of processes through which experience can have an effect on an individual's future behavior. As a central topic in psychology with relevance to many different subfields, learning has been much studied and much debated over the course of psychology's history. Three primary perspectives—behavioral, cognitive, and ecological—combine to give us a fuller view of learning and deeper insights into what it is, how it takes place, and which factors affect it.

The behavioral perspective characterizes learning in terms of observable stimuli and responses. Early behaviorists such as John B. Watson and B. F. Skinner insisted that what takes place inside the learner is irrelevant to scientific psychology because it cannot be observed and thus cannot be investigated scientifically.

One category of learning that has been intensively studied by behaviorists is classical conditioning, which involves the learning of reflexes. Ivan Pavlov discovered classical conditioning as a by-product of his research on digestive processes. He then switched his focus to this type of learning, analyzing the process through which it occurs and studying various phenomena of classical conditioning, such as extinction, spontaneous recovery, generalization, and discrimination. The chapter discusses conditioned emotional reactions and drug reactions in illustrating the practical significance of classical conditioning.

Unlike classical conditioning, which focuses on reflexive behavior, operant conditioning involves learning to perform certain actions in order to produce certain consequences: We study to get good grades, we buy food to alleviate hunger, we work for money, and so on. The most fundamental idea in operant conditioning is Edward Thorndike's law of effect. According to the law of effect, the probability of performing a given behavior in a given situation depends on the effects it has had in past experience in that situation. B. F. Skinner was the best-known investigator in this area and in fact coined the term *operant conditioning*. The basic concepts related to operant conditioning are reinforcers, shaping, extinction, schedules of partial reinforcement, discriminative stimuli, chaining, secondary reinforcement, and punishment. Operant conditioning has important practical applications, including behavior therapy and biofeedback training.

Advocates of the cognitive perspective contend that the very things behaviorists would leave out—those mysterious unseen processes inside the learner—are the things one must study to really understand learning. The essential point of the cognitive theorist is that learning involves information that is meaningful to the learner. It causes the learner to expect or predict certain things to happen under certain circumstances. The chapter explains how classical and operant conditioning can be understood from this perspective and presents evidence to support the cognitive view. The cognitive perspective has also been applied to place learning, with the work of Edward Tolman being especially prominent. Tolman showed that animals learning their way around mazes are actually forming cognitive maps—mental representations of spatial layouts. Another kind of learning that fits well with the cognitive viewpoint is learning based on watching what others do. Both animals and people are capable of such observational learning.

The ecological perspective emphasizes that specialized learning mechanisms have been developed through evolution to better enable animals to survive in their natural environment. This view makes sense of certain findings that are otherwise puzzling from the behavioral or cognitive perspective. For example, the ecological perspective helps to explain special cases of learning involving food aversion and food preference. It also helps us to understand why some stimuli work better than others in experiments that attempt to condition fear, what happens when baby birds become imprinted, and more.

LOOK over the table of contents for this chapter in your textbook before you continue with your study.

Notice that there are focus questions in the margins of the text for your use in studying the material. The following chart lists which Study Guide questions relate to which focus questions.

Focus Questions   Study Guide Questions

The Behavioral Perspective: Acquiring New
Responses to and for Stimuli
            1   3–4
            2–4   5–20
            5–9   21–29
            10–13   1–10
            14–21   11–28

The Cognitive Perspective: Acquiring Information
About the World
            22–29   1–15
            30   16–17
            31–33   18–26

The Ecological Perspective: Filling the Blanks in
Species-Typical Behavior Patterns
            34–39   1–9
            40–42   10–12

The Integrated Study Workout

Complete one section at a time.

The Behavioral Perspective on Learning— Classical Conditioning   (pages 97–105)

CONSIDER these questions before you go on. They are designed to help you start thinking about this subject, not to test your knowledge.

Can an emotional response like fear be learned? Can it be unlearned?

Why do we often start to salivate at the very sight of an advertisement for a tasty food?

Does classical conditioning have any practical applications?

READ this section of your text lightly. Then go back and read thoroughly, completing the Workout as you proceed.

Before we focus on the behavioral perspective, let us consider generally what learning is and how it fits into the field of psychology. Learning lies at the heart of psychology. Behavioral psychology and cognitive

psychology, for example, deal with it directly. But there is hardly an area that does not need to consider learning. The social psychologist, the personality theorist, and the clinical psychologist are all dealing with individuals who bring a history of learning to current situations.

Learning depends on mechanisms provided by natural selection. These mechanisms allow individual members of a species to adapt to the constant environmental change they will face in their lives.

1. Define *learning*, making sure to clarify all essential terms.

2. Indicate, by circling *yes* or *no*, whether the individual's behavior in each case is due to learning.

    Is it due to learning?

    Yes No **a.** A new employee in the customer service department watches videotapes of employees handling difficult customers effectively; then she handles her first grouch with aplomb by using the same techniques.

    Yes No **b.** A toddler touches a hot stove and then immediately withdraws his hand and starts crying.

    Yes No **c.** A student passes a bakery on the way to class one morning and finds that the sight of the fresh bread literally makes her mouth water.

    Yes No **d.** A child receives warm applause and praise after singing for dinner guests; then he volunteers to sing again on a similar occasion.

Behaviorism is an approach within psychology that has been important in several ways. It has helped to establish psychology as an objective, scientific endeavor as well as teaching us a great deal about learning.

3. Describe the major characteristics and goals of behaviorism.

4. Below are listed two forms of learning that have been intensively studied by behaviorists. Define each.

   a. classical conditioning

   b. operant conditioning

Behaviorists have spent decades studying classical conditioning—and with considerable success. They have discovered basic principles that underlie this type of learning and have developed some interesting and useful applications of those principles. In order to understand classical conditioning, you will need to learn some essential terminology—beginning with words such as *reflex.* Classical conditioning concerns the learning of reflexes.

5. Define *reflex.*

6. a. A(n) _____ is a particular, well-defined event in the environment.

   b. A particular, well-defined bit of behavior is a(n) _____ .

7. Give three examples of a stimulus and three examples of a response.

8. Why is it important to note that reflexes are mediated by the nervous system?

9. A decline in the magnitude of a reflexive response when the stimulus is repeated several times in succession is called _____ , which _____ (always/sometimes/never) qualifies as a form of learning.

Ivan Pavlov, a Russian physiologist, is a key figure in the study of classical conditioning. Even before he discovered classical conditioning, he was well-known for his staunch devotion to scientific rigor and for his research on digestive reflexes.

10. How did Pavlov come to discover classical conditioning?

A phenomenon that was at first only a nuisance soon attracted Pavlov's scientific eye. Once he realized he could study it as a reflex he began to analyze classical conditioning through a number of carefully controlled experiments. In his early experiments, he broke classical conditioning down into its elementary parts and gave them descriptive names. (See Figure 4.2 on text page 100 for help in answering the following questions.)

11. Explain the concept of a conditioned reflex. Why is the term *conditioned* used?

12. What is a conditioned stimulus? a conditioned response?

13. What is an unconditioned stimulus? an unconditioned response?

14. Identify the following aspects of Pavlov's classic experiment, in which a dog learned to salivate in response to a bell.

   a. The *conditioned reflex* involved was

   _____ .

   b. The *unconditioned stimulus* was

   _____ .

   c. The *unconditioned response* was

   _____ .

   d. The *conditioned stimulus* was the

   _____ .

   e. The *conditioned response* was

   _____ .

15. Trace the course of classical conditioning by answering the following questions about the same experiment you described in item 14 above.

   a. How did the dog respond to the food prior to its pairing with the bell?

   b. How did the dog respond to the bell prior to its pairing with the food?

   c. How did the dog respond to the bell after it was paired with the food?

16. The nature of the conditioned response is determined by the nature of the _____ .

17. Give examples of stimuli that can serve as conditioned stimuli. What are some different responses that can be conditioned?

Classical conditioning is not just a phenomenon that psychologists study in laboratories. It is something you encounter in everyday life.

18. Produce two simple examples of classically conditioned responses that a person or animal might make under appropriate circumstances. (See the examples on text page 101 and try to think of analogous situations.)

   a.

   b.

Long before Pavlov, philosophers had contemplated the nature of learning. Aristotle had proposed a law of learning called the law of association by contiguity. There is a certain similarity between this law and Pavlov's principle of conditioning—but there are also important differences.

19. State Aristotle's law of association by contiguity.

20. How was Pavlov's principle of conditioning similar to Aristotle's law? How was it different, and why is that difference critical?

Pavlov and his colleagues did hundreds of experiments on classical conditioning. In the course of that work, they uncovered a number of phenomena that are still considered of major importance. One issue—the permanence of conditioned reflexes (or the lack of permanence)—was of particular interest to Pavlov.

21. Answer the following questions concerning extinction. (*Note:* Students often make a leap from the term *extinction* to saying that a response has become "extinct." However, the proper terminology is to say a response has been *extinguished*.)

a. What is extinction and under what conditions does it occur?

b. Does extinction mean that the learning that took place has been totally erased? Explain.

Pavlov's team also studied the complementary phenomena of generalization and discrimination.

22. What is generalization? How does an organism's response change as the test stimulus becomes less and less similar to the actual conditioned stimulus?

23. Describe the procedure of discrimination training. How does it affect an organism's tendency to generalize?

24. How can classical conditioning and discrimination training be used to study an animal's sensory capabilities?

John B. Watson was a pioneer in the area of behaviorism and in the application of classical conditioning to human behavior.

25. Describe the work of John B. Watson and Rosalie Rayner on conditioned fear.

26. Give some other examples of conditioned emotional responses from everyday life. (Don't restrict yourself to examples involving fear.)

Some of the most fascinating and practical work in classical conditioning has involved conditioned drug reactions.

27. Describe the results of Pavlov's experiment on conditioned drug reactions.

28. What is a conditioned counteractive drug effect? (Be sure to describe the underlying mechanism.)

29. How can conditioned counteractive drug effects help to explain some drug overdose cases?

The Behavioral Perspective on Learning— Operant Conditioning (pages 105–117)

CONSIDER these questions before you go on. They are designed to help you start thinking about this subject, not to test your knowledge.

How do the consequences of a behavior affect the chances of that behavior occurring again?

How would a behaviorist explain the fact that some people study hard and others never open a book? that some people are compulsively neat and others are hopelessly messy? that some people save their money and others spend as if there were no tomorrow?

Can we learn to control internal bodily processes such as heart rate or blood pressure?

How can we develop desirable habits in ourselves and eradicate bad ones?

Is punishment always an effective way to handle a child's misbehavior? Are there preferable alternatives?

> *READ this section of your text lightly. Then go back and read thoroughly, completing the Workout as you proceed.*

Throughout each day, we engage in behaviors that have consequences. We turn a key in a lock and are thus able to open a door. We give money to a clerk and leave a store happily bearing some new treasure. We smile at someone and receive a smile in return. We try to carry too many books at once and watch them tumble into a heap at our feet.

1. Why are the terms *operant* and *instrumental* used to describe certain responses?

Edward Thorndike was studying learning at about the same time as Pavlov but was approaching it from a very different angle.

2. Describe Thorndike's basic experimental procedure.

3. Pavlov's training procedure allowed him to _____ the response he wanted, and he focused on stimuli that _____ (preceded/followed) that response. Thorndike, in contrast, had to wait until an animal _____ the response that led to the _____ of an open door and thus to food.

4. State Thorndike's law of effect.

Though B. F. Skinner did not originate the law of effect, he spent many years studying and extending this simple but powerful idea. In fact, he gave us some of the tools we use to study this type of learning and much of the language we use to talk about it.

5. Either describe or draw and label a Skinner box. Why is it a more efficient research tool than a puzzle box? (*Hint:* Look at Figure 4.8 on text page 108.)

6. *Operant conditioning* is a term coined by Skinner. You have already defined operant conditioning in item 4b on page 47, but it would be a good idea to look back at that definition now and write it below.

7. Define *reinforcer.*

Skinner argued that operant conditioning determines virtually all of our behavior. It may not seem to us that we are being controlled by relationships between our responses and their consequences, but that doesn't mean it isn't so.

8. Can people be operantly conditioned without even realizing it? Briefly describe the work of Ralph Hefferline in answering this question and relate it to the learning of motor skills.

Psychologists have taken the principles of learning discovered through research on operant conditioning and applied them to real-life problems such as smoking and headaches.

9. Briefly describe the work of a behavior therapist.

10. Explain how biofeedback training works and describe some of its uses.

Like classical conditioning, operant conditioning is associated with a number of behavioral phenomena. (*Note:* In several instances, the same term, such as *extinction*, is used in both classical and operant conditioning. Make sure you understand how the term applies in each case.)

11. Describe the technique of shaping. Why is it sometimes necessary? Give an example to illustrate how shaping might be carried out.

12. The absence of reinforcement for a response and the resulting decline in response rate are both called _____ .

13. Every occurrence of a particular response is reinforced in _____ reinforcement. In contrast, a response is reinforced only sometimes in _____ reinforcement.

Partial reinforcement is more precisely described in terms of four types of schedules, which are related to specific rates and patterns of responding in the individual being reinforced. The behavior produced by two of these schedules of reinforcement is especially resistant to extinction. Schedules are either fixed or variable and either ratio-based or interval-based.

14. Write the name of the schedule that applies in each of the cases below. The response alternatives are fixed-ratio (FR), variable-ratio (VR), fixed-

interval (FI), and variable-interval (VI). (See Figure 4.10 on text page 112.)

_____ a. A response must be emitted a certain average number of times before a reinforcer is given.

_____ b. A specific unchanging period of time following a reinforced response must elapse before another response is reinforced.

_____ c. Reinforcement becomes available only after some average amount of time has elapsed, but the exact amount of time at any given point is unpredictable for the learner.

_____ d. This schedule underlies many gambling systems and helps to explain gambling behavior.

_____ e. A specific unchanging number of responses must be made before reinforcement will be given.

15. In general, _____ (ratio/interval) schedules produce faster responding.

16. What is the partial-reinforcement effect? Which schedules produce the greatest resistance to extinction? Why?

In classical conditioning, the stimuli that are of interest to us precede the response. In fact, in this reflexive kind of responding the stimuli actually elicit the response. In operant conditioning, reinforcers are stimuli that follow the response. But operant behavior is also influenced by stimuli that precede it.

17. What is a discriminative stimulus?

18. How does operant behavior come under the control of a discriminative stimulus?

By definition, reinforcers are capable of affecting behavior, but reinforcers differ in that some are "born" and others are "made."

19. Describe chaining and mention one practical use of it.

20. Label the following reinforcers.

_____ a.   A stimulus that has acquired its reinforcing value through previous training

_____ b.   A stimulus that is reinforcing even without previous training

_____ c.   A secondary reinforcer, such as money, that can be saved and turned in later for another reinforcer

Reinforcement, which increases the chances that a particular response will occur, can be either positive or negative. It is important that you clearly understand what the terms *positive* and *negative* refer to (and what they don't refer to).

21. Define *positive reinforcement*. What is a positive reinforcer? Give two examples of positive reinforcement.

22. Define *negative reinforcement*. What is a negative reinforcer? Give two examples of negative reinforcement.

23. What do the terms *positive* and *negative* refer to in these cases? What do they not refer to?

In any discussion of how consequences affect future behavior, we must consider the case of punishment.

24. What is punishment? In what sense is it the opposite of reinforcement?

25. What is positive punishment? negative punishment? (*Hint:* Look at Figure 4.11 on text page 116.)

26. Recall from item 23 that the terms *positive* and *negative* refer to arrival and removal, respectively, not to the direction of change in behavior. A stimulus that serves as a positive reinforcer, such as money, can become a(n) _____ punisher. A stimulus that acts as a negative reinforcer, such as a queasy feeling in the stomach, can become a(n) _____ punisher.

Skinner and others have suggested that we might do better to use positive reinforcement rather than punishment in modifying the behavior of others, especially children.

27. Why might positive reinforcement be preferable to punishment in correcting a child's behavior?

28. Is punishment ever a good idea? Explain.

The Cognitive Perspective on Learning:
Acquiring Information About the World
(pages 118–130)

> CONSIDER *these questions before you go on. They are designed to help you start thinking about this subject, not to test your knowledge.*

What actually happens in the learner's mind when classical or operant conditioning takes place?

What would happen to the rate of operant responding if the magnitude of the reinforcer were suddenly increased or decreased?

When is it—and when is it not—a good idea to deliberately reinforce someone's behavior? For example, is it a good idea to give a child money for reading or for practicing the piano?

How do animals find their way around the environment? Do they learn a sequence of simple responses, such as "turn left," "turn left," "go through the door," "turn right"? Or do they learn something more sophisticated?

Can we learn just by watching someone else?

> READ *this section of your text lightly. Then go back and read thoroughly, completing the Workout as you proceed.*

The cognitive approach has some roots in behaviorism, by way of those behaviorists who called themselves *S-O-R*, as opposed to *S-R*, theorists. That little *O* in *S-O-R* represented a very significant departure from strict behaviorism, because it stood for the events occurring inside the organism, which mediate the relationship between stimulus and response. In the area of learning, the cognitive perspective focuses on mental events that take place inside the organism during learning.

1. How have cognitive psychologists and *S-O-R* theorists before them defended a scientific interest in mental constructs?

Cognitive theorists differ from traditional behaviorists in how they view conditioning. One important difference lies in their conception of the role of the stimulus.

2. According to cognitive theorists, behaviorists ignore a critical aspect of the stimulus, which is its _____ .

3. In an experiment involving human subjects and linguistic stimuli, Gregory Razran showed that meaning is critical in classical conditioning. Briefly describe this experiment.

4. How did Richard Herrnstein show that meaning is critical in classical conditioning, even when pigeons are the subjects and the stimuli are pictorial? What alternative explanation of the data did he rule out?

A major question in learning theory concerns the nature of the connection that is forged through classical conditioning. One camp has proposed an *S-R* interpretation, the other an *S-S* interpretation. (See Figure 4.13 on text page 120.)

5. According to the *S-R* view of classical conditioning, the animal learns a new

    _____ . According to the *S-S* view of classical conditioning, however, the animal

    learns a(n) _____ between

    _____ and _____ .

Considerable research has been done to settle the *S-R* versus *S-S* dispute. Robert Rescorla's work is illustrative.

6. Describe Rescorla's research procedure. Which position did his data support? What did the *other* theory predict?

The *S-S* view of classical conditioning is inherently more cognitive than the *S-R* view, because it assumes that the learner has a mental representation of the unconditioned stimulus.

7. Cognitive theorists describe this mental representation as a(n) _____ of the _____ .

8. How does expectancy theory help to explain why the conditioned response is often different from the unconditioned response?

9. How does Rescorla describe the learning organism in classical conditioning?

10. List three types of evidence supporting the notion that the learner uses the conditioned stimulus to predict the arrival of the unconditioned stimulus.

   a.

   b.

   c.

11. Why have some cognitive psychologists programmed computers to simulate expectation and prediction?

The cognitive viewpoint also provides insight into findings on operant conditioning.

12. What kind of mental representation or knowledge do cognitive theorists believe is involved in operant conditioning?

13. What are reward contrast effects? How do they support the cognitive view of operant conditioning?

14. How has Bitterman explained the fact that fish and reptiles do not show reward contrast effects? What evidence supports his view?

15. Explain the overjustification effect. What does it suggest about using rewards to influence people's behavior?

Edward Tolman provided considerable early support for the cognitive position through his work on place learning.

16. Contrast Tolman's view of maze learning with that of traditional behaviorists of his time. Briefly explain how Tolman supported his view.

17. Describe Tolman's work on latent learning. What question does this phenomenon help to settle?

24. Briefly discuss evidence that some behavior in wild chimpanzees depends on imitation.

Classical and operant conditioning are not the only categories of learning that have been extensively studied. Another important type of learning, especially in humans, is observational learning.

18. Define *observational learning*. List some species that have been shown capable of observational learning.

Albert Bandura, the foremost investigator of human observational learning, states that this type of learning has two functions. One is to learn specific motor skills and the other is to learn general modes or styles of behaving.

25. Give an example of a person learning each of the following through observation.

   a. a specific motor skill

19. It is generally believed to be

_____ and

_____ that make

observation helpful to the learner.

   b. a general mode or style of behavior

20. Explain and give examples for the terms used to answer item 19 above.

   a.

26. Summarize Bandura's experiment with the Bobo doll. Point out how it illustrates both functions of observational learning.

   b.

The Ecological Perspective on Learning: Filling the Blanks in Species-Typical Behavior Patterns
(pages 130–137)

21. What is imitation?

CONSIDER *these questions before you go on. They are designed to help you start thinking about this subject, not to test your knowledge.*

If nature were to build in certain kinds of specialized learning abilities, what types of activities do you think they might concern?

22. Imitation is cognitively _____ (simpler/more complex) than stimulus enhancement and goal enhancement.

How do animals know which foods are safe to eat and which are not?

23. Which species are known to be capable of imitation?

What would happen if a baby were allowed to choose its own food?

How do baby ducks know whom to follow around?

Can animals form mental maps of places to help them find their way around?

> READ *this section of your text lightly. Then go back and read thoroughly, completing the Workout as you proceed.*

Both the behavioral and cognitive perspectives have worked to develop general principles of learning that apply across situations.

1. The ecological perspective is also called the

   _____ .

2. How does the ecological perspective differ from the general-process perspective of behaviorists and cognitivists?

Finding food that is safe to eat is a significant undertaking for many species, especially omnivorous creatures such as rats and humans. The ecological perspective has helped to reveal some specific types of learning associated with this survival need.

3. How has food-aversion learning been demonstrated experimentally?

4. What are two characteristics that distinguish this type of learning from traditional examples of classical conditioning?

5. Why do the special characteristics of food-aversion learning make sense in the context of a natural environment?

Animals have to find foods that are not only safe but also nutritious. Apparently, learning is involved in food preference as well as food aversion.

6. How did an experiment show that rats will choose the food containing a vitamin they need? How can the rats' behavior be explained?

7. Describe Clara Davis's findings when she allowed babies to choose their own diets. Why should we be cautious in interpreting her results?

8. What evidence suggests that social learning plays a part in food selection?

9. How has natural selection prepared young omnivores to learn what to eat?

Nature seems to have equipped animals with other special learning abilities in addition to those involved in food selection.

10. Present evidence showing that some stimuli, such as snakes, can become conditioned fear stimuli more easily than others. Why is this the case?

11. Describe imprinting. What is meant by a critical period? Are all stimuli equally likely choices for young birds to be imprinted on?

12. What are some examples of special learning abilities in place learning?

> Be sure to READ the Concluding Thoughts at the end of the chapter. Note important points in your Workout. Then consolidate your learning by answering the focus questions in the margins of the text.

> After you have studied the chapter thoroughly, CHECK your understanding with the Self-Test that follows.

Self-Test 1

Multiple-Choice Questions

1. What term is defined as "any process through which experience at one time can alter an individual's behavior at a future time"?
   a. behaviorism
   b. learning
   c. reflex
   d. habituation

2. The law of association by contiguity originated with:
   a. Aristotle.
   b. John B. Watson.
   c. B. F. Skinner.
   d. Edward Thorndike.

3. A specific, well-defined event in the environment is called a(n):
   a. reflex.
   b. stimulus.
   c. operant.
   d. response.

4. In classical conditioning, a(n) _____ comes to elicit a response only as a result of training.
   a. conditioned stimulus
   b. unconditioned stimulus
   c. unconditioned response
   d. discriminative stimulus

5. Identification of specific learning mechanisms that have evolved to meet particular survival needs is the focus of the _____ perspective.
   a. operant conditioning
   b. cognitive
   c. behavioral
   d. ecological

6. Spontaneous recovery is defined as the:
   a. equivalent of extinction.
   b. restoration of an extinguished response after further pairing of the conditioned stimulus with the unconditioned stimulus.
   c. restoration of an extinguished response after the passage of time.
   d. restoration of the individual to the state that existed prior to conditioning.

7. We could best explain why someone might feel sleepy on returning to a room where he or she had frequently taken sedatives in terms of:
   a. a conditioned drug reaction.
   b. observational learning.
   c. spontaneous recovery.
   d. imprinting.

8. The law of effect lies at the heart of the form of learning called:
   a. classical conditioning.
   b. habituation.
   c. operant conditioning.
   d. observational learning.

9. The overjustification effect involves a change in the:
   a. amount of work that is required in order to be rewarded.
   b. meaning of a behavior and thus the likelihood of engaging in it.
   c. conditions under which a particular behavior will be rewarded.
   d. schedule of partial reinforcement, which results in greater resistance to extinction.

10. When the same stimulus serves as a secondary reinforcer for one behavior and as a discriminative stimulus for a subsequent behavior, we have an instance of:
   a. shaping.
   b. the blocking effect.
   c. partial reinforcement.
   d. chaining.

11. If the arrival of a stimulus following a response increases the likelihood of that response recurring, we know by definition that the stimulus is a:
   a. discriminative stimulus.
   b. secondary reinforcer.
   c. positive reinforcer.
   d. negative reinforcer.

12. Classical conditioning generally _____ occur if the conditioned and unconditioned stimuli are presented simultaneously, a fact supporting _____ views.
    a. does; *S-S*
    b. does; *S-R*
    c. does not; *S-S*
    d. does not; *S-R*

13. If reinforcement is based on the average number of responses produced (e.g., 10), with a different number of responses required on each occasion (e.g., 7, 11, 12), the learner is on a:
    a. fixed-interval schedule.
    b. fixed-ratio schedule.
    c. variable-interval schedule.
    d. variable-ratio schedule.

14. Rats deprived of the vitamin thiamine will:
    a. tend to eat all foods unselectively despite their nutritional deficiency.
    b. lose their ability to differentiate foods on the basis of taste and will thus fail to avoid poison.
    c. come to prefer foods containing thiamine after sampling various foods.
    d. consequently become incapable of learning operant responses.

15. Animals can more easily learn to:
    a. fear certain types of stimuli as compared to other types.
    b. avoid harmful foods if they become sick after eating them.
    c. choose the right foods if they observe an adult model doing so.
    d. do all of the above.

Essay Questions

16. What is generalization in classical conditioning? How can a learner be taught not to generalize?

17. Explain the difference between reinforcement and punishment, between positive and negative reinforcement, and between positive and negative punishment.

After you have assessed your understanding on the basis of Self-Test 1 and have tried to strengthen your preparation in any areas of weakness, GO ON to Self-Test 2.

Self-Test 2

Multiple-Choice Questions

1. A young man suffering from headaches is hooked up to a machine that presents a pleasant tone whenever he keeps the muscles in his forehead sufficiently relaxed. The man is undergoing:
    a. classical conditioning.
    b. biofeedback training.
    c. negative punishment.
    d. observational learning.

2. What kind of conditioning involves the learning of reflexes?
    a. habituation
    b. classical conditioning
    c. operant conditioning
    d. both classical and operant conditioning

3. A noise may startle you enough to make you jump. If it occurs several times, you will jump less and less each time. This is an instance of:
    a. a conditioned reflex.
    b. habituation.
    c. extinction.
    d. spontaneous recovery.

4. Stimuli similar to the conditioned stimulus are able to elicit the conditioned response in the phenomenon called:
    a. latent learning.
    b. habituation.
    c. generalization.
    d. discrimination.

5. You may find yourself salivating in response to a television commercial that shows a luscious dessert. This behavior would best be explained by:
   a. classical conditioning.
   b. operant conditioning.
   c. habituation.
   d. discrimination training.

6. One group of rats receives several food pellets for each response, while another group receives only one pellet for each response. When the first group is then treated like the second, they:
   a. stop responding altogether.
   b. continue to respond at a higher rate than the second group.
   c. drop to a response rate equal to that of the second group.
   d. drop to a response rate below that of the second group.

7. Which schedule of partial reinforcement underlies many gambling systems and may help to explain compulsive gambling?
   a. fixed interval
   b. fixed ratio
   c. variable interval
   d. variable ratio

8. Which of the following is true of a token?
   a. It elicits an operant response from an animal.
   b. It serves as a cue that reinforcement is available for a particular response.
   c. It tells an animal how long it must continue to respond before the next reinforcer will be delivered.
   d. It is a type of secondary reinforcer.

9. Sam has a habit of launching into long political tirades by saying, "Well, here's how I see it." As soon as she hears this, Betsy excuses herself. Betsy has learned to take advantage of a(n):
   a. conditioned stimulus.
   b. discriminative stimulus.
   c. observational response.
   d. response chain.

10. A stimulus that can serve as a positive reinforcer can:
   a. also serve as a positive punisher.
   b. also serve as a negative punisher.
   c. also serve as a negative reinforcer.
   d. only serve as a positive reinforcer.

11. Gregory Razran performed an experiment in which lemon juice was squirted into the mouths of college students just before a printed word was presented to them. He found that:
   a. the students could not be conditioned to verbal stimuli.
   b. the actual conditioned stimuli that elicited salivation were not the word meanings but the physical appearance of the words.
   c. students later generalized, salivating to the words that meant the same thing as the original words more than to sound-alike words.
   d. students could not learn to salivate in response to words, though they could learn other reflexive responses.

12. The technique in which successively closer approximations to the desired response are reinforced is:
   a. backward conditioning.
   b. discrimination training.
   c. continuous reinforcement.
   d. shaping.

13. In an experiment on place learning, rats were placed in a maze with three routes to the goal box containing the reward. After training, they preferred the shortest of the routes but would take the best alternative path if the preferred one were blocked at some point. This suggested that:
   a. their knowledge of the maze consisted of sequences of specific motor responses.
   b. their knowledge of the maze consisted of a mental representation of the maze's layout.
   c. they were operating at the level of trial and error, much like cats in a puzzle box.
   d. rats have an instinctive, unlearned ability to find their way to food.

14. A child who learns how to behave at a birthday party by seeing how other children behave is exhibiting:
   a. observational learning.
   b. classical conditioning.
   c. instrumental conditioning.
   d. biofeedback.

15. Imprinting:
    a. is a type of observational learning found in all species studied so far.
    b. occurs only during a critical period, which varies by species.
    c. occurs equally well if the stimulus is a human as when the stimulus is a female of the species.
    d. has not yet been reasonably explained in terms of adaptive value.

Essay Questions

16. Edward Tolman claimed that operant conditioning involves the learning of means-end relationships. Explain Tolman's view and present evidence for or against it.

17. Interpret and present an argument for the following statement: Learning mechanisms are products of natural selection and as such are suited to help a species deal with biologically important matters.

Answers

The Behavioral Perspective on Learning—Classical Conditioning

2. a. yes, b. no, c. yes, d. yes
6. a. stimulus
   b. response
9. habituation; sometimes
14. a. salivating in response to a bell
    b. food
    c. salivation
    d. bell
    e. salivation
16. unconditioned stimulus

The Behavioral Perspective on Learning—Operant Conditioning

3. elicit; preceded; emitted; consequence
12. extinction
13. continuous; partial
14. a. VR, b. FI, c. VI, d. VR, e. FR
15. ratio
20. a. secondary reinforcer
    b. primary reinforcer
    c. token
26. negative; positive

The Cognitive Perspective on Learning: Acquiring Information About the World

2. meaning
5. reflex; connection; conditioned stimulus; unconditioned stimulus
7. expectation; unconditioned response
19. stimulus enhancement; goal enhancement
22. more complex

The Ecological Perspective on Learning: Filling the Blanks in Species-Typical Behavior Patterns

1. specific-process perspective

Self-Test 1

1. **b.** (p. 97)

2. **a.** (p. 101)

3. **b.** (p. 98)

4. **a.** (p. 100)

5. **d.** (p. 97)

6. **c.** The conditioned response will also reappear if the conditioned stimulus is once again paired with the unconditioned stimulus, but spontaneous recovery refers specifically to the case in which the mere passage of time is sufficient to restore the extinguished response. (pp. 102–103)

7. **a.** The physical surroundings in which the drug is taken may act as a conditioned stimulus. (p. 105)

8. **c.** (pp. 107–108)

9. **b.** (p. 125)

10. **d.** (p. 114)

11. **c.** If the removal of the stimulus following the response had increased the likelihood of the response, we would have known the stimulus was a negative reinforcer. (p. 115)

12. **c.** A situation in which the conditioned and unconditioned stimuli occur together in time is not an effective means of producing classical conditioning. From the cognitive perspective—the *S-S* theory of classical conditioning—this makes sense. If the two are simultaneous, the conditioned stimulus cannot produce an expectancy that the unconditioned stimulus will occur. (p. 121)

13. **d.** (p. 112)

14. **c.** Food preferences of this sort seem to depend on consuming foods one or two at a time in order to isolate which ones lead to feeling healthier and which ones lead to feeling worse. (p. 132)

15. **d.** (pp. 130–134)

16. Generalization in classical conditioning is demonstrated when the learner produces a conditioned response to a stimulus other than the original conditioned stimulus. The strength of the subject's response to a new stimulus depends on its similarity to the actual conditioned stimulus: the closer it is to the conditioned stimulus, the closer the response will be to the usual conditioned response.

   A learner can be taught not to generalize through discrimination training. This procedure involves (1) pairing the conditioned stimulus with the unconditioned stimulus in further trials and (2) presenting the stimulus to which the learner generalized *without* the unconditioned stimulus. The learner eventually continues to respond to the conditioned stimulus and no longer generalizes to the other stimulus. (p. 103)

17. Reinforcement and punishment differ in terms of their effects on the likelihood of a behavior recurring. They not only differ in this regard; they are opposites. Reinforcement occurs when the consequences of a response increase the chances that the response will occur again, while punishment occurs when the consequences of a response decrease the chances that the response will occur again.

   Both positive and negative reinforcement involve increasing the likelihood of a response through the consequences of that response. But in positive reinforcement, the consequence involves the *arrival* of some stimulus, such as praise or money or food. In negative reinforcement, the consequence involves the *removal* of some stimulus, such as shock or a headache or forced confinement.

   Positive and negative punishment also both involve the same behavioral result—a decrease in the likelihood of the behavior. Positive punishment involves the *arrival* of some stimulus, such as shock or a headache or forced confinement, contingent on a behavior. Negative punishment involves the *removal* of a stimulus, such as praise or money or food. (pp. 115–116)

Self-Test 2

1. **b.** (pp. 110–111)

2. **b.** (p. 98)

3. **b.** (p. 99)

4. **c.** (p. 103)

5. **a.** (pp. 98–99)

6. **d.** (pp. 123–124)

7. **d.** The gambler is being influenced by the unpredictability of the reinforcement schedule. In the past, reinforcement sometimes occurred after the gambler played just once or twice, other times only after extended playing. One never knows, thinks the gambler, when the next win is due. (p. 112)

8. **d.** (p. 114)

9. **b.** (p. 113)

10. **b.** A positive reinforcer is one for which the learner is willing to work. It is also presumably a stimulus whose removal would be punishing—

hence, it is a negative punisher. Remember that the terms *positive* and *negative* refer to *presentation* and *removal*, respectively. *Reinforcer* and *punisher* refer to consequences that, respectively, *increase* and *decrease* the behaviors they follow. (p. 115)

11. **c.** Razran's results support the cognitive viewpoint because they show that what matters about the stimulus is its meaning. (p. 118)

12. **d.** (p. 111)

13. **b.** Such a mental representation of the spatial layout is called a cognitive map. (p. 126)

14. **a.** (p. 128)

15. **b.** (p. 135)

16. As a cognitively oriented theorist, Edward Tolman was comfortable interpreting behavioral phenomena in terms of mental entities. He was suggesting that what takes place through operant conditioning is the acquisition of knowledge by the learner, specifically knowledge about which action should lead to which result under which circumstances. The learner can then use that knowledge to fit current needs or desires and current conditions. In other words, the learner comes to know which means will lead to particular ends.

Tolman's view found substantial support. In one experiment, for example, hungry rats learned to lever-press for either sugar water or food. Then they were deprived of water and thus made thirsty. When tested with no reinforcement available, the thirsty rats that had learned to expect sugar water from lever presses performed this action much more than rats that had learned to expect dry food from the same action. Reward contrast effects provide another example suggesting that Tolman was right. Animals that have received a big reinforcer for an operant and are then switched to a small reinforcer don't respond as much as animals that received a small reinforcer all along. This makes sense if we assume that the animal had a certain conception of what ought to happen, but it doesn't make sense in strict *S-R* terms. (*Note:* The overjustification effect in humans also fits well with Tolman's view.) (pp. 123–125)

17. Natural selection operates under the pressure of the survival and reproductive needs of a particular species in a particular environment. It produces in each species tools for dealing with those needs in that environment. Learning mechanisms are examples of such tools. They are an inborn means of modifying behavior to suit the demands an organism faces in its lifetime.

A number of different findings in research on learning make sense if we view them in this ecological perspective. For example, there are apparently innate tendencies in learning that affect which stimuli can become conditioned fear stimuli. In an attempt to repeat the Watson and Rayner experiment using Little Albert, an experimenter tried to condition fear to blocks and pieces of fabric rather than to a rat. It didn't work. One explanation is that we are biologically predisposed to fear some things (like rats) but not other things (like blocks).

Research on food aversion provides another line of support for the ecological view. Food-aversion learning seems to be special—different in important ways from classical or operant conditioning. For example, the events that need to be linked through learning—the food and the subsequent illness—can be separated in time by a whole day. In fact, if the food tasting and the illness occur within a few minutes of one another, the food aversion will not be learned. In typical classical conditioning, on the other hand, the two events must occur close together in time if learning is to take place. (pp. 130–137)

Chapter 5   The Nervous System

READ the introduction below before you read the chapter in the text.

The nervous system is the basis of all that we refer to as psychological—thoughts, feelings, moods, behaviors. It coordinates and directs all of our actions. The most fundamental structure of the nervous system is a single cell called a neuron. Some neurons bring sensory information to the brain, others carry commands from the brain to muscles and glands, and still others serve communication functions entirely within the brain and spinal cord. Although neurons play different roles and come in a variety of sizes and shapes, all can be described in terms of the same functional parts, including dendrites, axons, and axon terminals. A neuron's dendrites receive incoming information; its axon carries electrical impulses; and its axon terminals release chemical messengers that influence other cells.

The nervous system consists of two main parts—the central nervous system (brain and spinal cord) and the peripheral nervous system (the nerves). The nerves connect the brain and spinal cord to sensory organs, muscles, and glands. Sensory neurons carry information to the central nervous system, and motor neurons carry commands from the central nervous system to muscles and glands.

In the central nervous system, the spinal cord functions as a conduit between the brain and many of the nerves in the peripheral nervous system. It is also responsible for organizing certain rhythmic movements and for mediating spinal reflexes—behaviors that can be triggered and carried through to completion without the help of the brain.

The brain controls all other behaviors. Beginning just above the spinal cord are the subcortical structures of the brain, such as the brainstem, cerebellum, thalamus, hypothalamus, and limbic system, each with particular functions. The cerebral cortex, the outermost and most massive part of the brain, is divided into two symmetrical hemispheres. The cortex is critical to high-level processes, such as language and decision making, as well as certain sensory and motor functions.

In many cases, the functions of the nervous system are organized hierarchically, with the most primitive, reflexive responses in the spinal cord at the lowest level and the most complex types of control in the cortex at the highest level. Movement control illustrates this hierarchical organization. Another characteristic of brain organization is that higher functions such as language are distributed asymmetrically across the left and right hemispheres.

The neuron is different from other cells of the body in that it is capable of carrying signals. Those signals take the form of electrical impulses, or action potentials, which involve the movement of electrically charged particles across the cell's membrane. These movements result in changes in the electrical balance across the membrane, carrying the impulses down the axon to the axon terminal, where, through synaptic transmission, the neuron sends messages to other cells. In synaptic transmission, minute quantities of chemical messengers called neurotransmitters flow across a tiny gap between cells. Fast and slow synapses differ in the nature of their effects on the "receiving," or postsynaptic, cell. Synaptic connections are significantly modified by learning.

Besides the nervous system, the other major mode of communication within the body is the hormonal system. Hormones are chemical messengers that are released from endocrine glands and other organs and are delivered to various target tissues through the bloodstream. They produce a variety of effects, playing important roles in the development of anatomical differences between males and females and in the body's response to stressful situations, for example.

The hormonal system and the nervous system are intimately related. In many ways, the hormonal system is under the control of the brain. Also, some hormones are chemically identical to neurotransmitters.

Drugs differ from hormones in that they are not produced inside the body but are introduced from outside. Like hormones, drugs are carried by the blood and taken up in target tissues of the body. Also like hormones, drugs can affect synaptic transmission, but the brain protects itself from some such substances by the blood-brain barrier. Drug tolerance and withdrawal symptoms are important phenomena related to the effects of some drugs on the body.

> LOOK over the table of contents for this chapter in your textbook before you continue with your study.

> Notice that there are focus questions in the margins of the text for your use in studying the material. The following chart lists which Study Guide questions relate to which focus questions.

Focus Questions	Study Guide Questions
Functional Organization of the Nervous System	
1–4	1–9
5–6	14–19
7	20–25
8–12	26–35
13–17	36–47
18–20	48–50
21–23	51–58
24–25	59–62
How Neurons Work and Influence Each Other	
26–28	1–13
29–30	14–19
31–34	20–27
How Hormones and Drugs Interact with the Nervous System	
35–39	1–10
40–42	11–24

The Integrated Study Workout

> Complete one section at a time.

Functional Organization of the Nervous System
(pages 143–165)

> CONSIDER these questions before you go on. They are designed to help you start thinking about the subject, not to test your knowledge.

What is a neuron? Is it the same as a nerve?

How do messages get from your feet or eyes or tongue to your brain? from your brain to your fingers?

How does the nervous system make your heart pound when you are scared? or make you want to get something to eat?

What part or parts of the brain are involved when you feel anger or joy?

How does the nervous system manage complex movement such as that involved in walking or skating?

> READ this section of your text lightly. Then go back and read thoroughly, completing the Workout as you proceed.

Despite the brain's rather unassuming appearance, even some ancients, such as the Greek physician Hippocrates, recognized it to be the organ of thought, feeling, and behavioral control. This represented a major difference of opinion, as other early thinkers credited the heart with these responsibilities. Students are often surprised to see that a psychology text includes a chapter on the brain (and the nervous system of which it is a part) because they expect that subject to be reserved for biologists. But if psychology is the science of mind and behavior, shouldn't we understand the organ that makes mind and behavior possible? Psychologists have answered "yes" to that question from the beginning, and the "yes" becomes increasingly insistent as new research uncovers more and more of the secrets of this amazing organ.

Let's begin with an overview of the nervous system.

1. Describe briefly the three kinds of work the nervous system must perform.

   a.

   b.

   c.

2. The central nervous system consists of the
_____ and the
_____ . The peripheral nervous
system includes the _____ that
extend from the central nervous system to the
rest of the body. (See Figure 5.1 on text page 144.)

In order to understand the way the nervous system
works, you must have a solid understanding of individual cells.

3. The basic units, the "building blocks," of the nervous system are called _____ .

4. These cells are specialized to carry
_____ rapidly from one place to
another within the body and to
_____ information from various
sources.

5. List and briefly describe three types of neurons
by function. Indicate how many of each type are
thought to exist in the human nervous system.
(See Figure 5.2 on text page 145.)

   a.

   b.

   c.

6. Different neurons have many of the same functional parts in common though they vary in anatomy and purpose. Label the diagram of a typical motor neuron below. This type of neuron is generally used to illustrate the basic parts of a neuron in textbooks. (See Figure 5.3 on text page 145.)

7. Each part of a neuron is specialized for some function. Write the name of the part that performs each of the following functions.

   _____ a. Thin, tube-shaped extensions that increase the surface area for receiving incoming signals from other neurons

   _____ b. A small swelling that can release a chemical substance onto a receiving cell, such as another neuron or a muscle cell

   _____ c. The widest part of the cell, which contains the cell nucleus and other basic machinery common to all cells

   _____ d. A thin, tubelike structure that carries electrical impulses from the cell body toward other cells

   _____ e. A casing that wraps tightly around the axons of some neurons

8. When a(an) _____ potential
reaches an axon terminal, it causes the release of a
_____ . This substance is passed to
a receiving cell at a _____ .
Interneurons and sensory neurons transmit their
chemical messengers to _____ ,
whereas motor neurons transmit theirs to
_____ and _____ cells.

9. Briefly compare sensory neurons, interneurons, and motor neurons in terms of their anatomy.

The incredible capabilities of the nervous system depend on its complex organization. The nervous system is divided into the central and peripheral nervous systems. In learning about the nervous system's organization, try to keep in mind the main functions of each structure and try to relate each structure to others you've studied. We will begin by looking more closely at the peripheral nervous system, which consists of all of the body's nerves. (Refer back to Figure 5.1 on text page 144.) We can differentiate two categories of nerves. In all cases, the nerves exist in pairs, with one left and one right member.

10. A bundle of axons of sensory or motor neurons outside the central nervous system is called a(n) _____ . (Be sure you understand the difference between a nerve and a neuron.)

11. Humans have _____ pairs of cranial nerves and _____ pairs of spinal nerves. Cranial nerves extend directly from the _____ and spinal nerves from the _____ .

12. Are cranial and spinal nerves exclusively sensory or motor? Explain.

13. Define *somatosensation*.

The motor portion of the peripheral nervous system can be subdivided into two subsystems that affect different types of structures.

14. What is the skeletal system?

15. What is the autonomic system?

16. Skeletal motor neurons _____ activity in the skeletal muscles. In contrast, autonomic motor neurons typically _____ activity in the visceral muscles, which have their own built-in nonneural mechanisms for generating activity.

The autonomic portion of the peripheral nervous system can be further subdivided into two opposing systems.

17. What does the sympathetic division do?

18. What does the parasympathetic division do?

19. When you are conversing comfortably with a friend, the _____ division is probably predominating. When you are viewing the climax of a suspenseful movie, the _____ division is probably predominating.

Now we will examine the various subdivisions of the central nervous system, starting with the spinal cord and moving up to the anatomical top of the system, the cerebral cortex.

20. In what sense is the spinal cord a conduit?

21. What is a tract? What are ascending tracts? descending tracts?

22. How is the level of spinal cord injury related to the severity of the resulting deficit? (See Figure 5.1 again.)

The spinal cord is not just a communication pathway between brain and spinal nerves. It organizes some behaviors on its own.

23. What are pattern generators, and what function do they serve?

The spinal cord directly controls some reflexive behaviors independent of the brain. These behaviors are called spinal reflexes.

24. What is a flexion reflex and why is it useful? Is it a response to feeling pain? How do you know?

25. What is the general anatomical arrangement underlying this spinal reflex? (Refer back to Figure 5.2 on text page 145.)

Moving up from the spinal cord, we turn to the organization of the brain.

26. Define *nucleus*. How does the organization of nuclei permit us to talk about the functions of relatively large areas in the brain?

All brain structures below the cerebral cortex are called subcortical structures. We will begin with those subcortical structures that lie nearest to the spinal cord—the brainstem and the thalamus. (See Figure 5.6 on text page 150.)

27. The parts of the brainstem are the

_____ , _____ ,

and _____ .

28. Compare the brainstem and spinal cord in terms of anatomy and functions.

29. Two kinds of reflexes organized by the medulla and pons are _____ reflexes and _____ reflexes.

30. Characterize the brainstem's control of movement by describing the behavior of an animal after its central nervous system is severed just above the midbrain.

31. Why is the thalamus considered a relay station?

Moving beyond the brainstem and thalamus, we come to the cerebellum and basal ganglia, both importantly involved in motor control. (See Figure 5.7 on text page 151.)

32. Answer the following questions about the cerebellum.

   a. The name *cerebellum* means _____ in Latin, and this part of the brain is so called because of its appearance.

   b. The cerebellum rests on the rear of the _____ .

c. Describe the most well-known function of the cerebellum. What happens when the cerebellum is damaged?

33. Answer the following questions about the basal ganglia.

a. The basal ganglia are located on each side of the _____ .

b. How is their role in motor control complementary to that of the cerebellum?

c. Tremors and difficulty starting and stopping movements are symptoms of _____ , which results from deterioration of a neural tract connecting the _____ to the basal ganglia.

d. Are the cerebellum and basal ganglia utilized only for sequencing and timing muscle movements? Explain.

At the next level up are the limbic system and the hypothalamus. (See Figure 5.8 on text page 153.)

34. Answer the following questions about the limbic system.

a. The term *limbic* comes from the Latin word for _____ . It divides the _____ parts of the brain from the cerebral cortex.

b. What is the general anatomical pattern of the limbic system?

c. Two important structures within the limbic system are the _____ and the _____ .

d. In general, structures of the limbic system help to regulate basic _____ and _____ .

e. Comment on the limbic system's connections to the nose and to the basal ganglia.

f. The _____ , a structure in the limbic system, is critical to the formation of memories.

35. Where is the hypothalamus? Why is it so very important, and how does it accomplish its tasks?

The evolutionarily newest part of the brain lies at the top of the brain.

36. The Latin word _____ means "brain"; the Latin word _____ means "bark." Thus the term _____ refers to the "bark," or outer layer, of the brain.

37. In size, the cerebral cortex is the _____ part of the human brain, accounting for about _____ percent of the brain's entire volume. Much of its surface area lies deep in _____ and is thus not visible in an undissected brain.

38. The cerebral cortex is divided into left and right halves, or _____ . In turn, each of these can be divided into four _____ .

39. Identify the lobes of the brain in the drawing below. (See Figure 5.9 on text page 154.)

a. _____

b. _____

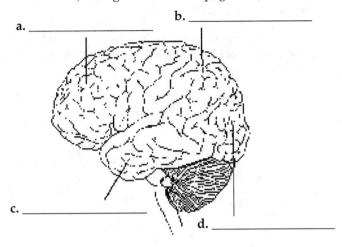

c. _____

d. _____

40. Identify the following different functional regions of the cortex by labeling the drawing below: primary sensory areas (including visual, auditory, and somatosensory areas) and primary motor areas. (Again see Figure 5.9.)

a. _____

b. _____

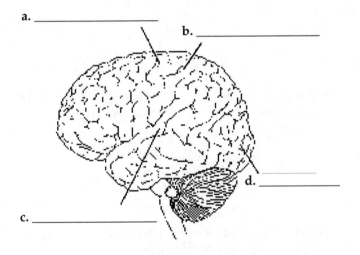

c. _____

d. _____

41. What are association areas, and what are their functions? How is the amount of association cortex in a given species related to the species' complexity? (See Figure 5.10 on text page 154.)

One way of approaching the complexities of the cortex is to think in terms of principles of organization, rather than physical divisions like right and left hemisphere.

42. What is the principle of topographic organization? Give one example to illustrate this principle.

43. Look at the maps of the somatosensory and primary motor areas of the cortex in Figure 5.11 on text page 155. Why do some body parts have greater representation than others? Why would species differ in terms of which body part has the greatest representation in these areas?

Now, let's concentrate on a more in-depth understanding of how the cortex is involved in motor control. (See Figure 5.12 on text page 156.)

44. The primary motor cortex, the basal ganglia, and the cerebellum are all involved in motor control. In what order do the structures exert their influence? How do we know?

45. Briefly describe the evidence showing that the motor cortex is critical for making delicate movements.

46. What roles do the premotor and supplementary motor areas of the cortex play in motor control? How do we know?

47. What role in motor control is played by association areas in the frontal lobes? in the parietal and temporal lobes?

Movement is behavior, whether it is something as dramatic and complex as a balance-beam routine or as subtle as a shift of the eyes. It is therefore worth understanding how the entire nervous system works to manage movement. This function of the nervous system also illustrates hierarchical control.

48. How do evolutionarily older and newer systems relate to one another in the movement-control hierarchy?

49. Figure 5.13 on text page 158 shows a functional hierarchy of movement control. Using this figure as an aid, describe what would be happening at the four levels of the hierarchy as a person thirsty after a long run spots a cool drink.

   a. at the first level (the top):

   b. at the second level:

   c. at the third level:

   d. at the fourth level:

50. Despite the elegance of a hierarchical explanation of nervous-system control over movement or some other activity, we do not have answers to all our questions. What type of question have we answered? What type of question have we not answered?

Even though the right and left hemispheres of the brain look like mirror images, their functioning is not the same in all regards.

51. Are the brain's two hemispheres isolated from one another? Explain.

52. In what ways are the hemispheres functionally symmetrical? functionally asymmetrical?

Split-brain studies provide some of the most compelling evidence for the functional differences between the hemispheres. These studies focus on individuals in whom the corpus callosum has been cut for medical reasons, thus effectively separating the hemispheres.

53. Describe a typical split-brain experiment and its results. (See Figures 5.15–5.17 on text pages 160–161.)

54. Are there individual differences in the right hemisphere's comprehension of language? Explain.

55. How do people who have had split-brain surgery manage in the everyday world?

Much of our understanding of association areas specialized for language has come from studies of people with relatively localized brain damage. (*Hint:* See Figure 5.18 on text page 162.)

56. A loss in language ability that results from brain damage is called _____ .

57. Distinguish between Broca's (nonfluent) aphasia and Wernicke's (fluent) aphasia. Be sure to comment on both cause and effect.

58. How do modern theories account for the pattern of deficits seen in Broca's aphasia? in Wernicke's aphasia?

Neuroimaging techniques now allow us to study the normal functioning of the brain. We no longer rely entirely on studies of people with brain damage.

59. What does PET stand for and how does it work?

60. What does fMRI stand for and how does this technique work?

61. How and why do PET and fMRI studies employ control conditions?

62. Briefly describe a study of language that used PET scans. Did it support the classic view of the roles played by Broca's and Wernicke's areas?

How Neurons Work and Influence One Another (pp. 165–177)

CONSIDER these questions before you go on. They are designed to help you start thinking about the subject, not to test your knowledge.

What actually happens when a neuron carries an electrical impulse?

How do neurons pass information among themselves?

Does experience have any effect on neurons, and, if so, how does it affect them?

READ this section of your text lightly. Then go back and read thoroughly, completing the Workout as you proceed.

As you have noted, neurons are designed to carry and to integrate information. Because these functions are so critical to everything we do—breathing, walking, smiling, writing, any activity you can name—it is important to understand them in greater detail. (See Figure 5.20 on text page 166 for the questions below.)

1. What is an action potential? Explain what it means to say that an action potential is "all or none."

2. What is the cell membrane? intracellular fluid? extracellular fluid?

3. Identify the electrically charged chemicals in the internal and external fluid environments of the inactive neuron. Also indicate their charge and location.

	Name	Type of charge	Location
a.			
b.			
c.			
d.			

4. Now place chemical symbols (e.g., Na$^+$) representing the various chemicals named above on the following diagram of an inactive (or resting) neuron.

5. What is the resting potential? How big is it? How is it relevant to the action potential?

The action potential can be broken down into two major phases: depolarization and repolarization. Now let's trace the events of an action potential in detail. (See Figure 5.21 on text page 167 for questions 6–8 below.)

6. Does the action potential occur in all parts of the axon simultaneously? Explain.

7. Answer the following questions about the depolarization phase of the action potential.

   a. What happens in the cell membrane to permit the action potential to occur at any given point along the axon?

   b. This allows _____ ions to rush into the neuron.

   c. Two forces cause this movement to take place. They are a(n) _____ and a(n) _____ force.

d. As a result of this movement, the electrical charge across the cell membrane becomes _____ .

8. Answer the following questions about the repolarization phase of the action potential.

   a. As the sodium channels close up, channels that permit only _____ ions to pass through open.

   b. Are these ions moving into or out of the cell? Why?

   c. As a result of this movement, the electrical charge across the cell membrane becomes _____ .

9. About how long does it take for an action potential to occur at a given point on the axon?

10. How does the cell restore the original balance of ions so that it can keep having action potentials?

11. What is a cell's threshold?

The speed with which an action potential can travel down an axon is affected by several factors.

12. Larger-diameter axons will conduct an action potential _____ than thinner ones. Another factor that affects the speed of conduction is the presence or absence of a(n) _____ . In cells with this type of insulation, the action potential does not move smoothly along the axon but rather _____ from one _____ to the next. The fastest neurons in the nervous system can carry an action potential at about _____ meters per second.

13. How could it be that you feel the pressure of a pinprick before you feel the pain of it?

Neurons are separated from one another (and from muscle or gland cells) by tiny gaps. Synaptic transmission is the nervous system's way of conveying information across those gaps by chemical means. (See Figure 5.22 on text page 169.)

14. Answer the following questions about structures involved in synaptic transmission.

    a. Synapses fall into two basic categories,
       _____ and _____ ,
       with _____ synapses being the best understood.

    b. The synaptic _____ is the tiny gap that separates the _____ membrane from the _____ membrane that it influences.

    c. The axon terminal of the presynaptic cell contains hundreds of minute globelike _____ , which hold chemical _____ .

    d. When a(n) _____ reaches the axon terminals, it causes the neurotransmitter to be released into the _____ , where it then diffuses through the fluid to reach the postsynaptic cell.

15. In general, how do neurotransmitter molecules have their effect on the postsynaptic cell?

It is important to consider neural activity in terms of the information being sent. A necessary distinction is that between excitatory and inhibitory synapses. At each of these types of synapses, a different type of signal is sent to the postsynaptic neuron. The two types of signals are designed to produce opposite effects in the postsynaptic cell.

16. Explain the mechanism by which these two types of synapses influence the postsynaptic cell.

    a. excitatory synapses

    b. inhibitory synapses

17. Why is it important to remember that each neuron receives input from many different synapses, often involving many different neurons? What ultimately determines the rate of action potentials in the postsynaptic neuron?

18. How do slow synapses differ from fast synapses?

19. Sustained effects on a person's behavior such as those involved in mood, pain sensitivity, or learning are due to activity at (fast/slow) _____ synapses.

As part of a living system, neurons can be modified by experience. They can change in size, shape, excitability, and patterns of connections. Every day we establish new synapses and eliminate others by the millions.

20. What brain differences were found in rats raised in enriched, as compared to deprived, environments?

21. Did the different types of environments affect the brains of adult mice or only the brains of young mice?

22. Can the mammalian brain produce new neurons after birth? Explain.

23. Is there evidence that practice at a given sensory discrimination task increases the number of neurons devoted to it? Explain.

More than 50 years ago, Donald Hebb proposed that some synapses grow stronger and more effective when pre- and postsynaptic neurons are active at the same time. Hebb's theory, which could help to explain classical conditioning and some other forms of learning, later received strong support from laboratory work on long-term potentiation, or LTP. (See Figure 5.25 on text page 173.)

24. According to Hebb, how might the strengthened synapse be related to learning?

25. Answer the following questions about long-term potentiation (LTP):

a. How is it produced in the laboratory?

b. How long might it last?

c. What is the actual mechanism involved in LTP? In other words, what happens when special receptors on the postsynaptic membrane receive the transmitter they are primed for?

26. Present evidence that LTP is actually involved in learning.

27. Answer the following questions about the gill-withdrawal reflex in *Aplysia*. (*Hint:* See Figure 5.27 on text page 175.)

a. Why have scientists chosen to study *Aplysia,* the sea slug?

b. How does classical conditioning of the gill-withdrawal reflex take place?

c. What are the neural mechanisms that provide the basis for such conditioning?

How Hormones and Drugs Interact with the Nervous System (pages 177–184)

CONSIDER these questions before you go on. They are designed to help you start thinking about the subject, not to test your knowledge.

What are hormones, and how do they affect the body's functioning?

How is the brain involved in hormonal effects?

How could a drug paralyze someone? affect someone's motor behavior? alter someone's mood?

Why do people sometimes need larger and larger doses of a drug?

What causes the unpleasant withdrawal symptoms associated with some drugs?

> READ this section of your text lightly. Then go back and read thoroughly, completing the Workout as you proceed.

Given that the heart is part of a vast circulatory system and that its vessels are easier to see than nerves, it is not surprising that early theorists considered it the seat of thought, emotion, and behavioral control. In fact, the circulatory system does play a communications role within the body. It is, however, a much slower messenger system than the nervous system.

1. _____ are chemical messengers secreted into the blood to act on specific _____ tissues.

2. Hormones, dozens of which have been identified, are secreted not only by _____ glands but also by other organs such as the brain and stomach. (See Figure 5.28 on text page 177.)

3. How are hormones and neurotransmitters alike? How are they different?

4. Give two arguments to support the idea that hormones and neurotransmitters have a common evolutionary origin.

Hormones affect behavior in a variety of ways. They can influence growth, metabolism, and brain states that correspond with drives and moods.

5. Explain how sex hormones can have long-term effects by influencing growth.

6. Hormones can also have shorter-term effects. How do adrenal hormones such as cortisol help in times of stress?

7. How do hormones exert an influence at the molecular level? How do peptides and steroids differ?

The hormonal system is not independent of the brain. In fact, it would be reasonable to say that the brain is the master of the hormonal system. (Refer to Figures 5.30 and 5.31 on text page 180.)

8. Why is the pituitary gland sometimes called the master endocrine gland? Where is it located?

9. Distinguish between the posterior and anterior lobes of the pituitary.

10. Briefly summarize a series of hormonal events that might occur in a frightening situation.

a.

b.

c.

d.

e.

The blood can carry chemical messengers other than hormones that affect the body's tissues, sometimes dramatically.

11. How are drugs similar to hormones? How are they different?

12. Identify several different ways in which drugs can be introduced into the body. Why might one method be preferred in a given set of circumstances?

13. What is the blood-brain barrier? What kinds of substances can generally pass easily through the barrier?

Drugs can have a variety of effects by altering synaptic transmission. Most drugs used by psychiatrists

and neurologists to affect mood or behavior work in this way.

14. List three ways that drugs can affect synaptic activity.

a.

b.

c.

15. Explain how a lock-and-key analogy can help us to understand one of the above modes of influence.

Drugs can influence behavior by affecting activity at any level of the neural hierarchy.

16. What is curare? At what level of the hierarchy does it act? How does it have its effects?

17. What is L-dopa? What is it used to treat? Where in the hierarchy does it have its effects? Why isn't dopamine itself used?

18. What are psychoactive drugs? At what level of the hierarchy do they work? What can they affect?

Tolerance, withdrawal symptoms, and addiction are three phenomena of drug use that can occur with pharmacological drugs as well as illicit "street" drugs. (Look at Table 5.1 on text page 183 to see how some psychoactive drugs affect us.)

19. Describe the phenomenon of drug tolerance.

20. What are withdrawal symptoms?

21. Are the occurrence of drug tolerance and withdrawal symptoms linked in any way? Explain.

22. Present a general theory that can explain both tolerance and withdrawal symptoms.

23. Briefly show how this theory can help to explain tolerance and withdrawal symptoms in the use of amphetamines.

24. Explain what it means to say that someone is addicted to a drug. Is addiction due solely to the attempt to avoid physiological withdrawal symptoms? Explain.

Be sure to READ the Concluding Thoughts at the end of the chapter. Note important points in your Workout. Then consolidate your learning by answering the focus questions in the margins of the text.

After you have studied the chapter thoroughly, CHECK your understanding with the Self-Test that follows.

Self-Test 1

Multiple-Choice Questions

1. The neurons that carry messages from the central nervous system to, say, your right leg are classed as:
   a. sensory neurons.
   b. interneurons.
   c. motor neurons.
   d. skeletal neurons.

2. In some cases, a myelin sheath is wrapped around a neuron's:
   a. dendrites.   **c.** cell body.
   b. axon.   **d.** cell nucleus.

3. The hypothalamus regulates the body's internal environment by:
   a. influencing the autonomic nervous system.
   b. controlling the release of some hormones.
   c. affecting drive states such as hunger and thirst.
   d. doing all of the above.

4. The nervous system is made up of the _____ and the _____ .
   a. skeletal motor system; autonomic nervous system
   b. central nervous system; peripheral nervous system
   c. peripheral nervous system; autonomic nervous system
   d. sympathetic nervous system; parasympathetic nervous system

5. An injury that severs the spinal cord will cause _____ ; the _____ the injury is, the more of the body it will affect.
   a. paralysis but not sensory loss; higher
   b. sensory loss but not paralysis; lower
   c. paralysis and sensory loss; higher
   d. sensory loss and paralysis; lower

6. A spinal animal's paw can be withdrawn from a sharp pin even though the brain never receives pain signals because this behavior is based on:
   a. an ascending reflex.
   b. a flexion reflex.
   c. cortical structures in the brain.
   d. subcortical structures in the brain.

7. Within the axon terminals are _____ , which store the _____ needed for synaptic transmission.
   a. vesicles; neurotransmitter
   b. nodes; neurotransmitter
   c. vesicles; sodium
   d. nodes; sodium

8. Parkinson's disease, which involves tremors and difficulty starting and stopping deliberate movements, stems from deterioration of neurons terminating in the:
   a. basal ganglia.   c. limbic system.
   b. cerebellum.   d. thalamus.

9. The part of the brain that plays a special role in the regulation of basic drives and emotions is the:
   a. limbic system.
   b. brainstem.
   c. cerebellum.
   d. corpus callosum.

10. Where are nerves found?
    a. only in the peripheral nervous system
    b. only in the brain
    c. only in the spinal cord
    d. in all parts of the nervous system

11. In the primary motor cortex, the amount of cortex devoted to each body part depends on the _____ of that body part.
    a. size   c. strength
    b. sensitivity   d. fineness of movement

12. During the depolarization phase of the action potential, _____ rush into the neuron.
    a. protein molecules   c. sodium ions
    b. potassium ions   d. chloride ions

13. A neuron's threshold is defined as the:
    a. strength of the action potentials that occur in that neuron.
    b. critical level of depolarization that must be reached before an action potential is triggered.
    c. number of action potentials that can take place in the neuron in a given unit of time.
    d. place on the neuron where action potentials begin.

14. The medulla, pons, and midbrain are all parts of the:
    a. limbic system.   c. thalamus.
    b. brainstem.   d. cerebellum.

15. Norepinephrine helps to illustrate the fact that:
    a. hormones target only one tissue each.
    b. hormones and neurotransmitters can be chemically identical.
    c. some hormones have their effects exclusively in the brain.
    d. neurohormones play a role in establishing the blood-brain barrier.

Essay Questions

16. Explain the process of synaptic transmission at fast synapses. How do excitatory and inhibitory synapses differ? What does it mean to say that the postsynaptic neuron integrates excitatory and inhibitory influences?

17. Discuss drug tolerance and withdrawal symptoms. Show how a single theory might explain both phenomena.

After you have assessed your understanding on the basis of Self-Test 1 and have tried to strengthen your preparation in any areas of weakness, GO ON to Self-Test 2.

Self-Test 2

Multiple-Choice Questions

1. The pituitary gland, located at the base of the brain:

    ✗ *P.179*

    a. is often called the "master endocrine gland" because of its control over other glands.
    b. nevertheless operates independently of the brain.
    c. does not actually manufacture any hormones but does direct the movement of many hormones.
    d. exerts its effects on the brain but not on any other part of the body.

2. The most basic unit of the nervous system is a:

    a. dendrite.   **c.** neuron.
    b. nerve.   d. tract.

3. In which type of neuron does stimulation come from a source other than neurons?

    a. motor neuron   **c.** sensory neuron
    b. interneuron   d. none of the above

4. When the neuron is inactive, the charge across the cell membrane is such that:

    a. the inside is about –70 millivolts relative to the outside.
    b. the inside is about –700 millivolts relative to the outside.
    c. the inside is about +70 millivolts relative to the outside.
    d. the inside is about +700 millivolts relative to the outside.

5. The sustained rhythmic movement of walking appears to be managed directly by:

    P.179 ✗

    a. nuclei in the limbic system.
    b. pattern generators in the spinal cord.
    c. cranial nerves.
    d. the cerebellum. — *thought that was fast movements*

6. The part of the brain located directly above the brainstem that serves as a major sensory relay station is the:

    a. pituitary.   c. amygdala.
    b. cerebellum.   **d.** thalamus.

7. Which part of the brain is considered a kind of computer or even a "little brain" that initiates and controls rapid movements?

    a. basal ganglia   c. frontal lobes
    b. cerebellum   d. brainstem

8. The cerebral cortex is divided into two _____ connected by _____ .

    a. lobes; the corpus callosum
    b. hemispheres; the corpus callosum
    c. primary sensory areas; lobes
    d. association areas; tracts

9. Studies of people who have had split-brain surgery have taught us a great deal about:

    a. the limbic system.
    b. cortical involvement in movement.
    c. topographic organization in the cortex.
    d. the asymmetry of the higher functions in the cortex.

10. Which part of the nervous system directly mediates the body's physiological response to a stressful situation by increasing heart rate, increasing blood pressure, releasing energy, and so on?

    a. excitatory nervous system
    b. sympathetic division of the autonomic system
    c. parasympathetic division of the autonomic system
    d. skeletal motor system

11. Sustained effects on a person's behavior can be produced by activity at _____ synapses.

    a. excitatory fast
    b. inhibitory fast
    c. slow
    d. peripheral

12. Experiments with rats and mice show that placing them in enriched (as compared to deprived) learning environments results in:

    a. no discernible differences in their brains.
    b. brain differences only if the experience occurs in infancy.
    c. thicker cerebral cortexes with more fully developed synapses.
    d. more numerous but smaller neurons in the cortex.

13. The brain and spinal cord together comprise the:

    a. autonomic nervous system.
    b. central nervous system.
    c. peripheral nervous system.
    d. sympathetic nervous system.

14. The hormones that can pass through cell membranes and activate or inhibit specific genes there are:

    a. neurohormones.   ✗ **c.** steroids.
    b. peptides.   d. releasing factors.

✗ p.179

15. Curare is a drug that paralyzes by blocking post-synaptic binding sites in:
  a. muscle cells.
  b. nerves in the spinal cord.
  c. neurons in the cerebellum.
  d. neurons in the motor cortex.

Essay Questions

16. What is meant by the term *hierarchical control of behavior*? How did such hierarchical control systems come to be?

17. What is aphasia? How are Broca's and Wernicke's aphasia different in their symptoms? Briefly summarize modern theories about the two brain areas involved in these types of aphasia. Have studies involving PET clearly supported such theories?

Answers

Functional Organization of the Nervous System

  2. brain; spinal cord; nerves

  3. neurons

  4. information; integrate

  7. a. dendrites
    b. axon terminal
    c. cell body
    d. axon
    e. myelin sheath

  8. action; neurotransmitter; synapse; neurons; muscle; gland

 10. nerve

 11. 12; 31; brain; spinal cord

 16. initiate; modulate

 19. parasympathetic; sympathetic

 27. medulla; pons; midbrain

 29. postural; vital

 32. a. little brain
    b. brainstem

 33. a. thalamus
    c. Parkinson's disease; brainstem

 34. a. border (or edge); evolutionarily older
    c. amygdala; hippocampus
    d. drives; emotions
    f. hippocampus

 36. cerebrum; cortex; cerebral cortex

 37. largest; 80; folds

 38. hemispheres; lobes

 39. a. frontal
    b. parietal
    c. temporal
    d. occipital

 40. a. motor
    b. somatosensory
    c. auditory
    d. visual

 56. aphasia

How Neurons Work and Influence One Another

  3. a. soluble protein molecules, negative, internal
    b. potassium ions (K^+), positive, greater internal concentration

c. sodium ions (Na$^+$), positive, greater external concentration

d. chloride ions (Cl$^-$), negative, greater external concentration

7. **b.** sodium

c. concentration; electrical

d. positive

8. **a.** potassium

c. negative

12. faster; myelin sheath; skips; node; 100

14. **a.** fast; slow; fast

b. cleft; presynaptic; postsynaptic

c. vesicles; neurotransmitters

d. action potential; synaptic cleft

19. slow

How Hormones and Drugs Interact with the Nervous System

1. Hormones; target

2. endocrine

Self-Test 1

1. **c.** (p. 144)

2. **b.** (pp. 144–145)

3. **d.** (p. 153)

4. **b.** (p. 144)

5. **c.** Severing the cord will cut through both ascending and descending tracts and will thus produce both sensory and motor deficits. The higher up in the cord the injury lies, the greater the number of spinal nerves that are cut off from the brain, and thus the greater the area of the body affected. (pp. 148–149)

6. **b.** The flexion reflex is an example of a spinal reflex. It is carried out independently of brain control. It makes adaptive sense that this defensive move should be handled by a spinal reflex since it can thus be accomplished faster, minimizing potential damage. (p. 149)

7. **a.** (p. 169)

8. **a.** (p. 152)

9. **a.** (p. 152)

10. **a.** (p. 146)

11. **d.** (p. 155)

12. **c.** (pp. 166–167)

13. **b.** (p. 168)

14. **b.** (p. 150)

15. **b.** (p. 178)

16. Synaptic transmission is the process through which a neuron sends a message to another cell, whether it be another neuron or a muscle or gland cell. When an action potential reaches the axon terminals of the "sending," or presynaptic neuron, it causes the release of the neurotransmitter from tiny vesicles in the axon terminals. The neurotransmitter acts as a chemical messenger that moves across the synaptic cleft, a tiny gap between the cells. The neurotransmitters at fast synapses are small and diffuse rapidly across this gap. When they reach the membrane of the "receiving," or postsynaptic, cell at a fast synapse, the molecules of the neurotransmitter are received at special binding sites. The process works something like fitting a key (the neurotransmitter molecule) into a lock (the binding site).

When the "key" fits into the "lock," the postsynaptic cell will contract if it is a muscle cell. If the postsynaptic cell is another neuron, the result is the opening of a gate that allows ions to pass through, thus causing a change in the electrical balance across the cell's membrane. The direction of change depends on whether the synapse is excitatory or inhibitory. At an excitatory synapse, positively charged sodium ions enter the cell and slightly depolarize it, thus pushing it toward an action potential. At an inhibitory synapse, the entry of negatively charged ions moves the cell farther away from the threshold level of depolarization needed to trigger an action potential, thus making one less likely. Since any given postsynaptic cell has many synapses, its rate of action potentials depends on the balance of activity at the various synapses. In other words, the neuron integrates the two types of inputs. (pp. 168–170)

17. Drug tolerance means that progressively larger doses of a drug must be taken in order to achieve the original effect. It occurs with repeated use of some drugs. Withdrawal symptoms are unpleasant and sometimes life-threatening effects that occur when use of some drugs is stopped. The symptoms are often the opposite of the effects produced by the drug. Both drug tolerance and withdrawal symptoms may arise as a result of a physiological response to prolonged use of the drug. The body appears to counteract the effect of those drugs that produce tolerance and withdrawal symptoms. When this happens, more of

the drug is needed to override the body's own counteractive effect. And withdrawal symptoms occur because, when the drug is stopped, only the counteractive force is left in effect. (pp. 182–184)

Self-Test 2

1. **a.** (p. 179)
2. **c.** (p. 144)
3. **c.** Sensory neurons receive their input, directly or indirectly, from whatever type of sensory stimulation they are specialized to respond to. (p. 144)
4. **a.** (p. 166)
5. **b.** Of course, the pattern generators exert their control under orders from the brain. You might say they are "deputized." (p. 149)
6. **d.** (p. 151)
7. **b.** (pp. 151–152)
8. **b.** (p. 159)
9. **d.** (pp. 160–161)
10. **b.** (pp. 147–148)
11. **c.** (p. 171)
12. **c.** (pp. 171–172)
13. **b.** (p. 144)
14. **c.** (p. 179)
15. **a.** (p. 182)
16. In hierarchical control, multiple behavior-control systems play a role in regulating behavior, each acting within a kind of chain of command. At the lowest level are systems involved in the actual execution of some response. Lower-level systems may be capable of carrying out some simple functions independently or semi-independently. An example would be a spinal reflex like a flexion reflex. But lower-level systems are also subject to control from higher levels. At the highest level of the hierarchy are systems involved in planning and motivation. These higher-level systems achieve their effects by acting upon the lower-level systems. Both cortical and subcortical structures are involved at the top levels of the hierar-

chy. Hierarchical control may have come about as evolution created more complex and sophisticated systems. Rather than replacing older, more primitive systems, the newer ones took control over the older ones. (pp. 157–159)

17. Aphasia is any type of loss of language ability resulting from brain damage. Broca's and Wernicke's aphasia (also called nonfluent and fluent aphasia, respectively) are two categories of aphasia, each associated with characteristic patterns of language difficulty and each stemming from damage to a particular area of the brain.

Damage to Broca's area, in the left frontal lobe, typically produces a tendency to speak in a labored way. The speech that the Broca's aphasic struggles to produce is generally telegraphic, that is, short utterances containing mostly content words such as nouns and verbs. A person with Broca's aphasia who wanted to stop and sit under a tree with a friend might express that desire in a minimal form such as "Sit tree." Language comprehension is generally fairly good, but comprehension of grammatically complex sentences is impaired. A sentence in which the individual word meanings are not enough to convey the sentence meaning may not be understood correctly. For example, the pursued and the pursuer would not be clear in the statement "The woman chased the dog."

A person with Wernicke's aphasia can speak with apparent fluency, but the speech is really only gibberish. It is full of articles, pronouns, prepositions, and nonsense words arranged in appropriate grammatical sequences, but has few content words such as nouns, verbs, and adjectives. The Wernicke's aphasic also has a serious deficit in language comprehension. This kind of aphasia is associated with damage to Wernicke's area, located in the left temporal lobe.

Contemporary theories propose that Broca's area is key for keeping in mind complex grammatical structures and that Wernicke's area is involved in relating the sounds of words with their meanings as well as finding words needed to express specific meanings. Evidence from neuroimaging studies is not entirely consistent with these views. (pp. 162–164)

Chapter 6   Mechanisms of Motivation, Sleep, and Emotion

READ *the introduction below before you read the chapter in the text.*

We can think of mental or behavioral states as the slow-moving components of psychological life that help modulate and direct the fast-moving parts, such as thoughts, perceptions, and actions. This chapter examines the physiological bases of several such states. One type of state—a motivational state or drive—is an internal condition that changes over time and orients an individual toward specific categories of goals, such as food, water, or a sexual partner. Physiological psychologists can learn about central (brain) states involved in drives by lesioning (destroying) brain tissue, stimulating an area of the brain, recording electrical brain activity, manipulating genes, and using advanced brain imaging equipment. They also study the influence of processes that are peripheral to (outside) the brain.

Hunger is one area in which such research has yielded major progress. It was once thought that the hypothalamus was a hunger-control center in the brain, with activity in one area increasing hunger and activity in another area suppressing it. We now know that the control of hunger is more complicated than that, involving several types of peripheral factors as well as specific areas of the brain. Research into obesity suggests that it may be related to heredity and that several physical consequences of weight gain (an increase in the number of fat cells) and loss (a reduction in basal metabolic rate) help to explain the difficulties of weight loss.

Physiological psychology has also helped us to understand the sex drive. Hormones play a major role in the sex drive after puberty, although adult sexuality in humans is not strictly tied to hormones. Testosterone, popularly considered a strictly male hormone, appears to be a key factor in the sex drive in women as well as in men. In humans and other animals, sexual differentiation early in an individual's development is due to hormones. Experiences that affect the prenatal hormonal environment may affect the individual's later sexual behavior as well as the development of the brain and genitals.

Another product of physiological research has been the discovery of systems in the brain that are responsible for pleasure or reward. Understanding their functioning may help us to better understand the mechanisms of drug addiction as well as more natural drives such as hunger and sex.

One of the most important tools in sleep research has been the electroencephalogram, or EEG, which provides a crude picture of brain activity. During the typical night's sleep, an individual goes through a well-ordered sequence of stages, each identifiable in part through the EEG pattern associated with it. Among the stages is REM sleep, so called because of the rapid back-and-forth eye movements that occur during this stage. It is during this stage that dreaming occurs. The restoration theory and the preservation and protection theory both help to explain why slow-wave sleep may have evolved. The first theory suggests that sleep is needed so that the body can recover from the day's wear and tear. The second suggests that sleep developed as a way for animals to conserve energy and to protect themselves at times of the day when activity would bring more risk than benefit. Sleep is an example of a circadian rhythm, an internally guided cycle that occurs on a 24-hour basis. Sleep deprivation affects some kinds of performance more than others and is a relative term, given that nonsomniacs function normally on very little sleep. Like hunger and sex, sleep is governed by specific brain mechanisms.

Arousal and emotion are the final states considered in this chapter. Arousal is a pattern of measurable physiological changes that helps prepare the body for "fight or flight." Emotion is a subjective feeling often accompanied by physiological arousal. In fact, some of the central theoretical issues in the study of emotion concern the relationship between emotion and arousal. Some evidence suggests that the amount of physiological arousal we feel and even our facial expression may contribute to our emotional experience. Emotion also involves specific brain areas and mechanisms.

LOOK over the table of contents for this chapter in your textbook before you continue with your study.

Notice that there are focus questions in the margins of the text for your use in studying the material. The following chart lists which Study Guide questions relate to which focus questions.

The Integrated Study Workout

Complete one section at a time.

Mechanisms of Motivation   (pages 187–208)

CONSIDER these questions before you go on. They are designed to help you start thinking about the subject, not to test your knowledge.

What internal factors cause a person to feel hungry?

What causes some people to become obese? What factors make it difficult for them to lose excess weight?

Does the sex drive work very differently in men and women? in humans and animals?

How can the pleasure we experience when a need is satisfied be explained physiologically?

READ this section of your text lightly. Then go back and read thoroughly, completing the Workout as you proceed.

The term *motivation*, as used in psychology, refers to a host of factors, some internal and others external, that cause an individual to engage in particular behaviors at particular times. But this definition is really too broad to be theoretically useful. Psychologists who study motivation prefer more specific terminology.

1. Define *motivational state*. Give one example. What term is a synonym for *motivational state*?

2. How do psychologists determine when an individual is in a particular motivational state?

3. Define *incentive*. Give one example. What terms are synonyms for *incentive*?

4. How are drives and incentives related? Give an example to illustrate your point.

A drive is a hypothetical inner state. Efforts to understand such states physiologically are efforts to make the hypothetical more concrete. Some psychologists have focused their attention on brain states. Others, such as Walter Cannon, described motivational states in terms of tissue needs.

5. Explain Cannon's concept of homeostasis. How, in Cannon's view, is homeostasis related to drives?

6. Briefly summarize some evidence suggesting that individuals behave in ways that fit their tissue needs.

The idea of homeostasis turned out to be more useful for understanding some drives than others. Even for the drives to which the concept applied well, its usefulness was limited.

7. Homeostasis is useful for explaining _____ drives, such as _____ , which involve tissue needs. It cannot explain _____ drives such as _____ .

8. Was it theoretically useful for psychologists to propose hypothetical needs for drives for which no tissue need could be identified? Why?

9. Why were definitions of drives based on tissue needs not entirely satisfactory even for regulatory drives?

Today, physiological psychologists generally think of drives in terms of brain states.

10. Explain the central-state theory of drives. What is a central drive system?

11. Describe the characteristics a set of neurons must have in order to serve as a central drive system.

12. What characteristics of the hypothalamus make it a suitable hub of many central drive systems?

Physiological psychologists seeking to identify central drive systems must have some methodological tools to find them.

13. Answer the following questions about lesions.

a. A lesion is an area of _____ .

b. Brain lesions can be produced in either of two ways: _____ , by delivering a current through a(n) _____ ; or _____ , by injection through a(n) _____ . A(n) _____ is used to help the researcher accurately lower the lesioning device into the brain.

c. Why are lesions typically made bilaterally?

d. What can be concluded if an animal with bilateral lesions in some area no longer shows a particular drive (but does respond to other incentives)?

14. Answer the following questions about stimulation.

a. Describe two methods used by physiological psychologists to stimulate specific brain areas.

b. What can be concluded if stimulation of a specific brain area causes an animal to engage in motivated behavior it was not previously exhibiting?

15. What are knockout animals, and how have they been used in motivational research?

Hunger is the drive that has received the greatest amount of attention from physiological psychologists. Our changing conception of the hypothalamus's role in hunger not only provides fascinating information about this important motivational system, it also vividly illustrates the scientific process. (See Figure 6.3 on text page 194 as you work through the items below.)

16. Early research suggested that a hunger center is located in the _____ and a satiety center in the _____ .

17. What patterns of research data seemed to support this theory? What observations then suggested that reality was more complicated than the theory suggested?

18. Answer the following questions about current views on the central drive system for hunger.

   a. What is the function of the tract running from parts of the brainstem through the lateral hypothalamus to the basal ganglia? What happens if lesions are made anywhere along this tract?

   b. Is there evidence that some lateral hypothalamic neurons really do play a special role in hunger? What is the role of neuropeptide Y?

c. What research technique did Edmond Rolls use, and what did he discover?

d. What is the current explanation of why bilateral lesions in the ventromedial hypothalamus cause animals to overeat and gain weight?

The central nervous system structures involved in hunger are sensitive to a variety of signals, though none by itself exerts total control. (Review Figure 6.4 on text page 195.)

19. Describe four types of influences on appetite.

   a.

   b.

   c.

   d.

Many people weigh more than they would like to. One aim of research on the motivational state of hunger has been to explain obesity.

20. How is obesity related to our evolutionary history and current environment?

21. At present, _____ percent of people in the United States are obese and _____ percent are overweight, based on BMI (or _____ _____ _____).

22. What primarily determines weight differences within a culture—genes or environment? Support your answer.

23. How do the Pima Indians illustrate the importance of environmental factors (including culture) on body weight?

Once a person has gained too much weight, it can be difficult (but not impossible) to shed the excess pounds.

24. How is the number of fat cells in the body related to the difficulty of losing excess weight?

25. How does weight loss affect basal metabolism? How does that affect further efforts to take off pounds?

26. How do most people who are successful at reducing their weight manage to do it?

27. Summarize expert advice for people who want to maintain a lower weight.

The sex drive has also received a great deal of attention from physiological psychologists. Just as with hunger, most of the research has been conducted on laboratory animals, usually rats. Because humans differ from other animals in both social and biological aspects of motivation, care must be taken in generalizing research findings to humans. However, humans do have something in common with other mammals in terms of basic physiological mechanisms. One important finding has been the existence of separate neural systems for male and female sex drives.

Puberty marks a great increase in sex hormone production in humans as well as in other mammals.

28. At puberty, males have increased amounts of _____ , which is produced by the _____ . Females have increased levels of _____ , produced by the _____ .

29. Both sexes also produce _____ in the _____ glands beginning at about 6 years old. Early sexual feelings and attractions, which begin at about age _____ in both boys and girls, are due to the hormone _____ .

30. Castration, the removal of the male's _____ , and thus the main supply of _____ , causes a _____ in the sex drive in men and male animals. The implantation of testosterone crystals in the _____ area of the hypothalamus _____ the male sex drive in various animals as do injections of testosterone for men as well as male animals.

31. Is testosterone critical for maintaining the sex drive in men? Explain.

32. What is the menstrual cycle? What is the estrous cycle?

33. Removal of the ovaries in most nonhuman female mammals causes the _____ of the sex drive; subsequent administration of estrogen (or estrogen and progesterone) _____ the sex drive. At least in rats, the _____ _____ in the female plays a role analogous to that of the medial preoptic area in males. In comparison to most other female mammals, female monkeys and apes are generally _____ (less/more) dependent on ovarian hormones for their sex drive, with copulation being possible throughout the _____ cycle.

In human females, sex drive is even more independent of the hormonal cycle. Research has not produced clear evidence that there is *any* consistent relationship between the two.

34. Which hormones play a larger role in women's sex drive? How do we know?

35. What does research on female musk shrews suggest about the evolution of sexual drive systems?

The presence or absence of testosterone has major influences even before an individual's birth.

36. Describe the role of testosterone in producing prenatal sexual differentiation.

37. How does prenatal stress affect the sexual development of male rats?

38. Why is a male rather than a female hormone critical to this early sexual differentiation?

The roots of sexual orientation are not fully understood, but research has begun to provide partial answers—and more questions.

39. Is sexual orientation due primarily to social learning? Support your answer.

40. Is there a genetic contribution to sexual orientation? Explain.

41. Describe Simon LeVay's findings on brain differences related to sexual orientation. Why must we be cautious about causal conclusions from this research?

Subjectively, we are aware of the relationship between a drive and the pleasure we feel upon satisfying that drive. Research in physiological psychology has advanced our understanding of the neural basis of pleasure and reward.

42. What did James Olds and Peter Milner discover in the 1950s?

43. How have people receiving electrical brain stimulation described the resulting feeling? Did they work compulsively for it?

44. What role do the median forebrain bundle and the nucleus accumbens play in rats' responses to brain stimulation? How might they be involved in the pleasure produced by drugs such as cocaine and opiates?

It is important to note that the brain areas underlying reward evolved to serve natural motivations—such as those directed toward sex or food—not motivations for electrical brain stimulation or drugs such as cocaine.

45. What evidence suggests that the neural circuitry involved in reward from brain stimulation also underlies natural drives?

Sleeping and Dreaming (pages 208–220)

CONSIDER *these questions before you go on. They are designed to help you start thinking about the subject, not to test your knowledge.*

What is sleep? Is it just a kind of "suspended animation" in which nothing much is going on?

How can psychologists learn anything about sleep, given that the sleeping person is, well, asleep?

What purpose does sleep serve? What physiological mechanisms cause us to sleep?

How much do people differ in the amount of sleep they need?

What is dreaming, and why does it happen? Does everyone do it?

What happens if a person goes without sleep for several days?

If people had no clues to night or day, would they still tend to sleep at the same time they ordinarily do?

READ *this section of your text lightly. Then go back and read thoroughly, completing the Workout as you proceed.*

Sleepiness can be thought of as a drive, since people will go to some trouble to achieve sleep, but sleep is also an altered state of consciousness. Because sleep involves little overt behavior that can be used to infer internal processes, scientists have developed ways to tap more subtle behavioral and physiological information. One of the most important tools at their disposal has been the EEG.

1. What is the electroencephalogram (EEG), and what is it measuring? (See Figure 6.13 on text page 209.)

2. For each of the following EEG patterns, note the frequency and amplitude of the waves and when each is likely to occur. (See Figure 6.14 on text page 210.)

   a. alpha waves

   b. beta waves

   c. delta waves

The EEG follows a regular sequence of changes in a sleeping person. The changes, which are gradual and continuous, are used by researchers to divide sleep into four stages. (See Figures 6.14 and 6.15 on text pages 210 and 211.)

3. The brief transitional stage between waking and sleeping is called _____ sleep.

4. As a person moves from stage 2 to stage 4, sleep becomes successively _____ . At the same time, other physiological indices of arousal such as heart rate and muscle tension _____ .

5. What happens after a person gets to stage 4?

6. REM is an acronym for _____ .

7. In what sense are there conflicting indicators of arousal during REM sleep (emergent stage 1 sleep)?

8. Stages 2, 3, and 4 are collectively referred to as _____ sleep.

9. A person goes through _____ sleep cycles in a typical night. A cycle consists of a progressive deepening of sleep, then progressive lightening, followed by _____ sleep. Each cycle lasts about _____ minutes. (Less/More) _____ time is spent in deep sleep with each successive cycle.

One of the mysteries that has interested not just scientists but people generally is why we have developed a need for sleep. Researchers have offered two possible explanations for the evolution of sleep.

10. Explain the restoration theory, and present two types of evidence that support it.

11. Explain the preservation and protection theory, and present two types of evidence that support it. How might this theory explain the typical 8-hour nighttime sleep pattern of adult humans?

We can generally understand more about a scientific phenomenon by looking at it in different ways. One useful way to think about sleep involves the fact that it is a biological rhythm.

12. What happens when animals are kept in an environment in which they have no cues to time of day? What happens with humans when time cues are removed?

13. A rhythmic change occurring on roughly a 24-hour cycle even without external 24-hour cues is called a(n) _____ . These are governed by cyclic changes in activity in the _____ .

14. Under normal environmental conditions, what cue resets the circadian clock daily? How can the cycle be artificially reset? Are there possible practical applications of this technique?

Most students have at some time or other experienced sleep deprivation, perhaps in studying for an exam or finishing a paper. (I hope that is not your current circumstance.)

15. What happens when people go 3 or 4 days without sleep? Does everyone suffer to the same degree from sleep deprivation?

16. What kinds of tasks are most affected by sleep deprivation? What kinds are least affected?

17. What is the most reliable effect of sleep deprivation? Is this effect simply related to the amount of sleep deprivation? Explain.

18. Describe a nonsomniac. How does nonsomnia compare with insomnia?

Dreaming is one reason that sleep has long fascinated us. In dreams, we may become a different character, overcome the limitations of time and space, experience bizarre happenings, and more.

19. How did Sigmund Freud explain the purpose of dreaming?

20. How do scientists study dreams?

21. Describe a true dream. How are true dreams related to REM sleep? Does everyone dream?

22. What kind of mental activity do people sometimes report when awakened from slow-wave rather than REM sleep? How effective is this mental activity compared to its daytime counterpart?

23. In the currently prevailing view, why do we have true dreams? Is there evidence consistent with this view? Explain.

24. Does the side-effect theory necessarily imply that dreams cannot be useful in understanding a person's mind?

25. Describe evidence suggesting a role for REM sleep in memory consolidation.

Just as the hunger and sex drives are regulated by neurons in the brain, so too is sleep. Sleep is not, as researchers once believed, a state that the brain enters when external stimulation is low. After all, we sometimes sleep with considerable stimulation around us and sometimes fail to sleep when stimulation is minimal.

26. Research on animals has uncovered several separate but interacting brain systems involved in sleep. Identify and describe each, making sure to specify its role and indicate the evidence for that role.

    a. suprachiasmatic nucleus

b. pineal gland

c. anterior hypothalamus

d. neural centers in the pons

2. When would it be better for a person to have an audience—when the task is to design a better mousetrap or to count how many mousetraps are in a box?

3. Explain the Yerkes-Dodson law. (See Figure 6.22 on text page 221.)

Arousal and Emotion   (pages 220–228)

> *CONSIDER these questions before you go on. They are designed to help you start thinking about the subject, not to test your knowledge.*

Do we perform better if we are super-relaxed, super-excited, or somewhere in between? Does the answer to the question depend on the kind of task we are performing?

Is emotion "all in the head," or does it have something to do with activity in the rest of the body as well?

Sometimes people who are feeling a little blue are told they will feel happier if they make themselves smile. Does this make any sense?

> *READ this section of your text lightly. Then go back and read thoroughly, completing the Workout as you proceed.*

If a police car pulls up behind you as you drive down the highway, its lights flashing and spinning, you will probably have more than a cognitive awareness of the event. Among other things, your heart may pound and your muscles may tense. These changes are part of the physiological arousal response.

1. Define and describe the arousal response.

4. Describe the effects of an arousal response that is too strong and prolonged.

The same stimuli that lead to high physiological arousal also lead to feelings. Arousal, emotions, and drives are all intimately related.

5. How does the text define *emotion*?

6. If someone asked you how many different emotions humans experience, what would be the wisest response?

One dimension of emotional experience is physiological. Psychologists have sought to understand the role that peripheral changes in heart rate, breathing rate, and muscle tension, for example, play in emotional feelings.

7. What position did William James take on this issue? Was his theory based on experimental data? How was he using the term *emotion*?

Stanley Schachter developed a theory of emotion similar to James's.

8. Describe Schachter's theory of emotion. How is it like James's theory? How does it differ? (See Figure 6.24 on text page 223.)

9. What laboratory evidence did Schachter provide to support his view?

In an emotional situation, the autonomic nervous system automatically triggers certain bodily responses. Depending on the stimulus and on your reaction to it, you may also lower your eyebrows in anger or lift the corners of your mouth in a smile. Paul Ekman asked whether facial expressions can contribute to emotion.

10. What evidence suggests that "putting on" a particular facial expression can affect mood?

11. What findings indicate that facial feedback may produce bodily states similar to those associated with the emotion depicted?

Emotion depends not just on peripheral processes, of course, but also on the brain, which not only produces the bodily changes but is responsible for experiencing the emotion.

12. According to the brain-based theory of emotion illustrated in Figure 6.28 (text page 226), the _____ is thought to be central in assessing the emotional significance of a stimulus and producing an immediate response. The _____ is critical for conscious emotional experience and more deliberate emotional behavior.

13. Describe what happens to emotional responsiveness when the amygdala is removed or damaged?

14. How do the results of prefrontal lobotomy verify the importance of the frontal lobes to emotion?

15. What evidence suggests that the left and right frontal lobes may be specialized for different emotions?

> Be sure to READ the Concluding Thoughts at the end of the chapter. Note important points in your Workout. Then consolidate your learning by answering the focus questions in the margins of the text.

> After you have studied the chapter thoroughly, CHECK your understanding with the Self-Test that follows.

Self-Test 1

Multiple-Choice Questions

1. Which of the following is *not* a sex hormone found in humans?
   a. testosterone
   b. estrogen
   c. DHEA
   d. Hey, you can't fool me—all of the above are human sex hormones.

2. According to Walter Cannon, tissue needs produce drives, which in turn produce behaviors that will restore:
   a. a central drive system.
   b. motivational states.
   c. incentive.
   d. homeostasis.

3. An example of a nonregulatory drive is the drive for:

   a. food.
   b. sex.
   c. both **a** and **b**.
   d. neither **a** nor **b**.

4. A brain structure that is the hub of many central drive systems is the :

   a. brainstem.
   b. cerebellum.
   c. thalamus.
   d. hypothalamus.

5. Which of the following statements is true of peripheral influences on hunger?

   a. Hunger is turned on or off exclusively by signals from the stomach.
   b. Despite popular belief, stomach fullness actually plays no part in signaling satiety.
   c. Hunger levels are affected by the amount of food molecules in the blood.
   d. The hunger drive is influenced by external stimuli only in the case of obese individuals.

6. The term *motivational state* is synonymous with:

   a. emotion.
   b. drive.
   c. incentive.
   d. arousal.

7. According to research described in the text, the hormonal changes that accompany a woman's menstrual cycle:

   a. cause her to experience peak sex drive during menstruation.
   b. cause her to experience a dramatically increased sex drive about the time of ovulation.
   c. cause her to experience an absence of sex drive during menstruation.
   d. have relatively little, if any, effect on her sex drive.

8. Electrical stimulation of reward mechanisms in the brain:

   a. has never been tried in humans.
   b. is not pleasurable enough to cause nonhuman animals to work for it.
   c. apparently is motivating because it directly produces effects normally produced by the satisfaction of natural drives.
   d. suggests that there is no genetic basis for pleasure.

9. The electroencephalogram, or EEG, measures _____ and has proved especially useful in studying _____ .

   a. gross electrical activity in the brain; sleep
   b. gross electrical activity in the brain; hunger
   c. electrical activity in an individual neuron; sleep
   d. electrical activity in an individual neuron; hunger.

10. Which stage of sleep is associated with REM?

    a. stage 1
    b. emergent stage 1
    c. stage 2
    d. stage 4

11. The pattern of measurable physiological changes that helps prepare the body for "fight or flight" is called:

    a. the circadian rhythm.
    b. the arousal response.
    c. emotion.
    d. the alertness mechanism.

12. Prolonged sleep deprivation in humans generally leads to:

    a. coma and death within 10 days.
    b. severe difficulty in the performance of tasks requiring physical skill or mental judgment.
    c. irritability, distorted perception, and difficulty carrying out simple, boring tasks.
    d. a paradoxical absence of sleepiness.

13. Extreme physical exercise is typically followed by lengthier, deeper sleep. This fact supports the _____ theory of sleep.

    a. restoration
    b. preservation and protection
    c. side-effect
    d. REM

14. According to the Yerkes-Dodson law, conditions of high arousal would be most likely to harm performance on a(n):

    a. high-energy physical task.
    b. instinctive or well-practiced task.
    c. task that demands persistence or endurance.
    d. task involving creativity or careful judgment.

15. Peripheral feedback contributes to the emotional experience, according to:

    a. James.
    b. Schachter.
    c. both **a** and **b**.
    d. none of the above.

Essay Questions

16. What is obesity? Explain three factors that may predispose a person to become and stay obese.

17. Discuss hormonal effects on the human sex drive after puberty. Be certain to deal with both the male and the female sex drive.

After you have assessed your understanding on the basis of Self-Test 1 and have tried to strengthen your preparation in any areas of weakness, GO ON to Self-Test 2.

Self-Test 2

Multiple-Choice Questions

1. A thirsty fan at a football game waits in line for a soft drink. In this example, the fan's thirst is a(n) _____ and the soft drink is a(n) _____ .
   a. reinforcer; incentive
   b. incentive; drive
   c. drive; incentive
   d. motivational state; drive

2. In terms of emotional experience, research suggests that the left and right frontal lobes:
   a. are not involved in emotion as was once thought.
   b. are responsible for immediate unconscious responses to emotional stimuli.
   c. differ in that one is specialized for positive emotions and one for negative emotions.
   d. are involved in emotional responses for women but not men.

3. Which of the following methods involves insertion of a cannula into the brain to destroy neurons whose cell bodies are near the cannula's tip?
   a. the electrical production of lesions
   b. the chemical production of lesions
   c. electrical brain stimulation
   d. chemical brain stimulation

4. In the area of sex, a basic difference between humans and other species is that:
   a. humans are much more stereotyped in their sexual behavior.
   b. the sex drive of human females is not limited to a specific time in their hormonal cycle.
   c. humans are not sexually differentiated as a result of prenatal hormones.
   d. the human sex drive typically is unaffected by the absence of sex hormones.

5. Animals with bilateral lesions to the lateral hypothalamus ignore food to the extent that they will starve if not fed through a stomach tube. This is because:
   a. the lateral hypothalamus is the hunger center and, once destroyed, can no longer produce the hunger drive.
   b. such lesions interrupt a tract serving general motor-activation functions for hunger and other drives.
   c. lesions in the lateral hypothalamus cause changes in digestion and metabolism.
   d. the brain can no longer send hunger signals to the stomach.

6. Injections of the hormone testosterone:
   a. will fail to restore the sex drive in men who have been castrated or who produce abnormally low levels of the hormone.
   b. lead to distortions of sexual orientation in heterosexual women.
   c. will be rejected by the immune systems of women because testosterone is an exclusively male hormone.
   d. will increase the sex drive in women who are experiencing low sex drive due to removal of the adrenal glands.

7. Large regular brain waves with a frequency of 8 to 13 cycles per second are called:
   a. alpha waves.
   b. beta waves.
   c. delta waves.
   d. REMs.

8. Simon LeVay has reported that a particular nucleus in the hypothalamus is:
   a. the same size in homosexual and heterosexual men.
   b. larger in homosexual men than in heterosexual men.
   c. smaller in women and homosexual men than in heterosexual men.
   d. destroyed by AIDS.

9. The administration of dopamine-blocking drugs will:
   a. cause animals who have learned to lever-press for food to nearly stop their lever-pressing and eating behaviors.
   b. enhance the effects of cocaine, amphetamines, and certain other illicit drugs.
   c. help an animal learn faster how to stimulate its reward centers electrically.
   d. cause animals who have learned to lever-press for food to exhibit this behavior at unusually high rates.

10. Prenatal differentiation of human males and females depends on the presence or absence of:
    a. estrogen.
    b. testosterone.
    c. dopamine.
    d. DHEA.

11. The sleep cycle can be reset through carefully timed:
    a. exposure to bright fluorescent light.
    b. changes in temperature.
    c. alterations in diet.
    d. mild electrical shocks.

12. True dreams occur during _____ sleep.
    a. slow-wave
    b. REM
    c. stage 2
    d. stage 4

13. The circadian clock is located in a specific nucleus in the:
    a. pons.
    b. cerebral cortex.
    c. hypothalamus.
    d. medulla.

14. Induced facial expressions can produce corresponding changes in:
    a. mood only.
    b. physiological response only.
    c. both mood and physiological response.
    d. self-reports of mood, but these have been shown to arise solely from subject expectations.

15. A set of neurons in which activity constitutes a drive is a:
    a. central drive system.
    b. motivational state.
    c. limbic system.
    d. homeostatic regulator.

Essay Questions

16. What is the function of slow-wave sleep? Offer evidence for any theories that you present.

17. What is the arousal response? What role does it play in emotion? Support your position.

Answers

Mechanisms of Motivation

7. regulatory; hunger; nonregulatory; sex

13. **a.** damage

   b. electrically; electrode; chemically; cannula; stereotaxic instrument

16. lateral area of the hypothalamus; ventromedial area of the hypothalamus

21. 22; 54; body mass index

28. testosterone; testes; estrogen; ovaries

29. DHEA; adrenal; 10; DHEA

30. testes; testosterone; decrease; medial preoptic; restores

33. elimination; restores; ventromedial area of the hypothalamus; less; hormonal

Sleeping and Dreaming

3. stage 1

4. deeper; decline

6. rapid eye movement

8. slow-wave

9. four or five; REM; 90; Less

13. circadian rhythm; nervous system

Arousal and Emotion

12. amygdala; frontal lobe

Self-Test 1

1. **d.** (p. 200)

2. **d.** (p. 189)

3. **b.** Nonregulatory drives are those whose purpose is other than to maintain internal bodily conditions within certain limits. In other words, nonregulatory drives exist for nonhomeostatic purposes. (pp. 189–190)

4. **d.** (p. 190)

5. **c.** (pp. 194–197)

6. **b.** (p. 187)

7. **d.** (p. 202)

8. **c.** (p. 206)

9. **a.** (pp. 208–209)

10. **b.** (p. 210)

11. **b.** (p. 220)

12. **c.** In fact, the difficulty with simple, boring tasks may be due to brief episodes of sleep during the performance of the task. (p. 214)

13. **a.** (p. 211)

14. **d.** (pp. 220–221)

15. **c.** (pp. 222–224)

16. Obesity is a condition in which a person has a BMI (body mass index) of 30 or more. Although it is possible for people to overcome the tendency to be obese, a number of factors make it difficult. One problem is that gaining weight increases the number of fat cells stored in the body. Altering the diet to lose weight doesn't decrease their number. It can only cause the fat cells to return to normal size. Another factor is that weight loss lowers basal metabolism so the body needs fewer calories to maintain itself and any additional calories are stored as fat. Obese individuals also may be strongly influenced by hereditary factors. Evidence from adoption studies shows that adopted children resemble their biological parents more than their adoptive parents where weight is concerned. If the biological parents were obese, then the individual is fighting against his or her genetic makeup in attempting to obtain a lower body weight. (pp. 197–198)

17. The hormone testosterone appears to be important for maintaining the sex drive in both men and women. Men who have been castrated or who produce abnormally low amounts of testosterone will show a decline in the sex drive and sexual behavior, though they will often not lose the drive entirely. If they receive injections of testosterone, their sex drive will be restored. At least in the case of noncastrated men with abnormally low levels of testosterone, injections specifically affect the desire for sex, not the ability to carry out sexual behavior.

   In women, the sex drive also appears to depend on some minimum level of testosterone in the body. Unlike females of other species, a woman's sex drive is not tied directly to cyclic fluctuations in female hormones such as estrogen. A woman whose ovaries have been removed, and who therefore is producing little estrogen or other ovarian hormones, will generally experience no decline in sex drive. However, a woman whose adrenal glands have been removed, and who therefore is producing no testosterone, will often experience a decline in sex drive. As with men, injections of testosterone restore the sex drive in such women. (pp. 200–202)

Self-Test 2

1. **c.** Remember that the drive, or motivational state, is the condition of the individual that causes the individual to orient toward some goal. The incentive is the external stimulus toward which motivated behavior is directed. (pp. 187–188)

2. **c.** (pp. 227–228)

3. **b.** Cannulas are used in chemical methods of lesioning and stimulation, but only in lesioning is there intentional destruction of brain tissue. Electrodes are used for electrically produced lesions and stimulation. (p. 191)

4. **b.** (p. 202)

5. **b.** (pp. 192–193)

6. **d.** (p. 202)

7. **a.** (p. 209)

8. **c.** Note that this correlational result does not allow us to conclude that this is a cause of male homosexuality. (p. 205)

9. **a.** Apparently, the dopamine blockers prevent the usual rewarding consequence that eating naturally produces. (p. 207)

10. **b.** (p. 203)

11. **a.** (p. 213)

12. **b.** Sleep thought, a type of mental activity different from true dreaming, occurs during slow-wave sleep, which includes stages 2 through 4. (p. 215)

13. **c.** Other neural controls for sleep are found in the anterior hypothalamus as well as in the brainstem and pineal gland. (p. 218)

14. **c.** (pp. 224–225)

15. **a.** (p. 190)

16. There are two major theories on the functions of slow-wave sleep. The restoration theory suggests that sleep is needed for the body to recover physically after a day of wear and tear. Several lines of evidence support this notion. One is the fact that sleep really is a time of rest in which the muscles are relaxed, the metabolic rate is slowed, and the brain is less active. Another is the fact that extreme physical exertion causes sleep to be deeper and a little longer, as if more repair is needed following harder wear and tear. Also, prolonged total sleep deprivation in rats led to a breakdown in tissues and eventually to death.

The preservation and protection theory is also supported by several different kinds of evidence. The theory states that sleep came about in evolution to conserve energy and to keep an animal relatively safe during that part of a 24-hour period when activity would be more risky than beneficial. Evidence for this theory comes primarily from comparing different species. For example, the theory helps to make sense of the fact that variations in sleep time between species correspond to feeding habits and ways of achieving safety. Animals who need to spend large amounts of time getting food and who are too big to hide easily during sleep do not sleep much. Animals who get all the food they need easily and who can sleep in a safely hidden place sleep for a good portion of a 24-hour period. This theory also helps to explain when members of a species tend to sleep as well as for how long. For example, species that need visual information to find food tend to be awake in daylight hours and asleep at night. (pp. 211–212)

17. The arousal response is a pattern of measurable physiological changes that occurs in response to some stimulus that provokes the individual to prepare for "fight or flight." The particular changes involved vary from individual to individual and from situation to situation, but often include such things as elevated heart rate, breathing rate, and blood pressure; diversion of blood to the skeletal muscles; increased muscle tension; the release of endorphins; and the narrow focusing of attention.

James's peripheral feedback theory suggests that emotion—the subjective feeling we have—is simply our awareness of the bodily changes we experience. Schachter's theory proposes that emotion is a product both of the arousal we experience and of an emotionally significant stimulus that causes us to interpret the arousal in emotional terms. According to this theory, the more arousal there is, the more intense the emotion we experience. Schachter found in a laboratory experiment that the intensity of his subjects' emotional response was heightened by epinephrine, which produces physiological arousal. (pp. 220–224)

Chapter 7

Smell, Taste, Pain, Hearing, and Psychophysics

> READ the introduction below before you read the chapter in the text.

Sensation occurs when a physical stimulus produces physiological responses in the sensory organs and brain that lead to a subjective, psychological experience of that stimulus. Perception is the more complex organizing and meaningful interpreting of sensory information, though the boundary between sensation and perception is blurry.

Sensations, in the form of sights, sounds, tastes, smells, and so on, are necessary for us to know about the world around us and even about our own bodies. Our various sensory systems actually have much in common. For example, all need certain types of neural structures: receptors, which respond directly to the stimulus; sensory neurons, which carry sensory information to the central nervous system; and still other cells that process sensory information in particular ways. Processes common to all of our senses include transduction (responding to a physical stimulus with electrical changes that can trigger neural impulses), coding (preserving information about the stimulus in patterns of neural activity), and adaptation (altering sensitivity to a stimulus with continued stimulation or lack of stimulation).

Smell is a chemical sense, with receptors designed to respond to the molecules of many different odorants. The human sense of smell is very useful and also quite sensitive. Smell receptors are distributed throughout the olfactory epithelium in the nose. Neural signals travel from these receptors to glomeruli in the olfactory bulb of the brain. Major pathways lead from there to the limbic system and hypothalamus, which may help to explain the powerful effect of smell on emotion and motivation. Another important destination for output from the olfactory bulb is the orbitofrontal cortex, where fine distinctions between odors are made and used to guide behavior.

Smell plays a significant role in our experience of flavor. In many animal species, pheromones provide a means of communicating with other members of the same species via smell. There is some limited evidence of human pheromones. Smell also appears to play a role in the selection of mates in humans as well as in mice, with individuals preferring mates who smell most different from them.

Taste, too, is a chemical sense. To be tasted, molecules must be dissolved in saliva and stimulate appropriate receptor cells in the taste buds, most of which are found on the tongue. Current thinking suggests that there are five basic taste sensations and five corresponding types of taste receptors: sweet, salty, sour, bitter, and umami.

Taste evolved to guide our food choices toward beneficial foods and away from harmful substances, such as poisons. Many harmful substances are experienced as bitter, and bitter foods are generally experienced as unpleasant and thus rejected. The sensitivity to bitter tastes is greater in carnivores than in herbivores, with omnivores falling somewhere in between. Bitter sensitivity also increases in women during early pregnancy to provide greater protection to the vulnerable fetus.

Pain is a body sense we may at times wish we didn't have; yet it is one with real survival value. The receptors for pain are the sensory neurons themselves, which have sensitive free nerve endings. There are two types of pain-sensory neurons, called C fibers and A-delta fibers. Different aspects of the pain experience are associated with different brain areas. The gate-control theory helps to explain pain and its inhibition. Pain relief may come from a number of natural sources, including endorphins, acute stress, and even our beliefs.

Sound waves—vibrations in the air or some other medium—are the stimuli that initiate responses in the ear. The chapter explains both the nature of sound waves and the workings of the human ear. Emphasis is placed on a structure called the cochlea, which is located in the inner ear, because it is in this coiled structure that transduction takes place. Two types of deafness—conduction deafness and sensorineural deafness—can occur, each resulting from a different type of malfunction in the ear. The basilar membrane, a structure in the inner ear, is the focus of theories of pitch perception; both the pattern and timing of its movement contribute to our ability to discriminate among pitches. Differences in timing and amplitude of the sound waves reaching the right and left ears help us to localize sounds.

The chapter concludes by introducing several questions addressed by the field of psychophysics, which attempts to relate characteristics of the stimulus to aspects of the resulting subjective experience. For example, one psychophysical question is: How weak can a stimulus be and still be detected? This question concerns the so-called absolute threshold. (Actually, it turns out to be a fairly arbitrary and unabsolute threshold, as you will see.) Psychophysics has been a fruitful area for those who appreciate mathematical precision in their answers.

> LOOK over the table of contents for this chapter in your textbook before you continue with your study.

> Notice that there are focus questions in the margins of the text for your use in studying the material. The following chart lists which Study Guide questions relate to which focus questions.

Focus Questions	Study Guide Questions
Overview of Sensory Processes	
1–4	1–6
The Chemical Senses	
5–10	1–12
11–12	13–22
Pain	
13–16	1–4
17–20	5–15
Hearing	
21–23	1–10
24–26	11–15
27–28	16–23
Psychophysics	
29–31	1–8
32–34	9–16

The Integrated Study Workout

> Complete one section at a time.

Overview of Sensory Processes   (pages 233–238)

> CONSIDER these questions before you go on. They are designed to help you start thinking about this subject, not to test your knowledge.

How can psychologists study a person's sensations, given that they're completely private experiences?

Are there really only five senses?

The eyes are certainly necessary for sight and the ears for hearing, but does seeing actually take place in the eyes? or hearing in the ears?

How can the wonderful smell of fresh coffee seem so vivid at first but become barely noticeable after a short while?

> READ this section of your text lightly. Then go back and read thoroughly, completing the Workout as you proceed.

The term *sensation* refers both to our elementary psychological experience of a stimulus, such as a light or sound, and to the basic physiological steps that allow us to respond to the stimulus. Sensation, and the kinds of questions scientists ask about it, can be more clearly understood if the process is broken down into three classes of events.

1. Indicate the three classes of events involved in sensation by filling in the diagram below.

    _____ → _____

    → _____

2. Direct physical measurement is possible for the first two classes of events in sensation. How do psychologists measure the third?

Different domains of inquiry focus on different types of relationships in the chain of events above.

3. Label each of the areas of study described below. (See Figure 7.1 on text page 234.)

    a. _____ deals with the relationship between the physiological response and the sensory experience.

    b. _____ concerns the relationship between the stimulus and the sensory experience.

    c. _____ focuses on the relationship between the stimulus and the physiological response.

Though we have a number of different senses, specifying a particular number would be arbitrary. Though each is unique in important ways, all senses have some things in common. For example, all depend on certain types of anatomical elements, which carry out particular types of functions. The senses also have some basic processes in common.

4. Name the three types of physiological structures common to all senses, and briefly state their respective functions.

       Structure   Function

a.

b.

c.

5. Define the following processes and give a specific example of each.

a. transduction

b. receptor potential

c. coding

d. sensory adaptation

6. In what part(s) of the sensory system does sensory adaptation take place?

The Chemical Senses   (pages 238–247)

> CONSIDER *these questions before you go on. They are designed to help you start thinking about this subject, not to test your knowledge.*

How sensitive is the human sense of smell?

Why are smells able to provoke powerful emotions and drives?
What makes some foods taste sweet and others salty or bitter?
How many types of taste sensations are there?
What is the evolutionary value of taste?

> READ *this section of your text lightly. Then go back and read thoroughly, completing the Workout as you proceed.*

Both smell and taste are specialized to respond to chemical molecules. Though keener in many other species, the sense of smell in humans is actually quite sensitive and very useful. Smell is handled by the olfactory system.

1. Note two facts that underscore the sensitivity of human smell.

2. The _____ contains the sensitive ends of about _____ olfactory sensory neurons. Each of these ends contains 5-10 hairlike _____ and each of those contains many _____ sites capable of binding the molecules of specific odorants. The axons of the sensory neurons pass into the _____ in the brain, where they synapse with other neurons in structures called _____ .

3. How does transduction occur in the olfactory system?

4 Describe the variety and organization of receptor sites, sensory neurons, and glomeruli.

5. How do quantitative and qualitative coding take place in the olfactory system?

6. Where does output from the glomeruli go in the brain, and why are these pathways important?

   a.

   b.

The senses of taste and smell are more closely linked than many people realize.

7. How is it possible to smell food in the mouth?

8. Describe two kinds of evidence that smell contributes significantly to the experience of flavor.

In many species, smell is the basis of a communications system. A specific chemical called a pheromone is released by an animal to influence the behavior or physiology of other members of its species.

9. What is the vomeronasal organ found in most mammalian species?

10. Describe the current state of research on human communication by means of pheromones.

Obviously, we are capable of recognizing other people by their faces and by their voices, but what about recognizing them by their odor?

11. Can humans identify other people by their smell? Support your answer.

12. What is the major histocompatibility complex (MHC)? How and why might it affect mating preferences in mice? Is there evidence of the same preference pattern in humans?

Some species walk on their taste receptors and others carry them all over their bodies, but in humans, they are found exclusively in the mouth—mainly on the tongue, but also on the roof of the mouth and in the opening of the throat. The taste receptors are organized somewhat like the segments of an orange in spherical structures called taste buds. There are 50–150 receptor cells in each of the thousands of taste buds in a person's mouth.

13. Western taste researchers formerly believed that there were four basic taste sensations corresponding to four types of taste receptors. Each type of receptor was named after the type of sensation it produces when activated. Those four tastes were:

_____   _____

_____   _____

14. Why do we now believe there are five basic types of taste sensation and taste receptors? What is the fifth?

15. What is necessary for a substance to be tasted?

16. What constitutes transduction in the sense of taste? Is it the same for all types of receptors? Explain.

17. Below list the types of taste receptor cells and the types of stimuli that activate them.

    a.

    b.

    c.

d.

e.

18. How are the different types of taste receptors distributed over the tongue?

19. Where is the primary taste area in the cerebral cortex and how is it organized?

Taste evolved in order to guide our eating behavior—drawing us to some substances and away from others. Of course, the taste preferences that were most useful for our evolutionary ancestors may no longer be ideal in an environment where candy and potato chips fill store shelves. Generally speaking, we find salty, sweet, and umami tastes pleasant and sour and bitter tastes unpleasant. The text presents an evolutionary perspective on the rejection of bitter-tasting foods (the bitter rejection response). It also points out that learning can override the bitter rejection response, leading us to eat some foods that are safe and nutritious though bitter-tasting—like brussels sprouts or spinach.

20. Explain in evolutionary terms why we may experience so many chemically diverse substances as bitter?

21. Among carnivores, omnivores, and herbivores, which are most sensitive to bitter tastes? How can we make sense of that?

22. Why is a woman's sensitivity to bitter tastes increased during the first 3 months of pregnancy?

Pain   (pages 247–253)

> *CONSIDER these questions before you go on. They are designed to help you start thinking about this subject, not to test your knowledge.*

The usefulness—and the pleasures—of senses such as taste and hearing are obvious, but why should pain exist?

Is there a sense organ for pain? Where does this type of sensation originate?

Why might a person who has been badly injured not feel pain until later?

Can our beliefs affect pain?

> *READ this section of your text lightly. Then go back and read thoroughly, completing the Workout as you proceed.*

Pain is a biologically useful and highly motivating, though generally unwanted, type of sensation. It is a body sense that is related to other somatosenses such as the senses of touch and temperature. Like the receptors for these senses, pain receptors are actually specialized parts of sensory neurons, not separate cells. (See Figure 7.8 on text page 248.)

1. Pain neurons have sensitive terminals called

   _____ , which are found in

   _____ from which pain is sensed.

2. Distinguish between C fibers and A-delta fibers. Indicate the types of stimuli that activate them, and specify the type of pain associated with each.

   a. C fibers

   b. A-delta fibers

As with other senses, pain depends not only on specialized peripheral neurons but also on specialized areas of the brain. (See Figure 7.9 on text page 249.)

3. For each brain area below, describe the type of pain experience associated with it and the evidence that supports that association.

   a. somatosensory cortex

   b. areas of the limbic system and insular cortex

   c. prefrontal cortex

4. The fact that the experience of pain does not always come from pain receptors is illustrated by

   an experience called _____ .

The very same pain stimulus doesn't always produce the same level of pain. Ronald Melzack and Patrick Wall proposed the gate-control theory to explain the extent to which pain will or will not be felt. The theory is well supported by physiological evidence.

5. Explain the basic premise of the gate-control theory.

Because pain was designed to serve a protective function—by alerting us to physical damage or disease and motivating us to behave in certain ways—the body has mechanisms to enhance pain.

6. How and why does illness produce a general increase in pain sensitivity?

7. How and why does injury lead to a localized increase in pain sensitivity?

8. Why have surgeons increasingly turned to local anesthetics?

The periaqueductal gray (PAG) in the midbrain is a major center for pain inhibition.

9. Discuss the role of the PAG in gate control.

10. What happens to pain levels when the PAG is stimulated electrically? by morphine? by endorphins?

11. Do opiates and endorphins work only in the PAG? Explain.

Nature has provided us with several psychologically medicated mechanisms of pain reduction.

12. Describe the phenomenon of stress-induced analgesia.

13. Describe evidence suggesting that stress-induced analgesia is mediated at least partly by endorphins.

14. Can pain be reduced through the power of belief or faith? Explain.

15. What do endorphins have to do with placebo-induced pain reduction?

Hearing (pages 253–263)

> CONSIDER these questions before you go on. They are designed to help you start thinking about this subject, not to test your knowledge.

Where in the ear does the neural response to sound occur?

What causes deafness? Why does a hearing aid help some people with impaired hearing and not others?

What makes some sounds high, such as those of a piccolo, and others low, such as those of a tuba? What makes them loud or soft?

> *READ this section of your text lightly. Then go back and read thoroughly, completing the Workout as you proceed.*

As in every sensory system, hearing is specialized to respond to a particular type of stimulation. In order to understand this sense, you must understand the nature of its stimulus—sound waves. (See Figure 7.11 on text page 254.)

1. Sound occurs when an object produces _____ of the air or some other medium, which can be described in terms of _____ with a given height and rate of movement.

2. We experience the intensity, or _____ , of the sound (measured in_____) as _____ .

3. The rate at which a sound wave travels is called its _____ and is measured in units called _____ . This aspect of the sound stimulus corresponds to what we hear as _____ . Humans hear sounds varying from 20 up to _____ .

4. Most natural sounds are more complex than a(n) _____ tone, which is a constant-frequency wave of vibration that can be described as a sine wave.

In order to understand the sense of hearing, you must also know something about the parts of the ear. The ear is commonly divided into three major sections, each with its own functions. (See Figure 7.12 on text page 255.)

5. The outer ear, which consists of the _____ and the _____ , is separated from the middle ear by the _____ , which is also called the _____ . The function of the outer ear is to _____ sound inward.

6. The middle ear contains the _____ (more specifically called the _____ ,

_____ , and _____), which essentially transfer vibration from the eardrum to the much smaller _____ window. The middle ear's main function is to increase the _____ that sound waves exert on the inner ear.

7. Identify and describe the following parts of the inner ear. (See Figures 7.13 on text page 256.)

    a. cochlea

    b. basilar membrane

    c. hair cells

    d. tectorial membrane

    e. auditory nerve

8. Briefly describe the process of transduction in the inner ear.

Two types of deafness can occur, each stemming from a different physiological problem.

9. What problem underlies conduction deafness? Is there any help for this problem? Explain.

10. What problem underlies sensorineural deafness? What kind of device can help this problem? How much help can the best devices provide?

A major task for scientists studying sensation is to understand how the nervous system codes various aspects of the stimulus. In the study of hearing, interest has centered on how frequency is coded to produce the experience of pitch.

11. How does the ear code various frequencies to allow pitch perception, according to Georg von Békésy? (See Figure 7.14 on text page 258.)

12. Has subsequent research confirmed Békésy's hypothesis? What has been revealed about the inner row of hair cells?

13. Explain how Békésy's traveling-wave hypothesis partially accounts for asymmetry in auditory masking. (See Figure 7.15 on text page 259.)

14. How does his hypothesis fit with the fact that aging reduces sensitivity to higher frequencies more than to lower frequencies?

15. Explain how the timing of activity in the basilar membrane plays a role in pitch perception of sounds below about 4000 Hz.

Information delivered to the brain by the auditory nerve receives extensive processing in the auditory cortex. Many cells there are specialized to respond only to very specific types of auditory information—a narrow range of frequencies, for example, or a brief burst of sound. Through the combined pattern of activity in these cells, the brain extracts information about different aspects of the sound.

16. What does it mean to say that neurons in the primary auditory cortex are tonotopically organized?

17. Four types of information (in addition to loudness and pitch) that the brain extracts about sound are _____ , _____ , _____ , and _____ .

18. Can the response characteristics of neurons in the auditory cortex be modified by experience? Support your answer.

Imagine you were hiking and heard a threatening rattle. It would certainly be a good idea not to come closer to that sound source. Our ability to discern where sounds are coming from is clearly important—so important that we are born with it. It even helps in ways that may not be obvious, such as mentally separating the conversation we want to listen to from the other conversations at a restaurant.

19. Localization of sounds depends in part on the relative _____ of the sound waves reaching the two ears. Sound from a source directly in front of us will be received _____ by the two ears, but sound coming from slightly farther to the left will arrive at the _____ ear sooner than it will arrive at the other ear, with the difference ranging from a few to about 700 _____ .

20. Describe neurons in a way station of the auditory system that might respond differentially based on such timing differences.

21. How does amplitude play a role in sound localization?

22. How can we distinguish between a sound that is coming from directly in front of and one from right behind us?

Our auditory system, under some circumstances, creates the compelling impression that we have heard something that was not physically present.

23. Describe the phenomenon of phonemic restoration. Why might the auditory system produce this effect?

Psychophysics   (pages 263–271)

> CONSIDER these questions before you go on. They are designed to help you start thinking about this subject, not to test your knowledge.

What's the smallest amount of light a person can see? the smallest amount of sound a person can hear?

How can we study human sensations (which are private experiences) precisely enough to make trustworthy measurements?

Are any general psychophysical relationships pretty much the same for everyone? Or is everyone so different that a scientific law would be impossible to establish?

Why does changing lighting from a 50- to a 100-watt bulb make a bigger difference in brightness than changing from a 150- to a 200-watt bulb?

> READ this section of your text lightly. Then go back and read thoroughly, completing the Workout as you proceed.

Psychophysics involves the relationship between physical characteristics of a stimulus and the psychological experiences that it produces. The physical characteristics of the stimulus can be measured directly, but experience must be measured indirectly. One major psychophysical question is: What is the weakest stimulus that can be detected in a particular sensory system, for example, vision?

1. What does the term *absolute threshold* refer to? Why is the absolute threshold not really "absolute"?

2. In general, how is a person's absolute threshold for a particular kind of stimulus determined? (See Figure 7.19 on text page 265.)

According to signal-detection researchers, stimulus detection depends on more than sensory sensitivity.

3. What is the other major factor? Why is this especially important in real-life tasks?

Psychophysicists use a procedure in which there are four categories of response—hits, misses, false alarms, and correct rejections—to obtain separate measures of sensory sensitivity and response bias.

4. Complete the following matrix of possible signal-detection outcomes by entering hit, miss, and so on, in the appropriate box. (See Figure 7.20 on text page 266.)

	Actual stimulus condition	
	Present	Absent
Subject says present		
Subject says absent		

5. Why would both hits and false alarms increase with a liberal response strategy? decrease with a conservative response strategy?

6. To derive d', a true measure of sensitivity, researchers compare the proportion of _____ to _____ .

A second question asked by psychophysicists is: How different must two stimuli be in order to be noticeably different?

7. What is a difference threshold, or jnd? Is the difference threshold a statistical concept like the absolute threshold? Explain.

8. Express Weber's law as a formula, defining each element. Now state the same law verbally.

Another major interest in psychophysics has been the way sensation increases with increasing stimulus intensity. Gustav Fechner in the nineteenth century and S. S. Stevens in the twentieth century both produced elegant mathematical descriptions of this relationship.

9. On what theoretical unit did Fechner base his law? What important assumption did he make about this unit?

10. State Fechner's law mathematically. According to Fechner, to what is the magnitude of the sensory experience proportional?

11. Why is it useful that the law involves a logarithmic transformation?

Stevens went on to do what Fechner believed could not be done: He tested the validity of Fechner's work experimentally.

12. Describe the subject's task in Stevens's method of magnitude estimation.

13. If Fechner's law were correct, what relationship should Stevens have found in his subjects' magnitude estimations? What did he find instead?

14. What kind of mathematical relationship best describes Stevens's results?

15. Is the exponent (p) greater or less than 1 for most of the various types of stimuli Stevens investigated? When p is less than 1, does a given increase in stimulus intensity produce equal sensory effects at the high and low ends of the scale? Explain. What about cases in which p is greater than 1?

16. Why did Stevens think nature would produce senses that follow power laws?

> *Be sure to READ the Concluding Thoughts at the end of the chapter. Note important points in your Workout. Then consolidate your learning by answering the focus questions in the margins of the text.*

> *After you have studied the chapter thoroughly, CHECK your understanding with the Self-Test that follows.*

Self-Test 1

Multiple-Choice Questions

1. The basic sequence of events in sensation is (1) physical stimulus → (2) physiological response → (3) sensory experience. Psychophysics is concerned with:
   a. only 2.
   b. the relationship between 1 and 3.
   c. the relationship between 2 and 3.
   d. the relationships among 1, 2, and 3.

2. There is a limited number of basic taste sensations and types of receptors. They are:
   a. sweet, salty, and sour.
   b. sweet, salty, sour, and umami.
   c. sweet, salty, sour, bitter, and umami.
   d. sweet, salty, sour, bitter, and creamy.

3. The main function of the ear's ossicles is to:
   a. transmit the pattern of sound waves from the outer to the inner ear without modification.
   b. decrease the pressure of sound waves before they reach the delicate inner ear.
   c. increase the pressure that incoming sound waves place on the inner ear.
   d. lower the frequency of incoming sound waves to reduce wear and tear on the auditory nerve.

4. Békésy found that high-frequency sounds cause:
   a. the basilar membrane to vibrate equally over its whole length.
   b. the basilar membrane to vibrate maximally near its proximal end, that is, near the oval window.
   c. the basilar membrane to vibrate maximally near its distal end.
   d. the two ends of the basilar membrane to vibrate more than the middle.

5. Conduction   deafness   occurs   when   the _____ become(s) rigid.
   a. basilar membrane   c. hair cells
   b. tectorial membrane   d. ossicles

6. Which of the following statements is true of stress-induced analgesia?
   a. It is at least partially the result of endorphins in the brain.
   b. It is purely psychological and unrelated to physiological mechanisms of pain.
   c. It has not been found to occur under controlled laboratory conditions.
   d. It occurs in humans but not in other animals.

7. Sally smells a great cup of coffee being delivered to her table. The transduction necessary for that sensory experience to take place occurs in her:
   a. vomeronasal organ.
   b. olfactory bulb.
   c. glomeruli.
   d. olfactory epithelium.

8. Glomeruli are located:
   a. in the olfactory epithelium.
   b. in the olfactory bulb.
   c. on the tongue and soft palate.
   d. in the vomeronasal organ.

9. In signal-detection tasks, _____ and _____ are compared in order to derive a true measure of sensitivity called _____ .
   a. hits; false alarms; d'
   b. hits; misses; d'
   c. hits; false alarms; the absolute threshold
   d. hits; misses; the absolute threshold

10. List the following categories of animals in terms of increasing sensitivity to bitterness:
    a. herbivores, omnivores, carnivores.
    b. omnivores, herbivores, carnivores.
    c. carnivores, omnivores, herbivores.
    d. omnivores, carnivores, herbivores.

11. The amplitude of a sound is:
    a. a dimension of psychological sensation.
    b. related to what the hearer experiences as loudness.
    c. the rate at which the sound waves are traveling.
    d. measured in units called hertz.

12. Which of the following is true of pain receptors?
    a. They are the same ones used for touch and temperature.
    b. They are found only in the skin and joints.
    c. They are specialized endings of the pain sensory neurons.
    d. They are short, thick neurons with special encapsulated endings.

13. Research on mice has shown that they prefer to mate with opposite-sex mice that:
    a. smell most like them.
    b. smell most different from them.
    c. have the least amount of body odor.
    d. have the greatest amount of body odor.

14. The strong association we experience between smells and emotional/motivational states is supported anatomically by connections between the:
    a. vomeronasal organ and the somatosensory cortex.
    b. vomeronasal organ and the amygdala.
    c. glomeruli and the limbic system and hypothalamus.
    d. glomeruli and the frontal lobes.

15. In a room with 20 lit candles, we must add 2 to get a jnd. How many would Weber's law say we have to add to a set of 100 candles to get a jnd?
    a. 2   c. 10
    b. 5   d. 20

Essay Questions

16. What are three different aspects of our conscious pain experience? With which brain areas are they associated?

17. What is an absolute threshold? Why isn't it really "absolute"? How do we define the absolute threshold for a given type of stimulus?

> *After you have assessed your understanding on the basis of Self-Test 1 and have tried to strengthen your preparation in any areas of weakness, GO ON to Self-Test 2.*

Self-Test 2

Multiple-Choice Questions

1. The PAG (periaqueductal gray):
   a. acts as a gate controller for pain.
   b. causes pain to be felt more intensely when it is activated.
   c. reduces pain when it is inhibited.
   d. gives pain its motivational and emotional facets.

2. The process by which a receptor cell produces electrical changes in response to a physical stimulus is called:
   a. sensory adaptation.
   b. coding.
   c. perception.
   d. transduction.

3. The absolute threshold for a given type of sensation depends on all of the following *except*:
   a. particular characteristics of the test stimulus (such as the frequency of a sound when hearing is being tested).
   b. the conditions under which the test is made.
   c. the person being tested.
   d. the jnd for that particular type of sensation.

4. A higher tone cannot mask a lower tone very effectively because:
   a. the basilar membrane vibrates more intensely for lower tones than for higher ones.
   b. the area of the basilar membrane that responds to high tones is completely separate from the area that responds to low tones.
   c. the part of the basilar membrane that responds most to low tones is unaffected by higher tones and is thus "out of their reach."
   d. our ears are insensitive to higher frequencies.

5. Why is it sensible in evolutionary terms that carnivores are the most sensitive to bitter tastes?
   a. Because meat is more likely than plants to contain poisonous substances.
   b. Because poisonous plants can generally be identified and rejected based on vision and smell, so bitter taste sensitivity is redundant in herbivores.
   c. Because the poisons found in meats are less common than those found in plants but are far more lethal.
   d. Because herbivores cannot afford to reject all bitter plant foods, since their diet is restricted to plants and not all bitter plants are poisonous.

6. The major histocompatibility complex is used by mice to help them "sniff out" potential mates that are:
   a. most genetically different from themselves.
   b. most genetically similar to themselves.
   c. maximally receptive to sex at a given time.
   d. already carrying the offspring of another mouse.

7. Which category of taste receptors is key to avoiding the ingestion of harmful substances:
   a. sour
   b. bitter
   c. umami
   d. salty

8. How are different types of taste receptors distributed over the tongue?
   a. Different types of receptors are concentrated in different areas of the tongue.
   b. Each taste bud contains an equal proportion of each type of taste receptor.
   c. Different types of receptors are evenly distributed over the tongue.
   d. Sweet receptors are distributed uniformly over the tongue, but the other types of receptors are concentrated in specific areas of the tongue.

9. In the sensory system for pain, A-delta fibers are:
   a. fast-conducting.
   b. activated by chemical changes in damaged tissue.
   c. associated with diffuse, lasting pain.
   d. the receptive endings for C fibers.

10. Pauletta feels refreshed and happy whenever she smells new-mown grass. Her emotional response to the smell stimulus involves activity in these parts of her olfactory system (in order):
    a. glomeruli, olfactory bulb, limbic system
    b. olfactory epithelium, limbic system, prefrontal cortex
    c. olfactory bulb, olfactory epithelium, prefrontal cortex
    d. olfactory epithelium, glomeruli, limbic system

11. In research done on human mothers and their newborn babies, it was found that:
    a. the mothers generally could not identify their own babies based on smell alone.
    b. the infants showed no sign of recognizing their mothers based on smell alone.
    c. smell is critical to mother-infant bonding.
    d. mothers and infants quickly learned to identify one another by smell.

12. Our ability to localize sound depends:
    a. exclusively on timing differences between what the left and right ears hear.
    b. exclusively on amplitude differences between what the left and right ears hear.
    c. on both timing and amplitude differences between what the left and right ears hear.
    d. on neither the timing nor amplitude of the sound as once thought, but rather on timbre.

13. Measurement of sensory experience is:
    a. not possible.
    b. irrelevant because sensory experience is a purely psychological creation with no objective reality.
    c. not only precise but also objective.
    d. accomplished indirectly by observing what the subject says and does.

14. The function of the eardrum is to:
    a. vibrate in response to incoming sound waves.
    b. transduce sound.
    c. increase the frequency of incoming sound waves.
    d. relieve pressure created by waves in the cochlea.

15. Signal-detection theory suggests that, when you are in the shower, whether or not you think you hear the phone ringing depends on:
    a. your sensitivity.
    b. whether you are expecting a call.
    c. whether you are motivated not to miss the call.
    d. all of the above.

Essay Questions

16. Describe the theoretical concepts necessary to explain the full range of our ability to discriminate pitch.

17. What are endorphins? How do they have their effect? What evidence suggests that they are involved in stress-induced analgesia?

Answers

Overview of Sensory Processes

1. physical stimulus; physiological response; sensory experience

3. a. sensory physiological psychology
   b. psychophysics
   c. sensory physiology

The Chemical Senses

2. olfactory epithelium; 10 million; cilia; receptor; olfactory bulb; glomeruli

13. sweet, salty, sour, bitter

Pain

1. free nerve endings; all parts of the body

4. phantom-limb pain

Hearing

1. vibrations; waves

2. amplitude; decibels; loudness

3. frequency; hertz; pitch; 20,000 hertz

4. pure

5. pinna; auditory canal; eardrum; tympanic membrane; funnel

6. ossicles; hammer; anvil; stirrup; oval; pressure

17. location in space; timbre; time of onset and offset; inflection

19. timing; simultaneously; left; microseconds

Psychophysics

6. hits; false alarms

Self-Test 1

1. **b.** (p. 234)

2. **c.** (pp. 243–244)

3. **c.** (p. 256)

4. **b.** Békésy found that the effects of sounds of various frequencies differ in the total area of the basilar membrane stimulated and in the place of maximal vibration. For example, low sounds produce vibration in a larger portion of the membrane and also produce peak vibration nearer the distal tip. (pp. 257–258)

5. **d.** (p. 257)

6. **a.** (p. 252)

7. **d.** Since the receptors for smell are located in the olfactory epithelium, transduction necessarily occurs there. (p. 238)

8. **b.** (p. 239)

9. **a.** (p. 265)

10. **a.** This answer is counterintuitive. Be sure you can make sense of it. (p. 246)

11. **b.** Amplitude is the physical dimension of sound related to the psychological dimension of loud-ness. Frequency is the physical dimension of sound related to the psychological dimension of pitch. (p. 254)

12. **c.** (p. 248)

13. **b.** (p. 243)

14. **c.** (p. 240)

15. **c.** Weber believed that the amount that must be added to the original stimulus to produce a jnd was a constant proportion of the original stimulus. So, if we had to add 2 to 20, the proportion would be 1/10. This proportion would also apply to 100 candles. Thus, we would need to add 1/10 of 100, or 10. (pp. 266–267)

16. Our conscious experience of pain involves several different aspects. The immediate motivation we feel to escape the pain depends on the limbic system and on the insular cortex. Our ability to perceive the sensation of pain in the first place is due to the somatosensory cortex. A third aspect of pain is cognitive in nature. We worry about the future or about the meaning of the pain. The prefrontal lobes are essential to this aspect of pain experience. (p. 249)

17. An absolute threshold is not truly absolute—clear and permanently fixed—for several reasons. For one thing, different people have different absolute thresholds. For example, an older person might have a higher absolute threshold for hearing than does a younger person, who might in turn have a higher absolute threshold than do some of her peers. Also, other aspects of the stimulus besides intensity may play a part in determining the threshold. In hearing, it depends on the frequency of the sound, for example. The conditions under which the test is made, such as the amount and type of background noise, can also make a difference. And finally, since we depend on behavior to infer the absolute threshold and since behavior is variable, we define the absolute threshold statistically. Since we cannot say that one level of intensity produces no detections and another level just above it produces 100 percent detections, we arbitrarily define the absolute threshold as the level of stimulus intensity that produces 50 percent correct detection. (p. 264)

Self-Test 2

1. **a.** The PAG, when it is activated, blocks the progress of pain messages at the point where they would enter the central nervous system. (p. 251)

2. **d.** (p. 236)

3. **d.** (p. 264)

4. **c.** One tone masks another when the wave it sets up in the basilar membrane interferes with the wave set up by the masked tone. Higher tones affect only the near portion of the basilar membrane. Therefore, they cannot disrupt the distal area of the membrane that responds to low tones. (p. 259)

5. **d.** (p. 246)

6. **a.** (p. 243)

7. **b.** (p. 245)

8. **c.** For years, many textbook authors have incorrectly stated that answer a. is the case, though researchers have known otherwise for a long while. (p. 245)

9. **a.** Alternatives **b** and **c** describe C fibers, not A-delta fibers. (p. 248)

10. **d.** (pp. 238–240)

11. **d.** (pp. 242–243)

12. **c.** (pp. 261–262)

13. **d**. (p. 234)

14. **a.** The eardrum performs an important function, but the nature of its response to sound is merely mechanical, not neural. It is the middle ear that serves to increase the pressure exerted by sound waves on the inner ear and the inner ear where transduction occurs. (p. 255)

15. **d.** (p. 265)

16. Two kinds of theories of pitch discrimination are necessary. Békésy's traveling-wave theory suggests that sounds produce traveling waves in the basilar membrane, with different frequencies having maximal effects in different areas. The waves produced by high frequencies create maximal vibration in the near, or proximal, portion of the basilar membrane, and lower frequencies peak toward the distal end. The brain can then interpret sounds as higher or lower depending on the location of the most rapid firing. For sounds below 4000 Hz, the *timing* of the activity in the basilar membrane also determines the pitch we hear. Basically, frequency of firing in the auditory neurons will match the frequency of the incoming stimulus. (pp. 257–260)

17. Endorphins are chemicals produced by the body that play an important role in pain reduction. They behave much like drugs such as morphine. We believe endorphins reduce pain by stimulating the PAG, a site also responsive to morphine. Activation of the PAG inhibits pain signals at the point where they enter the central nervous system. Endorphins are also thought to act in the spinal cord and lower brainstem where pain neurons enter. Experimental evidence that endorphins mediate the phenomenon of stress-induced analgesia comes from a study of rats that were shocked (the stressor) and were then shown to be insensitive to pain for a short time after (the analgesia). Rats that had been given a drug that blocked either the action or release of endorphins did not show any such analgesic effect of stress. (pp. 251–252)

Chapter 8   Vision

READ the introduction below before you read the chapter in the text.

The discussion of vision begins with a description of the basic workings of the eye. The retina, the part of the eye that includes the receptor cells capable of responding to light, contains two types of visual receptors—rods and cones—each underlying a kind of visual subsystem with particular strengths and weaknesses. The rods enable us to see in very dim light, but we must rely on the cones to see color and fine detail. Color vision involves neural mechanisms in the eye and higher up in the nervous system that code information provided by the light stimulus. This section continues by discussing how the visual system enhances contrast for sharper vision and how the brain processes information about visual features. It concludes by presenting evidence for two visual pathways in the brain—a "what" pathway for identifying objects and a "where" pathway for locating objects.

Pattern perception and object recognition involve both top-down and bottom-up processing. In top-down processing, our knowledge helps us to interpret incoming information. In bottom-up processing, we register and integrate sensory data. At the most elementary level, these data are primitive parts called features. The perception of patterns and objects consists of a continuous interaction of top-down and bottom-up processing. The chapter introduces work by several theorists who focus on different levels of form. Anne Treisman, for example, concentrates on the early process of detecting and combining simple features. Irving Biederman proposes that there are components of form somewhere between simple features and complex wholes that are important for our perceptual processes. And Gestalt theorists emphasize whole forms.

The chapter then turns to the spatial perception of objects. We use various cues to help us make determinations about depth and size. For example, binocular disparity—the slight difference in the views our two eyes receive—is a major cue to depth. In general,

the closer an object is, the more different the two views will be. In some cases, the study of spatial aspects of perception has progressed through the study of visual illusions. For example, psychologists have gained a better understanding of how we perceive size by studying errors in judgment. A case in point is the moon illusion, in which the moon looks much larger near the horizon than high in the sky, even though the size of the retinal image cast by the moon remains the same. Theorists try to explain this and other systematic errors in spatial perception not just to uncover the reasons for the illusions but to reveal something about the normal mechanisms of perception.

An underlying theme worth following carefully is the perceptual system's use of information about relationships among various aspects of a scene. The chapter presents two views of the way we make use of relational information. The unconscious-inference theory hypothesizes that unconscious mental "calculation" is necessary. The direct-perception theory maintains that we are biologically designed to pick up such relational information effortlessly.

LOOK over the table of contents for this chapter in your textbook before you continue with your study.

Notice that there are focus questions in the margins of the text for your use in studying the material. The following chart lists which Study Guide questions relate to which focus questions.

Focus Questions	Study Guide Questions
Physiological Foundations for Seeing	
1–3	1–3
4–6	4–10
7–13	11–20
14–18	21–29
19–22	30–39
Seeing Patterns and Recognizing Objects	
23–28	1–17
29–33	18–25

The Integrated Study Workout

Complete one section at a time.

Physiological Foundations for Seeing
(pages 275–297)

CONSIDER these questions before you go on. They are designed to help you start thinking about this subject, not to test your knowledge.

Which part of the eye is able to respond to light? What do the other parts do?

When you enter a dark, crowded movie theater, you may be unable to see the bucket of popcorn in your hand; yet, moments later, you see well enough to find an unoccupied seat. Why is that?

How does the brain process the signals it receives from the eye in order to give us such incredibly detailed and subtle views of the world?

How do we see color? Why are some people color-blind? What does a color-blind person "see"?

READ this section of your text lightly. Then go back and read thoroughly, completing the Workout as you proceed.

Most species—even single-celled organisms—have some light sensitivity because such sensitivity is highly adaptive. But the rudimentary photoreceptors of, say, an earthworm are a far cry from the refined visual system of a human being.

1. How might eyes like ours have evolved?

Some parts of the eye are designed for responding to light with neural signals. Others are designed for focusing the light on the cells that are light sensitive.

2. Match the parts of the eye with their descriptions. (See Figure 8.1 on text page 276.)

_____ A doughnut-shaped ring of muscle fibers that opens or closes to control the amount of light entering the eye

_____ Transparent tissue at the front of the eye whose curved surface begins to focus incoming light

_____ A thin membrane at the back of the eye's interior that contains vision receptors

_____ A hole that admits light into the eye

_____ A structure that carries visual information from the eye to the brain and causes a blind spot where it leaves the eye

_____ A tiny retinal area specialized for high visual acuity

_____ A flexible structure that can become rounder or flatter to focus on objects at different distances

_____ Type of receptor cell that permits sharply focused color vision in bright light

_____ Type of receptor cell that permits vision in dim light

a. pupil
b. retina
c. cones
d. lens
e. fovea
f. rods
g. iris
h. cornea
i. optic nerve

3. Briefly describe the process of transduction in vision.

Rods and cones underlie two separate but coordinated systems that together allow us to see over an enormous range of light intensities.

4. Describe the difference between these two systems by filling in the table that follows.

	Rods (scotopic vision)	Cones (photopic vision)
Sensitivity to light		
Acuity		
Color vision capability		
Distribution over retina		

In light adaptation, the eyes become less sensitive; in dark adaptation, they become more sensitive. This is due primarily to changes in the photochemicals inside rods and cones and shifting between rod and cone vision.

5. When do we undergo light adaptation? dark adaptation?

6. What happens to the photochemicals in rods and cones in bright light?

7. State one reason that cones are more sensitive than rods in bright light.

8. What happens to the photochemicals in rods and cones in darkness?

9. In what sense is dark adaptation a two-part process? (See Figure 8.5 on text page 279.)

Rods and cones send information on to bipolar cells, which in turn send information on to ganglion cells. The axons of ganglion cells form the optic nerve. Horizontal and amacrine cells make other neural connections within the retina. (See Figure 8.6 on text page 280.)

10. Using the concepts of receptive fields and neural convergence, explain how the increased sensitivity and reduced acuity of rods are really two sides of the same coin. (See Figure 8.7 on text page 281.)

The world we see is full of color. Our experience of color depends on the wavelengths of light reaching our eyes. An object absorbs some wavelengths from the light falling on it and reflects others, depending on its pigments. With vision as with hearing, it is necessary to understand the nature of the stimulus for which the sense is specialized.

11. Light can be thought of in terms of particles called _____ . It can also be thought of in terms of _____ , which provides the most useful perspective for understanding vision, especially color vision.

12. Light varies in _____ from about 400 to 700 nanometers (nm).

13. Visible light is a small range of wavelengths within the _____ spectrum, which also includes x-rays and radio waves.

14. Answer the following questions about subtractive color mixing. (See Figure 8.9 on text page 283.)

    a. Subtractive color mixing involves mixing _____ .

    b. Under what circumstances would the mixture appear green?

15. Answer the following questions about additive color mixing. (Spend some time studying the standard chromaticity diagram in Figure 8.11 on text page 284.)

    a. Additive color mixing involves mixing _____ .

    b. State the three-primaries law of color vision.

    c. State the law of complementarity.

d. Why do we say that these two laws represent psychological, not physical, facts?

Two theories—the trichromatic and opponent-process theories—have been advanced to explain the behavioral and physiological aspects of color vision.

16. Explain the trichromatic theory developed by Thomas Young and Hermann Helmholtz. How well does this theory fit with the discovery of three types of cones? (See Figure 8.12 on text page 285.)

17. What is a dichromat? Why is the most common type of dichromat more likely to be male than female? What colors will a red-green color-blind person find hard to distinguish?

The trichromatic theory of color vision doesn't explain everything as nicely as it does the three primaries law and certain types of color blindness.

18. What observation was Ewald Hering trying to explain with his opponent-process theory of color vision? What was Hering's explanation?

19. How does the opponent-process theory explain the complementarity of afterimages?

20. Are the trichromatic and opponent-process theories considered to be contradictory? Explain.

Our visual system is designed to provide us with the information we need to survive. That entails the ability to identify objects. Though the fact that objects may differ in color or brightness helps, we also need information about contour to identify objects around us. Contour is so important that the visual system enhances contrast to "sharpen" contours for us. Stephen Kuffler's work has helped us to understand how the receptive fields of ganglion cells help to accomplish this sharpening.

21. Define the term *contour*.

22. Diagram and explain the functioning of a ganglion cell's receptive field with an *on* center and an *off* surround. Be sure to explain how this arrangement produces heightened contrast. (See Figures 8.15–8.17 on text pages 289–290.)

Using cats and monkeys as subjects, Hubel and Wiesel studied the receptive fields of cells in the primary visual area of the cortex. They discovered that these receptive fields were arranged differently from those of retinal ganglion cells. (See Figure 8.19 on text page 291.)

23. Briefly describe the retinal receptive fields for edge and bar detectors.

24. Explain how edge and bar detectors are sensitive to orientation.

25. What did Hubel and Wiesel find about orientation sensitivity as they moved from one column of cortical cells to another?

The same cortical neurons studied by Hubel and Wiesel are also sensitive to spatial frequency.

26. Which of the patterns below has higher spatial frequency?

a.

b.

27. *Spatial frequency* is defined as the number of _____ per unit distance in the pattern's retinal image.

28. List two reasons that vision researchers are interested in spatial frequency.

The visual system is particularly attuned to change and contrast because these provide the greatest information. It deals efficiently with uniform surfaces.

29. What is the process of surface interpolation, and how might it be valuable?

The cortical neurons discussed so far are found in the primary visual cortex. A great deal of visual processing is carried out elsewhere in the cortex. Output from the primary visual area is carried to the rest of the occipital lobe and to the temporal and parietal lobes. In fact, 25-40 percent of the human cortex is devoted to processing visual information. These areas tend to involve much more specialized processing than that in the primary visual area.

30. List some of the types of information for which areas outside the primary visual cortex are specialized.

31. Present evidence for the existence of such specialized visual processing in these areas.

Ungerleider and Mishkin proposed an influential theory suggesting that visual processing areas outside the primary area are organized along two rather distinct pathways or streams—a "what" pathway and a "where" pathway. Evidence for the existence of these pathways comes from single-cell recordings in monkeys, from neural imaging studies of people, and from the particular deficits suffered by people with brain damage in these areas. The "what" pathway, which involves shape perception and object identification, runs from the lower occipital lobe into the temporal lobes.

32. What is visual agnosia? Where is the damage that produces this type of deficit?

33. Distinguish between the following forms of visual agnosia.

   a. visual form agnosia

   b. visual object agnosia

34. How does the existence of these two forms of visual agnosia shed light on the visual perception of an object?

35. What is prosopagnosia and what does its existence imply?

The "where" pathway runs from the upper occipital area into the parietal lobe.

36. Bilateral damage in the "where" pathway disrupts the ability to _____ objects and to _____ one's own actions appropriately.

37. According to Milner and Goodale, what is the primary purpose of the "where" stream?

38. In addition to providing conscious information about an object's location, the "where" pathway provides unconscious information about an object's _____ and _____ .

39. What is the evidence for the statement made in item 38 above?

Seeing Patterns and Recognizing Objects
(pages 297–307)

> CONSIDER *these questions before you go on. They are designed to help you start thinking about this subject, not to test your knowledge.*

How do we decide whether the object we're looking at is a tree, a trumpet, or a teapot?

Since the typical visual scene is full of many parts— lines, curves, textures—how do we know what goes with what?

Do we automatically see the "big picture" when we look at an object, or do we first have to see the smaller parts of the object and put them together somehow?

Can anything other than the "objective facts" of a stimulus affect the way we perceive it?

> READ *this section of your text lightly. Then go back and read thoroughly, completing the Workout as you proceed.*

Pattern perception and object recognition are often described in terms of an interplay of bottom-up and top-down processes. That interplay constitutes a kind of unconscious problem solving designed to answer the question: "What am I looking at?"

1. Define and give a synonym for each of the following terms.

    a. bottom-up processes

    b. top-down processes

2. Can computers accomplish object recognition with only bottom-up processes?

3. Give a simple account of the interplay between bottom-up and top-down processes that might occur as someone identifies an apple. (See Figure 8.23 on text page 298.)

Some theorists have focused on bottom-up processing, attempting to understand how parts are put together to form higher-level structures in perception. Anne Treisman, for example, has studied the lowest-level parts or features and theorized about how they are picked up and integrated.

4. Name the two stages in Treisman's feature-integration theory.

    stage 1: _____

    stage 2: _____

5. Distinguish between serial and parallel processing. When is feature processing serial and when is it parallel, according to Treisman? (See Figure 8.24 on text page 299.)

6. Describe some research evidence supporting Treisman's theory.

Treisman has pointed out a phenomenon that she calls *illusory conjunctions*.

7. What are illusory conjunctions, and why do they occur? Describe the case of a man who was especially prone to them.

Gestalt psychologists were among those who took a strong stand on the nature of perception in the early twentieth century, and their influence has lasted. They emphasized the holistic nature of perception.

8. What earlier position were the Gestalt psychologists challenging? What was the Gestalt viewpoint?

9. The Gestalt psychologists are responsible for a well-known saying: "The whole is different from the sum of its parts." Explain this statement. Try to produce an example that illustrates the point.

10. The German word *gestalt* means _____
_____ .

Gestaltists believed that we tend innately to use certain principles of grouping to organize what we see.

11. Identify the following principles of grouping by writing the correct term in the blank provided. (See Figure 8.26 on text page 301.)

_____ a. Elements closer to one another are grouped together as part of the same object.

_____ b. When lines cross, line segments are put together perceptually so that smooth, unbroken lines are formed.

_____ c. Stimuli are perceptually organized in ways that maximize symmetry, simplicity, and predictability.

_____ d. Gaps in a form's border are ignored.

_____ e. Like objects are grouped together, separate from unlike objects.

_____ f. Stimuli moving in the same direction at the same rate are seen as part of a single object.

The Gestalt psychologists also pointed out our tendency to automatically divide a scene into a more important part (the object to which we attend) and a less important part (the background). (See Figures 8.27 and 8.28 on text page 302.)

12. The object to which we attend is called the _____ , while the rest of the scene is the _____ .

13. This automatic process is guided by certain cues in the stimulus. For example, _____ is a cue that will cause a surrounded form to be seen as the _____ and the surrounding form as the _____ .

14. When cues are insufficient, object and background may exchange roles, sometimes at the will of the perceiver. This is what occurs in _____ figures.

The visual system's orientation toward whole, organized patterns and objects is so strong that we may perceive wholes where they do not physically exist.

15. In the visual stimulus above, you may see a white triangle even though there is no continuous edge outlining this "triangular" area. This phenomenon is called _____ .

16. How might we explain this illusion in terms of:

   a. bottom-up processes?

   b. top-down processes?

17. Look at Figure 8.30a and 8.30b on text page 303. Which type of explanation (bottom-up or top-down) best accounts for 8.30b creating a stronger illusion?

Irving Biederman's theory of object recognition proposes that there is a level of structure between the kind of primitive features that Treisman has studied and whole, real-world objects like faces, houses, or flowers. Using components at this intermediate level of form helps to simplify the job of perception, according to Biederman.

18. Explain the basic idea behind Biederman's recognition-by-components theory.

19. Define the term *geons*. What role do they play in perception? How many different geons are in Biederman's suggested list?

20. Briefly describe two pieces of evidence that support Biederman's theory.

Eleanor Gibson proposes that our ability to perceive and discriminate can be altered through experience and is related to feature perception.

21. Define the term *distinctive features*. What part does Gibson suggest they play in perceptual learning?

22. Think of two professions in which a high degree of perceptual learning must underlie the skill demonstrated. Briefly explain each choice. (See page 132 for sample answers.)

   a.

   b.

23. Does being able to use distinctive features effectively necessarily mean that one can describe them? Explain.

The identification of objects is also affected by context and even by the object's movement.

24. Briefly describe evidence that context affects perception. Be sure to explain the role of top-down processes in such context effects. (See Figure 8.33 on text page 306.)

25. Summarize Gunnar Johansson's research on the role of stimulus movement in perception.

Seeing in Three Dimensions and Seeing Constancies (pages 307–319)

> *CONSIDER these questions before you go on. They are designed to help you start thinking about this subject, not to test your knowledge.*

How can people tell how big a given object is?

Why does a person who has the use of only one eye, perhaps because of blindness or having to wear an eyepatch, find it harder to perceive depth?

Why is the experience of depth partly missing in paintings, photographs, and movies? On the other hand, what allows them to give as much of an impression of depth as they do?

Can the eye be fooled in judging such things as size?

> *READ this section of your text lightly. The go back and read thoroughly, completing the Workout as you proceed.*

As modern psychologists have attempted to understand how we manage to perceive the visual world, they have found Helmholtz's nineteenth-century notions about unconscious inferences consistently valuable.

1. Explain the concept of unconscious inference.

The retina directly represents only two dimensions—an up-down dimension and a side-to-side dimension. Where do we get the information that allows us to see depth? The answer lies in a variety of depth cues that fall into two categories—binocular cues and monocular cues. Binocular cues require both eyes, but monocular cues are available even when we're depending on one eye.

2. Define the following two binocular depth cues, making sure to note which is more important.

   a. eye convergence

   b. binocular disparity

3. What is stereopsis? How is this ability exploited to create illusions of depth in a stereoscope? in autostereograms?

Motion parallax is an important monocular depth cue that is present only when one is moving through real three-dimensional space.

4. Define motion parallax in general terms. Now describe a specific scene in which a person has a clear experience of motion parallax and a consequent sense of depth.

5. How is motion parallax similar to binocular disparity?

Unlike motion parallax, most monocular depth cues can help to convey a sense of depth in the two-dimensional realm of pictures. Monocular cues that function in this way are called pictorial cues for depth.

6. Name the monocular cue represented in each of the following descriptions. (See Figure 8.38 on text page 312.)

_____ a. A tree appears closer to the horizon than the house it shades and thus looks farther away.

_____ b. Railroad tracks appear to get closer and closer together with increasing distance.

_____ c. The bricks in a campus sidewalk look smaller, more densely packed together and less defined the farther away they are.

_____ d. A person sees a car and a billboard and, because the retinal image of the car is bigger, the car appears closer.

_____ e. A vase in the middle of a table is partially hidden by a hat, so we see the hat as being closer to us.

_____ f. A photographic portrait shows two people side-by-side. The eyes of one appear deep-set, sunken in shadow, whereas the other has eyes that appear to protrude with only a hint of shadow.

The perception of an object's size is closely related to the perception of distance.

7. What is size constancy? How can distance cues sometimes play a part in promoting or interfering with size constancy? (See Figures 8.40 and 8.41 on text page 313.)

Psychologists have often tried to understand size perception by seeking to explain size illusions. One proposed explanation for a number of size illusions is that we unconsciously process depth cues that then lead us to erroneous conclusions.

8. Briefly describe the following size illusions or draw a rough sketch of each, as you prefer. (See various illustrations on text pages 314 and 315.)

a. Müller-Lyer illusion

b. Ponzo illusion

c. moon illusion

9. How does the depth-processing theory explain the following illusions?

   a. Ponzo illusion

   b. Müller-Lyer illusion

   c. moon illusion

10. Why is the depth-processing theory problematic as an explanation of those illusions? How do proponents defend the depth-processing explanation?

In the perception of depth, size, and other aspects of the visual world, it seems that information about relationships is often critical. Two theoretical approaches to the issue of relational information have informed much of the thought on perceptual issues. The text compares them in terms of the way each explains visual constancies.

11. Define the term *visual constancies*.

12. State the major premise of Helmholtz's unconscious-inference theory. Explain how the theory can be applied to two of the following: size, shape, or lightness constancy.

13. State the major premise of Gibson's direct-perception theory. Why is it called an ecological theory? Show how the theory can be applied to two of the following: size, shape, or lightness constancy.

14. What theory was a precursor to Gibson's direct-perception theory? What criticisms did Hering and Helmholtz level against each other's theories?

15. How can the two theoretical perspectives be seen as complementary?

Be sure to READ the Concluding Thoughts at the end of the chapter. Note important points in your Workout. Then consolidate your learning by answering the focus questions in the margins of the text.

After you have studied the chapter thoroughly, CHECK your understanding with the Self-Test that follows.

Self-Test 1

Multiple-Choice Questions

1. Anne Treisman has developed a theory about the bottom-up aspect of form perception. She proposes that there are two different steps, first _____ and then _____ .
   a. feature detection, which involves parallel processing; feature integration, which involves serial processing
   b. feature detection, which involves serial processing; feature integration, which involves parallel processing
   c. feature integration, which involves parallel processing; feature detection, which involves serial processing
   d. feature integration, which involves serial processing; feature detection, which involves parallel processing

2. In the retina, _____ synapse on _____ , which in turn synapse on _____ .
   a. rods; cones; ganglion cells
   b. rods and cones; ganglion cells; bipolar cells
   c. rods and cones; bipolar cells; ganglion cells
   d. ganglion cells; rods and cones; the optic nerve

3. A biologist watches a group of twenty penguins moving toward the water for feeding. The group then splits into two groups, some moving to the left and some to the right. What Gestalt principle helps the biologist to perceive that there are two groups now instead of one?
   a. good continuation   c. good form
   b. similarity   d. common movement

4. In _____ , figure and ground may switch roles.
   a. the Ponzo illusion
   b. illusory contours
   c. a reversible figure
   d. illusory conjunctions

5. The distinctive features that we use in skilled perceiving:
   a. are necessarily available to consciousness.
   b. depend on the types of distinctions we need to make.
   c. are usually easily verbalized by experts in this perceptual skill.
   d. are primitive features that we need not learn to detect.

6. The retina is designed to produce a neural response to light, while the rest of the eye is designed primarily to:
   a. focus light on the retina.
   b. filter incoming light.
   c. transduce light.
   d. separate light into different wavelengths.

7. Which of the following is true of dark adaptation?
   a. It involves reduced sensitivity with increased time in the dark.
   b. It involves changes in cones as well as rods.
   c. It depends primarily on chemical changes in ganglion cells.
   d. It is due to the breakdown of photopigments in cones.

8. If we simultaneously view pictures of the same object taken from slightly different angles, looking at one picture with the left eye and the other with the right eye, we may see the object in depth. Our ability to perceive depth based on this type of cue is called:
   a. occlusion.
   b. convergence.
   c. stereopsis.
   d. pictorial cues.

9. When you're riding through the countryside, telephone poles move by at a pretty fast clip; trees some distance from the road move more slowly; and hills in the distance pass by more slowly still. This experience is a product of:
   a. binocular disparity.
   b. linear perspective.
   c. occlusion.
   d. motion parallax.

10. The Ponzo and Müller-Lyer illusions are illusions of _____ that have been fairly well explained by _____ theory.
    a. shape; depth-processing
    b. shape; recognition-by-components
    c. size; depth-processing
    d. size; recognition-by-components

11. Which of the following statements is true of people with red-green color blindness?
    a. They may be completely unaware that they have defective color vision.
    b. They are more likely to be female than male.
    c. They have a defective or missing blue cone.
    d. They can distinguish only colors in the red-to-green part of the spectrum.

12. Which theorist most vigorously promoted the idea that perception must be considered ecologically?
   a. Gibson
   b. Helmholtz
   c. Treisman
   d. all of the above

13. A ganglion cell's receptive field consists of:
   a. those rods and/or cones from which it receives input.
   b. the portion of the stimulus from which it receives input.
   c. the part of the ganglion cell that synapses on other cells.
   d. an area in the cerebral cortex to which it sends sensory information.

14. The notion that color vision is mediated by three different types of receptors is known as:
   a. the law of complementarity.
   b. the three-primaries law.
   c. additive color mixing.
   d. trichromatic theory.

15. Hubel and Wiesel showed visual stimuli to cats and monkeys while recording electrical activity in the cells of their visual cortex. They were interested in discovering how the visual system accomplishes:
   a. transduction.
   b. adaptation.
   c. coding.
   d. depth perception.

Essay Questions

16. Present Biederman's recognition-by-components theory of object recognition. Cite one type of evidence in support of the theory.

17. What is the meaning of the Gestalt psychologists' statement that "the whole is different from the sum of its parts"? What is the status of the *whole* in the Gestalt conception of object perception?

After you have assessed your understanding on the basis of Self-Test 1 and have tried to strengthen your preparation in any areas of weakness, GO ON to Self-Test 2.

Self-Test 2

Multiple-Choice Questions

1. Eye convergence is:
   a. a monocular depth cue in which lines move closer together, thus giving an appearance of depth.
   b. a binocular depth cue in which we unconsciously rotate the eyes inward as we focus on an object.
   c. poorer for closer objects than for more distant ones.
   d. the most powerful binocular depth cue available to us.

2. If the time to locate a target increases in direct proportion to the number of distractors, this indicates that the perceiver is:
   a. doing serial processing, that is, attending to one item at a time.
   b. doing parallel processing, that is, attending to all items at the same time.
   c. doing parallel processing, that is, attending to one item at a time.
   d. doing serial processing, that is, attending to all items at the same time.

3. The Gestalt psychologists believed—in contrast with the structuralists—that we automatically and immediately perceive:
    a. features.
    b. whole patterns and objects.
    c. components.
    d. sometimes a, sometimes b, sometimes c.

4. When you see a highway sign for a deer crossing, the deer symbol is immediately perceived as the object of interest while the rest of the sign appears to exist as merely a backdrop behind the symbol. This exemplifies:
    a. illusory conjunctions.
    b. illusory contours.
    c. the figure-ground relationship.
    d. relative size.

5. In Biederman's theory of object perception, geons are:
    a. primitive features.
    b. complex whole shapes such as flowers and faces.
    c. basic geometric forms that can be combined to create more complex forms.
    d. irregular, almost random shapes.

6. An entomologist can easily distinguish among many types of beetles that would look alike to most people. According to Eleanor Gibson, the entomologist has learned the _____ of these insects.
    a. distinctive features   c. shape constancy
    b. primitive features   d. geons

7. Hubel and Wiesel discovered cells in the cortex that are maximally responsive to:
    a. bars of light or dark at specific orientations.
    b. roughly circular spots of light at specific locations on the retina.
    c. simple shapes such as circles and triangles.
    d. contours that curve in a particular direction.

8. Which of the following statements is true of depth perception?
    a. It is possible only with two eyes.
    b. It is possible with one eye, but better with both eyes.
    c. It is equally good with both eyes or with just one.
    d. None of the above is true.

9. The wavelength of visible light ranges from about:
    a. 20 to 20,000 nm.   c. 100 to 1000 nm.
    b. 400 to 700 nm.   d. 700 to 1400 nm.

10. Which of the following statements regarding size perception is true?
    a. When we are dealing with familiar visual objects such as a car, a telephone, or a person, our previous knowledge of the object's size surprisingly plays no part in size perception.
    b. We can accurately judge the size of objects, familiar or unfamiliar, with or without cues to the object's distance.
    c. We judge size directly from the size of the retinal image, with a larger image meaning a larger object and a smaller image meaning a smaller object.
    d. We can perceive the size of even familiar objects incorrectly if distance cues mislead us.

11. The direct-perception theory emphasizes the _____ of stimulus information, whereas the unconscious-inference theory emphasizes its _____ .
    a. static nature; dynamic nature
    b. absolute qualities; relative qualities
    c. sufficiency; insufficiency
    d. lower-level structure; higher-level structure

12 The unconscious-inference theory is most closely associated with:
    a. James Gibson.
    b. Anne Treisman.
    c. Donald Broadbent.
    d. Hermann von Helmholtz.

13. The "where" pathway of the visual system leads from the occipital lobe to the _____ lobe.
    a. prefrontal
    b. frontal
    c. parietal
    d. temporal

14. The trichromatic and opponent-process theories of color vision:
    a. are contradictory and have both been proved wrong by recent physiological data.
    b. are contradictory and only trichromatic theory is supported by physiological data.
    c. are contradictory and only opponent-process theory is supported by physiological data.
    d. are complementary and both have been supported by physiological data.

15. The visual system is designed to:
  a. reduce contrast.
  b. preserve exact levels of physical contrast.
  c. exaggerate contrast.
  d. accomplish all of the above under different circumstances.

Essay Questions

16. Compare rods and cones in terms of acuity and then in terms of sensitivity. Explain how the concept of neural convergence can be used to help explain these differences.

17. Give a general definition of a visual constancy. Then discuss shape constancy specifically. How is shape constancy explained by unconscious-inference theory? by direct-perception theory?

Answers

Physiological Foundations for Seeing

  2. g; h; b; a; i; e; d; c; f
11. photons; waves
12. wavelength
13. electromagnetic
14. a. pigments
15. a. colored lights
26. pattern **a.**
27. repetitions
36. locate; guide
38. size; shape

Seeing Patterns and Recognizing Objects

  4. stage 1: feature detection; stage 2: feature integration
10. organized whole
11. a. proximity, **b.** good continuation, **c.** good form, **d.** closure, **e.** similarity, **f.** common movement
12. figure; ground
13. circumscription; figure; ground
14. reversible
15. illusory contours
22. Examples of professions that require a high degree of perceptual learning include musicians, who must learn to recognize and distinguish chords in notation, for example; dog breeders, who must learn to distinguish a champion from an also-ran; and radiologists, who must learn to distinguish a pattern in images that is cause for concern from one that is not.

Seeing in Three Dimensions and Seeing Constancies

  6. a. position relative to the horizon
  b. linear perspective
  c. texture gradient
  d. relative image size for familiar objects
  e. occlusion
  f. differential lighting of surfaces

Self-Test 1

  1. a. According to Treisman, serial processing (as compared with parallel processing) is indicated when the time it takes to find a target increases proportionally with the number of distractors. (pp. 298–299)

2. **c.** Photoreceptors (rods and cones), bipolar cells, and ganglion cells essentially make up three different layers of the retina. (p. 280)

3. **d.** (p. 301)

4. **c.** (p. 302)

5. **b.** The distinctive features of teeth for a dentist may be different from those for most other people. The distinctive features used become less and less available to consciousness with increased skill levels. (pp. 305–306)

6. **a.** (p. 276)

7. **b.** Dark adaptation involves increasing sensitivity with time in the dark. Improvement over the first 7 or 8 minutes or so results from a change in cones, whereas further and even greater improvements result from changes in the rods. (p. 279)

8. **c.** (p. 309)

9. **d.** Motion parallax and binocular disparity are somewhat related, but motion parallax arises because the two eyes of a stationary perceiver occupy different positions. Also note that motion parallax as described in the question would be experienced monocularly. (p. 311)

10. **c.** (pp. 314–315)

11. **a.** People who are red-green color-blind are generally male because of the nature of the genetic transmission of the defect. Red-green color-blind people are one type of dichromat. The defective or missing cone is either a red or a green one; its absence produces abnormalities in the way these people see colors in the red-to-green part of the color spectrum. But because visual experience is private, they cannot compare their color vision directly with that of normal individuals and thus may not realize there is a problem. (pp. 285–286)

12. **a.** (p. 317)

13. **a.** (p. 289)

14. **d.** (p. 285)

15. **c.** (pp. 290–291)

16. Biederman suggests that when we recognize a three-dimensional object, we do so by first accomplishing an intermediate goal—the recognition of simpler components. We then use the arrangement of those component shapes to recognize the whole object. Biederman argues that using a finite set of shapes such as these components simplifies the job of object recognition. The components, which he calls geons, function somewhat like an alphabet of form. Combining a few geons gives us a recognizable form just as combining a few letters gives us a recognizable word. He suggests there are only 36 different geons. One type of evidence for the theory is the existence of people with visual-object agnosia who can perceive simple forms (like geons) but can't combine them. (pp. 303–305)

17. When Gestalt psychologists said, "the whole is different from the sum of its parts," they meant something is added. The whole cannot be reduced to a catalog or a "line-up" of parts. It is an organization of those parts into a pattern or form. In fact, the Gestalt psychologists believed the whole that is created by the arrangement of parts is the first thing we see when we perceive an object. To them, it is the primary—the most important—thing. They believed we are biologically designed to be able to perceive incoming information in simple, holistic ways. (pp. 300–301)

Self-Test 2

1. **b.** The other binocular depth cue—binocular disparity—is much more important. (p. 308)

2. **a.** This makes sense because, for example, it takes twice as long to check 10 items serially (one item at a time) as it does to check 5. If parallel processing were being used, all 5 or all 10 items would be checked simultaneously and the number of items would not affect processing time. (p. 299)

3. **b.** (p. 300)

4. **c.** (p. 302)

5. **c.** They are combined to create more complex forms like faces or flowers. (p. 304)

6. **a.** (pp. 305–306)

7. **a.** (pp. 290–291)

8. **b.** It is possible with one eye, but without binocular disparity, we are lacking a powerful cue to depth. (pp. 308–311)

9. **b.** Remember that the visible spectrum is just a small part of the entire electromagnetic spectrum. (p. 282)

10. **d.** (p. 313)

11. **c.** (pp. 316–317)

12. **d.** (p. 316)

13. **c.** (p. 295)

14. **d.** (p. 288)

15. **c.** The visual system, through such mechanisms as ganglion receptive fields, sharpens contrast. (p. 289)

16. Rods are more sensitive than cones, but cones have higher acuity than rods do. Different levels of neural convergence help to produce both the sensitivity and the acuity difference. Neural convergence refers to the way that many receptor cells feed information to fewer sensory neurons. If many photoreceptors feed information to a single ganglion cell, there is high convergence. This is typical of rods. By contrast, if only a few receptors feed information to a single ganglion cell, there is low convergence. This is typical of cones. Another way to say this is that ganglion cells receiving input chiefly (or entirely) from rods have larger receptive fields than those connected mainly (or entirely) to cones. With high convergence, a single ganglion cell will benefit from the combined sensitivity of a number of receptors. However, it will also lose acuity for the following reason. If only a few receptors are feeding information to each ganglion cell, as with cones, the distinct spatial layout of the stimulus can be preserved. For example, if ganglion cell X responds, it had to get its stimulation from receptors A, B, or C. If there is high convergence, however, the ganglion cell's firing doesn't "tell" the brain as much about what spatial location on the retina was the source of that stimulation. It could have been any of twenty different receptors. So spatial detail is lost. (pp. 280–281)

17. We are dealing with a visual constancy when some aspect of the retinal image changes and yet our perception stays the same. In shape constancy, for example, the shape of the retinal image of an object changes as its orientation in three-dimensional space changes. Yet we perceive its shape as remaining the same. Unconscious-inference theory would say that we mentally calculate how far different parts of the object are from us in various orientations and take this into account, with the result that perceived shape stays the same. Direct-perception theory would say that we directly pick up higher-order information that easily and consistently tells us about the shape of the object regardless of its rotation in space. For example, in the case of a square rotated in space, we would be picking up not only the borders of the square but also textural information about the surface itself that would allow us to see that the object was square. Specifically there would still be an equal number of texture units along each side. (pp. 316–318)

Chapter 9   Memory and Consciousness

| READ *the introduction below before you read the chapter in the text.*

Memory holds a central place in cognitive psychology. All of our cognitive activities—such as reasoning, understanding, perceiving, planning—and indeed most of our physical activities—such as speaking, playing sports, or driving—depend on memory. The most influential and widely accepted theory of memory, the modal model, proposes that memory consists of sensory memory, working memory, and long-term memory, each with its own characteristics and functions. The model also describes control processes, which handle information within stores or transfer information from one store to another.

Sensory memory is the first component of the memory system in which incoming information is registered. It holds a good deal of information, but very briefly. Each sensory system has its own sensory store. Visual sensory memory, also called iconic memory, and auditory sensory memory, also called echoic memory, have received the most study.

A large array of stimuli are available to us at any given moment in the sensory stores but only some can be sent on to working memory via the control process called attention. How do we select what we will attend to? A number of theories have been proposed to explain attention. Though they differ in important ways, they generally contain these basic components: first, a large-capacity compartment that does an automatic preliminary analysis of sensory input; then a selection mechanism that determines which input goes on for further processing; and finally, a limited-capacity compartment in which input receives more thorough, effortful processing. Several studies show that consistent practice can make a task that once required effort (and thus attention) one that can be carried out automatically. The Stroop effect suggests that what becomes automatic may become obligatory, potentially interfering with performance on certain tasks.

Working, or short-term, memory is the component of memory in which conscious thought occurs. It is the main "workplace" of the mind. Information enters from either sensory or long-term memory. Working memory is itself thought to consist of several components. Baddeley proposed that these are the phonological loop, the visuospatial sketch pad, and the central executive. Neuroimaging studies have shown that perceptual tasks—such as checking for a detail on a picture—may involve the same brain areas as purely mental tasks that are analogous—such as checking for a detail on a mental picture.

Long-term memory is the more permanent large-scale repository of knowledge. Long-term memory for information is best achieved through elaboration, which involves thinking about the information. Memory can be made more efficient through various organizational strategies. For example, by packaging information so that each item is a larger unit called a chunk, we can fit more information into memory. Techniques involving visualization, such as the keyword method for learning foreign-language vocabulary, can also help.

What causes us to forget? Decay theory suggests that memory just fades with time and disuse. Interference theories maintain that other information in memory may get in the way of our remembering the information we want. Retrieval-cue theories suggest that the memories we want may be stored but cannot be accessed because we lack the appropriate cues. The effectiveness of retrieval cues depends on mental associations and the organization of long-term memory. As the chapter makes clear, remembering is not just the passive replaying of some sort of mental "tape." Rather, it is a constructive process in which retrieved information is pieced together and inferences are drawn. This constructive nature of memory is adaptive, but it also opens the door to potential distortion.

While the modal model described at the beginning of the chapter works well for explicit memory, it is not so useful for implicit memory. Explicit memory involves making the remembered information consciously available. Implicit memory, in contrast, influences perception, thought, or behavior without the stored information itself entering consciousness. Evidence for the existence of these two broad classes of memory—explicit and implicit—includes findings from neuropsychological research. Neuropsychological evidence also supports the difference between working memory and long-term memory as well as different types of explicit memory.

LOOK over the table of contents for this chapter in your textbook before you continue with your study.

Notice that there are focus questions in the margins of the text for your use in studying the material. The following chart lists which Study Guide questions relate to which focus questions.

Focus Questions	Study Guide Questions
Overview: An Information-Processing Model of the Mind	
1–5	1–10
Sensory Memory and Attention: The Portal to Consciousness	
6–7	1–8
8–11	9–20
12–13	21–25
Working Memory: The Active, Conscious Mind	
14–15	1–4
16–17	5–8
18–19	9–12
Encoding Information into Long-Term Memory	
20	1–3
21	4–6
22–24	7–9
25	10–12
Retrieving Information from Long-Term Memory	
26	1–3
27–28	4–7
29–32	8–14
33–37	15–22
Multiple Memory Systems: Beyond the Modal Model	
38–43	1–9
44–48	10–15

The Integrated Study Workout

Complete one section at a time.

Overview: An Information-Processing Model of the Mind (pages 325–329)

CONSIDER these questions before you go on. They are designed to help you start thinking about this subject, not to test your knowledge.

What is memory?

How is it that a person can remember some information for a lifetime and forget other information seconds after acquiring it?

Are there different forms of memory?

How is memory related to consciousness?

READ this section of your text lightly. Then go back and read thoroughly, completing the Workout as you proceed.

Before outlining the theoretical model of memory that organizes most of the chapter—and most research on memory—the text clarifies some terms.

1. How is memory related to learning?

2. How is the term consciousness defined in the text?

The dominant theory of memory since the 1960s—the modal model of the mind—proposes that memory is made up of several interacting components. The model has led to intensive study of those proposed components, of their interactions, and of the very idea that memory is actually divided in such a fashion. Keep in mind as you study that the model is just that—a model—not reality itself.

3. Broadly defined, what is memory?

4. What is a model in the context of cognitive psychology?

5. The term *modal* in "modal model of memory" simply means _____ .

6. The three components of memory (or memory stores) proposed by the modal model are

_____ , _____ ,

and _____ memory.

7. The modal model characterizes each component in terms of its _____ ,

_____ , and _____ .

8. In general terms, what do control processes do? What are some specific examples?

9. Describe the nature and function of each of the memory stores. Be certain to make clear the differences among them.

   a. sensory memory

   b. working memory

   c. long-term memory

Information can move from one store to another by means of specific control processes. (See Figure 9.1 on text page 326.)

10. Label each of the following with the control process being described:

   _____ a. is the control process that moves information from working memory into long-term memory.

   _____ b. is the control process that moves information from long-term memory into working memory.

   _____ c. is the control process that moves information from the sensory memory into working memory.

Sensory Memory and Attention: The Portal to Consciousness (pages 329–336)

> CONSIDER these questions before you go on. They are designed to help you start thinking about this subject, not to test your knowledge.

How can we even know that sensory memory exists?
How long does sensory memory last?
What purpose does sensory memory serve?

> READ this section of your text lightly. Then go back and read thoroughly, completing the Workout as you proceed.

Each sensory system (vision, hearing, smell, taste, and touch) appears to have its own form of sensory memory. Psychologists have investigated visual and auditory sensory memory much more than the other types of sensory memory.

1. *Visual* sensory memory is also called

   _____ , and the brief memory

   trace it holds is called the _____ .

2. According to _____ , the first psychologist to suggest the existence of sensory memory, the icon lasts for about

   _____ of a second.

3. How did Eriksen and Collins demonstrate the picturelike nature of iconic memory?

4. How might iconic memory play a role in normal visual perception?

5. Another name for *auditory* sensory memory is
_____ , and the brief memory trace
it holds is called the _____ .

6. How long is the echo estimated to last and how
has that been established experimentally?

7. Why might the echo last longer than the icon?

8. What does the phonemic restoration effect suggest about echoic memory?

Attention is the process by which the mind selects
from among the stimuli available in sensory memory
those that will enter working memory. We can only
consciously perceive and think about those that are
selected and passed on in this way. A number of different theories of attention have been proposed. (See
Figure 9.3 on text page 331.)

9. What do different theories of attention have in
common? Be sure to explain how they portray
attention.

10. What is preattentive processing, and why is it
such a key concept in theories of attention?

11. In general, how do the various theories of attention differ?

12. Distinguish between two categories of theories of
attention.

Psychologists have learned a good deal about attention from studies of selective listening and viewing.

13. Describe the cocktail-party phenomenon.

14. What is shadowing?

The typical experiment on selective listening is one in
which a subject hears two tape-recorded messages at
the same time and is asked to shadow one. In the case
of dichotic listening studies, the two messages are
presented through separate earphones.

15. According to early experiments, what affects the
ease of shadowing? And what do people notice
about the unattended message? Be specific.

16. How did Donald Broadbent account for this pattern of results in his filter theory of attention?

17. Is there any evidence from subsequent research that the unattended message is processed for meaning? Support your answer with evidence and be specific.

Studies of selective viewing have provided findings analogous to those of selective-listening studies.

18. How do the methods and findings of selective-viewing studies compare to the methods and findings of selective-listening studies? Give specific examples.

The existence of priming helps to emphasize a serious defect in the modal model—its failure to consider *unconscious* effects of sensory input.

19. What is priming?

20. Describe an experiment that provides evidence for priming of concepts in long-term memory without conscious awareness of the priming stimuli.

Some of the most practical findings in research on attention concern the effects of practice on our ability to process information.

21. What is the benefit of making a routine task automatic?

22. Describe evidence from Ulrich Neisser and colleagues showing that practice can allow us to perform two tasks simultaneously. How is that result interpreted?

Though automatic, unconscious processing has obvious advantages, the Stroop interference effect illustrates a major disadvantage. In the Stroop technique, subjects are shown a series of stimuli, including color names, each printed in a particular ink color. For example, the word "blue" might be printed in red ink. (See Figure 9.7 on text page 335.)

23. Describe the subject's task in a Stroop experiment.

24. When are subjects slowest at performing that task?

25. What disadvantage of automaticity is illustrated by the Stroop interference effect? In other words, what causes the effect?

Working Memory: The Active, Conscious Mind
(pages 336–340)

> CONSIDER these questions before you go on. They are
> designed to help you start thinking about this subject, not
> to test your knowledge.

If someone were to say a string of 11 digits to you,
could you remember the string exactly?

When you are mentally repeating a phone number
you've just looked up, what is happening in your
memory?

What is a mental image? When we "look at" a mental
picture of, say, our living room, is that anything like
actually looking at our living room?

> READ this section of your text lightly. Then go back and
> read thoroughly, completing the Workout as you proceed.

Just as memory in general is thought to involve separate but interacting components, so too is working
memory thought to consist of such components.
Alan Baddeley has proposed an influential theory of
working memory that consists of three components—
the phonological loop, the visuospatial sketch pad,
and the central executive.

1. The phonological loop is responsible for

   _____ by means of

   _____ .

2. Define *the span of short-term memory.*

3. Baddeley suggests that such measures as digit or
   word span are actually measuring the span of the
   phonological loop of working memory. Describe
   evidence that the span of short-term memory is
   related to subvocal repetition.

4. In everyday life, how might we utilize the phonological loop of working memory?

In working memory, we also deal with mental pictures.

5. The visuospatial sketch pad is responsible for
   holding and potentially manipulating

   _____ .

6. Give three examples of tasks in which you might
   depend on the visuospatial sketch pad. Make
   sure at least one example is original and not from
   the text.

7. What evidence supports the notion that the
   phonological loop and the visuospatial sketch
   pad are really separate and can operate independently of one another?

8. How did Stephen Kosslyn show that there is
   some similarity between examining a visual
   image and examining an actual picture? (See
   Figure 9.8 on text page 338.)

Neuroimaging studies and studies of people with
specific types of brain damage have helped us to
understand how mental performance of a task (such
as subvocal speech) is like actual overt performance
of the task (speech).

9. What do neuroimaging studies show about the brain areas involved in mental rehearsal of words and in mental rehearsal of a melody?

10. Describe two types of evidence that the "what" and "where" visual pathways are also involved in mental imagery tasks.

Though most of this section has focused on the other two components of working memory, the central executive is extremely improtant.

11. The central executive is thought to be responsible for _____ and _____ . (Refer back to text page 336 if necessary.)

12. Which area of the brain is critically involved in the activity of the central executive component? How do we know?

Encoding Information into Long-Term Memory
(pages 340–346)

> CONSIDER these questions before you go on. They are designed to help you start thinking about this subject, not to test your knowledge.

Why don't we remember everything we've ever noticed or thought about?

How can we improve our memory performance?

In what ways is an expert's memory different from a novice's?

> READ this section of your text lightly. Then go back and read thoroughly, completing the Workout as you proceed.

One of the most interesting areas of research on memory—and one especially relevant to students—concerns the kind of processing that can help to encode information into long-term memory.

Both Hermann Ebbinghaus, a pioneering memory researcher, and later researchers found evidence that the amount of repetition an item receives in working memory promotes encoding into long-term memory. But other research emphasizes that merely holding information in working memory does not guarantee its transfer to long-term memory.

1. Briefly describe Ebbinghaus's method and his evidence that repetition leads to better long-term memory.

2. Have you had experiences like Edmund Sanford's that suggest repetition is just not enough to produce long-term memory? Explain.

3. A failing of the _____ model is that it did not distinguish between two forms of rehearsal as we do today. The process by which information is held in short-term memory is _____ rehearsal. The process of encoding information into the long-term store involves _____ rehearsal. Some of the most effective activities to accomplish the latter are _____ , _____ , and _____ .

4. What is elaboration (or elaborative rehearsal)? What is its immediate goal? What is its "bonus" effect?

5. Briefly describe three examples of experimental evidence from school settings and the laboratory that show that elaboration is valuable.

a.

b.

c.

6. How does your textbook author recommend you approach studying?

Organizing information—which requires elaboration, of course—is a useful strategy for increasing the efficiency of memory. It helps to create connections among items that would otherwise be separate.

7. What is chunking? How and why is it related to memory efficiency?

8. How does chunking help to explain experts' outstanding memory for information in their particular field? Be sure to use the concept of long-term working memories.

9. What is hierarchical organization? Does this type of organization improve long-term memory performance? Explain.

Visualization has also been found to be an important aid to long-term memory.

10. How does Paivio explain the value of imagery in enhancing long-term memory performance? What are some findings his theory helps to explain?

11. Why else might mental imagery be a way to improve memory?

12. Describe the key-word method. If you have any foreign-language vocabulary, show how the key-word method could be applied to learning a specific word. (See Figure 9.12 on text page 346.)

Retrieving Information from Long-Term Memory (pages 346–355)

CONSIDER these questions before you go on. They are designed to help you start thinking about this subject, not to test your knowledge.

Why do we forget?

What kinds of cues can help us to probe our memories most effectively?

Can a memory be altered by information learned later? For example, could an attorney's misleading questions affect a witness's memory of an accident?

READ this section of your text lightly. Then go back and read thoroughly, completing the Workout as you proceed.

Somehow we are more likely to complain about the occasional failures of our memories than to applaud the frequent successes. Psychologists have tried to discover some of the reasons underlying those failures—the kind we tend to notice, such as the outright inability to retrieve desired information, as well as the less detectable cases of distortion in memory.

1. What do Ebbinghaus's forgetting curves teach us about the relationship between time and forgetting? what about the work of H. P. Bahrick and colleagues on memory for former high school classmates? (See Figure 9.13 on text page 347.)

2. Define the terms below.

   a. decay theory

   b. interference theories

   c. retrieval-cue theories

3. Why is decay theory untestable?

4. Define the following two types of interference. (See Table 9.1 on text page 348.)

   a. retroactive interference

   b. proactive interference

5. Indicate whether each real-life case below represents retroactive interference (RI) or proactive interference (PI).

   _____ a. A student who has studied French and now studies Spanish cannot recall the Spanish verb for "to know" because the French verb keeps coming to mind.

   _____ b. An engineer who has just moved to a new firm slips and calls the new boss by the old boss's name.

   _____ c. A senior dormitory resident cannot remember the name of a freshman-year roommate.

6. How might proactive interference explain the rapid forgetting Ebbinghaus discovered in his list-learning studies?

7. How does one theory use the idea of distinctiveness to explain when interference effects will be more or less severe?

Who was your first-grade teacher? What is one of your favorite books? How many times have you read it? Who is the main character? What does the word *stirrup* mean? What countries border France? Our long-term memories allow us to answer innumerable questions, skip from topic to topic, make sensible associations, and much more. Retrieval cues are apparently critical to our ability to gain access to long-term memories. And the organization of memory is critical to the effectiveness of retrieval cues. The manner in which information is organized determines what will and what will not be an effective way to find that information in the system. The sophisticated organization of memory largely explains our flexible retrieval abilities. Some of the basic principles of association were originally proposed by Aristotle.

8. State Aristotle's principle of association by contiguity. What ability can it help to explain?

9. What was Aristotle's principle of association by similarity? Why was it proposed?

10. Describe William James's views on the roles of contiguity and similarity in the organization of memory.

A common way of portraying the mind's vast, organized store of knowledge is a network in which concepts are linked by pointers (associations). (See Figure 9.15 on text page 350.)

11. What led Allan Collins and Elizabeth Loftus to develop their model? Briefly describe the model.

12. Why is the term *spreading activation* used to describe the model?

13. What is the encoding-specificity principle? Discuss a research finding consistent with this principle.

14. Define and give an example of context-dependent memory. How is it a special case of encoding-specificity?

Remembering is an active, rather than a passive, process. It is not like replaying a tape recording or even like reading words we have written down.

15. Explain what it means to say that memory entails construction. What are some of the consequences of memory's constructive nature?

16. Identify the following:

_____ a. One's general mental representation or concept of a class of object, scene, or event that one uses to recognize and understand examplars of that class

_____ b. A schema that involves the organization of events in time rather than objects in space

17. We might very well have _____ to represent such events as football games, final exams, and vacations. We might represent such concepts as continents, dogs, furniture, and vehicles in _____ .

18. Briefly describe how Frederick Bartlett used "The War of the Ghosts" to illustrate the power of culture-specific schemas on memory.

Suggestion and imagination may sometimes become factors in memory construction.

19. How did Elizabeth Loftus and J. C. Palmer show that the construction of memories can be affected by information acquired after the original experience?

20. According to Loftus and others, when is memory distortion most likely?

Some studies appear to show that strong suggestion can cause some people to "remember" childhood events—such as getting lost in a mall or spilling the punch at a wedding—that never happened.

21. How did Hyman and Pentland show that deliberately imagining such an event can make subjects more likely to report that it actually happened?

22. How are source confusion and social pressure thought to be involved in instances of remembering things that never occurred?

Multiple Memory Systems: Beyond the Modal Model (pp. 355–363)

CONSIDER these questions before you go on. They are designed to help you start thinking about this subject, not to test your knowledge.

Can knowledge in memory affect our perception or thought only if it becomes conscious?

Isn't there something fundamentally different about memory for the meaning of the word "dance" and memory for how to dance?

Why is it that we can sometimes fail to recall someone's phone number verbally and yet can quickly dial the number?

READ this section of your text lightly. Then go back and read thoroughly, completing the Workout as you proceed.

As mentioned earlier, though the modal model accounts well for many memory phenomena, it falls short when we consider memory that does not involve the conscious mind. (Examine Figure 9.18 on text page 356.)

1. Label the following types of memory.

   a. _____ is memory in which the remembered information enters consciousness; it is tested by directly asking the person to recall or report the information. It is also called _____ memory.

   b. _____ , on the other hand, involves previously acquired information that affects behavior or thought without itself entering consciousness. It is also called _____ memory.

2. How are the two types of memory assessed?

3. How do implicit and explicit memories differ in terms of their context-dependence?

There are two types of explicit memory differentiated by cognitive psychologists.

4. Describe each of the following:

   a. episodic memory

   b. semantic memory

5. Can an episodic memory become a semantic memory? Explain.

Implicit memory can also be subdivided.

6. List three types of implicit memory, and define them as necessary.

7. How do some experiments with artificial grammars illustrate the implicit nature of rule-based procedural memories?

8. Why is priming considered implicit?

9. How might priming be important in everyday life? Why was it important to the development of network models of semantic memory?

Evidence for the reality of distinctions between working- and long-term memory and between explicit and implicit memory is available from neuropsychological studies.

10. Who is H. M., and how does his case support a clear distinction between working and long-term explicit memory? What neural structures were implicated in encoding explicit long-term memories?

11. What other evidence indicates that the hippocampus and nearby structures are involved in encoding explicit long-term memories?

12. Are these same structures critical for creating or using implicit memories? Support your position with evidence.

There is also neuropsychological evidence suggesting that episodic and semantic memory involve different neural systems.

13. What does a disorder called developmental amnesia reveal about the role of the hippocampus in episodic as compared to semantic memory?

14. What evidence suggests that the prefrontal cortex is more critical to episodic than to semantic memory?

15. How might the role of the prefrontal cortex in episodic memory help to explain such diverse issues as childhood amnesia, age-related memory declines, and human self-awareness?

Be sure to READ the Concluding Thoughts at the end of the chapter. Note important points in your Workout. Then consolidate your learning by answering the focus questions in the margins of the text.

After you have studied the chapter thoroughly, CHECK your understanding with the Self-Test that follows.

Self-Test 1

Multiple-Choice Questions

1. According to the modal model of memory, memory is made up of a(n):
   a. attentive memory, short-term memory, and long-term memory.
   b. sensory memory, working memory, and short-term memory.
   c. sensory memory, working memory, and long-term memory.
   d. episodic memory, procedural memory, and semantic memory.

2. A brief, picturelike trace of a visual stimulus is held in _____ memory.
   a. episodic
   b. implicit
   c. context-dependent
   d. iconic

3. Information passes into working memory from:
   a. short-term memory.
   b. sensory memory.
   c. long-term memory
   d. both b and c.

4. The span of short-term memory is probably really measuring the capacity of:
   a. the central executive.
   b. the visuospatial sketch pad.
   c. procedural memory.
   d. the phonological loop.

5. Studies of selective listening and viewing have typically found that subjects can later report:
   a. absolutely nothing about the unattended material.
   b. some physical characteristics of the unattended material.
   c. only the meaning of the unattended material.
   d. none of the above, since selective listening and selective viewing have virtually opposite patterns of results.

6. Suppose you have been introduced to a friend of a friend, and you repeat that person's name in your mind over and over with no elaborative processing. This approach is most likely to serve as:
   a. maintenance rehearsal.
   b. encoding rehearsal.
   c. chunking.
   d. echoic memory.

7. Suppose that Stroop stimuli, such as the word *red* printed in green ink, are presented to a variety of subjects. Who among the following should be *most* susceptible to the Stroop effect in this case?
   a. a normal adult reader of English
   b. a young child who is just beginning to read English
   c. a Chinese person who speaks English but does not read it
   d. a normal adult reader of English who is looking at the stimuli with her head tilted 90 degrees to the side

8. A woman receives a secret PIN number for using her bank's cash machines. She remembers the number, 111621, as 11 (the month of her birth), 16 (sweet sixteen), and 21 (the age of majority). This woman is using _____ to enhance her memory performance.
   a. episodic memory
   b. dual coding
   c. chunking
   d. context dependence

9. A boy studying Spanish mentally pictures a cart full of letters in order to remember *carta*, the Spanish word for "letter." This student is employing:
   a. the key-word method.
   b. hierarchical organization
   c. echoic memory.
   d. a script.

10. The idea that unused memories are forgotten due to the passage of time is known as _____ theory and is _____ today.
   a. decay; not testable
   b. decay; supported by much research evidence
   c. interference; not testable
   d. interference; supported by much research evidence

11. According to the Collins and Loftus network model of memory organization, hearing the word *table* facilitates subsequent recognition of *chair* through the process of:
   a. visualization.
   b. elaborative rehearsal.
   c. spreading activation.
   d. procedural memory.

12. Suppose a subject is given a list of words for later recall. Next to each word is another word, which the subject is simply asked to read. One of the words to be recalled is *jam* and the word beside it is *strawberry*. Considering the principle of encoding specificity, what would make the best retrieval cue for *jam* at recall time?
    a. trouble
    b. traffic
    c. strawberry
    d. All of the above would be equally effective.

13. Frederick Bartlett asked subjects to listen to "The War of the Ghosts" and later retell the story from memory. He found that subjects:
    a. had excellent memory for the story, retelling it in the very same terms in which they heard it.
    b. distorted the story in accordance with their own culture-based schemas.
    c. used their schemas to accurately relate the meaning of the story in different words.
    d. could not retain any aspect of the story.

14. Neisser and other researchers have shown that with extensive practice on certain tasks, what was once _____ can become _____ .
    a. preattentive; controlled
    b. preattentive; controlled
    c. semantic; episodic
    d. implicit; explicit

15. Neuropsychological studies have provided evidence suggesting that:
    a. there really is no distinction between working and long-term memory.
    b. implicit and explicit memories are encoded by way of different neural paths.
    c. episodic and semantic memories are encoded through the same neural mechanisms.
    d. both a and b are true.

Essay Questions

16. Distinguish between explicit and implicit memory, giving examples of each. Present one piece of evidence to support the reality of this distinction.

17. Explain Broadbent's filter theory of attention, and broadly describe findings from attentional studies that fit well with this theory. Similarly, describe findings that convince us that the theory is nevertheless wrong as it stands.

After you have assessed your understanding on the basis of Self-Test 1 and have tried to strengthen your preparation in any areas of weakness, GO ON to Self-Test 2.

Self-Test 2

Multiple-Choice Questions

1. Which of the following statements regarding sensory memory is true?
    a. Apparently, only vision and hearing have sensory-memory systems.
    b. We are generally conscious of iconic memory.
    c. Information in the visual sensory store is still in visual form.
    d. Rehearsal can help to keep information in sensory memory longer.

2. The phonemic-restoration effect helps to demonstrate that echoic memory:
    a. does not exist separately from iconic memory.
    b. is not an entirely passive store.
    c. has its own neural structures in the temporal lobe.
    d. lasts only one-third of a second.

3. Which of the following is considered the seat of conscious thought?
    a. long-term memory
    b. short-term memory
    c. working memory
    d. both b and c, which are two names for the same memory component

4. According to Baddeley, what refreshes information in the phonological loop, helping us to hold the information there longer?
   a. coordination with the visuospatial sketch pad
   b. subvocal repetition
   c. attention
   d. retrieval

5. Encoding is the control process that:
   a. maintains information in working memory.
   b. maintains information in sensory memory.
   c. transfers information from sensory to working memory.
   d. transfers information from working to long-term memory.

6. Which of the following statements concerning rehearsal is true?
   a. Maintenance rehearsal is the best means of accomplishing encoding.
   b. Maintenance rehearsal and encoding rehearsal are one and the same.
   c. Elaborative rehearsal is accomplished unconsciously.
   d. Elaborative rehearsal promotes encoding better than repetition does.

7. Gail routinely greeted her professors by name when she met them on campus. But when she encountered one of them at the local movie theater, she couldn't think of the person's name. In fact, she wasn't quite sure if it was the same person. What could best explain this?
   a. context-dependent memory
   b. retroactive interference
   c. proactive interference
   d. temporal lobe amnesia

8. The notion that forgetting occurs because other memories get in the way of our ability to retrieve a given memory is the essence of:
   a. implicit-memory theory.
   b. dual-coding theory.
   c. interference theory.
   d. decay theory.

9. If you get a new phone number and have trouble remembering it because your old phone number keeps coming to mind instead, you are experiencing the problematic effects of:
   a. retroactive interference.
   b. proactive interference.
   c. iconic memory.
   d. echoic memory.

10. If you were to study by outlining a chapter using several levels of headings, from more general to more specific, you would be using _____ to aid your memory.
    a. the key-word method
    b. proactive grouping
    c. memory construction
    d. hierarchical organization

11. A type of schema that organizes events in time rather than objects in space is called a(n):
    a. script.   c. episodic memory.
    b. procedural memory.   d. pointer.

12. The role of the prefrontal cortex in episodic memory can help to explain:
    a. childhood amnesia.
    b. why aging causes declines in episodic memory sooner than semantic memory.
    c. the uniquely human capacity for self-reflection.
    d. all of the above.

13. Which of the following is a type of explicit memory?
    a. episodic memory
    b. nondeclarative memory
    c. sensory memory
    d. memories produced by classical conditioning

14. What kind of information in your memory allows you to be a skillful dancer?
    a. procedural   c. semantic
    b. declarative   d. episodic

15. Priming is based on a type of _____ memory.
    a. explicit   c. working
    b. procedural   d. implicit

Essay Questions

16. What is the span of short-term memory? How does chunking affect the amount of information that can be held in short-term memory? Can chunking make a substantial difference in the amount of information short-term memory can hold? Explain.

17. Explain Aristotle's concepts of association by contiguity and association by similarity. Give examples of each. Is the notion of mental associations still important in modern theories of memory organization? Explain.

Answers

Overview: An Information-Processing Model of the Mind

5. standard

6. sensory; short-term or working; long-term

7. function; capacity; duration

10. encoding; retrieval; attention

Sensory Memory and Attention: The Portal to Consciousness

1. iconic memory; icon

2. George Sperling; one-third

5. echoic memory; echo

Working Memory: The Active, Conscious Mind

1. holding verbal information; subvocal repetition

5. visual and spatial information

11. coordinating mental activities; bringing new information into working memory from the sensory and long-term stores

Encoding Information into Long-Term Memory

3. modal; maintenance; encoding; elaboration; organization; visualization

Retrieving Information from Long-Term Memory

5. **a.** PI, **b.** PI, **c.** RI

16. **a.** schema, **b.** script

17. scripts; schemas

Multiple Memory Systems: Beyond the Modal Model

1. **a.** Explicit memory; declarative

   b. Implicit memory; nondeclarative

Self-Test 1

1. **c.** (p. 326)

2. **d.** (p. 329)

3. **d.** Information coming in from the outside world passes through sensory memory before it can be transferred to working memory. Information in long-term memory must enter working memory in order to be consciously processed. For example, in order to think about an event that happened to you last week or to form a mental image of a friend's face, you must process information from the long-term store in working memory. Remember that working memory is also called short-term memory. (p. 327)

4. **d.** (p. 337)

5. **b.** (p. 333)

6. **a.** (p. 341)

7. **a.** (pp. 335–336)

8. **c.** (p. 343)

9. **a.** This particular technique is the key-word method described in the text, which employs visualization to enhance memory. (p. 345)

10. **a.** (p. 347)

11. **c.** (p. 350)

12. **c.** Though **a** and **b** are conceptually related to the word *jam*, the encoding-specificity principle states that the best retrieval cues are those that were present at encoding. (p. 350)

13. **b.** (pp. 352–353)

14. **a.** (p. 335)

15. **b.** Neuropsychological research has suggested that all of the distinctions mentioned in the alternatives (working and long-term memories, implicit and explicit memory, and episodic and semantic memories) have some physiological basis. (pp. 360–361)

16. Explicit memory is memory in which the remembered information enters consciousness. It is tested by asking a person to recall or report the information of interest. Explicit memory is well accounted for by the modal model. Implicit memory involves stored information that can influence behavior or cognitive processes without

entering consciousness. Episodic memory, such as your memory for the last movie you saw, is a type of explicit memory. Procedural memory, such as your knowledge of how to drive a car, would be considered an example of implicit memory. One kind of evidence for the distinction comes from amnesic patients who cannot create new long-term memories of the explicit type but can create new implicit ones. (pp. 355–362)

17. Broadbent proposed that there is an attentional filter that acts as a kind of tuner between the first, or preattentive, processing compartment and the second, or attentive, processing compartment. He suggested that all information at the preattentive stage is processed for physical features such as color or location or loudness. Stimuli with the "right" physical characteristics are selectively allowed into the next compartment for further processing; other stimuli cannot get through the filter. This theory fits with the research finding that people can successfully select a message based on its physical characteristics, such as pitch. But it can't explain the findings that show some aspects of meaning coming through from the unattended message. (pp. 331–332)

Self-Test 2

1. **c.** (p. 330)
2. **b.** (p. 331)
3. **d.** (p 327)
4. **b.** (p. 337)
5. **d.** (p. 328)
6. **d.** (pp. 341–342)
7. **a.** (p. 351)
8. **c.** (p. 347)
9. **b.** (pp. 347–348)
10. **d.** (p. 344)
11. **a.** (p. 352)
12. **d.** (p. 362)
13. **a.** (p. 356)
14. **a.** (p. 357)
15. **d.** (p. 358)

16. The term *span of short-term memory* refers to the number of pronounceable items that can be held in short-term memory at one time and repeated back after a brief delay. Even though the number of items that can be held stays roughly the same, the effective capacity of short-term memory can be improved by increasing the amount of information packed into each item. This is called chunking. For example, the letters c, i, a, f, b, i could be remembered not as six individual letters but as two acronyms—CIA and FBI. With this method, it is possible to dramatically improve memory performance. One man, after weeks of practice, managed to increase his digit span (the number of digits he could repeat after hearing them just once) to 80. His incredible performance was achieved by grouping digits together in meaningful chunks that he classified as running times, dates, etc. Chunking also seems to be a consequence of becoming an expert. Expert chess players can reproduce a briefly displayed layout of a chess game better than people less experienced at chess. This ability was attributed to the fact that they could chunk meaningful combinations of pieces on the board. When a random layout of chess pieces was shown, in which no such meaningful combinations would be likely, experts did no better than other players. (pp. 337, 343–344)

17. Aristotle suggested that memory is organized in terms of associations. An association exists between two pieces of stored information if the thought of one tends to evoke the thought of the other. Association by contiguity occurs when information is associated because of co-occurrence in a person's experience. For example, dentists might be associated with drills for this reason because the two have been experienced together (that is, contiguously) in the past. Association by similarity is involved in those cases of association based on some shared property. For example, bathtubs and oceans might be associated because both contain water. The idea of mental associations is still central to modern theories of memory organization, such as the Collins and Loftus spreading-activation model. (pp. 349–350)

Chapter 10   Intelligence and Reasoning

READ *the introduction below before you read the chapter in the text.*

Chapter 10 opens with a discussion of intelligence testing. The testing methods most familiar today were pioneered by Alfred Binet. Binet developed his test to identify schoolchildren who were not thriving in the French educational system. Performance on IQ tests, not surprisingly, is moderately predictive of school performance. Lewis Terman and David Wechsler are among those who have adapted Binet's approach and versions of their tests are in use today.

One major question about the structure of intelligence is whether it consists of a single mental ability or different abilities. A statistical method called factor analysis has been applied to the pattern of scores on different subtests of standardized intelligence tests to reveal the structure of intelligence. With this technique, Charles Spearman found evidence of both a general intelligence, which he called *g*, and a number of specific types of intelligence, which he referred to as *s*. Raymond Cattell proposed that *g* itself actually had two aspects, not just one. He called these two aspects fluid intelligence and crystallized intelligence. Researchers looking for the properties of the mind that underlie general intelligence have considered mental speed, working memory capacity and what Robert Sternberg calls mental self-government.

The chapter next explores the nature-nurture debate regarding intelligence, explaining the central concept of heritability. Heritability and environmentality are complementary concepts; both terms are used to refer to the degree to which genetics (or environmental factors) are responsible for the variation in IQ (or some other trait) seen in a given population. Unfortunately, there have been significant misunderstandings and misuses of the concept of heritability. In particular, it has been inappropriately used to try to explain average IQ differences between racial or cultural groups, such as that between American blacks and whites, as genetic in origin. Much evidence favors environmental explanations of such differences.

Varieties of intelligence are highlighted in the following section of the chapter. Neuropsychological studies of people with left- or right-hemisphere brain damage and retarded savants suggest the existence of separate mental abilities. The ecological approach emphasizes that intelligence is not only demonstrated in classrooms but in an infinite variety of situations. This approach has been valuable in pointing out that standard mental tests may fail to adequately measure the intelligence exhibited on the job, and may incorrectly represent the intelligence of people from other cultures, particularly non-Western cultures. Studies of experts reveal just how critical practice is to the development of extremely high levels of performance.

A major function of the human intellect involves solving problems that depend on logical reasoning. Inductive reasoning entails reasoning from specific facts or observations to general conclusions. Research on inductive reasoning has identified several kinds of biases in thinking. Deductive reasoning involves reasoning from premises that are assumed to be true to a conclusion that logically follows from them. Research suggests that people who reason successfully on deductive problems often use visual imagery to aid their thinking. Problem solving can include many types of problems—syllogisms used to test deductive reasoning, math story problems, a game of chess, crossword puzzles, even how to write a novel or be a happier person. Psychologists have described several ways in which people can be more effective problem solvers, such as avoiding rigid thinking patterns (called mental set), using analogies, and establishing subgoals.

A major issue in the study of language is linguistic relativity, the notion that thought may be shaped and even limited by the language of the thinker. Higher-order mental processes are more susceptible to linguistic influence than are sensory processes. For example, mathematical thinking has been found to be related to the way a given language represents numerical concepts in words. Language also appears to aid or impede some problem-solving tasks. It can even affect our tendency to think in sexist ways.

LOOK over the table of contents for this chapter in your textbook before you continue with your study.

Notice that there are focus questions in the margins of the text for your use in studying the material. The following chart lists which Study Guide questions relate to which focus questions.

Focus Questions	Study Guide Questions
Problems of Identfying and Measuring Intelligence	
1–3	1–12
4–8	13–29
The Nature-Nurture Debate Concerning IQ	
9–13	1–13
14–17	14–18
Varieties of Intelligence	
18–19	1–4
20–23	5–9
How People Reason and Solve Problems	
24–28	1–6
29–30	7–12
31–36	13–26
Roles of Language in Thought	
37–40	1–7

The Integrated Study Workout

Complete one section at a time.

Problems of Identfying and Measuring Intelligence   (pages 367–376)

CONSIDER these questions before you go on. They are designed to help you start thinking about this subject, not to test your knowledge.

How did intelligence tests originate?

What underlying mental qualities cause one person to score higher than another on intelligence tests?

Can performance on intelligence tests really predict anything about performance outside the testing room?

READ this section of your text lightly. Then go back and read thoroughly, completing the Workout as you proceed.

Historically, there have been different approaches to the study and measurement of intelligence, each with its own view of what intelligence is. When Mark

Snyderman and Stanley Rothman asked over 1000 experts what abilities they considered important aspects of intelligence, they found considerable agreement on some aspects (such as abstract reasoning and problem solving) and much less on others (such as sensory acuity and goal directedness). Today's intelligence tests can be traced back to the pioneering work of Alfred Binet and his assistant Theophile Simon in France.

1. What was Binet's conception of intelligence?

2. Why was the Binet-Simon Intelligence Scale originally developed?

3. What kinds of items did Binet and Simon include on their test? How were items selected? Were the kinds of items used consistent with the purpose of the test? Explain.

4. Explain the concept of mental level (also called mental age).

In North America, the first widely used intelligence test was Lewis Terman's modification of the Binet and Simon scale. It was called the Stanford-Binet Scale because the work was conducted at Stanford University. The test score was expressed as an IQ.

5. The formula for IQ is _____ . IQ stands for _____ .

Revisions of the Stanford-Binet Scale are widely used today, but revisions of David Wechsler's test are even more commonly used. Both are individually administered intelligence tests.

6. Why did Wechsler originally design his test?

7. The acronyms *WAIS-R* and *WISC-III* stand for

   _____ and

   _____ , respectively.

8. How is the meaning of IQ in Wechsler's test different from its original meaning? Why would the original meaning have been absurd in an adult test?

Psychologists in the field of intelligence testing must ask themselves whether their tests provide useful and trustworthy information—that is, whether they really tell us about a person's intelligence.

9. The extent to which a test measures what it is

   supposed to measure is its _____ .

10. How well do IQ scores correlate with school grades?

11. Why is it harder to determine how well IQ predicts achievement outside of school?

12. What evidence suggests that IQ can help to predict on-the-job performance? Does it predict equally well across all occupations? across all stages of employment?

Scientists have long debated the essential nature of intelligence, an issue that also affects the measurement of intelligence.

13. How did Galton view intelligence? Did his research bear out this view?

Does it make sense to summarize a person's intelligence with a single number? Or does this misrepresent something as complex as the intellect? The answer depends on whether one believes intelligence to be unitary, a collection of separate abilities, or some combination of the two. An important tool for studying the structure of intelligence is factor analysis, a method invented by Charles Spearman. (See Figure 10.2 on text page 372.)

14. What did Spearman agree with in Galton's approach? in Binet's approach?

15. Explain the basic purpose and rationale underlying factor analysis.

16. What did Spearman refer to as *g*? What suggested to him that *g* existed?

17. What did Spearman refer to as *s*? What suggested to him that there was such a thing as *s*?

18. How does Spearman's *g* relate to Galton's concept of intelligence?

Raymond Cattell, a student and colleague of Spearman, developed his own modified version of Spearman's theory of intelligence. He distinguished between two kinds of general intelligence. (See Figures 10.4 and 10.5 on text page 374.)

19. Define the following two forms of *g*.

   a. fluid intelligence (g_f)

   b. crystallized intelligence (g_c)

20. Describe two types of evidence that led Cattell to make this distinction.

21. Cattell noted that _____ intelligence depends on _____ intelligence.

What really underlies general intelligence? One goal is to identify elementary cognitive correlates of intelligence. Many of the research findings in this area highlight the importance of mental speed, a notion that echoes Galton's idea of mental quickness.

22. Summarize evidence that general intelligence is correlated with mental speed.

23. Why might one think that working-memory capacity underlies differences in intelligence?

24. Why would we expect working-memory capacity to be related to mental speed? What evidence supports this idea?

Other researchers have explored individual differences more complex than variables like mental speed. Robert Sternberg sees intelligence as "mental self-government."

25. What does Sternberg mean by "mental self-government"?

26. What are metacomponents? What does the term *meta-* mean in this context? Give some examples of tasks performed by metacomponents.

27. Describe some evidence supporting Sternberg's theory.

28. How might Sternberg's theory help to explain correlations between IQ and mental speed or working-memory scores?

29. Provide evidence that the frontal lobes are crucially involved in intelligence.

The Nature-Nurture Debate Concerning IQ
(pages 377–385)

> CONSIDER *these questions before you go on. They are designed to help you start thinking about this subject, not to test your knowledge.*

Is the variation in intellectual ability among individuals due more to nature or to nurture? How can we discriminate between the two influences?

Are there average differences in IQ between racial or cultural groups? How could we interpret any such differences rationally?

> READ *this section of your text lightly. Then go back and read thoroughly, completing the Workout as you proceed.*

The familiar concept of a nature-nurture debate began with Galton's theories about the hereditary basis of variations in intelligence. The essential question of nature versus nurture is often misunderstood, with one version being a reasonable question to ask and the other being absurd. To clarify the distinction between the reasonable question and the absurd one, consider the rectangle analogy presented in Figure 10.6 on text page 377.

1. State the essential nature-nurture question in its two forms as applied to the matter of intelligence.

   a. absurd version

   b. reasonable version

Heritability is the concept that scientists use to frame the nature-nurture question regarding intelligence or any other characteristic that varies among individu-

als. Like the nature-nurture question itself, the concept of heritability is often misunderstood. It is worth your time to be clear about it.

2. Define *heritability.*

3. Heritability can be expressed quantitatively by means of the heritability coefficient, abbreviated h^2. Fill in the terms in the formula below.

   $h^2 = \underline{\hspace{3cm}} = \underline{\hspace{3cm}}$

4. Give the heritability coefficient that would correctly describe each of the following situations.

   _____ a. None of the observed variance in the population is due to genetic differences.

   _____ b. Seventy percent of the observed variance in the population is due to genetic differences.

   _____ c. All of the observed variance in the population is due to genetic differences.

   _____ d. Forty percent of the observed variance in the population is due to environmental differences.

5. Logically, when we measure heritability, we are also measuring _____ .

The study of twins has been a valuable avenue for estimating the heritability of IQ.

6. Why are twins particularly valuable subjects in the attempt to tease apart genetic and environmental contributions to IQ variation?

7. What did Galton conclude in his pioneering study of twins? Has recent research supported Galton's conclusions? Explain.

One approach to estimating heritability coefficients is to compare identical twins raised together with fraternal twins raised together. The rationale is that while both types of twins share an environment, identical twins have twice the genetic relatedness that fraternal twins have. The former are 100 percent related and the latter only 50 percent related, just like any other pair of biological siblings.

8. In general, how do IQ correlations between identical twins raised together compare to IQ correlations between fraternal twins raised together? What does this suggest about the heritability of IQ?

9. Is IQ heritability as estimated in these studies equal for children and adults?

A different approach is to measure the correlations between identical twins who have been adopted at a young age into separate homes.

10. What is the average heritability coefficient found in these studies prior to 1993?

11. Are fluid and crystallized intelligence equally heritable?

Many studies of IQ correlations show that the effect of a shared family environment has only a temporary effect on IQ. A direct method for addressing the impact of shared environment on IQ is to study biologically unrelated people who are adopted into the same home.

12. What is the IQ correlation for such individuals in childhood? in adulthood?

13. How might we explain the transient effect of a shared family environment on IQ?

Heritability coefficients are legitimately applied only within the population studied. In general, the heritability estimates discussed so far came from white, North American or European populations in the upper two-thirds of the socioeconomic scale.

14. If heritability coefficients were estimated for the broadest range of the human population, how would those estimates compare to the ones just discussed?

One focus in IQ research has been average differences between racial or cultural groups. Though the difference between American blacks and whites has attracted particular attention, racial or cultural comparisons often show differences in average IQ.

15. What is the average difference in IQ points between American blacks and whites?

16. Why doesn't it make sense to use heritability within groups to assess the reasons for differences between groups?

17. Present two lines of evidence that the black/white IQ difference represents cultural rather than genetic effects.

    a.

    b.

18. Is there a historical trend in IQs? Describe the findings and explain their implications.

Varieties of Intelligence (pages 385–390)

> CONSIDER *these questions before you go on. They are designed to help you start thinking about this subject, not to test your knowledge.*

Is intelligence a single ability that one has more or less of? Or is intelligence a collection of several qualitatively different abilities?

Is there truth to the popular notion that the right and left hemispheres of the brain have different intellectual strengths?

Does a retarded person with a remarkable musical gift simply perform by memorization? Or does such a person really think intelligently in this particular area?

Do people in different cultures reason the same way? Do their environments affect the types of intellectual abilities they develop?

> READ *this section of your text lightly. Then go back and read thoroughly, completing the Workout as you proceed.*

The issue of singular versus multiple intelligence has already been raised in the discussion of Spearman's factor-analysis work. Spearman proposed the existence of both general intelligence and specific factors that influence performance on particular subtests. But note that scores on some sets of subtests seem to cluster together, having higher correlations among themselves than they do with scores on other subtests. This suggests that each cluster measures a different type of intelligence. Cattell's distinction between fluid intelligence and crystallized intelligence arose from finding such clusters of related performance.

1. What two distinguishable factors did Philip Vernon identify?

A different approach to understanding the varieties of intelligence comes from neuropsychology. Researchers in this field often study individuals with brain damage and people with unusual patterns of intellectual development.

2. What does the pattern of intellectual capabilities and deficits in people with brain damage imply about the nature of intelligence?

3. Is there evidence that the left and right hemispheres are associated with different aspects of intelligence? Explain.

Specialized intellectual abilities are most dramatically illustrated by retarded savants.

4. Do these individuals simply perform by rote, or are they behaving intelligently in their area of specialty? Support your answer.

The ecological approach suggests that intelligence is a property not of the individual but of the individual in a particular environmental context. Therefore, the types of intelligence that exist are infinite in number just as the number of person-context combinations is infinite.

5. Discuss research showing that people may demonstrate intelligence in their work that might not be evident in more formal tests.

We all know that practice plays a role in the development of skills. Someone who practices guitar once a month is not going to play as well as someone who practices daily.

6. Discuss the relationship between practice and expert performance.

7. Are the skills that experts develop in their field easily generalized to other areas? Explain.

Researchers who take an ecological perspective have concluded that culture affects an individual's approach to an intelligence test.

8. What kinds of results have led to this conclusion?

9. Present evidence suggests that a cultural group's environment and lifestyle may be related to the mental abilities that its members develop.

How People Reason and Solve Problems
(pages 390–399)

CONSIDER *these questions before you go on. They are designed to help you start thinking about this subject, not to test your knowledge.*

Are human beings really capable of being logical?

Do we tend to make certain types of mistakes in our reasoning or are our errors just random?

How can we improve our problem-solving performance?

READ *this section of your text lightly. Then go back and read thoroughly, completing the Workout as you proceed.*

Though cognitive psychologists, like philosophers, are interested in reasoning, their orientation to the topic is different. Psychologists seek to understand how people typically reason, not to describe ideal logic. In fact, they have found that humans are not ideal logic machines whether they are engaging in deductive or inductive reasoning.

1. Inferring a new principle or proposition from specific facts or observations is called

_____ or _____ .

Psychologists such as Amos Tversky and Daniel Kahneman have explored inductive reasoning with problems that resemble those that people face in everyday life. They have been especially interested in identifying the kinds of information people tend to use or tend to ignore in making judgments.

2. Define the two kinds of information named below, and illustrate each in terms of the librarian-or-salesperson problem in the text.

a. representativeness

b. base rate

3. What evidence suggests that people tend to ignore base rates and overemphasize representativeness?

4. How does availability bias thinking?

5. What is confirmation bias? How has it been demonstrated in experiments?

6. Could confirmation bias occur because it is adaptive in daily life? Explain.

Psychological research has also focused on deductive reasoning.

7. Deciding logically that a given conclusion inevitably follows from premises that are assumed to be true is called _____ reasoning.

8. Describe each of the following types of deductive-reasoning problems:

a. series problem

b. syllogism

c. conditional reasoning problem (See page 395.)

9. Does research suggest that people solve deductive-reasoning problems through formal logic? Explain.

One alternative to formal logic theories of human reasoning comes in the form of mental-model theories.

10. How do people accomplish deductive reasoning in the view of Phillip Johnson-Laird?

11. What evidence supports the mental-model view?

12. Are mental models visual in nature? Explain.

The purpose of reasoning is, of course, to solve problems. Problem solving has long been a focus of psychologists, who have asked, for example, What gets in the way of our solving problems and what helps us to succeed?

13. Define the term *problem*.

14. The three elements that all problems have in common are _____ ,
_____ , and _____ .

15. What must one do to solve a problem? Which of these steps are most critical for many problems?

Habits are often helpful results of learning, but they can sometimes set up barriers to effective problem solving. Before proceeding, look at Figure 10.12 on text page 395 and follow the directions in the figure caption. Now do the same with Figure 10.13 on text page 396.

16. Define the concept of mental set, and show how it applies to the nine-dot problem.

17. Define the type of mental set known as functional fixedness, and show how it applies to Duncker's candle problem.

18. Can a lighthearted mood help to overcome mental set? How is this related to Gestalt views on achieving insight?

Analogies can be powerful aids to problem solving; some famous examples of successful problem solving, such as Darwin's theory of natural selection, illustrate this point nicely.

19. What are analogies, and how can they help a problem solver?

Sometimes a problem is difficult because the problem solver must work with a great deal of information and find some way to represent it efficiently.

20. How do experts differ from novices with regard to selecting and representing information?

21. What general point about organizing information is illustrated by the stick-configuration problem, presented in Figure 10.14 on text page 397?

22. A(n) _____ is any rule that, if followed correctly, will eventually lead to solving the problem. A(n) _____ is any rule that allows one to reduce the number of operations tried in solving a problem; in other words, it is a kind of _____ . The success of human problem solving is particularly related to the use of successful

_____ .

23. Give examples of an algorithmic approach and a heuristic approach.

Sometimes the gap between a problem's initial state and its goal state is too great to be negotiated in a single step. Subgoals provide a useful means of bridging such a gap.

24. Explain and give an example of the concept of subgoals.

25. A(n) _____ problem clearly states the initial state, goal, and permissible operations. A(n) _____ problem leaves one or more of these unclear. Balancing your checkbook is an example of a(n) _____ problem. Achieving financial security is a(n) _____ problem.

26. How is it possible for subgoals to impede progress toward a goal?

Roles of Language in Thought (pages 399–403)

> CONSIDER these questions before you go on. They are designed to help you start thinking about this subject, not to test your knowledge.

Can the language we speak affect our thoughts or make some thoughts more likely than others?

Can sexist language, such as the use of *man* to refer generically to all humans, promote sexist thinking?

> READ this section of your text lightly. Then go back and read thoroughly, completing the Workout as you proceed.

Humans are unique in possessing verbal language. The ability to use this highly flexible, abstract, symbolic mode of communication has enormous implications for human life. Language allows us to span distance, time, and the limitations of our personal experience. It is the means by which cultures are developed and passed on. It is a foundation for much of our thought. Psychologists and others have theorized about the relationship between language and thought for many years.

1. What is suggested in the theory of linguistic relativity proposed by Edward Sapir and Benjamin Whorf?

Linguistic relativity may help to explain cultural differences in math ability.

2. How does the Worora language illustrate an obvious effect of language on mathematical thinking?

3. How might language differences account for the superior mathematical performance of Asian children compared with American and European children? What evidence supports this explanation?

Bilinguals are especially helpful subjects in studies of linguistic relativity.

4. What research problem is overcome by studying bilinguals?

5. Describe research showing that one's language may affect one's impressions of other people.

Language can also affect performance on logic and insight problems.

6. What verbal habit did researchers promote to help people approach the candle problem more effectively?

The possibility exists that we can deliberately affect our thinking by altering our language. That idea provides part of the motivation for the current attempt to eliminate certain sexist constructions in the English language. An example of such a construction is the use of *man* to mean both humans in general and human males in particular.

7. Describe research showing that such generic use of the term *man* or *he* does, in fact, affect thinking.

> *Be sure to READ the Concluding Thoughts at the end of the chapter. Note important points in your Workout. Then consolidate your learning by answering the focus questions in the margins of the text.*

> *After you have studied the chapter thoroughly, CHECK your understanding with the Self-Test that follows.*

Self-Test 1

Multiple-Choice Questions

1. Snyderman and Rothman asked specialists in the field of intelligence to indicate those human abilities that were important elements of intelligence. Nearly everyone in the study indicated all of the following *except*:
   a. abstract reasoning.
   b. problem solving.
   c. sensory acuity.
   d. capacity to acquire knowledge.

2. Asking whether an intelligence test really measures what it is supposed to measure is a question about the test's:
   a. representativeness.   c. factor analysis.
   b. validity.   d. *g.*

3. The technique known as *factor analysis* is a powerful means of determining the _____ of intelligence.
   a. biological basis   c. degree
   b. evolutionary origins   d. basic components

4. According to Spearman, the lack of perfect correlation among various mental tests is accounted for by:
   a. *g.*
   b. *s.*
   c. varying math ability.
   d. mental level.

5. Researchers trying to correlate simple behavioral measures with intelligence have often converged on _____ in one form or another.
   a. mental speed
   b. the size of long-term memory
   c. deductive reasoning
   d. word associations

6. Studies of the on-the-job intellectual performance of electricians would most probably be conducted by researchers interested in:
   a. representativeness.
   b. availability bias.
   c. environmentality measurements.
   d. the ecological perspective on intelligence.

7. Amos Tversky and Daniel Kahneman have suggested that people tend to _____ base rates.
   a. overestimate
   b. underestimate
   c. ignore
   d. pay too much attention to

8. A person who reasons from the premises *All birds can fly* and *Chickens are birds* that *Chickens can fly* has:
   a. engaged in deductive reasoning.
   b. engaged in inductive reasoning.
   c. fallen prey to the availability bias.
   d. fallen prey to the confirmation bias.

9. Consistent with Phillip Johnson-Laird's hypothesis, research has shown that college students reason better with syllogisms that are easier to:
   a. pronounce.
   b. visualize.
   c. state in terms of a mental set.
   d. combine into one sentence.

10. Charles Darwin's use of selective breeding by horticulturists to help him understand natural selection illustrates the power of:
    a. subgoals.
    b. algorithms.
    c. metacomponents.
    d. analogies.

11. A strategy for solving an anagram (a scrambled-word problem) that involves producing all possible sequences of the letters in the anagram will eventually guarantee a solution. It is thus a(n):
    a. heuristic.
    b. analogy.
    c. algorithm.
    d. mental set.

12. Comparison of African-Americans and the Buraku in Japan suggests that black/white IQ differences in the United States are due to:
    a. poorer educational opportunities for Blacks.
    b. the genetic endowment of the two groups.
    c. unfair testing.
    d. blacks' occupying a castelike status.

13. Retarded savants:
    a. have high *g*.
    b. depend on rote learning for performance in their specialties.
    c. behave intelligently in a particular intellectual realm.
    d. readily break out of mental set.

14. Until age 50, _____ increases.
    a. mental speed
    b. crystallized intelligence
    c. working-memory capacity
    d. fluid intelligence

15. The idea that language can affect thinking is known as _____ and is associated with _____ .
    a. linguistic relativity; Binet
    b. linguistic relativity; Whorf and Sapir
    c. heuristic thought; Sternberg
    d. heuristic thought; Wechsler

Essay Questions

16. What is heritability? Why and how is heritability affected by the amount of environmental variation among the group being tested? How can heritability be high within two groups and yet not account for differences between those groups?

17. Describe Binet's conception of intelligence. How were his views consistent with his goals and methods in developing an intelligence scale?

> *After you have assessed your understanding on the basis of Self-Test 1 and have tried to strengthen your preparation in any areas of weakness, GO ON to Self-Test 2.*

Self-Test 2

Multiple-Choice Questions

1. The "10-year rule" proposed by Ericsson emphasizes that _____ is critical to the attainment of expert status in a field.
    a. age
    b. practice
    c. advanced education
    d. abstract thought

2. Alfred Binet and Theophile Simon developed the Binet-Simon Intelligence Scale by trying out items similar to those found in schoolwork and:
    a. keeping only those that could be answered by about 50 percent of the children.
    b. making them easier or harder to accommodate children of different mental ages.
    c. dropping those that did not correlate well with simple measures of mental speed and sensory acuity.
    d. keeping only those that distinguished between children rated high and those rated low by teachers.

3. Which of the following correctly represents the *original* meaning of IQ?
   a. mental age divided by chronological age times 100
   b. chronological age divided by mental age times 100
   c. mental age divided by the number of items correctly answered times 100
   d. the number of items correctly answered divided by chronological age times 100

4. IQ scores on standard intelligence tests are correlated with school grades:
   a. only weakly.
   b. moderately.
   c. almost perfectly.
   d. not at all.

5. According to Raymond Cattell, mental ability derived directly from previous experience is classified as:
   a. crystallized intelligence.
   b. fluid intelligence.
   c. comprehension.
   d. irrelevant to a consideration of intelligence.

6. If an entire population were genetically identical, heritability in its members would:
   a. be zero.
   b. be 50 percent.
   c. be 100 percent.
   d. depend on the trait in question.

7. Overall, twin studies suggest that the heritability of IQ falls roughly in the range:
   a. 0.00 to 0.25.   c. 0.50 to 0.75.
   b. 0.25 to 0.50.   d. 0.75 to 1.00.

8. Researchers have found that the Kpelle people of Nigeria:
   a. were unable to sort by taxonomic category as Westerners typically do.
   b. could sort by taxonomic category but preferred to sort in another way.
   c. typically sorted by taxonomic category just as Westerners do.
   d. could not sort at all unless they were given a set of categories.

9. Alan believes that a classmate who is a somewhat flamboyant nonconformist is an English major when in fact he is a chemistry major. Alan's error illustrates:
   a. overreliance on representativeness.
   b. overreliance on base rates.
   c. confirmation bias.
   d. availability bias.

10. Carrie is nervous about boarding her flight to Denver because of a highly publicized plane crash the previous week. We could best explain her apprehension in terms of:
    a. mental set.
    b. availability bias.
    c. a syllogism.
    d. an analogy.

11. A problem, by definition, has all of the following *except*:
    a. a goal state.   c. possible operations.
    b. an initial state.   d. algorithms.

12. Suppose a person going to a birthday party needs something to protect a carefully wrapped present from the rain but overlooks an unused plastic trash bag lying on the counter. This person has illustrated the problem of:
    a. functional fixedness.
    b. representativeness.
    c. induction.
    d. availability bias.

13. Imagine that a group of genetically diverse children from a variety of different backgrounds are randomly assigned to two school systems, one excellent and one poor. Differences in academic performance between the two school systems would be due primarily to:
    a. genetic variability among the children.
    b. variability in the backgrounds of the children.
    c. the different environments of the school systems.
    d. mental set.

14. Sunita has been assigned a lengthy term paper in her history class. First, she breaks the task down into smaller steps—like choosing a topic, selecting relevant books at the library, etc. She has made good use of:
    a. factor analysis.
    b. algorithms.
    c. subgoals.
    d. metacomponents.

15. Which of the following would be *least* likely to show evidence of linguistic relativity?
    a. pitch perception
    b. reasoning about syllogisms
    c. impressions of other people
    d. judgments of guilt or innocence

Essay Questions

16. What is confirmation bias? Give an example from laboratory research.

17. What is deductive reasoning? Explain Phillip Johnson-Laird's hypothesis about why some people solve syllogisms better than other people. What evidence suggests that Johnson-Laird's hypothesis might be correct?

Answers

Problems of Identifying and Measuring Intelligence

5. (mental age/chronological age) × 100; intelligence quotient

7. Wechsler Adult Intelligence Scale, Revised; Wechsler Intelligence Scale for Children, Third Edition

9. validity

21. crystallized; fluid

The Nature-Nurture Debate Concerning IQ

3.
$$h^2 = \frac{\text{variance due to genes}}{\text{total variance}} = \frac{\text{variance due to genes}}{\text{variance due to genes} + \text{variance due to environment}}$$

4. **a.** 0.00

   b. 0.70

   c. 1.00

   d. 0.60

5. environmentality

How People Reason and Solve Problems

1. inductive reasoning; hypothesis construction

7. deductive

14. initial state; goal state; permissible operations

22. algorithm; heuristic; shortcut; heuristics

25. well-defined; ill-defined; well-defined; ill-defined

Self-Test 1

1. **c.** (p. 367)

2. **b.** (p. 370)

3. **d.** Factor analysis can help to reveal the essential makeup of intelligence in terms of general ability and component mental abilities. (p. 372)

4. **b.** (p. 372)

5. **a.** This represents a revival of Galton's earlier thinking, which is now supported by research data. (pp. 374–375)

6. **d.** (pp. 387–388)

7. **c.** (pp. 391–392)

8. **a.** (p. 393)

9. **b.** (p. 394)

10. **d.** (p. 397)

11. **c.** (p. 398)

12. **d.** (p. 383)

13. **c.** (p. 386)

14. **b.** (p. 374)

15. **b.** (p. 400)

16. Heritability, the central concept of nature-nurture debates, is the extent to which genetic differences in a group of individuals can account for observed differences in some characteristic. Heritability is logically and necessarily influenced by the amount of environmental variation within the group. For example, suppose the members of a group were exposed to identical environments and still differed in some trait. We would have to assume that the differences were due to genetic variation.

One can look at the formula for the heritability coefficient to see this point another way. This statistic essentially defines heritability as the amount of genetic variation divided by the amount of total variation (that is, genetic variation plus environmental variation—the only two possibilities). If environmental variation (variation being expressed statistically as variance) were nonexistent in a particular case, then the denominator would equal the numerator and thus heritability would be 1.00, the highest possible. The smaller the amount of environmental diversity, the higher the heritability coefficient will be; conversely, the greater the environmental diversity, the lower heritability will be. Heritability can be high within groups and low or nonexistent between them if the individuals within a group have very similar environments and the two groups have different environments. In fact, heritability within groups tells us nothing about the causes of differences between those groups. (pp. 378–381)

17. Binet thought of intelligence as a collection of various higher-order mental abilities that might be only loosely related to one another. He also emphasized the importance of the environment in shaping intelligence.   In fact, his test was intended to identify children who were not benefiting as much as they should from schooling so that they could receive special attention and thereby increase their intelligence. The questions and problems on the test assessed memory, vocabulary, common knowledge, number usage, and other higher-level intellectual functions. Items were selected by pretesting on schoolchildren of various ages and comparing results with teachers' ratings of the children's classroom performance. Only items answered correctly by high-rated children more often than by low-rated children were retained. Both the nature of the items and their manner of selection made them consistent with Binet's goals and his concept of intelligence. (pp. 368–369)

Self-Test 2

1. **b.** (p. 388)

2. **d.** Binet realized the circular nature of this selec-

tion procedure but also saw the advantages of a single standard test that could be used on many different children in different circumstances. Further, since he was trying to produce a valid test of academic ability, he needed to compare it with an accepted measure of such ability. (p. 368)

3. **a.** Don't forget that Wechsler, in developing his adult intelligence test, kept the term *IQ* because of its familiarity to the public but changed its meaning. An IQ score was no longer produced by dividing mental age by chronological age. Rather, 100 was the IQ score associated with whatever level of performance was average for a particular age group; better or poorer performance received correspondingly higher or lower scores. (p. 369)

4. **b.** (pp. 370–371)

5. **a.** (p. 373)

6. **a.** Genetic variation can't explain variation on a trait if genetic variation doesn't exist! (p. 378)

7. **c.** (p. 380)

8. **b.** The Kpelle clearly had a different notion of what constituted intelligent behavior, since they would sort by taxonomic category only when they were asked to sort the way a stupid person would. (p. 390)

9. **a.** (pp. 391–392)

10. **b.** (p. 392)

11. **d.** (p. 395)

12. **a.** Mental set is a situation in which we have difficulty breaking free of existing habits of thought to find a solution. Functional fixedness is a special case of mental set in which a habit of thought makes it harder to think of using objects for unaccustomed purposes. (p. 396)

13. **c.** (p. 378)

14. **c.** (pp. 398–399)

15. **a.** (pp. 400–401)

16. Confirmation bias is the normal human tendency to look for confirmation rather than disconfirmation of a hypothesis. This is despite the fact that, logically, no amount of confirmation can prove a hypothesis true and that disconfirmation has the power to rule *out* a hypothesis. Peter Wason asked subjects to guess the rule that the experimenter was using to generate sequences of three numbers, such as 5-7-9. The subjects could test their hypotheses by generating sequences of their own and having the experimenter say whether they fit his rule or not. Subjects tended to generate sequences consistent with their own hypothe-

ses rather than sequences that could tell them if the hypothesis was wrong. (pp. 392–393)

17. Deductive reasoning involves reasoning from premises assumed to be true to a conclusion that logically follows from them. It is often tested in logic problems such as syllogisms or series problems. An example would be "All fish are scaly (major premise); Cedric is a fish (minor premise); therefore, Cedric is scaly (conclusion)." In this case, the conclusion does follow logically from the premises. Johnson-Laird suggested that peo- ple who solve deductive-reasoning problems suc- cessfully do so by creating and then examining a mental model, often in the form of a visual image. Research evidence to support this idea comes from studies in which people have been shown to do better with syllogisms in which the premises are easy to visualize. Also, the ability to solve syl- logisms is more strongly correlated with visual- spatial ability than with verbal ability. (pp. 393–395)

Chapter 11   The Development of Thought and Language

READ the introduction below before you read the chapter in the text.

Chapter 11 explores the development of mental abilities during infancy and childhood. Babies are born with certain sensory and perceptual capabilities, which develop further during infancy—roughly the first 18 to 24 months of life. These abilities are exploited even by newborns as they seek to explore the world around them. Soon after birth, infants show an interest in controlling their environment and reveal a preference for novel over familiar stimuli. As they gain the ability to coordinate different parts of their bodies, such as eyes and hands, they actively examine objects.

Though they do not require adult encouragement to explore, infants begin at about 6 to 12 months to use social cues to guide their exploration. Even very young infants seem to understand some basic physical principles of the world though they may be too young to act on that knowledge in certain ways. For example, they may know an object still exists though it has been hidden but may be unable to reach for it. Studies using the visual cliff apparatus have shown that infants learn to fear and thus to avoid apparent drop-offs through experience in self-produced locomotion. Self-produced actions play a central part in the theory of Jean Piaget, a major theorist in the area of cognitive development.

Jean Piaget has suggested that the growth of the child's ability to think logically occurs in four stages: sensorimotor, preoperational, concrete operational, and formal operational. The movement from one stage to the next involves the emergence of new types of schemes in the child's thinking. Schemes are something like mental blueprints for organized patterns of action. The two complementary processes of assimilation and accommodation advance the child's thinking. Theorists from the information-processing perspective attempt to understand cognitive development in terms of developmental changes in the components of the mind, such as working memory. They also claim that development is more domain-specific than Piaget claimed. Annette Karmiloff-Smith emphasizes the redescription of mental representation in development. Theorists from the sociocultural perspective emphasize that cognitive development occurs in a particular cultural and social context. Lev Vygotsky, the theorist generally credited with originating this perspective, stressed the importance of the relationship between language and thought in human cognitive development.

The child's acquisition of language is one of the most amazing aspects of cognitive development. In general, developmentalists believe that it depends both on innate mechanisms that predispose the child to learn language and on an environment that supports such learning. Young infants can distinguish phonemes, the basic units of speech sound. Early in life, infants begin to coo and babble, two forms of vocalization that prepare them for later speech and appear to be types of play. Children move on to acquire words, slowly at first and then at a faster pace. At first they speak one word at a time, but they soon learn to produce progressively longer utterances that are meaningful and indicate some understanding of the rules of grammar. A number of observations suggest that children do not simply mimic the speech around them but infer the underlying rules of language. Efforts to teach nonvocal forms of language to chimpanzees and other nonhuman primates have generally shown that, while they can learn to use symbols in a referential way, they cannot acquire more than a slight knowledge of grammar.

LOOK over the table of contents for this chapter in your textbook before you continue with your study.

Notice that there are focus questions in the margins of the text for your use in studying the material. The following chart lists which Study Guide questions relate to which focus questions.

Focus Questions	Study Guide Questions
Learning, in Infancy, About the Physical World	
1–4	1–9
5–8	10–20
Development of Reasoning	
9–11	1–8
12–17	9–17
18–21	18–21
22–26	22–30
Development of Language	
27–29	1–9
30–35	10–21
36–38	22–29
39–41	30–33

The Integrated Study Workout

Complete one section at a time.

Learning, in Infancy, About the Physical World
(pages 410–417)

CONSIDER these questions before you go on. They are designed to help you start thinking about this subject, not to test your knowledge.

How can psychologists learn about an infant's perception or knowledge if the infant can't tell them about what it perceives or knows?

Does an infant know better than to crawl over a sudden drop-off? Must an infant have experience with falling before it will avoid such a drop-off?

Can an infant who sees an interesting object—say, a bright red ball—continue to think about it once it has disappeared?

READ this section of your text lightly. Then go back and read thoroughly, completing the Workout as you proceed.

Developmental psychologists seek to understand the changes in abilities and disposition that come with increasing age. Development is shaped not only by what occurs during an individual's lifetime, but also by evolutionary and cultural forces. Developmental psychologists have most often focused their efforts on infancy and childhood, though adult development has received some attention. Two key interests have been the development of thought and the development of language.

The foundations are laid in infancy with the exploration of the physical world.

1. *Infancy* is defined as the first _____ to _____ months after birth.

2. Describe the infant's sensory preparedness for being an explorer.

3. What evidence suggests that infants prefer novel stimuli? How is this preference used by psychologists as an assessment tool?

4. Discuss evidence that even young infants are interested in controlling their environment and respond emotionally to gaining or losing control.

5. Briefly note the infant's exploratory behavior at each age:

   a. 5 days old

   b. a few weeks old

   c. 2 to 3 months old

d. 4 months old

e. 5 to 6 months old

6. What constitutes examining, and how do we know that it involves active mental processing?

7. Present evidence that infants adjust their examining to fit the object's properties.

8. Do infants need to be taught or encouraged to examine the objects available to them? Support your answer.

Infants, beginning at about 6 to 12 months, use what they see adults do to guide what *they* do.

9. Name and describe three ways that infants use social cues to guide their behavior.

a.

b.

c.

Adults share certain assumptions about the nature of physical reality. We expect these core principles always to be true.

10. What is the origin of such knowledge? Describe two contrasting views.

a. empiricist philosophers, such as Locke and Berkeley

b. nativist philosophers, such as Descartes and Kant

Though psychologists have not resolved the nativist-empiricist debate, they have shown that humans exhibit knowledge of physical reality beginning at a very young age.

11. What is the most common method used today to assess early knowledge of physical principles? Be sure to explain the rationale.

12. What are some core principles that even 3- to 4-month-olds appear to possess based on this method?

According to Jean Piaget, a pioneer in developmental research, object permanence develops only gradually during the first year and a half of life.

13. The core principle that says objects continue to exist even when out of view is called

_____ .

14. Briefly describe Piaget's three hidden-object tasks and give the age at which infants typically succeed at each. (See Figure 11.2 on text page 415.)

    a. simple hiding problem

    b. changed hiding-place problem

    c. invisible displacement problem

15. How does Renée Baillargeon explain the discrepancy between results from Piaget's studies and those from selective-looking studies?

16. What is another possible explanation for the apparent discrepancy in results?

17. How might the development of self-produced locomotion lead to an improvement in retrieving hidden objects?

When infants begin to move around on their own, they face a new set of potential opportunities for learning and new dangers as well—electric outlets, hot ovens, sharp-edged tables, and sudden drop-offs. Psychologists use the visual cliff to study the growth of infants' wariness of heights.

18. Describe the visual cliff. What did Eleanor Gibson and Richard Walk discover about crawling infants' reactions to height in their experiment with the visual cliff? (See Figure 11.3 on text page 416.)

19. How did Campos and Bertenthal study 6- to 7-month-olds on the visual cliff? How did non-crawlers and crawlers differ in their responses, and how was the difference interpreted?

20. Is the experience of falling necessary for infants to develop fear of the visual cliff? Support your answer, and provide two proposed explanations —one cognitive and one evolutionary.

Development of Reasoning (pages 417–434)

CONSIDER these questions before you go on. They are designed to help you start thinking about this subject, not to test your knowledge.

What aspect of the child's experience promotes the development of new capabilities in logical thinking?

How are changes in a child's memory and mental speed related to changes in the child's ability to think logically?

What role does language play in the development of thought?

How does a child's social world support cognitive development?

Do young children have any conception of other people's psychological or subjective reality?

READ this section of your text lightly. Then go back and read thoroughly, completing the Workout as you proceed.

As they grow older, children become increasingly logical in their thinking, and thus more capable of solving problems. Developmental psychologists want to know how to describe these changes in logical capabilities and how to explain their occurrence. Jean Piaget is widely regarded as the most influential theorist in this area of research.

1. What was Piaget's basic approach? his most fundamental idea?

2. What is a scheme? How does the nature of schemes change with development?

3. Complete the following sentences.

   a. _____ is the process by which experiences are incorporated into existing schemes.

   b. _____ is the change in an existing scheme or set of schemes that results from the assimilation of an event or object.

4. Identify each of the following descriptions as focusing primarily on assimilation or accommodation. (Note that each example involves both processes.)

   _____ A child sees a woodcarving of a human figure and thinks of it as a doll.

   _____ A child discovers that the pencil scribblings she has produced can be erased.

   _____ A child is surprised to hear a neighbor's cat "meow" given that it looks a lot like a "doggy."

5. What are operations? operational schemes? Why did Piaget consider operations so important?

Piaget developed a four-stage theory of the child's developing understanding. In Piaget's theory, transition to a given stage is gradual and is based on the child's thoughts and activities at the previous stage. Children may move ahead on some categories of problems before they progress to new schemes with other categories. The four stages are loosely associated with ages, but children vary in their rate of progress. According to Piaget, all children must go through the four stages in order, however.

6. Characterize each of the following stages, being careful to indicate the kind of scheme associated with each, the kinds of abilities they support, and the way that advancement to the next stage is promoted.

   a. sensorimotor stage (birth to about 2 years old)

   b. preoperational stage (about 2 to 7 years old)

   c. concrete-operational stage (about 7 to 12 years old)

   d. formal-operational stage (from onset of adolescence through adulthood)

Piaget's theory is widely admired even today, but, like any scientific theory, it has its limitations. The process whereby theories are developed, criticized, defended or modified, and so on, is part of the nature of the scientific endeavor.

7. Why is Piaget's work so admired?

8. List and explain three types of criticisms of Piaget's theory. Where possible, describe evidence supporting the critics' point of view.

   a.

   b.

   c.

The information-processing perspective approaches cognitive development not in terms of the whole mind, as Piaget did, but rather in terms of interacting mental components. These mental components are organized as a system for handling information, analogous to a computer. From this perspective, cognitive development can be explained in terms of changes in the components or changes in the rules or strategies.

9. Why are developmental changes in working memory thought to be particularly important?

10. Summarize Juan Pascual-Leone's theory, and describe evidence that appears to support it.

11. How might working-memory improvements be due to an increase in processing speed? What evidence suggests that the faster processing results from biological maturation?

Developmental changes in working-memory capacity and processing speed are "all-purpose" changes, affecting many intellectual processes. Some researchers have explored the acquisition of more specific capabilities of the mind—rules and strategies that might apply to only a select type of problem.

12. Summarize Robert Siegler's work on the development of the ability to solve balance-beam problems. (See Figure 11.6 on text page 425.)

13. How does Siegler's account illustrate the fundamental difference between the information-processing and Piagetian approaches?

Annette Karmiloff-Smith has built on Piaget's notion that information in the mind is restructured in the process of development. She combines that idea with modern concepts of domain-specific development and implicit versus explicit memory.

14. What is redescription?

15. Distinguish between proceduralization and explicitation, and state the value of each.

16. Using the case of block balancing in 4-, 6-, and 8-year-olds, show how explicitation may initially have a cost.

17. In general, does development proceed according to stages, according to Karmiloff-Smith?

Still another view of cognitive development is offered by the sociocultural perspective. Lev Vygotsky is usually regarded as the originator of this perspective.

18. On what points did Vygotsky agree with Piaget? How did they differ in their views on the aspects of the environment most relevant to development?

19. Why are language in general and the internalization of speech in particular so important to cognitive development, in Vygotsky's view?

20. How did Piaget interpret children's noncommunicative speech? How did Vygotsky reinterpret this phenomenon? Describe some evidence consistent with Vygotsky's view.

Vygotsky proposed that growth occurs first at the social level and only then at the individual level. Moreover, the developing child's thought occurs not in a void but rather in a *particular* social and cultural context. The child's experience is structured by a variety of social routines—making a purchase at a store, hearing a bedtime story, and going to the movies in some cultures; hunting, building shelters, and ceremonial dancing in others.

21. Vygotsky used the term _____ _____ to refer to the difference between what a child can do alone and what that child can do together with someone more competent. The child's ability grows, in this view, through _____ , largely in the form of _____ . In contrast to Piaget's conception of the child as a little _____ , Vygotsky saw the child as a(n) _____ .

Another fact of social life is that children learn *about* other people as well as from them.

22. In what sense are we all everyday psychologists?

23. What evidence suggests that children start to interpret the behavior of others in terms of mental constructs beginning quite early in life?

A child's understanding that people's actions are related to their beliefs takes time to develop. For example, 3-year-olds seldom explain someone's behavior in terms of beliefs. It takes even longer for the child to understand that a person's beliefs can be incorrect.

24. How do 3- and 4-year-olds differ in terms of their performance on the container test? the displacement test? Is the difference in their performance simply a function of memory?

25. Describe evidence that pretend play is a precursor to understanding false belief.

26. Alan Leslie suggests an evolutionary explanation for the occurrence and importance of pretend play. What is his position? What other sorts of logical reasoning might pretend play help to foster?

The failure to understand other people's minds—or even to recognize that there are other minds to understand—characterizes a congenital disorder called autism.

27. Describe the diagnostic features of autism.

28. How did the vocabulary development of Clara Park's daughter, Elly, demonstrate a difference in her understanding of the physical world and the psychological world?

29. Autistic people generally perform poorly on false-belief tests or tests involving deception. How did autistic children averaging 12 years old compare to normal 4-year-olds on false-belief tests? What does their performance on false-picture tests suggest?

30. How does research on autistic children's play support Leslie's idea about the developmental basis for understanding false beliefs and other nonliteral mental states?

Development of Language (pages 435–447)

CONSIDER these questions before you go on. They are designed to help you start thinking about this subject, not to test your knowledge.

Can children respond to language even before they are born?

What do the babbling and cooing of young infants have to do with language development?

How is it possible that children who have not mastered the intricacies of dressing themselves or using eating utensils can produce and understand something as complex as language?

Is there any evidence that nonhuman animals are capable of learning language?

> *READ this section of your text lightly. Then go back and read thoroughly, completing the Workout as you proceed.*

Perhaps the most incredible feat of the developing human mind is its rapid progress toward the mastery of language. Children typically acquire considerable facility with their native language before they can manage many other, simpler tasks.

1. Most developmentalists agree that language learning requires a combination of _____ mechanisms that predispose children to it and a(n) _____ that provides models and opportunities for practice.

Though there are about 3000 different languages, all have so much in common that we can reasonably speak of human language in a generic sense.

2. Entities that stand for other entities are called _____ . _____ , the smallest meaningful units in a language, are symbols that stand for ideas, events, objects, and so on. For example, the word *unhappiness* contains _____ such units (*un-*, *happy*, and *-ness*). The main meaning of a sentence is carried by _____ , which include nouns, verbs, adjectives, and adverbs. In English, conjunctions, prepositions, articles, and some prefixes and suffixes are classified as _____ ; though they primarily serve grammatical functions, they also contribute to _____ .

3. What does it mean to say that a morpheme is arbitrary? Why is arbitrariness important?

4. What does it mean to say that a morpheme is discrete?

5. How do arbitrariness and discreteness distinguish linguistic symbols from nonverbal communication signals?

Language can be described in terms of a four-level hierarchy. Units at each level of the hierarchy can be combined to form the units of the next-higher level.

6. From the highest to the lowest level of the hierarchy, the units are _____ , _____ , _____ or _____ , and _____ , which are the elementary vowel and consonant sounds of a language. The rules that specify the permissible ways to arrange units at one level of the hierarchy in order to produce the next-higher level constitute the _____ of the language. These rules, which exist in some form in all languages, include rules of phonology, which pertain to combining _____ ; rules of morphology, which pertain to combining _____ ; and rules of _____ , which pertain to combining words into phrases and sentences.

7. Why is such a hierarchical organization powerful?

8. Is grammar something one learns in school? Support your answer.

9. How is tacit knowledge of grammar demonstrated?

Speech sounds appear to have special status in human development.

10. Summarize evidence that infants are sensitive to and interested in speech stimuli as soon as they are born and possibly even while they are still in the womb.

11. Describe one experimental technique used in research on infants' abilities to distinguish phonemes. What do such experiments suggest about the abilities of infants up to 6 months of age? What happens to their abilities after the age of 6 months?

A familiar (sometimes all-too-familiar) form of infant vocalization is crying. Other types of infant vocalization are cooing and babbling.

12. Repeated, drawn-out vowel sounds, such as *oooh-oooh*, are referred to as _____ ;

_____ consists of repeated consonant-vowel sounds, such as *baa-baa*. Cooing begins to appear at about _____ months and gradually changes to babbling between the ages of _____ and _____ months. Cooing and babbling occur most often when the infant is happy and seem to be forms of _____ that have evolved to _____ the vocal apparatus.

13. Are cooing and babbling influenced by the speech sounds infants hear around them? Explain your answer and be sure to compare the development of deaf and hearing children.

A child's first words are generally greeted with great parental excitement and pride. The psychologist studying language development, however, must be somewhat more rigorous than the typical parent in deciding what counts as a word!

14. Distinguish between a performative and a true word.

15. Describe the rate of growth of the child's vocabulary. Do children acquire most of their new words through explicit instruction? Explain.

16. How do children determine what aspect of the environment a new word refers to?

17. A child's application of the term *car* to a truck or bus would be an instance of

_____ . In contrast, a child who fails to include a picture of a chicken in a stack of pictures of birds is showing evidence of a(n)

_____ of the term *bird*.

18. How does Eve Clark explain overextensions?

A major step in language development is taken when the child begins to put words together to form rudimentary sentences. This usually occurs at about 18 to 24 months.

19. What kinds of words do children tend to include in early sentences? Do they use word order correctly to indicate their meaning?

20. What evidence has shown that young children learn grammatical rules rather than simply imitating what they hear? (See Figure 11.11 on text page 441.)

21. Support the argument that children *discover* the rules of their language.

The process of language development is promoted by both internal and external supports. Some theorists emphasize the internal support provided by human biology.

22. Identify some ways in which humans are specially equipped for language.

23. In what sense was the approach to grammar developed by Noam Chomsky, a linguist, inherently psychological?

24. Chomsky's concept of the LAD, or

_____ _____ , refers to the entire set of innate mechanisms for a child's language acquisition. It includes the foundations for _____ as well as mechanisms that guide learning of the child's own particular native language.

25. What has Derek Bickerton concluded from studying the development of creole languages?

26. How does the development of sign language in Nicaragua support Bickerton's contention that children play a crucial role in imposing grammar in a new language?

27. Describe evidence for the critical-period hypothesis.

Other theorists point out that the social environment is also necessary to the development of language.

28. Define the *LASS*. How is it demonstrated in our culture?

29. How can social-learning theorists make sense of language development in Kalikuli infants?

Language is considered uniquely human. Only humans acquire such a complex communication system, one based on symbols and grammar, as a normal part of development. But many people have wondered whether it is possible for other species to acquire language under special circumstances. Most efforts to answer this question have focused on chimpanzees or other species of apes. Because these animals lack the vocal apparatus for speech, most efforts have used nonvocal language systems.

30. Who was Washoe? What did the Gardners teach her?

31. What LASS did Sue Savage-Rumbaugh provide for the bonobo Kanzi?

32. What kinds of linguistic accomplishments has Kanzi demonstrated?

33. Summarize the overall findings from studies of language learning in apes.

> *Be sure to READ the Concluding Thoughts at the end of the chapter. Note important points in your Workout. Then consolidate your learning by answering the focus questions in the margins of the text.*

> *After you have studied the chapter thoroughly, CHECK your understanding with the Self-Test that follows.*

Self-Test 1

Multiple-Choice Questions

1. Infants' use of a caregiver's emotional expressions to gauge the possible safety or danger of their own actions is called _____ and begins _____ .
   a. joint visual attention; soon after birth
   b. joint visual attention; by the time they can crawl or walk on their own
   c. social referencing; soon after birth
   d. social referencing; by the time they can crawl or walk on their own

2. Autistic children have particular difficulty in:
   a. exploring the physical world.
   b. conceptualizing other people's minds.
   c. discontinuing pretend play.
   d. learning to stop lying and engaging in other forms of deception.

3. Young infants will generally look longer at _____ than at _____ .
   a. homogeneous stimuli; patterned stimuli
   b. novel stimuli; familiar stimuli
   c. dark, rounded shapes; bright, angular shapes
   d. stimuli that are controlled by others; stimuli they control themselves

4. Eleanor Gibson and Richard Walk showed that infants who were experienced crawlers would:
   a. refuse to crawl over the visual cliff unless their mothers called to them.
   b. crawl slowly and carefully over the visual cliff.
   c. refuse to crawl over the visual cliff.
   d. crawl quickly and readily over the visual cliff once they felt the glass support.

5. Piaget referred to the child's ability to think of an object that is not immediately present as:
   a. object permanence.
   b. displacement.
   c. objectification.
   d. overextension.

6. Which of the following is true of infants tested shortly after birth for their response to speech sounds?

   a. They show a preference for human speech over instrumental music.
   b. They show no preference for the sound of the mother's voice over the voice of another woman.
   c. They show a preference for the voices of children over those of adults.
   d. All of the above are true.

7. A child's application of the term *kitty* to cats, dogs, and stuffed bears can be described as:

   a. overextension.   c. a performative.
   b. underextension.   d. a LAD.

8. With regard to children's language acquisition, Noam Chomsky contends that:

   a. children's general intelligence is enough to help them acquire language.
   b. children have a set of innate learning aids that specifically help them to acquire language.
   c. learning is not involved in the acquisition of language.
   d. children do not acquire language rules but merely learn to repeat what they hear and are reinforced for producing the sounds.

9. Which of the following is true of young children's earliest word combinations?

   a. They typically use only content words.
   b. They must be explicitly taught to combine words.
   c. Their word order is essentially random.
   d. They generally use the passive voice before the active voice.

10. Studies of language learning by chimpanzees and other species of apes:

    a. have repeatedly shown that they are incapable of using language symbolically and of learning rules of grammar.
    b. have recently led researchers to conclude that they are fully capable of both basic symbolic usage and grammar.
    c. have consistently shown that they are capable of learning grammar but incapable of using language symbolically.
    d. have led to the general conclusion that they can use language symbolically but have only the slightest capacity for grammar.

11. Piaget's theory has been criticized for:

    a. overestimating age differences in ways of thinking.
    b. overspecifying the process of change.
    c. overestimating the role of the social environment.
    d. all of the above.

12. In Piaget's theory, the capacity for thinking hypothetically comes when children:

    a. reach the formal-operational stage.
    b. develop schemes.
    c. understand reversible actions.
    d. are capable of communicative speech.

13. Which approach attempts to understand specific changes in the child's cognitive abilities in terms of specific changes in the mind's components?

    a. the Piagetian approach
    b. the information-processing approach
    c. the sociocultural approach
    d. all of the above approaches

14. The view that a broad range of problems can be solved through general principles once the appropriate stage of development has been reached is held by _____ and disputed by _____ .

    a. Piaget; information-processing theorists
    b. Piaget; sociocultural theorists
    c. information-processing theorists; Piaget
    d. information-processing theorists; sociocultural theorists

15. The Soviet psychologist Lev Vygotsky suggested that:

    a. thought involves a hidden form of the muscular movements that are part of speech.
    b. language is separate from thought in very young children but gradually comes to be used for private thought.
    c. language plays little or no role in the development of thought.
    d. thought cannot occur in the absence of some linguistic symbol system.

Essay Questions

16. Describe the development of the young infant's abilities to distinguish and produce phonemes.

17. Discuss Jean Piaget's beliefs about the role of action in cognitive development during the sensorimotor stage. Be sure to include in your discussion the concept of schemes.

> *After you have assessed your understanding on the basis of Self-Test 1 and have tried to strengthen your preparation in any areas of weakness, GO ON to Self-Test 2.*

Self-Test 2

Multiple-Choice Questions

1. The physical structure of morphemes need not be similar to the concept they stand for; in other words, morphemes are:
   a. discrete.   c. grammatical.
   b. arbitrary.   d. literal.

2. Lev Vygotsky used the analogy of a(n) _____ to characterize the developing child.
   a. scientist   c. apprentice
   b. sponge   d. computer

3. What leads to wariness of heights as indicated by the visual cliff?
   a. physical maturation reached by 9 months
   b. experience with falling
   c. experience with self-produced locomotion
   d. social experience, such as seeing parental concern when the infant is near a drop-off

4. Piaget used hiding problems to test the development of:
   a. conservation.   c. reflexive actions.
   b. object permanence.   d. operations.

5. Which of the following statements is *not* true of babbling?
   a. It consists of consonant-and-vowel sounds such as *baa-baa-baa*.
   b. Deaf infants begin to babble at the same age as infants who can hear.
   c. Infants babble only the sounds heard in their own native language.
   d. Babbling is a form of vocal play.

6. An infant who reliably produces a wordlike sound in a particular context but does not use the word as a symbol is producing a(n):
   a. overextension.
   b. grammatical morpheme.
   c. performative.
   d. lexigram.

7. The fact that children overgeneralize the past tense *-ed* ending to create such utterances as "He comed over" helps to illustrate the fact that they:
   a. prefer their own individual speech patterns to adult speech patterns.
   b. tend to overextend more than underextend.
   c. must reach the stage of formal operations before they can acquire an understanding of syntax.
   d. learn grammatical rules rather than simply mimic what they hear.

8. The case of the girl known as Genie provides evidence _____ the idea that _____ .
   a. for; children acquire language rules
   b. against; children acquire language rules
   c. for; there is a critical period for some aspects of language acquisition
   d. against; there is a critical period for some aspects of language acquisition

9. The fact that in our culture adults speak much more simply and clearly to young children than they do to other adults supports the idea of:

   a. a LAD.
   b. a LASS.
   c. syntax.
   d. a pidgin language.

10. In Piaget's theory, as children become mentally free from the strict control of the here and now, they enter which stage of cognitive development?

    a. sensorimotor
    b. formal operational
    c. concrete operational
    d. preoperational

11. According to Piaget, schemes are associated with which stage of development?

    a. sensorimotor
    b. concrete operational
    c. formal operational
    d. all of the above

12. Piaget refers to change in an existing scheme that results from incorporating new experiences as:

    a. an operation.
    b. assimilation.
    c. accommodation.
    d. proceduralization.

13. Juan Pascual-Leone proposed that the most significant change underlying cognitive development is a gradual, maturational increase in the:

    a. speed of retrieval from long-term memory.
    b. capacity of working memory.
    c. tendency to use rote rehearsal.
    d. motivation behind problem solving.

14. Robert Siegler's research on children's ability to solve balance-beam problems showed that the children could:

    a. not profit from feedback regardless of which rule it disconfirmed.
    b. profit from feedback regardless of which rule it disconfirmed.
    c. profit from feedback that disconfirmed their current rule and confirmed the next rule in the developmental sequence.
    d. profit from feedback that disconfirmed their current rule and also disconfirmed the next rule in the developmental sequence.

15. The sociocultural perspective points out that children learn better when they work on problems:

    a. alone.
    b. with peers at the same level of understanding.
    c. with a younger child whom they can teach.
    d. with parents or older children who are more competent.

Essay Questions

16. Describe the visual-cliff apparatus. How do crawling infants respond to the cliff when given the opportunity to crawl over it? What is their emotional response to the cliff, and what leads to this response? Support your answer with research evidence.

17. Discuss the opposing views of Lev Vygotsky and Jean Piaget on the phenomenon of noncommunicative speech.

Answers

Learning, in Infancy, About the Physical World

1. 18; 24

13. object permanence

Development of Reasoning

3. a. Assimilation

   b. Accommodation

4. assimilation; accommodation; accommodation

21. zone of proximal development; collaboration; dialogue; scientist; apprentice

Development of Language

1. innate; environment

2. symbols; morphemes; three; content morphemes; grammatical morphemes; meaning

6. sentences; phrases; words *or* morphemes; phonemes; grammar; phonemes; morphemes; syntax

12. cooing; babbling; 2; 4 and 6; vocal play; exercise

17. overextension; underextension

24. language-acquisition device; universal grammar

Self-Test 1

1. d. (p. 412)

2. b. (pp. 432–434)

3. b. This fact is interesting in its own right, but it is also important because it provides a methodological tool. The infant's preference for novelty can be used to test the infant's ability to discriminate between the familiar stimulus and the novel one. If the infant prefers the new stimulus, it must be able to tell that it is different from the previous stimulus or, in other words, novel. (p. 410)

4. c. Infants will refuse to crawl over even when their mothers call to them. (p. 416)

5. a. His tests of this ability, however, may not reveal the infants' knowledge as well as selective-looking studies. (p. 414)

6. a. (p. 437)

7. a. (p. 440)

8. b. Chomsky dubbed this set of special language-learning aids the LAD, or language-acquisition device. (p. 442)

9. a. (p. 440)

10. d. (p. 446)

11. a. (p. 421)

12. a. (p. 420)

13. b. (p. 422)

14. a. Piaget's approach is holistic, referring to global changes in the mind that allow wide-ranging and new problem-solving capabilities. Information-processing theorists, in contrast, are concerned with changes in individual components of the mind and believe that children learn specific rules that better equip them to handle particular classes of problems. (p. 424)

15. b. (p. 427)

16. Even very young infants are able to distinguish among phonemes, the elementary vowel and consonant sounds that make up speech. Infants under 6 months of age can detect differences between very similar speech sounds. After the age of 6 months, they start to lose the ability to distinguish subtly different sounds that constitute different phonemes in other languages but belong to the same phoneme category in their native language. This loss actually represents an adaptive change.

Infants can also produce a wide variety of phonemes in their cooing and babbling. Cooing, which starts at about 2 months, consists of the repetition of long, drawn-out vowels (such as *ooooh-ooooh*). Babbling involves consonant-and-vowel combinations (such as *gaaa-gaaa* or *paatooo*) and starts between 4 and 6 months. Both are forms of vocal play that help to exercise the vocal apparatus in preparation for speech. The phonemes that the infant produces initially do not appear to come from experience but rather are genetically based. Evidence for this comes from the fact that deaf infants coo and babble as many different sounds as hearing babies and from the fact that young infants' sounds are not much influenced by the particular language they hear. A baby who hears English spoken in the home will produce not only the phonemes of English but also the phonemes of other languages. But this changes by 8 months of age, when babbling begins to resemble the language the baby hears both in rhythm and pitch patterns. By about 10 months, the hearing child's babbling increasingly reflects the syllables and words of the child's native language. Deaf infants begin to babble manually if exposed to sign language. (pp. 437–439)

17. In Piaget's view, action is synonymous with knowledge during infancy. The infant is initially incapable of representing objects and events in terms of mental symbols. During the sensorimotor period, he or she internalizes actions as schemes, mental blueprints for action. In other words, the infant can think about objects and events in terms of action schemes, such as schemes for sucking, kicking, grasping, and so on. Objects become assimilated into schemes for the actions that can be performed on them. Sensorimotor schemes only allow the child to think about objects that are present. (pp. 417–418)

Self-Test 2

1. **b.** (p. 436)

2. **c.** Piaget thought of the child as a little scientist. (p. 429)

3. **c.** (pp. 416–417)

4. **b.** (p. 414)

5. **c.** (p. 438)

6. **c.** (p. 439)

7. **d.** (p. 441)

8. **c.** (p. 444)

9. **b.** (p. 444)

10. **d.** (p. 419)

11. **d.** (pp. 419–420)

12. **c.** Assimilation is matching a new experience to an existing scheme. Accommodation occurs when the object assimilated does not quite fit the scheme to which it is matched and so the scheme must be modified accordingly. (p. 418)

13. **b.** Pascual-Leone referred to this capacity as *M* space, or mental space. (p. 423)

14. **c.** Siegler suggested that children move sequentially through a series of four rules and that they cannot use feedback that would require them to skip over the next rule in the sequence. (p. 424)

15. **d.** (p. 427)

16. The visual-cliff apparatus is a glass-topped table that produces the illusion of a drop-off of several feet. Infants who are experienced crawlers will refuse to crawl over the visual cliff even when their mothers call to them. The reason for the avoidance of the visual cliff is apparently fear, as indicated by other research. In this research, it was found that infants responded differently to the sight of the cliff depending on their experience with self-produced locomotion. Those 6- to 7-month old infants who had learned to crawl (or been given experience moving in a walker) showed increased heart rate when placed directly over the cliff. Infants without such movement experience responded with interest rather than fear, judging by their decreased heart rate when similarly placed. (pp. 416-417)

17. Piaget observed that 4- to 6-year-old children often produce speech that does not take other people into account. What they say is not tailored for the comprehension of another person. For example, it may occur when the child is alone. When the child is with others, the topic of one child's speech may have no relation to the topic of another child's speech, even though they are working or playing side by side. Or one child may say something that has no apparent referent, such as "I see where it is." Piaget labeled this "noncommunicative speech" and thought it represented a lack of understanding of language's purpose.

Vygotsky, on the other hand, felt that language (rather than action, as in Piaget's theory) was the foundation of thought, and thus of cognitive development. In his view, what Piaget called noncommunicative speech was the child's thinking out loud, using language as a support to thought. Vygotsky explained the decline in this form of speech in terms of the child's progress at internalizing language. By the age of 7, the child could depend on inner speech or verbal thought, rather than audible speech, to aid thinking. (p. 428)

Chapter 12 Social Development

READ *the introduction below before you read the chapter in the text.*

We are all social beings who must continue to adapt to the social environment throughout our lifetimes. Several theoretical approaches offer different perspectives on social development. Psychodynamic theorists, such as Sigmund Freud and Erik Erikson, emphasize the role of drives, biological maturation, and universal sequences in social development. A biological emphasis is also present in the thinking of John Bowlby and Melvin Konner, who analyze social development in evolutionary terms. Urie Bronfenbrenner, who exemplifies the cultural perspective, emphasized the role of the social environment and cross-cultural differences. Cognitive theorists, such as Jean Piaget and Lev Vygotsky, stress the role of intellectual growth in social development.

Attachment is a major focus of infant social development. The term *attachment* refers to the emotional bonds that infants develop toward principal caregivers, usually their mothers. Research on humans and other primates indicates that physical contact with the caregiver is an important element of attachment. Human infants first show signs of attachment at about the time they begin to crawl, which makes evolutionary sense. Secure attachment in infancy is associated with greater confidence and sociability and with better emotional health and problem-solving performance later in childhood. The quality of care is a major influence on the quality of attachment. Cross-cultural differences in infant care are considerable. Western cultures are in many ways less indulgent of infants' desires.

Childhood is a time when powerful forms of socialization are at work. Among the earliest influences are interactions with caregivers. Children seem to be predisposed toward prosocial behaviors such as giving and helping but must also learn to restrain themselves and learn compliance. Theorists have devised ways of categorizing different styles of parental discipline and have argued that some styles are more effective than others. Theorists generally agree that play serves developmental functions but disagree about what they are. Some theorists emphasize its value as a means of learning about social roles and rules and about morality; others, its usefulness in skill development and the transmission of culture. Age-mixed play has some powerful benefits. Gender is also a factor in socialization. Gender enters into treatment of boys and girls by parents, by teachers, and by children themselves.

Adolescence lasts from the first signs of puberty until an individual is accepted as a full member of adult society. During adolescence, individuals typically become more independent of parents and more dependent on peers. Theorists have tried to explain the increased recklessness and violence of this period in terms ranging from a quest for or reaction against adult roles to a genetically ordained struggle for status. Adolescence is also a time in which individuals may have gained the intellectual capabilities that permit sophisticated moral reasoning, as described in Lawrence Kohlberg's theory of moral reasoning. Problems of emerging sexual relationships are compounded by the continuing sexual double standard and cultural messages glorifying sex. The choice in favor of sexual restraint or promiscuity may reflect adaptive strategies and evolutionary pressures.

Adulthood centers largely around the themes of love and work. In many ways, adult romantic love is similar in form to infant attachment. Research suggests that mutual liking, commitment, good communication, and understanding are among the characteristics of happy marriages. Because work is such a large part of adult life, job satisfaction is very important to life satisfaction and it appears to derive largely from occupational self-direction. Men and women differ in the satisfaction they derive from work at home versus work out of the home. The chapter concludes with a look at old age and points out that life satisfaction in later years is often greater than younger people would predict. Older people are also more focused on the present and less afraid of dying than younger people are.

LOOK over the table of contents for this chapter in your textbook before you continue with your study.

Notice that there are focus questions in the margins of the text for your use in studying the material. The following chart lists which Study Guide questions relate to which focus questions.

Focus Questions	Study Guide Questions
Conceptions of Social Development	
1–2	1–5
3–4	6–8
5	9–11
Infancy: Using Caregivers as a Base for Growth	
6–12	1–14
13–16	15–20
Childhood: Learning to Play by and with the Rules	
17–22	1–14
23–27	15–21
28–32	22–28
Adolescence: Breaking Out of the Cocoon	
33–38	1–13
39–41	14–18
Adulthood: Finding Satisfaction in Love and Work	
42–43	1–5
44–45	6–9
46	10–14

The Integrated Study Workout

Complete one section at a time.

Conceptions of Social Development
(pages 451–455)

CONSIDER these questions before you go on. They are designed to help you start thinking about this subject, not to test your knowledge.

Is culture a major factor in the ways people develop socially? What about evolutionary influences? cognitive growth?

What drives dominate or direct social development?

Do all people go through a similar progression in their social development?

READ this section of your text lightly. Then go back and read thoroughly, completing the Workout as you proceed.

Through all the phases of life, an individual is enmeshed in a social world to which he or she must adapt. Social development, which involves the changing nature of our relationships through life, has been approached from three theoretical perspectives. One perspective emphasizes innate drives or instincts and biological maturation. One of the earliest theories from this perspective was Freud's.

1. Sigmund Freud's _____ theory of personality emphasized _____ human drives, particularly the _____ and _____ drives.

2. What type of learning is at the heart of social development in Freud's view? When and in what social context do the most critical aspects of this learning take place?

Erik Erikson's theory is also a psychodynamic theory. Like some other theories influenced by Freud's thinking, it was expanded to include a larger age range and other types of drives. Today, Erikson's is the most influential developmental theory from this perspective.

3. What is a psychosocial stage in Erikson's theory? How does the resolution of each stage affect subsequent development?

4. List Erikson's stages. (See Table 12.1 on text page 453.)

   Stage 1

   Stage 2

   Stage 3

   Stage 4

   Stage 5

Stage 6

Stage 7

Stage 8

Other biological theories of development were strongly influenced by Darwinian concepts and by the ethologists who applied such thinking to the study of animal behavior.

5. How does John Bowlby illustrate the influence of ethology on developmental psychology? What evolutionary perspective does Melvin Konner offer?

Whereas the biological perspective emphasizes the similarities that all humans share as a result of evolution, the cultural perspective often focuses on cross-cultural differences. From this viewpoint, development occurs in a cultural context and that context must itself be understood in order to understand social development.

6. How might a theorist from the cultural approach challenge the universality of Erikson's eight stages?

7. What does Urie Bronfenbrenner's term *social ecology* mean?

8. Describe briefly each of the concentric rings in Bronfenbrenner's model, beginning with the innermost circle and moving outward. Provide a brief description next to each term. (See Figure 12.1 on text page 454.)

immediate environment

relationships among immediate environments

social context

cultural context

A third approach emphasizes the impact of cognitive growth on the individual's social thought and behavior.

9. Explain Piaget's argument that social development depends on cognitive development.

10. How did Vygotsky's developmental theory combine the cognitive and sociocultural perspectives?

11. Must we consider the three theoretical approaches to social development strictly as competitors? Explain.

Infancy: Using Caregivers as a Base for Growth
(pages 455–463)

> CONSIDER *these questions before you go on. They are designed to help you start thinking about this subject, not to test your knowledge.*

Does a caregiver "spoil" a child by being very responsive?

How do Western cultures compare to other cultures in terms of infant care?

Why do some infants cling to a security blanket?

> READ *this section of your text lightly. Then go back and read thoroughly, completing the Workout as you proceed.*

Human infants are born with a biological preparedness for identifying their caregivers, developing an emotional bond with them, and eliciting their help.

1. Describe the preferences and emotional signals that help infants to build bonds with their caregivers. What term is used to refer to such emotional bonds?

Attachment is observed not only in human infants. Harry Harlow's experimentation on attachment in rhesus monkeys is classic.

2. Discuss the method and results of Harry Harlow's experiment on infant monkeys' attachment to surrogate mothers. (See Figures 12.2 and 12.3 on text pages 456 and 457.)

The concept of attachment is central to John Bowlby's theory of development. Bowlby, like Harlow, developed his theory in the 1950s, but he focused on human infants.

3. What observations did Bowlby make about the behavior of attached children?

A strengthening of infants' attachments to their primary caregivers occurs at about 6 to 8 months of age. Because these attachment behaviors have been noted in a variety of cultures and in other species of mammals, they are thought to have a strong biological basis.

4. Describe some specific behaviors that indicate infants' attachment to primary caregivers.

5. Discuss the emergence of these behaviors from an evolutionary perspective.

Some means of measuring attachment is needed in order to study it objectively.

6. Name and describe the most commonly used method for measuring attachment.

7. How do the responses of securely attached infants differ from those of infants who are not securely attached? (Distinguish between infants with an avoidant attachment and those with an anxious resistant attachment.)

8. How common is each type of attachment in middle-class North American infants?

9. What are some limitations of the strange-situation test?

Psychologists have attempted to learn more about both the causes and the effects of attachment.

10. What behaviors in the caregiver are correlated with secure attachment?

11. How are these correlations interpreted by Bowlby and Ainsworth? What are some alternative interpretations?

12. How did research by Dymphna van den Boom support Ainsworth's and Bowlby's interpretation?

13. Summarize other evidence that the sensitivity and responsiveness of the caregiver affect attachment.

Many psychologists have suggested that the quality of an infant's early attachment has long-term consequences.

14. What is some evidence that early attachment influences psychological functioning in later childhood and young adulthood? Why must we be cautious about cause-effect conclusions?

Cross-cultural studies show large differences in the way infants are cared for. In contrast to other cultures, Western culture is notable for its relative lack of physical contact between infant and caregiver. For example, infants and young children in Western society typically sleep alone, whereas infants in a great many other cultures typically sleep with their mothers or other related adults.

15. According to a cross-cultural interview study, how did Mayan and American women differ in beliefs as well as in sleeping practices? What findings suggest that co-sleeping may be beneficial for children?

16. How might sleeping arrangements be related to attachment to an inanimate object?

17. Why have some psychologists chosen to study hunter-gatherer societies?

18. How are infants cared for in !Kung society? in Efe society? among the Aka?

19. Does indulgent infant care lead to spoiled or overly dependent children? Explain.

20. How does such early indulgence seem to be related to the size of extended families?

Childhood: *Learning to Play by and with the Rules*   (pages 463–476)

> CONSIDER *these questions before you go on. They are designed to help you start thinking about this subject, not to test your knowledge.*

Are children naturally selfish or naturally giving?

Is it better to be a firm, no-nonsense, no-explanations-given type of parent, or are other styles of discipline more effective?

What functions are served by children's play?

If you could design the ideal school, what would it be like?

In what ways do adults treat boys and girls differently? What are some of the consequences of this differential treatment?

> READ *this section of your text lightly. Then go back and read thoroughly, completing the Workout as you proceed.*

During childhood, powerful forces of socialization are at work. But the child is not a passive object of socialization. Rather, the child actively uses the resources of the social environment, including caregivers, peers, and others, to achieve socialization.

1. What kind of learning is referred to as socialization?

The text focuses on the child's socialization between the ages of about 1 and 12 years. During the earliest part of this period, most social interactions are with the child's caregivers. Even in this earliest period, researchers find the foundations of giving, helping, and caring.

2. Do very young children enjoy or resist giving? Support your answer with evidence.

3. How does the !Kung culture compare to ours in terms of the attention paid to children's giving?

4. Do children of this young age join in to help with adult tasks?

5. How might empathy be related to children's giving and helping? What evidence suggests that empathy begins in infancy?

6. Have securely attached children been found to be more giving and helpful to others?

Children not only develop prosocial behaviors such as giving but must also learn to deal with situations in which they *cannot* do what they want or must do something they would rather not do.

7. Discuss the role of social referencing in the child's development of self-restraint. Be sure to comment on the child's tendency to negotiate.

8. How are the child's temperament and attachment related to compliance?

9. Is there a sense in which guilt can be socially and personally constructive? When does the child begin to show a capacity for guilt?

One classic topic of socialization research has been parenting styles, particularly styles of parental discipline. Martin Hoffman and Diana Baumrind have each analyzed discipline and found that certain approaches are associated with more positive outcomes.

10. Label the following techniques of discipline identified by Hoffman.

_____ The use or threatened use of punishment and reward to control the child's behavior

_____ A form of verbal reasoning in which the parent leads the child to think about his or her actions and their consequences for others

_____ A style in which parents often unconsciously express disapproval of the child, not just of the undesirable behavior

11. Which technique does Hoffman favor? Why? Is there evidence to support his view? Is power assertion ever necessary?

12. Label the three discipline styles identified by Baumrind.

_____ Parents were the most tolerant of their children's disruptive behaviors and least likely to discipline them

_____ Parents were more concerned with helping the child to acquire and use principles of right and wrong than they were with pure obedience

_____ Parents wanted obedience for its own sake and often used power assertion to get it

13. What was Baumrind's main finding? How do her findings fit with Hoffman's categorization?

As you know, we must exercise caution when interpreting correlations between parents' disciplinary styles and children's behavior. No causal relationship is established simply by a correlation. More recent research has helped to reveal more about who is influencing whom.

14. Describe evidence that:

   a. children's behavior influences the parents' disciplinary style.

   b. parents' disciplinary style influences children's behavior.

Children are strongly oriented toward other children, and after the age of 4 or 5 they spend most of their waking hours with peers. Much of that time is spent in play, which serves development in a number of ways. Play occurs in comparable forms in every culture studied.

15. Four universal forms of play are:

   a.

   b.

   c.

   d.

Karl Groos contended that play can be understood in evolutionary terms.

16. Why do children (as well as the young of other mammalian species) play, according to Groos? What is some evidence supporting this view?

Play occurs in a cultural as well as an evolutionary context.

17. Describe evidence that play reflects the culture in which it occurs. How might it also help to shape that culture?

Piaget proposed that social play helps the child to better understand rules, social roles, and morality.

18. According to Piaget, how does play allow the child to develop the ability to reason about right and wrong?

19. Is play inherently free and spontaneous in Lev Vygotsky's view? Explain. What evidence supports Vygotsky's view?

Play among children of mixed ages appears to be especially valuable for children's development.

20. Describe some of the special qualities and advantages of age-mixed play.

21. How does the example of the Sudbury Valley School in Massachusetts suggest the educational value of age-mixed play?

In every culture studied, boys and girls differ, and so do their experiences of life. Different biology can explain some but not all of the disparities.

22. Distinguish between the terms *sex* and *gender*.

23. On average, how do boy and girl infants differ behaviorally?

Differential treatment of boys and girls by adults begins very early indeed. To some extent, this may reflect responsiveness to actual differences in the children, but it also stems in part from adult expectations based on gender.

24. List some examples and mention possible consequences of how adults respond differentially to boys and girls.

25. How is culture related to the differential treatment of boys and girls?

Children play a significant part in shaping their own gender-related behavior.

26. What is gender identity? How do children actively adapt to and assert their own gender identity?

Children reinforce gender distinction through their peer groups. Boys and girls interact more with members of their own gender. A preference for same-sex playmates is present even at age 3 but peaks between ages 8 and 11.

27. Why is the tendency toward gender segregation stronger in girls in early childhood but stronger in boys later in childhood?

Some have suggested that the peer groups of boys and girls are really different subcultures.

28. Compare the world of boys and the world of girls as described by some social scientists. How might this view exaggerate the typical differences?

Adolescence: Breaking Out of the Cocoon
(pages 476–485)

CONSIDER these questions before you go on. They are designed to help you start thinking about this subject, not to test your knowledge.

Is the classic image of the adolescent as a rebel really accurate?

What role do peers play in the lives of adolescents?

Is there still a double standard of sexuality for adolescent girls and boys?

Why are some adolescents so reckless or even delinquent?

What is the developmental basis of morality and of moral reasoning? What leads some young people to act out of extraordinary idealism?

READ this section of your text lightly. Then go back and read thoroughly, completing the Workout as you proceed.

Adolescence, a bridge between childhood and adulthood, begins at the onset of puberty and ends when a person is considered a full member of adult society. Developmental psychologists generally agree that adolescents actively move away from their childhood identities and toward independent adult identities, though most disavow Erikson's notion of an identity *crisis*.

1. Why is adolescence longer in our culture compared to earlier times and to other cultures?

2. Adolescence as a time of rebellion is a popularly accepted notion. In what sense do adolescents "rebel"? In what sense do they not? Is conflict linked more to age or to physical maturation?

As adolescents move toward independence from their parents, they become increasingly dependent upon their peers.

3. Present some evidence of this shift from parental to peer dependence. What does emphasis on the peer group promote?

Though adolescence may be more difficult and turbulent in Western than in non-Western cultures, it is not equally so for all individuals. But for those on one end of the spectrum, adolescence is marked by increased recklessness and delinquency, especially among young males.

4. What are some characteristics of adolescent cognition and motivation that have been noted as potential explanations for such behavior?

5. How does Terrie Moffitt explain adolescent recklessness and delinquency? What evidence does she present?

6. What alternative position is taken by Judith Harris, and how does her theory account for such risky behaviors as train surfing?

7. Following the lead of Wilson and Daly, argue for an evolutionary explanation of increased risk taking and violence among young males.

8. Are females also more violent on average in adolescence? Explain.

Idealism and increasing moral vision distinguish adolescence as well. The roots of morality lie in the ability to reason logically, according to Lawrence Kohlberg.

9. Briefly describe Kohlberg's research method. What aspect of people's responses was of greatest interest to Kohlberg?

10. In what sense do Kohlberg's five stages represent a true developmental progression, according to Kohlberg? How do the stages reflect a broadening social perspective? (See Table 12.2 on text page 481.)

11. What is the motivating force that pushes a person on to the next stage of moral reasoning? Does everyone eventually reach Stage 5? Explain.

12. Is moral reasoning necessarily related to moral behavior? Explain.

13. How did Daniel Hart and his colleagues approach the study of moral development? What has been found to promote exceptional moral commitment?

Sexuality is a topic that must be addressed in any full consideration of adolescence; after all, the beginning of adolescence coincides with the onset of puberty. With the physical changes that permit reproduction come powerful drives and emotions, as well as potentially troublesome behaviors. In modern cultures, a prolonged period of sexual maturity before adulthood is reached may contribute to problems associated with emerging sexual relationships. So may the attitudes that exist within those cultures.

14. How might cultural attitudes and messages lead to a greater incidence of early sexual intercourse and a higher rate of teen pregnancy?

15. Is there really a sexual double standard for girls and boys? Explain.

16. List some factors that may lead to the high frequency of date rape.

17. How would Robert Trivers explain the greater desire for uncommitted sex among males?

Though nature may have created certain tendencies toward sexual behavior that differ between males and females, those tendencies can be moderated by the social environment. For example, the restraint—or lack of it—on the part of one sex may help to determine the sexual strategy of the other sex. Patricia Draper and Henry Harpending suggest that childhood cues, such as the presence or absence of a caring father in the home, may incline individuals toward either restraint or promiscuity.

18. Explain the theory offered by Draper and Harpending, and comment on the evidence available for it.

Adulthood: Finding Satisfaction in Love and Work (pages 486–492)

CONSIDER these questions before you go on. They are designed to help you start thinking about this subject, not to test your knowledge.

What makes some marriages happy and others unhappy?

What contributes most to satisfaction in work?

How does becoming a parent affect a marriage?

What can make old age a happier time of life?

Do elderly people fear death more than others?

READ this section of your text lightly. Then go back and read thoroughly, completing the Workout as you proceed.

Love and work are the joint themes of adult development. Romance and marriage are found in all cultures studied, and psychologists have sought to understand the essentials of both.

1. List the characteristics that seem to be common both to romantic love and to infant attachment. Is the quality of attachment in infancy related to the quality of later romantic attachment?

In the study of love relationships, psychologists have asked why some marriages work while others do not.

2. What do studies of happily married couples reveal about them?

3. How do husbands and wives tend to differ in terms of attention to the relationship?

Parenthood can affect the marital satisfaction experienced by couples.

4. How is marital satisfaction affected by parenthood? Why? Who tends to be more affected—men or women?

5. Why is marital harmony particularly important during child-rearing years?

Working outside the home is a fact of life for most men and women in the United States, but it is a happier fact for some than for others.

6. What are some factors positively associated with job satisfaction? What term does sociologist Melvin Kohn apply to this set of job characteristics?

7. How does high occupational self-direction affect workers? their children? Were these effects dependent on salary level or job prestige?

Women who work outside the home often have two roles—their outside employment and their work at home. And they often feel torn between the two sets of obligations.

8. Among couples in which husband and wife both work outside the home, are household duties evenly divided? Explain your answer.

9. Where are husbands and wives happier—working at home or working out of the home? What might explain this?

Given current estimates of life expectancy, today's college student can reasonably hope to live well past retirement age—in fact, past the age of 80.

10. Old age is undeniably a period that involves loss, but is old age as bad as it seems to the young? Explain.

11. Label the theories of aging briefly described below.

_____ Elderly people gradually and voluntarily withdraw from the world around them into a more subjective, inner world.

_____ Elderly people prefer to remain involved in the world and are happier when they can remain so.

_____ Elderly people become more focused on the present than on preparing for the future as the "size" of that future decreases.

12. What observations fit well with Carstensen's socioemotional selectivity theory?

Death awaits everyone eventually, but with advancing age one grows ever closer to that point.

13. Do the elderly fear death more than people in other age groups? Explain.

14. Does everyone approach death in essentially the same way—by going through a sequence of stages, for example, or by reviewing his or her life? Support your answer.

Be sure to READ the Concluding Thoughts at the end of the chapter. Note important points in your Workout. Then consolidate your learning by answering the focus questions in the margins of the text.

After you have studied the chapter thoroughly, CHECK your understanding with the Self-Test that follows.

Self-Test 1

Multiple-Choice Questions

1. Freud's and Erikson's theories of development are similar in that they:
   a. both emphasize the importance of continued development in adulthood.
   b. both give sexuality a central role in development.
   c. both portray social development as involving drives.
   d. both propose that development occurs in stages that may take place in different orders in different individuals.

2. Bronfenbrenner uses the term *social ecology* to mean:
   a. the whole network of people as well as the social setting to which a developing person must adapt psychologically, which varies across cultures.
   b. those essential aspects of any social environment that underlie social development and that are the same across cultures.
   c. only those aspects of society that affect the developing child without the child actually coming into direct contact with them.
   d. the set of beliefs, values, and accepted ways of behaving that characterize the historically connected group of people to which the child and the child's family belong.

3. The willfulness of the 2-year-old is moderated in the third year of life by the gradual development of a capacity for:
   a. social referencing.
   b. guilt.
   c. negotiation.
   d. trust.

4. Mary Ainsworth's strange-situation test is used to:
   a. measure the developing child's ability to become involved in various kinds of play.
   b. promote the developing adolescent's resistance to peer pressure.
   c. enhance the developing child's ability to engage in moral reasoning.
   d. measure the developing infant's attachment to a person.

5. Cross-cultural research has shown that Western culture is atypical in that Western parents generally:
   a. require young children to sleep in a different room from adults.
   b. employ an authoritarian style of parenting.
   c. use power assertion to gain behavioral compliance from children.
   d. give in most readily to demands for attention from young children.

6. Martin Hoffman described one type of parental discipline in which parents use verbal reasoning to lead the child to think about his or her actions and their consequences. He called this type of discipline:
   a. authoritarian.
   b. permissive.
   c. induction.
   d. power assertion.

7. In the view of Lev Vygotsky, the most important function of play is that it:
   a. promotes spontaneity and creativity.
   b. provides a time of relaxation and release for children, who outside of play experience considerable pressure to learn and to become socialized.
   c. allows children to express deep, unconscious wishes and conflicts and thereby helps to alleviate emotional problems.
   d. gives children a context for learning about rules and social roles.

8. Which of the following is true of self-imposed gender segregation in children?
   a. Boys avoid girls more than the reverse throughout childhood.
   b. Girls avoid boys more than the reverse throughout childhood.
   c. Boys avoid girls more than the reverse in early childhood, but girls become the more avoidant gender later in childhood.
   d. Girls avoid boys more than the reverse in early childhood, but boys become the more avoidant gender later in childhood.

9. Studies show that adolescent rebellion is primarily directed against:
   a. school authorities rather than parents.
   b. peers rather than authority figures.
   c. ethical or political injustices in society rather than family matters.
   d. parental constraints on personal freedom rather than parental values.

10. Research suggests that there _____ a double standard of sexual behavior for boys and girls and that this may tend to _____ acts of sexual aggression.
    a. is still; contribute to
    b. is still; prevent
    c. is no longer; contribute to
    d. is no longer; prevent

11. The fact that newborns cry reflexively in response to other babies' crying has been suggested as evidence of the early roots of:
    a. social referencing.
    b. empathy.
    c. compliance.
    d. rebellion.

12. In his studies of moral development, Lawrence Kohlberg was mainly interested in:
    a. the decision someone reached about resolving a dilemma.
    b. the reasoning involved in reaching a decision about a dilemma.
    c. the action someone had taken in a real-life moral dilemma.
    d. the empathy people expressed for those involved in the dilemma.

13. Older workers generally have _____ job satisfaction compared to younger workers.
    a. equal
    b. lower
    c. higher
    d. more variable

14. Interviews with exceptionally morally committed young people show that they are primarily motivated by:
    a. a selfless sense of duty.
    b. abstract principles of right and wrong.
    c. positive aspects of their self-image.
    d. the desire for adult approval.

15. Carstensen's socioemotional selectivity theory of aging suggests that as people get older, they become increasingly focused on:
    a. their inner, subjective world.
    b. connecting in new ways with the world around them.
    c. death.
    d. the present.

Essay Questions

16. Discuss infant attachment in terms of its nature, causes, prerequisites, and results.

17. What qualities tend to distinguish happy marriages?

After you have assessed your understanding on the basis of Self-Test 1 and have tried to strengthen your preparation in any areas of weakness, GO ON to Self-Test 2.

Self-Test 2

Multiple-Choice Questions

1. In contrast to Freud, Erikson emphasizes:
  a. drives for sex and aggression.
  b. social drives.
  c. the biological basis for drives.
  d. early childhood experience.

2. In Harry Harlow's study of attachment in infant monkeys, attachment:
  a. was based purely on whichever surrogate "mother" provided nutrition.
  b. developed toward the wire "mother" but not the cloth "mother."
  c. developed toward the cloth "mother" but not the wire "mother."
  d. was based on whichever surrogate "mother" the infant was first exposed to.

3. Bowlby believes that infant attachment is based on:
  a. sociocultural learning.
  b. biological factors arising through natural selection.
  c. the earlier phenomenon of social referencing.
  d. a combination of reward and punishment from the mother or other caregiver.

4. Angela promptly comforts her infant son whenever he shows signs of distress. Research suggests that this is likely to:
  a. spoil the child.
  b. develop an unhealthy dependence in the child.
  c. promote secure attachment.
  d. promote insecure attachment.

5. Martin Hoffman uses the term *love withdrawal* to refer to a disciplinary style in which parents:
  a. use their superior strength or control of resources to induce the child to behave in ways they find acceptable.
  b. express disapproval of the child, not just of the child's specific unacceptable actions.
  c. use verbal reasoning to lead the child to think about his or her actions and the consequences of those actions.
  d. ignore or excuse their children's misbehavior without any attempt at correcting it.

6. Diana Baumrind found that nursery school children were most likely to show positive qualities if their parents applied a disciplinary style she called:
   a. authoritative.
   b. authoritarian.
   c. power assertion.
   d. permissive.

7. Karl Groos emphasized that play stems from:
   a. drives that lead the young of a species to practice skills required for survival and reproduction.
   b. the dictates of the cultural context to which each child must adapt himself or herself.
   c. the need for all cultures to refresh and advance themselves through the innovative play of youth.
   d. the social need for bonding with peers rather than family members of widely varying ages.

8. Which of the following is emphasized as a key element in the educational effectiveness of the Sudbury Valley School?
   a. age-mixed play
   b. a progressive age-based curriculum based on extensive research into the intellectual capabilities of children at various ages
   c. organized group activities tailored to each child's strengths and weaknesses, both intellectual and social
   d. more frequent formal evaluation than is found in most schools

9. Which of the following correctly describes a research finding about the ways that adults respond differently to boys and girls?
   a. They play more gently with infant girls than with infant boys.
   b. They talk more to infant girls than to infant boys.
   c. They offer help and comfort more often to girls than to boys.
   d. All of the above.

10. Draper and Harpending propose that the presence of a caring father in the home tends to lead to increased _____ in adolescence.
    a. sexual restraint
    b. promiscuity
    c. parental dependence
    d. gender differentiation

11. Romantic love has been likened to:
    a. a form of role play.
    b. a permissive style of parenting.
    c. attachment in infancy.
    d. cooperation in hunter-gatherer societies.

12. Researchers have found that in happy marriages:
    a. husband and wife highly value their independence.
    b. the couples argue much less than couples in unhappy marriages.
    c. husband and wife like each other as friends.
    d. the couples pull apart during hard times to avoid stressing the marriage.

13. Husbands are more likely than wives to:
    a. prefer their at-home work to their out-of-home work.
    b. report decreased marital satisfaction during childrearing years.
    c. notice their spouse's unspoken needs.
    d. prefer an indulgent parenting style.

14. Social referencing is especially important in the development of:
    a. helping behavior.
    b. creativity.
    c. restraint.
    d. romantic love.

15. Research suggests that life satisfaction in old age is _____ younger people would expect it to be.
    a. much lower than
    b. somewhat lower than
    c. about what
    d. higher than

Essay Questions

16. What is the major function of play, according to Lev Vygotsky? Is there evidence to support his view? Explain.

17. Discuss Lawrence Kohlberg's theory of the development of moral reasoning. Be sure to include in your answer the primary goal of the theory, Kohlberg's methodology, the basic tenets of the theory, and some criticisms of the theory.

Answers

Conceptions of Social Development

1. psychodynamic; universal; sexual; aggressive

Childhood: Learning to Play by and with the Rules

10. power assertion; induction; love withdrawal
12. permissive; authoritative; authoritarian
15. **a.** rough and tumble
    b. constructive
    c. sociodramatic
    d. formal games

Adulthood: Finding Satisfaction in Love and Work

11. disengagement; activity; socioemotional selectivity

Self-Test 1

1. **c.** Though they both emphasized inner drives, Freud focused on sexual and aggressive drives, and Erikson on a set of social drives. (pp. 451–452)

2. **a.** The social ecology includes **c**, which is the social context, and **d**, which is the cultural context. (p. 454)

3. **b.** (p. 466)

4. **d.** (p. 458)

5. **a.** This may be related to a research finding that blanket attachments are more common in North American infants than in infants of other cultures who generally sleep in the same room with a mother or other close adult relative. (p. 460)

6. **c.** Induction is also the style that Hoffman most favors. (p. 466)

7. **d.** (p. 470)

8. **d.** (p. 474)

9. **d.** (p. 477)

10. **a.** (p. 483)

11. **b.** (p. 465)

12. **b.** Kohlberg, whose work was influenced by that of Piaget, was interested in the development of the ability to *think* about moral situations. He was therefore most interested in the thought processes involved in reaching a conclusion, not the conclusion itself. (pp. 480–481)

13. **c.** (p. 491)

14. **c.** For example, they may see themselves as individuals who set a good example. (p. 482)

15. **d.** (p. 491)

16. Attachment is the emotional bond that an infant develops toward a primary caregiver. It is strongest between the ages of about 8 months and 3 years. The infant expresses distress when the object of attachment leaves, especially in an unfamiliar or frightening situation, and pleasure when he or she is nearby. The infant is more likely to explore an unfamiliar environment with the object of attachment present and looks to that person for reassurance in the presence of a stranger.

    John Bowlby, who originated research in this field, believed it to be based in evolution. Infants who behaved in an attached way were more likely to survive into adulthood and reproduce. Longitudinal research indicates that infants who consistently receive comfort and prompt responsive reactions when they cry are more likely to be securely attached. Early measures of attachment are correlated with positive outcomes later in childhood, such as greater confidence, problem-solving ability, and emotional health. The warmth and security of romantic attachment in adulthood may also be related to early attachment. Such findings do not show a causal role of attachment in producing such outcomes, however. (pp. 456–460)

17. Studies show that happily married people genuinely like each other, regarding their spouses as friends and confidants as well as marriage partners. They also appear to have an extraordinarily high commitment to the marriage, each individual being willing to give more than his or her share during rough periods in the relationship. In terms of communication patterns, happily married people are willing to listen to each other, show respect for the other partner's views, and focus on the present issue under discussion rather than have a hidden agenda of "winning" or bringing up old hurts. Partners in happy marriages also intersperse their communications, even in arguments, with positive comments and humor. (pp. 487–488)

Self-Test 2

1. **b.** (p. 452)

2. **c.** Harlow concluded that the contact comfort afforded by the cloth, but not the wire, "mother" was more important to attachment than feeding was. (p. 456)

3. **b.** (p. 457)

4. **c.** (p. 459)

5. **b.** (p. 467)

6. **a.** Be sure you can distinguish between authoritarian and authoritative parenting styles. Authoritar*ian* parents value control for its own sake and use a high degree of power assertion. Authoritat*ive* parents value good behavior more than control itself and prefer induction but will use power assertion when necessary. (p. 467)

7. **a.** (p. 469)

8. **a.** (pp. 471)

9. **d.** (p. 473)

10. **a.** (p. 484)

11. **c.** (p. 486)

12. **c.** (p. 487)

13. **a.** (p. 489)

14. **c.** (p. 466)

15. **d.** (p. 490)

16. Vygotsky, who generally emphasized the importance of the social world to development, felt that social play is critical to the socialization process. He argued that play is not the context in which children are most free and spontaneous, as popular belief would have it. Rather, play is a context in which children learn to govern their behavior according to rules of social behavior and according to the social roles they act out. A child playing the role of a robber in cops and robbers, for example, would be forced to think about what it means to be a robber—what behavior makes a person a robber, how a robber interacts with other people such as police, and so on. The child would also have to fit his or her behavior to that role as it is understood. This ability to assume roles later spills over into the child's nonplay activities, as the child begins to move into such social roles as student or junior gardener or pet caretaker. Research consistent with Vygotsky's position suggests that children actually do think about and enforce rules in their social play. Further, the amount of sociodramatic play children engage in is correlated with their social competence. (pp. 470–471)

17. Kohlberg recognized that moral development is at least in part the development of the ability to think logically about moral situations. He sought to understand this aspect of moral development by asking people what the protagonists of hypothetical moral dilemmas should do and why. His interest was not so much in the conclusions subjects reached but in the nature of the reasoning they used to reach those conclusions.

    On the basis of such research, Kohlberg proposed that there is an invariant sequence of stages through which moral development proceeds. Initially, an individual thinks only of himself or herself. In the fifth and highest stage, which is not attained by everyone, universal moral principles are the basis of judgment. Progression from the first to the fifth stage involves a growing inclusiveness of others in the social world. As the limitations of one stage become evident, the individual is drawn toward the next stage.

    Kohlberg's theory is not without critics. Some note that it is biased toward males, others that it is biased toward Western cultures. (pp. 480–481)

Chapter 13   Social Perception and Attitudes

READ *the introduction below before you read the chapter in the text.*

A major focus of social psychology is the study of the mental processes and systematic biases underlying perceptions of the social world, which includes ourselves as well as other people. Many social judgments depend on interpreting the causes of behavior. A decision about the causes of a behavior is called an *attribution.* Harold Kelley has developed a model of the logic involved in making attributions. Fritz Heider, a pioneer in this area, claimed that we have a natural tendency to attribute behavior to the characteristics of the person who is behaving, though we sometimes attribute behavior to the situation. Various factors, including culture and the identity of the person behaving, affect our tendency to make attributions to the person or to the situation. Biases toward personality or situational attributions, as well as a number of other biases in our social thinking, are more likely to occur if we engage in automatic processing than if we engage in controlled processing.

Just as we form schemas for trees, modes of transportation, and furniture, we form schemas—organized sets of information or beliefs—for people. The person schema you have for an individual helps you to interpret and organize new information about that individual, though it can also distort your perceptions of the person. This distortion often occurs because we are unduly influenced by first impressions, which may be superficial, deriving from physical appearance for example, or may simply be wrong. Stereotypes, which are schemas about groups of people, can distort our impressions of individual members of those groups even if we consciously combat the influence of cultural stereotypes in our thinking.

Our self-concepts and behavior are affected by other people's expectations of us, such that expectations can become self-fulfilling prophecies. In a variety of ways, we come to view ourselves by looking at what the social world around us seems to reflect back about us. Charles Cooley called this the looking-glass self. Our own active comparisons of ourselves to others also help to determine our self-concepts. The particular reference group to which we compare ourselves may affect how smart, how tall, or how talented we think we are. In Western cultures, people have a tendency to enhance their views of themselves in a number of ways—for example, seeing their successes as due to themselves and their failures as due to the situation. People in Eastern cultures are not similarly disposed. Individuals appear to have more than one self-concept, with different "selves" for different social roles. Social roles are more important to the creation of a self-concept in some cultures than in others.

Attitudes are beliefs or opinions that have an evaluative component. The attitudes we have toward objects, events, people, concepts, and so on serve several functions. Our most central attitudes, called *values*, are important elements of our self-concepts and can help to predict behavior. Cross-cultural research suggests that certain values cluster together in a universal pattern—the value wheel. Our attitudes can be shaped by the social groups with which we identify. The drive to reduce cognitive dissonance, the psychological discomfort that exists when there is disagreement among our beliefs, attitudes, and/or behaviors, can also have interesting effects on our attitudes. For example, if we freely perform some behavior contrary to our attitudes with no obvious incentive, we may change our attitudes to be more consistent with the behavior. We may also blame victims—victims of violence or illness, for example—for their own misfortune in order to preserve our belief that the world around us is just and fair. The formation of attitudes may involve virtually no thought (as in classical conditioning), minimal thought (as in the use of decision rules or heuristics), or systematic, logical thought. We are more likely to devote systematic, logical processing to matters that have high personal relevance to us.

LOOK *over the table of contents for this chapter in your textbook before you continue with your study.*

Notice that there are focus questions in the margins of the text for your use in studying the material. The following chart lists which Study Guide questions relate to which focus questions.

Focus Questions	Study Guide Questions
Perceiving and Evaluating Other People	
1–7	1–16
8–10	17–21
11–12	22–26
13	27–29
Perceiving and Evaluating the Self	
14–15	1–5
16–18	6–10
19–21	11–15
Attitudes: Beliefs Tinged with Emotion	
22–24	1–6
25	7–8
26–29	9–15
30–32	16–20
33–35	21–25

The Integrated Study Workout

Complete one section at a time.

Perceiving and Evaluating Other People
(pages 497–508)

CONSIDER these questions before you go on. They are designed to help you start thinking about this subject, not to test your knowledge.

If someone throws a tantrum, gives a lot of money to charity, or trips on the stairs, how do we decide what caused this behavior—is it the individual's personal characteristics, the situation, or something else?

Are our perceptions of other people unduly influenced by such factors as physical appearance?

How do our culture's stereotypes of certain groups—of women, blacks, students, or southerners, for example—affect the way people perceive individual members of those groups?

READ this section of your text lightly. Then go back and read thoroughly, completing the Workout as you proceed.

We are social creatures, dependent upon human community. Our cognitive capabilities are constantly being applied to the social world in which we find ourselves. We strive to understand such things as what other people want, how they're likely to behave, how we should or actually do relate to them, what our culture expects of us, and so on.

1. Define the term *social psychology*.

2. Briefly explain Fritz Heider's term *naïve psychologists*.

One area of investigation in social psychology is person perception—the ways we perceive, understand, and evaluate other people and ourselves.

3. In the area of person perception, what is meant by the term *bias*?

4. When are people most susceptible to the influences of social biases?

5. Why are social psychologists interested in the biases that affect social judgments?

Because behavior is observable and personality is not, we must decide what, if anything, a given behavior indicates about a person. The study of attributions—inferences about the causes of behavior—was pioneered by Fritz Heider.

6. What do we tend to remember later, a person's behavior or our attribution?

7. According to Heider, what is a major problem we face in making attributions?

Heider's work was elaborated upon by Harold Kelley, who produced a model of the logic that might be involved in the attribution process.

8. There are three types of information people would ideally take into account in making an attribution. Write three general questions that you might ask to obtain this information. (See Figure 13.1 on text page 499.)

   a.

   b.

   c.

9. For each of the examples below, indicate the kind of attribution that would logically be made on the basis of the information provided. (S = situational; PG = personality, general; PP = personality, particular; N = no basis for attribution)

   Attribution

   _____ a. Ruth is arguing with her mother, something she often does. Ruth rarely argues with other people, and other people rarely argue with Ruth's mother.

   _____ b. Cally has missed her bus home. She is usually a few minutes early for the bus.

   _____ c. Gene has criticized his friend for not trying hard enough in his classes, but the friend doesn't hear this from anyone else. Gene regularly criticizes this friend—and his sisters, and the president, and the janitor, and the clerk at the video store, and . . .

   _____ d. Richard almost always slows down and looks both ways before driving through a particular intersection, even when he has the green light. So do many other drivers.

Heider suggested that people give too much weight to personality factors and too little to the situation. This is called the person bias.

10. What is some evidence for the existence of the person bias?

11. Why is this bias sometimes called the fundamental attribution error? Is it really so fundamental? Explain.

12. What factors promote a person bias? a situation bias? How did an experiment demonstrate these influences?

13. Briefly describe a two-stage model of the attribution process.

14. Is the tendency toward the person bias equally likely across cultures? Support your answer.

15. The _____ bias is stronger and the _____ bias weaker when we make attributions about ourselves than when we make them about others. This difference is called the _____ .

16. Explain the knowledge-across-situations hypothesis, and describe an observation consistent with it. Now do the same for the visual-orientation hypothesis.

The organized set of information or beliefs that we have about a person can be thought of as a schema for that person. The schema we already have may influence our interpretation of the person's behavior and of new information we receive about the person.

17. Briefly describe the method and results of an experiment on student perceptions of a guest lecturer at MIT.

18. Why are first impressions often hard to change?

A person's appearance is often the first information we have about him or her. It may influence the construction of our initial schema of the person and thereby have undue influence on our perception of that person.

19. Describe and provide evidence for each of the following.

   a. attractiveness bias

   b. baby-face bias

20. How has Zebrowitz applied the baby-face bias to explain perceived psychological differences between the sexes?

21. Briefly put our bias toward infant facial features in an ethological and evolutionary context.

Preconceptions influence our evaluation not only of an individual person but also of whole groups of people.

22. A schema for a whole group of people is called a(n) _____ .

23. Distinguish among public, private, and implicit stereotypes.

24. How is priming used to reveal implicit stereotypes? What have such studies shown?

25. Can implicit stereotypes promote prejudiced actions and attributions even in people who appear not to hold conscious prejudices? Support your answer.

26. How is susceptibility to such influences related to automatic versus controlled processing?

What we believe and expect can affect the behavior of others as well as our own behavior, in a sense creating reality. And those powerful beliefs and expectations may be wrong.

27. What are self-fulfilling prophecies?

28. How did Rosenthal and Jacobson produce a classic demonstration of self-fulfilling prophecies in the classroom?

29. Describe evidence that gender stereotypes can also lead to self-fulfilling prophecies.

Perceiving and Evaluating the Self
(pages 508–517)

CONSIDER *these questions before you go on. They are designed to help you start thinking about this subject, not to test your knowledge.*

How do we arrive at a sense of who we are as individuals? Are we influenced by the ways others view us? Do we compare ourselves to others to see how we "measure up"?

How are our social roles related to our self-concepts? Was Shakespeare right when he wrote, "All the world's a stage, and all the men and women merely players"?

READ *this section of your text lightly. Then go back and read thoroughly, completing the Workout as you proceed.*

Unlike the members of most other species, we humans have a rich conceptual representation of ourselves. The roots of that representation are evident even in infancy.

1. Describe the rouge test and how it has been used to demonstrate species differences in self-recognition.

We are obviously not born with a self-concept, and we do not pluck one out of thin air. Instead, our views of ourselves arise at least in part from the social world around us.

2. Explain Charles Cooley's concept of the looking-glass self.

3. Summarize evidence suggesting that our self-concepts and behavior can be affected by others' evaluations of us. Also indicate the limitations of this type of influence.

William James suggested that each of us has not just one self-concept but many. This idea has been further developed by psychologists who stress the relationship between self-concept and social roles.

4. Describe weblike models of the self-concept in which self-perceived traits are associated with particular social roles. Show how such an idea might apply to your own self-concept. (See Figure 13.7 on text page 511.)

5. Does having multiple self-concepts associated with different roles add to psychological stress? Explain.

The self-concept is produced in part from the fact that we actively measure ourselves against others to determine how smart we are, how good-looking, how happy, how resourceful, and so on. This process is called social comparison.

6. Define the term *reference group*.

7. What evidence supports the role of the reference group in forming a self-concept?

8. How can our selection of a reference group affect our self-esteem? Support your answer with research findings. What reference group do you use when thinking of your athletic ability? of your academic ability? of your appearance?

Are you a child of Lake Wobegon? Apparently most of us see ourselves as above-average to such an extent that we create a statistical joke.

9. Present four possible explanations for the better-than-average phenomenon, and give evidence if available.

a.

b.

c.

d.

10. Briefly discuss the idea that the better-than-average and self-serving biases so common in Western culture are not universal.

Our social nature is reflected not only in the formation of the self-concept but in its content.

11. Distinguish between personal identity and social identity.

12. How flexible are we in thinking of ourselves in terms of both personal and social identities? Why might this be adaptive?

13. How could the success of a group with which we identify either boost or lower our self-esteem?

14. Do people extend to their groups the types of attributional biases that favor themselves as individuals?

15. Explain Triandis's distinction between individualist and collectivist cultures. Discuss the costs and benefits of the two perspectives. How does this difference in cultural perspective relate to people's self-descriptions?

Attitudes: Beliefs Tinged with Emotion
(pages 517–530)

CONSIDER these questions before you go on. They are designed to help you start thinking about this subject, not to test your knowledge.

What are attitudes? Why and how do we form them?

Are our attitudes influenced by the attitudes of groups that we want to think well of us, such as fraternity brothers, fellow English majors, or people in the photography club?

If you don't really like someone but you do him or her a favor anyway, could doing so change your attitude toward that person?

How well can we predict someone's behavior by knowing his or her attitudes?

How are our perceptions of people colored by misfortunes they have suffered? For example, do we view rape victims differently because they have been raped? or cancer victims differently because they have developed cancer?

READ this section of your text lightly. Then go back and read thoroughly, completing the Workout as you proceed.

The study of attitudes is of central importance in social psychology because attitudes tie individuals to the whole social world. One can have attitudes toward birthday parties, police, justice, the man at the corner market, aerobic dance, fruitcake, and so on, ad infinitum.

1. Define the term *attitude*.

2. Name the function of the attitude described in each case below.

_____ **a.** Attitudes can serve to ally us with a particular group. If Helen wants an environmentalist group to think well of her, she may be quick to mention her aversion to nonrecyclable materials.

_____ **b.** We may adopt an attitude because it provides a sense of consistency or helps us to feel better about ourselves or to feel less anxious or upset. If Sam is told by an insensitive kindergarten teacher that he has no sense of rhythm, he may develop a negative attitude toward music or dance.

_____ **c.** An attitude toward some particular object can help to determine our behavior toward that object. If Josh has a negative attitude toward boxing, he doesn't need to question whether he should spend money for tickets to a boxing match.

_____ **d.** Attitudes can help us to define who we are and to give meaning to our lives. If Roberta has a strong sense of herself as an actively involved citizen, her attitude toward voting is likely to be strongly positive.

Our most central attitudes—the general, relatively abstract attitudes that pertain to our sense of right and wrong and to our personal and societal goals—are called values. Values form an important part of the self-concept.

3. How did Shalom Schwartz come to the conclusion that values are organized in a pattern that is universal? Describe that pattern.

4. How did he explain the universality of the value wheel? What two dimensions seem to underlie the value wheel?

5. How does the importance assigned to particular value types differ cross-culturally?

6. What evidence suggests that the values people hold can help to predict their behavior?

Social groups play an important part in shaping and maintaining our attitudes.

7. Why might people tend to have attitudes similar to those of the people with whom they live or interact?

8. Describe the method and findings of the Bennington College study and its follow-ups.

We all have attitudes about many, many things. Sometimes our attitudes and beliefs fit harmoniously with one another and with our behavior—but sometimes they do not.

9. Define the term *cognitive dissonance*, and state the fundamental tenet of Leon Festinger's theory of cognitive dissonance. Is dissonance reduction always adaptive?

10. Describe research evidence showing that people sometimes avoid dissonant information.

11. Do people usually feel more confident of a decision just before or just after they have made it? Why?

12. What is the insufficient-justification effect? Give an example.

13. Describe three conditions that promote the insufficient-justification effect.

Sometimes we use attitudes as a kind of psychological shield against the uncertainty and risk of life. Unfortunately, this can lead us to unintentionally "justify" injustice.

14. What is the just-world bias?

15. How can the just-world bias lead to blaming the victim? Give two examples.

When social scientists first began to study attitudes, they assumed that attitudes would predict behavior. Early research profoundly challenged this assumption, but later research has shown that there are many cases in which attitudes *are* related to behavior.

16. Were attitudes toward cheating correlated with cheating behavior in Corey's classic study? Explain.

The question asked by social psychologists these days is not *whether* attitudes and behavior are correlated but *when*—that is, under what conditions.

17. Briefly describe evidence showing that attitude-behavior correlations are stronger when people are reminded of their attitudes shortly before taking action.

18. When are attitude-behavior relationships strongest, according to Russell Fazio? What is his reasoning?

Another complication in the attitude-behavior relationship is that attitudes are, of course, not the only thoughts involved in the decision to behave in a certain way.

19. According to Ajzen's theory of planned behavior, the conscious intention to behave in a particular way depends on three things:

   a. one's _____ , which is one's desire to act in a certain way;

   b. _____ , defined as one's beliefs about what others who are important at the moment might think; and

   c. _____ , one's sense of being able or not able to carry out the action.

20. According to Ajzen's model, which of the three types of thoughts has the greatest impact on a given behavioral decision? Does research support his view?

Thought is not only important to applying attitudes; it can also be an important factor in the formation of attitudes—but not always. Sometimes little or no thought is required.

21. Explain how classical conditioning can be regarded as an automatic attitude-formation system.

22. How do advertisers exploit classical conditioning to shape our attitudes? Does research suggest that such attitude manipulation can be effective?

23. What evidence suggests that no conscious thought is required in forming attitudes through classical conditioning?

In other cases, a deliberate thought is involved in forming an attitude.

24. How do heuristics, or decision rules, provide a way to evaluate information and form an attitude with minimal thought? Give three examples of such decision rules.

Systematic, logical thought is used in the development of some attitudes.

25. When are we most likely to engage in such systematic thought in attitude formation, according to the elaboration likelihood model? What evidence supports this view? (See Figure 13.12 on text page 528.)

Be sure to READ the Concluding Thoughts at the end of the chapter. Note important points in your Workout. Then consolidate your learning by answering the focus questions in the margins of the text.

After you have studied the chapter thoroughly, CHECK your understanding with the Self-Test that follows.

Self-Test 1

Multiple-Choice Questions

1. If we have an organized set of information or beliefs about someone, we have a(n):
   a. stereotype.   c. attribution.
   b. value wheel.   d. schema.

2. According to Harold Kelley, if John regularly feels happy in situation A and if most other people also feel happy in situation A, then John's happiness in situation A will be attributed to:
   a. general aspects of John's personality.
   b. situation A.
   c. the combination of John's personality and this particular situation.
   d. chance.

3. Social psychologists have found that first impressions:
   a. are actually easy to change because they are often sketchy.
   b. resist change because subsequent information is interpreted to be consistent with the existing view.
   c. have a lasting effect only if confirmed by later independent judgments.
   d. are easily changed if they are positive but not if they are negative.

4. When we watch someone carry out an action, we are looking more at the person than at the environment; but when we ourselves carry out an action, we see the environment, not ourselves. This point has been used as a possible explanation of:
   a. the self-effacing bias.
   b. the actor-observer discrepancy.
   c. multiple selves.
   d. knowledge across situations.

5. Research has shown that a person bias in making attributions is:
   a. so strong that it is virtually universal.
   b. more likely if the explicit task focuses on personality rather than situational assessment.
   c. more likely if subjects have little opportunity or motivation to go beyond automatic mental processes.
   d. both b and c.

6. Priming has been used to reveal the impact of:
   a. public stereotypes.
   b. private stereotypes.
   c. implicit stereotypes.
   d. explicit stereotypes.

7. In an experiment, subjects who can see themselves in a mirror are more likely to:
   a. behave in accordance with their attitudes.
   b. express their stereotypes openly.
   c. change their attitudes.
   d. justify their attitudes.

8. The idea that we form the self-concept by considering the ways other people react to us is referred to as:
   a. social identity.   c. social comparison.
   b. social adjustment.   d. the looking-glass self.

9. People in Eastern cultures are more likely than those in Western cultures to:
   a. describe themselves in terms of their social roles and groups.
   b. exhibit a self-serving attributional bias.
   c. have a just-world bias.
   d. make the fundamental attribution error.

10. Values are a subcategory of:
    a. attributions.
    c. personality traits.
    b. attitudes.
    d. none of the above.

11. A person with a firm belief that he or she is dominant will tend to project the characteristic of dominance more strongly if:
    a. another person perceives him or her as dominant.
    b. another person perceives him or her as submissive.
    c. that belief is implicit.
    d. that trait goes against social norms.

12. The common desire for cognitive consistency can lead us to:
    a. avoid information that would conflict.
    b. firm up an attitude.
    c. change an attitude.
    d. do all of the above.

13. The Bennington College study demonstrated that:
    a. social groups play an important part in changing attitudes.
    b. social groups play little part in changing attitudes.
    c. cognitive dissonance plays an important part in changing attitudes.
    d. cognitive dissonance plays little part in changing attitudes.

14. People tend to use automatic or superficial approaches to attitude construction *except* when messages have:
    a. high personal relevance.
    b. high complexity.
    c. the voice of authority behind them.
    d. vivid arguments.

15. In an early study of the relationship between attitudes and behavior, it was found that college students:
    a. with strong anticheating attitudes were just as likely to cheat as those with weak anticheating attitudes.
    b. with strong anticheating attitudes were much less likely to cheat than those with weak anticheating attitudes.

   c. who cheated were likely to change their attitudes to be less negative toward cheating.
   d. who did not cheat were likely to believe that other students were also unlikely to cheat.

Essay Questions

16. How is a person's self-concept affected by other people's perceptions and expectations? Cite research evidence to support your answer.

17. Discuss Icek Ajzen's theory of planned behavior.

After you have assessed your understanding on the basis of Self-Test 1 and have tried to strengthen your preparation in any areas of weakness, GO ON to Self-Test 2.

Self-Test 2

Multiple-Choice Questions

1. An inference about the cause of a particular behavior is called a(n):
   a. impression.
   b. attribution.
   c. schema.
   d. expectation.

2. Suppose subjects in an experiment are given evidence regarding either a crime of negligence or a crime of deliberate deception. Baby-faced defendants would be more likely than mature-faced defendants to be found:
   a. innocent of either charge.
   b. innocent, but only for a crime of deliberate deception.
   c. guilty of a crime of negligence but not a crime of deliberate deception.
   d. guilty of a crime of deliberate deception but not a crime of negligence.

3. People are more likely to judge their close friends' behavior as dependent on the situation than they are to judge a stranger's behavior as dependent on the situation. This supports the _____ an explanation of the _____ .
   a. visual-orientation hypothesis; fundamental attribution error
   b. visual-orientation hypothesis; situation bias
   c. knowledge-across-situations hypothesis; actor-observer discrepancy
   d. knowledge-across-situations hypothesis; effects of prior information

4. Adults in India were _____ likely than American adults to attribute behaviors to personality, a finding that _____ the fundamental attribution error.
   a. more; supports
   b. more; challenges
   c. less; supports
   d. less; challenges

5. The big-fish-in-a-little-pond effect illustrates the importance of _____ to _____ .
   a. one's reference group; self-esteem
   b. one's reference group; attitude formation
   c. self-enhancing biases; self-esteem
   d. self-enhancing biases; attitude formation

6. The just-world bias may help to explain:
   a. the influence of social norms.
   b. the better-than-average effect.
   c. the use of reference groups in attitude formation.
   d. blaming the victim.

7. By placing a dot of rouge on children's or animals' faces before they look in a mirror, researchers have found that:
   a. only humans recognize themselves.
   b. only humans and great apes, such as chimpanzees, recognize themselves.
   c. most vertebrates, including cats and dogs, recognize themselves.
   d. most species that exhibit some type of social organization recognize themselves.

8. Which of the following messages to children has been shown experimentally to produce the greatest improvements in math performance?
   a. telling the children why math is important
   b. telling the children they should try to become good at math
   c. telling the children they are good at math
   d. telling the children they should try to do their best in everything

9. Collectivist cultures generally have _____ conflict within groups and _____ conflict between groups.
   a. less; less
   b. less; more
   c. more; more
   d. more; less

10. According to research based on Ajzen's theory of planned behavior, the most influential determinant of behavior:
    a. is a person's attitude.
    b. is the subjective norm.
    c. is an individual's perceived control.
    d. can be any of the above, depending on various factors.

11. The role of attitudes in guiding behavior with respect to the object of the attitude is referred to as the _____ function.
    a. defensive
    b. social-adjustive
    c. utilitarian
    d. value-expressive

12. Systematic, logical analysis of the message content occurs in:
    a. classical conditioning.
    b. the application of heuristics.
    c. both a and b.
    d. neither a nor b.

13. An awareness of disagreement or lack of harmony among the attitudes or beliefs in one's mind creates psychological discomfort. This condition is called:
    a. the fundamental attribution error.
    b. cognitive distinctiveness.
    c. cognitive dissonance.
    d. cognitive bias.

14. If a person is induced to behave in a way that is contrary to his or her attitude, and lacks any obvious way to justify that behavior, the person's attitude will tend to:
    a. move in a direction consistent with the behavior.
    b. become strengthened in the direction of the original attitude.
    c. remain unchanged because of the conflict between thought and behavior.
    d. become neutralized so that it is neither positive nor negative.

15. Milton Rokeach found that he could predict people's _____ by asking them to rank-order their _____ .
    a. attitudes; social roles
    b. attitudes; personality traits
    c. behavior; values
    d. behavior; personality traits

Essay Questions

16. Discuss self-enhancing and self-effacing biases in the context of culture.

17. Create an everyday scenario in which a person bias in attribution is extremely likely. Be certain to point out three factors in your scenario that would tend to produce this bias.

Answers

Perceiving and Evaluating Other People

9. a. PP, b. N, c. PG, d. S
15. situation; person; actor-observer discrepancy
22. stereotype

Attitudes: Beliefs Tinged with Emotion

2. a. social adjustive
   b. defensive
   c. utilitarian
   d. value expressive
19. a. attitude
    b. subjective norm
    c. perceived control

Self-Test 1

1. d. (p. 503)
2. b. (p. 499)
3. b. (p. 503)
4. b. (p. 502)

5. **d.** If the task focuses on the situation and offers little chance or reason to use controlled processing, a situation bias is shown. (p. 500)

6. **c.** Implicit stereotypes can affect automatic processing even in people who consciously reject those stereotypes. (p. 506)

7. **a.** (p. 525)

8. **d.** In this case, the "mirror" is the social world and we come to see ourselves in the image that it seems to reflect back to us. (p. 509)

9. **a.** In fact, people in Eastern cultures are *less* likely to do **b** or **d**. (p. 516)

10. **b.** (p. 517)

11. **b.** (p. 510)

12. **d.** (pp. 520–522)

13. **a.** At least partly because the Bennington College students continued to have a liberal reference group after college, their liberal attitudes persisted. (pp. 519–520)

14. **a.** (p. 528)

15. **a.** (p. 525)

16. One way in which the social world influences the self-concept is through the expectations other people have of us. Someone's beliefs about us can affect his or her behavior toward us, which can affect how we see ourselves and how we behave—in other words, it can lead to a self-fulfilling prophecy. This is one example of the "looking-glass self" in operation.

    In Rosenthal and Jacobson's study, elementary school teachers were told that a group of students were about to undergo an intellectual growth spurt when in reality these children were just randomly selected. Several months later, these children showed superior gains in academic performance and IQ. Further research showed that the teachers' expectations caused them to act differently toward the children, by praising their work more often or giving them more challenging assignments, for example. This different treatment may well have caused the children to regard themselves more positively and to act in ways consistent with their improved self-concept.

    The ways that other people describe us are also a means by which the social world reflects to us who we are. Children told that they are neat or that they are good at math appear to modify their self-concepts accordingly and then behave in ways that fit those beliefs about themselves. (pp. 507–510)

17. Ajzen pointed out that a person's intentional behaviors depend in part, but not entirely, on the person's attitudes, that is, on their desire to behave that way or not to. Other kinds of thoughts and judgments also enter into the decision about how to act. Specifically, Ajzen theorized that the decision about how to behave depends also on (1) the subjective norm, which is the person's belief about what other people who are important at the moment would think about a given action, and (2) perceived control, which is the person's sense of being able or not able to carry out the action. For example, suppose a high school student comes from a family in which adults routinely choose professions such as medicine or the law. The student might feel very negative about the idea of such a career and very positive about a career in forestry, might feel fully capable of success in forestry, and yet not move toward the preferred occupation because of the subjective norm. Any of the three factors may predominate in determining behavior depending on a host of factors. (p. 526)

Self-Test 2

1. **b.** (p. 498)

2. **b.** Because people tend to perceive baby-faced individuals as more naive, honest, helpless, kind, and warm than mature-faced individuals of the same age, it is harder to believe them guilty of a crime of deliberate deception. (p. 504)

3. **c.** (p. 502)

4. **d.** (pp. 500, 501)

5. **a.** (p. 512)

6. **d.** Blaming victims for whatever has happened to them helps to avoid a belief that would be dissonant with the belief in a just world. (p. 524)

7. **b.** (pp. 508–509)

8. **c.** When children are led to believe that they are good at math, they apparently incorporate that belief into their self-concept. They expect more of themselves and try to live up to those expectations. (pp. 509–510)

9. **b.** (p. 516)

10. **d.** (p. 526)

11. **c.** (p. 517)

12. **d.** (pp. 527–528)

13. **c.** (p. 520)

14. **a.** This is termed the insufficient-justification effect. (p. 522)

15. c. (p. 519)

16. People often demonstrate a bias in their perceptions of themselves. However, the tendency depends at least in part on culture. People in North America tend to show a self-enhancing bias, seeing themselves in a rather rosy, positive light. One example is the better-than-average bias, in which *most* people see themselves as above average—a statistical impossibility. Another is the self-serving attributional bias, in which people see their successes as due to themselves and their failures as due to the situation. This tendency is so prevalent that failure to demonstrate it is considered by some psychologists a sign of depression. Japanese subjects, in contrast, seem to be more realistic or even biased in the opposite direction at times. Japanese students showed no sign of the better-than-average bias when evaluating their intellectual abilities relative to their classmates. When administered the Twenty Statements Test, Japanese students gave twice as many negative as positive self-statements, the reverse of what American students in the study did. (pp. 512–514)

17. In her hometown of Pittsburgh, Pennsylvania, Sandra is looking for someone from whom she might borrow some change for bus fare. She is feeling tired and stressed after being in an unfamiliar part of town and having her ride home fail to show up. She can see the bus at a red light two blocks away. While looking for someone on the street who seems approachable, she sees a woman grab a shopping bag from an old man's hand and rush off. Sandra later tells her sister that she saw a thief steal a shopping bag from an old man. What Sandra didn't see was that the bag was originally in the woman's possession and the man had quietly taken it when she set it down to rummage for her car keys in her purse. Sandra has incorrectly attributed the bag-grabbing incident to the woman's dishonesty when in fact it was due to the situation she was in.

The tendency to make a person attribution in this scenario was increased by (a) the fact that Sandra is an American and the person bias is stronger in that culture than in some other cultures; (b) the fact that the woman was a stranger to her rather than a friend whom she had observed in a number of situations; and (c) the fact that Sandra made a quick and automatic judgment about the situation given her fatigue, the time pressure she was under, and the incident's relative unimportance to her. (A fourth factor would be that her task—finding someone who looked as if he or she might help her out—already had her oriented to assessing people.) (pp. 498–501)

Chapter 14   Social Influences on Behavior

READ *the introduction below before you read the chapter in the text.*

Emotions and emotional expressions play a fundamental role in social life. A simple smile, for example, serves as a social signal. Such social signals can help to communicate the psychological state or desires of one individual to others and help them to respond in ways that lead to greater social binding, behavioral coordination, and mutual beneficence. Emotions that concern our relationships—such as guilt or embarrassment—can motivate useful social behaviors.

As participants in a social world, we are all influenced by a host of social pressures that may take a variety of forms—such as direct or indirect requests, commands, expectations, and so on. These pressures need not be real, only perceived, in order to affect us. Kurt Lewin, a pioneer in this area of social psychology, viewed these pressures as a field of forces that act together to push or pull individuals in various directions. His field theory is a foundation for Bibb Latané's social impact theory, which specifies the variables that can increase or decrease the impact of social forces.

Our behavior can also be affected by the mere presence of other people. In social facilitation, performance with onlookers present is superior to performance when alone. In social interference, performance suffers when others are present. Robert Zajonc has explained both phenomena in terms of the effects of arousal on the performance of different kinds of tasks.

Our interest in the judgments other people make about us can affect us in a number of ways. For example, we try to project a certain view of ourselves to others, a tendency psychologists call impression management. People high in a personality characteristic called self-monitoring are especially concerned with impression management.

Why do people conform? Solomon Asch expected to find that people would not conform to the judgment of a majority when a simple perceptual task was involved. To his surprise, he found that people often *did* conform to the opinion expressed by the majority—even if they knew it was wrong. Conformity can help to explain a commonly observed phenomenon in which people fail to help someone in apparent trouble if there are multiple witnesses.

Many decisions are the product not of individuals but of groups working together. Group discussion can sometimes polarize attitudes; if people who agree on some matter get together to discuss it, they will generally emerge with a more extreme version of their original opinion. Groupthink is a faulty mode of thinking that may result when members of a cohesive group place unanimity above the realistic appraisal of alternatives.

Social psychologists have found that people have a general tendency to comply with requests, although they can be more or less compliant depending on a number of factors. Certain techniques can induce greater compliance and are sometimes exploited by people whose job it is to persuade us to behave in certain ways, such as to buy a given product.

People may be particularly likely to comply when the request is perceived as an order from an authority. A classic series of experiments by Stanley Milgram revealed that ordinary people will under some circumstances obey orders that they consider wrong, even if they believe another person will be seriously harmed as a result. Some theorists have applied these experimental results to real-world situations such as the Nazi Holocaust. The ethics of the experiments themselves have, however, been questioned.

Social dilemmas pit self-interest against the good of the group. Cooperation to promote the good of the group is more likely if there is an opportunity to establish reciprocity or if people share a group identity. Setting up superordinate goals that unite groups in a common pursuit can reduce conflict and increase cooperation.

LOOK *over the table of contents for this chapter in your textbook before you continue with your study.*

Notice that there are focus questions in the margins of the text for your use in studying the material. The following chart lists which Study Guide questions relate to which focus questions.

Focus Questions	Study Guide Questions

Emotions as Foundations for Social Behavior
| 1–5 | 1–4 |
| 6–8 | 5–9 |

Social Pressure: How Our Concern for Others' Judgments Affects Our Actions
9–12	1–10
13–16	11–18
17–21	19–24
22–24	25–28

Influence of Others' Requests
| 25–27 | 1–4 |
| 28–31 | 5–9 |

To Cooperate or Not: The Dilemma of Social Life
32–36	1–5
37–39	6–8
40–42	9–13

The Integrated Study Workout

Complete one section at a time.

Emotions as Foundations for Social Behavior
(pages 533–539)

CONSIDER these questions before you go on. They are designed to help you start thinking about this subject, not to test your knowledge.

Can emotion be contagious? Does laughter or anger really tend to spread among people in a group?

Do unpleasant emotions such as guilt or embarrassment nevertheless have social value?

When do people experience pride? When is it "safe" to express one's pride?

READ this section of your text lightly. Then go back and read thoroughly, completing the Workout as you proceed.

A social species such as ours has a number of requirements: socially binding drives to draw people together; behavioral coordination; and, most fundamentally, mutual beneficence, which means that group members help one another more than they harm one

another. Emotions play an important part in helping people come together and get along with each other.

1. Defend this statement: "Emotions are foundations for social behavior."

2. How can someone's emotional expressions help to promote that individual's welfare within the group? Can those emotional expressions promote the welfare of others? Explain.

3. Differentiate between the smile of greeting and the smile of happiness. Are greeting smiles social signals? What about smiles of happiness? Support your answer.

4. What is emotional contagion, and why is it valuable socially? How might it be related to the ability to lead others? Can it occur unconsciously?

Some emotions arise from self-consciousness. Though they may sometimes involve discomfort, they can help us to get along with others.

5. What are two primary means by which self-conscious emotions have been studied?

6. Explain the causes and social functions of the following self-conscious emotions, providing evidence for your statements.

   a. guilt

   b. shame

   c. embarrassment

7. When do we experience pride? How are we served by the *expression* of pride? By the *feeling* of pride?

8. Pride can be considered the opposite of
   _____ ; while pride increases
   _____ , its opposite emotion
   diminishes it.

9. Describe the sociometer theory of self-esteem, and give evidence to support it.

Social Pressure: How Our Concern for Others' Judgments Affects Our Actions (pages 539–551)

CONSIDER *these questions before you go on. They are designed to help you start thinking about this subject, not to test your knowledge.*

What kinds of social pressures might affect a person's decision to either go to medical school or become a high school biology teacher?

Can social pressures be studied through experiments?

How can people stand by and watch someone in trouble—someone apparently having a heart attack or being robbed, for example—without doing anything to help?

Can the opinions expressed by a majority cause people to say things that are contrary to their beliefs just so they will fit in? Can the majority cause them to change their minds about what is true?

What kinds of conditions can lead to poor group decision making? What can promote good group decision making?

READ *this section of your text lightly. Then go back and read thoroughly, completing the Workout as you proceed.*

The individual living in the midst of the social world is subject to a multitude of pressures from that world, some real and others imagined. We may feel pressure to be polite, to marry, to go into the family business, or to wear a certain style of clothing. The concept of social pressure figures in a number of theories.

1. State the basic ideas of Kurt Lewin's field theory.

Bibb Latané's social impact theory elaborates on Lewin's thinking.

2. What are three factors that affect the degree of social impact a person feels as a result of social pressure, according to Bibb Latané?

   a.

b.

c.

The results of Latané's research on stage fright were consistent with his theory.

3. Indicate whether each factor below produces an increase or a decrease in stage fright.

    _____ **a.** increased status of audience

    _____ **b** increased size of audience

    _____ **c.** increased number of performers on stage

4. Make up two original examples of situations in which Latané's theory would apply.

Our behavior can be powerfully affected by the presence of others who are observing and/or evaluating our performance.

5. Complete the following statements.

    a. _____ is the tendency to perform a task better in front of others than when alone.

    b. _____ is a decline in performance when others are present as compared to performance when alone.

6. How did Robert Zajonc relate the occurrence of social facilitation at some times and social interference at other times to the nature of the task? to arousal?

7. Present some evidence in support of Zajonc's view.

8. Explain how the presence of others might lead to increased arousal in humans. Provide supporting evidence.

9. How might a shift in attention be involved in social interference?

10. Explain how the concepts of challenge and threat are used in a recent modification of Zajonc's theory.

For a variety of reasons, we are interested in others' impressions of us, and we do not generally leave those impressions to chance. In fact, behavior can to some extent be regarded as performance.

11. Define *impression management*.

12. What metaphor did Erving Goffman use to characterize impression management? In what sense might his analogy be misleading? What alternative metaphor is offered in the text?

Our concern for impression management varies depending on the audience.

13. Which types of "audiences" lead us to engage in more impression management? Why?

Impression management also varies across individuals and cultures.

14. How is the personality dimension of shyness related to impression management?

15. The personality dimension called _____ has to do with the degree to which people project a varied impression of themselves as they go from one audience to another. _____ scrutinize themselves, evaluating how they look to the current audience and adjusting accordingly. _____ are less vigilant, being more consistent across different audiences.

16. What kinds of questions are asked in Mark Snyder's test of self-monitoring?

17. How do high and low self-monitors differ in terms of their social lives and preferences?

18. Briefly discuss differences between Eastern and Western cultures in regard to impression management.

How are people who are asked to express a view influenced by the views expressed by others around them? Does the majority opinion alter what people believe? Or does it change only what they say? These are some of the questions addressed in research on social conformity.

19. Distinguish between informational and normative influences on conformity.

20. Briefly describe the basic procedure and results of Solomon Asch's conformity studies.

21. How did Asch test the relative importance of informational and normative influences in his studies, and what did he find? Be sure to mention the variable of task difficulty considered in later studies.

In Asch's basic research, the confederates were unanimous in giving the wrong answer. Other experiments have examined the influence of a minority opinion.

22. What happens to conformity if one of the confederates disagrees with the rest? Does this also occur if the dissenting confederate simply gives a different wrong answer?

23. Is the impact of a minority opinion due to its effect on normative or informational influences? Explain.

24. If you were the victim of an accident, would you be more likely to receive help if there were one witness or more than one? Why? Support your answer.

Group discussions, such as those that take place in creating a new product's marketing plan, in a school committee on campus crime, or in a congressional task force, also involve the influence of social pressure. A well-documented phenomenon in group discussion is the polarization of attitudes.

25. Define *group polarization*. Give an example of group polarization from research. How can it have important consequences in everyday life?

26. How is group polarization explained in terms of informational and normative influences? (Be sure to name and describe three specific hypotheses that concern normative influences.)

Depending on a number of factors, groups can produce decisions that are better or worse than those made by individuals. Irving Janis explored causes of bad group decisions by studying some notorious government decisions, such as those involved in the Bay of Pigs invasion and the Watergate burglary and cover-up.

27. Explain Janis's concept of groupthink, and present evidence supporting his view. When is the tendency toward groupthink strongest?

28. List some factors that tend to promote better group decisions.

Influence of Others' Requests   (pages 551–559)

> *CONSIDER these questions before you go on. They are designed to help you start thinking about this subject, not to test your knowledge.*

How can salespeople sometimes manipulate us into buying things that we don't want or need?

Why do people still obey the orders of authorities when they believe those orders to be wrong, even unethical? What factors help people to resist obeying such orders?

> *READ this section of your text lightly. Then go back and read thoroughly, completing the Workout as you proceed.*

Both research and everyday experience reveal that most people have a tendency to comply with direct requests. In fact, they seem to need a good excuse before they feel free to refuse. As you know, people are motivated to reduce cognitive dissonance, the discomfort experienced when one's beliefs clash with one another or with one's behavior. Robert Cialdini has shown that cognitive dissonance is the basis for some techniques that people use to increase compliance to their requests.

1. For each of the following, give a general description, an example, and an explanation for its effectiveness.

  a. Four-walls technique

b. Foot-in-the-door technique

Another basis for gaining compliance is the reciprocity norm.

2. Describe the reciprocity norm and give an example of how it can be exploited to gain compliance.

3. What happens if the foot-in-the-door technique and pregiving are combined? What does this tell us about the means by which each technique works?

4. What is psychological reactance? Describe two ways in which an understanding of this tendency can help us to gain compliance.

Obedience is defined as compliance with a request that is perceived as an order from an authority figure or leader. Though obedience is often positively valued as necessary to social order, it can in some cases lead to nightmarish behavior, such as that exhibited in the Nazi Holocaust. Stanley Milgram carried out a classic study of obedience—one that had disturbing results.

5. Describe the method and result of Milgram's study.

6. How consistent is this finding? Is it dependent on using a particular type of subject? Explain.

7. State five factors that are important in explaining the obedience found in experiments such as Milgram's. Where possible, indicate evidence that supports these explanations.

a.

b.

c.

d.

e.

8. Summarize the *ethical* criticisms of Milgram's obedience studies. Are these criticisms valid? Support your answer.

9. Summarize criticisms of Milgram's obedience studies that are based on their dissimilarity to real-world situations. Do you think these criticisms are valid?

To Cooperate or Not: The Dilemma of Social Life (pages 559–567)

> CONSIDER these questions before you go on. They are designed to help you start thinking about this subject, not to test your knowledge.

What causes conflict between groups of people?

What makes people work together?

> READ this section of your text lightly. Then go back and read thoroughly, completing the Workout as you proceed.

People have a variety of goals in life. Sometimes their goals are shared and other times their goals conflict.

1. What are social dilemmas? How might such dilemmas be a matter of human survival? Give three examples of social dilemmas.

Psychologists have often studied people's choices in social dilemmas through prisoner's dilemma games.

2. Explain the basic prisoner's dilemma game as played in a psychology laboratory. How do players in a one-shot game tend to play if they are anonymous, unable to converse, and motivated to maximize their personal gain? Does this serve them well? Explain.

3. Why are players more likely to cooperate in an iterative (repeated) prisoner's dilemma game?

4. Why was Rapoport's TFT program so successful?

Public-goods games are social-dilemma games that permit any number of players, unlike the two-person prisoner's dilemma games.

5. Describe a typical public-goods game. Which is more likely to cooperate—a small group or a large one? Why?

Often, the choices people make indicate that they are not motivated purely by immediate self-interest. Through evolution, cultural history, and personal experience, we come to take into account longer-term interests that frequently rely on good social relations. Many aspects of human social nature can be thought of as adaptations for cooperating in social dilemmas.

6. How do real-life social dilemmas compare to laboratory games with regard to accountability, reputation, and reciprocity? How do such factors explain the general tendency to help others if the cost to ourselves is small and inhibiting factors are absent?

7. Discuss some ways that emotions tend to promote cooperation.

Recall the distinction between personal identity and social identity presented in Chapter 13. A person's social identity is related to the tendency to cooperate.

8. Define social identity and describe research showing its impact on cooperation in social-dilemma games.

Group identification can unfortunately also lead to conflict between different groups. Muzafer Sherif and colleagues conducted the Robbers Cave experiment in order to study conflict and ways of resolving that conflict.

9. How did the experimenters establish groups?

10. What resulted from the series of competitions between the groups?

11. List some methods tried in this and similar experiments that did *not* work as a means of reducing intergroup hostility.

12. What strategy for reducing intergroup hostility was successful? Explain.

The historical record—and, sadly, the current evening news—shows that intergroup conflict can escalate to overwhelming, often tragic, proportions.

13. How can historical and psychological research combine to help us understand intergroup atrocities?

Be sure to READ the Concluding Thoughts at the end of the chapter. Note important points in your Workout. Then consolidate your learning by answering the focus questions in the margins of the text.

After you have studied the chapter thoroughly, CHECK your understanding with the Self-Test that follows.

Self-Test 1

Multiple-Choice Questions

1. Bibb Latané's social impact theory is an elaboration of:
   a. Leon Festinger's cognitive dissonance theory.
   b. Kurt Lewin's field theory.
   c. Robert Zajonc's theory of social facilitation and interference.
   d. Robert Cialdini's work on social compliance.

2. Jackson, who suffers from stage fright, is about to deliver a dramatic speech. Which of the following circumstances would tend to *minimize* Jackson's stage fright, according to Latané's research?
   a. having only a few people in the audience
   b. being alone on stage rather than having other actors present
   c. having respected local actors in the audience rather than just fellow students
   d. both **a** and **b**.

3. In social impact theory, the immediacy of a source:
   a. depends on the extent of the target's fear, admiration, respect, or need for that person.
   b. can increase if the source is physically near or has simply been brought to mind.
   c. refers to how recently the target has been exposed to the source.
   d. is unrelated to the amount of social impact that the source exerts.

4. A salesperson who gets potential customers to say things consistent with the idea that owning the product would be a good thing is using the _____ technique.
   a. reciprocity-norm   c. foot-in-the-door
   b. reactance   d. four-walls

5. In Milgram's classic study _____ percent of subjects went all the way to the most severe level of punishment.
   a. 5   c. 35
   b. 15   d. 65

6. Which of the following self-conscious emotions is thought to motivate the repair of relationships?
   a. pride   c. guilt
   b. shame   d. embarrassment

7. Strong ethical objections have been raised to:
   a. Cialdini's work on principles of compliance.
   b. Zajonc's work on social interference and facilitation.
   c. Asch's work on conformity.
   d. Milgram's work on obedience.

8. Which of the following has *not* been supported as a partial explanation of the obedience shown in experiments such as those conducted by Stanley Milgram?
   a. the subjects' prior beliefs about authority
   b. the sequential nature of the task
   c. the experimenter's acceptance of responsibility
   d. the sadistic tendencies of the subjects

9. People who are high self-monitors:
   a. have little interest in impression management.
   b. are highly consistent across various audiences.
   c. choose friends on the basis of common values.
   d. have more friendships but they are less intimate ones.

10. According to the _____ theory, self-esteem functions as a gauge of the extent to which we are likely to be accepted or rejected by others.
    a. emotional contagion
    b. social facilitation
    c. reciprocity
    d. sociometer

11. People seem to have a greater desire to impress:
    a. close friends.
    b. family members.
    c. acquaintances.
    d. both **a** and **b**.

12. Reciprocity can help to explain:
    a. the foot-in-the-door technique.
    b. the four-walls technique.
    c. cooperation in an iterative prisoner's dilemma game.
    d. all of the above.

13. People who share the same view initially will tend to hold a more extreme version of that view after discussing the subject with one another. This phenomenon is called:
    a. social facilitation.
    b. normative influence.
    c. group polarization.
    d. groupthink.

14. In real-life social dilemmas, cooperation is promoted by:
    a. emotions, both positive and negative.
    b. a sense of personal accountability.
    c. a shared social identity.
    d. all of the above.

15. TFT offers:
    a. a strategy for eliciting cooperation in social-dilemma games.
    b. a way of measuring self-monitoring.
    c. a means of reducing conformity behavior in groups.
    d. a foolproof means of gaining compliance in a sales situation.

Essay Questions

16. How did Solomon Asch study conformity in the laboratory, and what was his basic finding? Why did subjects conform? What factor was found to help subjects resist conformity?

17. What are two possible explanations of group polarization? Indicate whether each explanation is normative or informational.

After you have assessed your understanding on the basis of Self-Test 1 and have tried to strengthen your preparation in any areas of weakness, GO ON to Self-Test 2.

Self-Test 2

Multiple-Choice Questions

1. According to Latané's social impact theory, _____ increases with an increase in the number of_____ .
   a. social facilitation; sources
   b. social facilitation; targets
   c. social pressure; sources
   d. social pressure; targets

2. Social psychology suggests that emotional contagion is:
   a. a myth and not an actual psychological phenomenon.
   b. possible for negative but not positive emotions.
   c. of value in promoting coordinated social action.
   d. a type of self-conscious emotion.

3. An interviewer conducting a survey asks Max for a few seconds of his time and Max consents. Then Max is asked to respond to 10 yes-or-no questions and he agrees. Finally, the interviewer works up to the primary aim, asking for a half-hour interview in Max's home. The interviewer is using the _____ to gain compliance.
   a. four-walls technique
   b. reciprocity norm
   c. foot-in-the-door technique
   d. phenomenon of reactance

4. Which of the following sales techniques is believed to work on the principle of cognitive dissonance?
   a. foot in the door   c. pregiving
   b. four walls   d. both a and b

5. Students who were asked to produce philosophical counterarguments did worse when in the presence of other people than when alone. This experimental result illustrates:
   a. social comparison
   b. the occurrence of cognitive dissonance.
   c. social interference.
   d. the phenomenon of groupthink.

6. Public-goods games are used to study:
   a. social facilitation.
   b. social interference.
   c. compliance.
   d. cooperation.

7. Researchers have found that the relative amount of informational as compared to normative influence on conformity varies depending on the:
   a. personal persuasiveness of individuals in the majority.
   b. difficulty of the task.
   c. gender of confederates and subjects.
   d. amount that subjects are being paid.

8. Jim, Anne, and Karen believe that the workers in their factory should unionize. They believe this even more firmly after talking together about the issue. This could be explained in terms of:
   a. groupthink.
   b. group polarization.
   c. social facilitation.
   d. none of the above.

9. Group polarization results because people tend to conform to a mentally exaggerated version of their group's opinion, according to the _____ hypothesis.
   a. one-upmanship   c. informational
   b. group-stereotyping d. reciprocity

10. The kind of thinking that arises when people immersed in a cohesive ingroup strive for unanimity more than for realistic appraisal of alternatives for action is called:
    a. groupthink.
    b. deindividuation.
    c. superordinate goal construction.
    d. obedience.

11. Garrett Hardin's "The Tragedy of the Commons" illustrates the dynamics of:
    a. obedience to authority.
    b. stereotyping.
    c. social dilemmas.
    d. compliance.

12. Players are most likely to cooperate in a(n):
    a. one-shot prisoner's dilemma game.
    b. iterative prisoner's dilemma game.
    c. brief, anonymous encounter with a stranger.
    d. social-dilemma game in which players see themselves as individuals rather than group-mates.

13. What led to intergroup hostility in Sherif's Robbers Cave experiment?
    a. competitive games between groups
    b. group solidarity
    c. psychological reactance
    d. the reciprocity norm

14. In his Robbers Cave experiment, Sherif successfully ended intergroup hostilities between the boys by:
    a. arranging for joint participation in pleasant activities.
    b. setting up individual rather than group competitions.
    c. establishing superordinate goals.
    d. arranging peace meetings between group leaders.

15. Shekiah has many friends but isn't very close to any of them. She pays a lot of attention to how she looks, talks, and acts so that she comes across well with different groups of people. Shekiah is probably:
    a. a low self-monitor.
    b. a high self-monitor.
    c. a social facilitator.
    d. a social inhibitor.

Essay Questions

16. Summarize the method and results of Stanley Milgram's classic study of obedience. Give two explanations that have been offered for these results.

17. Define the terms *social facilitation* and *social interference*. How did Zajonc explain these phenomena and thereby predict when each would occur? How have more recent theorists built on Zajonc's foundation?

Answers

Emotions as Foundations for Social Behavior

8. shame; self-esteem

Social Pressure: How Our Concern for Others' Judgments Affects Our Actions

3. **a.** increase, **b.** increase, **c.** decrease

5. **a.** social facilitation

 b. social interference

15. self-monitoring; High self-monitors; Low self-monitors

Self-Test 1

1. **b.** (p. 539)

2. **a.** Social impact increases as the number of sources increases and as the number of targets decreases. Thus, the circumstance described in **a** would tend to make things easier for Jackson, while those described in **b** and **c** would tend to worsen his stage fright. (p. 540)

3. **b.** (p. 540)

4. **d.** (p. 552)

5. **d.** (p. 557)

6. **c.** (pp. 536–537)

7. **d.** (p. 558)

8. **d.** The subjects did not comply because they enjoyed harming the "learner"; they clearly showed evidence of distress as they carried out the experimenter's orders. The impact of Milgram's finding stems from the fact that these *were* normal subjects. Their behavior is something that normal people are capable of. (pp. 556–559)

9. **d.** (p. 544)

10. **d.** (p. 538)

11. **c.** (p. 543)

12. **c.** Both **a** and **b** are produced by cognitive dissonance. (p. 561)

13. **c.** (p. 548)

14. **d.** (pp. 563–565)

15. **a.** (pp. 561–562)

16. Solomon Asch started out by trying to demonstrate that people will not conform when objective evidence is clear-cut. He arranged for each subject to join a group of people who appeared to be fellow subjects but who were in reality confederates of the experimenter. On each trial, subjects (real and fake alike) were to compare a standard line to a set of three comparison lines and to indicate the one line that was the same length as the standard. The task was extremely simple. The real subjects were seated so that they were the next to last to give their answers. The confederates had been instructed beforehand to give the same wrong answer on certain trials.

 Most subjects were influenced by the clearly wrong answers of the confederates, at least sometimes. Some conformed to the unanimous wrong answer on every one of these trials. Subjects apparently conformed primarily because of the normative influence of the group. When subjects were led to believe that they were late and should therefore give their answers in writing rather than aloud, the level of conformity dropped dramatically. Research suggests that conformity is due mostly to normative influence on easy tasks but mostly to informational influence when the task is difficult. Having another person disagree with the majority opinion apparently helps subjects to resist compliance. (pp. 545–547)

17. Group polarization may be due to the tendency of like-minded people to present arguments favoring their own position but not the opposite

view. As a result, each member will only be persuaded to hold his or her original position more firmly. This is an informational effect. The one-upmanship hypothesis, a normative hypothesis, suggests that people may try to outdo one another in the extremity of their support for the common view. People have been found to admire views that agree with their own but are more extreme. (pp. 549–551)

Self-Test 2

1. **c.** It decreases with a greater number of *targets*. (p. 540)

2. **c.** (p. 535)

3. **c.** (p. 552)

4. **d.** (pp. 552–553)

5. **c.** According to Robert Zajonc, the presence of others can lead to either social facilitation or social interference, depending on the task. If the task is well learned, simple, or instinctive, social facilitation results. Zajonc explains the difference in terms of the increased arousal produced when others are present. High arousal typically improves performance on simple, well-learned tasks and harms performance on complex or poorly learned tasks (such as producing a philosophical counterargument). (p. 541)

6. **d.** (p. 562)

7. **b.** (p. 547)

8. **b.** (p. 548)

9. **b.** Both **a** and **b** are normative hypotheses about the causes of group polarization. (p. 549)

10. **a.** (p. 550)

11. **c.** (p. 559)

12. **b.** Here, reciprocity has a chance to develop cooperation. (pp. 561–562)

13. **a.** (p. 565)

14. **c.** (p. 566)

15. **b.** (p. 544)

16. Stanley Milgram had subjects take the role of teacher, while the role of learner—supposedly played by another subject—was actually played by a confederate of the experimenter. The learner was placed in a separate room and the real subject stayed with the experimenter. The subject's job was to read questions on a verbal-memory test and to shock the learner when he made an error. (The shocks were, of course, not real.) As the experimental session progressed with the learner making many mistakes, the shock level was increased and the learner began to show signs of distress, then to scream for the shocks to stop, and finally to fall silent. If the subject hesitated to continue the shocks at any point, the experimenter responded with firm prompts demanding cooperation.

Sixty-five percent of the subjects continued to the highest level of shock, despite apparent reluctance to do so. This result has been partially explained in terms of subjects' preexisting beliefs about the appropriateness of obeying authorities, especially if they represent a valued endeavor such as science. Another factor that seems to be important is the degree to which the experimenter appears to accept responsibility. In a similar experiment in which subjects were told they should accept responsibility for the learner's welfare, obedience was sharply reduced. (pp. 555–559)

17. In a variety of tasks, the presence of others has been found to improve performance relative to performance when subjects are alone. This well-established effect is known as social facilitation. However, another well-established effect appears to contradict social facilitation. Social interference is a frequently replicated phenomenon in which the presence of others causes performance to worsen relative to performance when subjects are alone.

Robert Zajonc suggested that the task determines which phenomenon will result. Social facilitation will occur when tasks are dominant (for example, well learned or simple), whereas social interference will occur when tasks are nondominant (for example, unfamiliar or complex). The underlying explanatory concept is arousal. The presence of other people increases physiological arousal. High arousal is known to affect simple or well-learned tasks positively and complex or unfamiliar tasks adversely. Psychologists believe the increased arousal in the presence of other humans is due to evaluation anxiety.

A more recent modification of Zajonc's theory proposes that social facilitation occurs when the situation is experienced by the subject as a challenge, whereas social interference occurs when it is experienced as a threat. Different physiological patterns of arousal occur in the two types of situations. Research has supported this view. (pp. 541–542)

Chapter 15   Personality

READ *the introduction below before you read the chapter in the text.*

Psychologists use the term *personality* to mean an individual's general style of interacting with the world, especially with other people. Theories of personality are efforts to systematically describe and explain variations among people in this general style of behaving.

Trait theories focus on describing individual differences by attempting to specify the most fundamental dimensions underlying personality. A trait is a relatively stable predisposition to behave in a certain manner. Trait theorists distinguish between surface traits, which are linked directly to observable behaviors, and central traits, which are the most basic dimensions of personality. Trait theorists typically collect data using paper-and-pencil questionnaires and subject the results to factor analysis. Pioneering this general approach, Raymond Cattell described personality in terms of sixteen dimensions, while Hans Eysenck claimed that only two dimensions are really necessary. Many trait researchers today believe that there are five basic traits, which they call the Big Five. Some major issues for trait theorists are the consistency of traits over time, their consistency across situations, their heritability, and their physiological bases.

A useful approach to the issue of personality variation is to consider it from the evolutionary perspective, which requires us to ask how personality differences are adaptive and what might lead to the adaptations. Personality variation, like all other forms of diversity produced by genetic mechanisms, allows the investment in offspring to be protected, essentially by hedging one's bets in an uncertain and ever-changing world. Both genetic diversity and developmental flexibility allow individuals to develop strategies that promote their survival and reproduction within various niches. People may specialize in ways that suit their birth-order niche in the family and even carve out a unique niche for themselves by contrasting themselves with siblings. Biological sex and cul-turally defined gender may lead us to become different based on the different niches they cause us to occupy.

Freud's personality theory and his approach to psychotherapy are both called psychoanalysis, which is considered a psychodynamic theory—that is, one that focuses on mental forces. In this theory, unconscious motivation is the main cause of behavior; people are often unaware of or wrong about their true motivations because sex and aggression—the chief forces motivating us, according to Freud—are unacceptable to the conscious mind. However, mental association, dreams, and mistakes such as speech errors (Freudian slips) can give clues to the contents of the unconscious. In order to reduce the anxiety that unacceptable aspects of ourselves produce, we use self-deceptive defense mechanisms. Alfred Adler, Karen Horney, and Erik Erikson also developed psychodynamic theories, retaining Freud's core idea of unconscious mental forces but differing in their emphasis on social rather than sexual/aggressive drives.

Social-cognitive theories of personality are distinguished by using traditional areas of laboratory research, such as learning, cognition, and social influence, as well as clinical data. Julian Rotter's concept of locus of control, the tendency to believe that rewards are or are not usually controllable by one's own efforts, is an example of a cognitive construct used as a personality variable. A related idea is Albert Bandura's concept of self-efficacy, the belief in one's own ability to perform specific tasks. Social-cognition research suggests that a positive, optimistic outlook is associated with various benefits.

Humanistic theories of personality were born out of a conviction that certain other theories essentially dehumanized people. Humanistic theories emphasize those characteristics of people that are uniquely human. They typically have a phenomenological orientation, which means that they emphasize subjective mental experience; they are generally holistic, looking at the whole person rather than analyzing the person into components; and they are concerned with people's tendency to actualize themselves, that is, to grow and to realize their individual potential. Carl Rogers and Abraham Maslow are pioneers of this approach. Based on the life stories people tell, Dan McAdams has proposed that personal myth is an important construct for understanding personality.

> LOOK over the table of contents for this chapter in your textbook before you continue with your study.

> Notice that there are focus questions in the margins of the text for your use in studying the material. The following chart lists which Study Guide questions relate to which focus questions.

The Integrated Study Workout

> Complete one section at a time.

Personality as Behavioral Dispositions, or Traits (pages 573–584)

> CONSIDER these questions before you go on. They are designed to help you start thinking about this subject, not to test your knowledge.

Can the fundamental ways in which personalities differ be efficiently summarized in terms of two dimensions? in terms of five? Or does it take many more dimensions to do the job?

Can we predict that a person who is polite in dealing with employers will be polite with store clerks? with children? with coworkers?

Will a person who is suspicious today tend to be suspicious 20 years from now?

How much of a role does heredity play in determining the personality differences among individuals?

> READ this section of your text lightly. Then go back and read thoroughly, completing the Workout as you proceed.

George is shy, Susan reckless, and Sam friendly. As social beings, we are constantly making judgments about people's personalities—that is, about their style of interacting with the world in general and other people in particular. Psychologists seek to understand personality in a more formal, systematic way. Trait theories have the description and measurement of individual differences in personality as their main purpose.

1. Define the term *trait*, and distinguish traits from states.

2. Are traits all-or-none characteristics—that is, does a person have a trait or not have a trait? Do traits *explain* individual differences?

Trait theories are designed to summarize personality differences efficiently and succinctly. They share the basic assumption that traits and related behaviors are hierarchically organized.

3. Distinguish between surface and central traits. Give examples of two surface traits and of the central trait to which they are linked.

4. Give a general description of the components and development of a trait theory.

5. What is the primary goal of trait theories?

Raymond Cattell, a pioneer of the trait approach to personality, describes personality in terms of sixteen dimensions, or central traits. His was the first prominent trait theory. (See Table 15.1 on text page 575.)

6. How did Cattell's background in chemistry influence his thinking?

7. How did Cattell develop his theory?

8. Describe the results of Cattell's research.

Hans Eysenck took an approach similar to Cattell's but used factor analysis differently and produced a theory involving far fewer central traits. The Eysenck Personality Inventory is still used today.

9. Describe the dimensions Eysenck identified, and indicate the surface traits associated with the extreme on each continuum.

   a. introversion–extroversion

   b. neuroticism–stability

   c. psychoticism–nonpsychoticism

Some trait theorists consider Cattell's theory too complex and Eysenck's too simple. Factor-analytic studies using more sophisticated procedures have produced results that are remarkably consistent, even when testing was conducted in different countries, with different languages, or with children rather than adults. The five traits revealed in these studies are called the Big Five. (See Table 15.2 on text page 577.)

10. What are the five central traits of the Big-Five theory? What do they have in common with two of Eysenck's dimensions?

Suppose we can describe a person in terms of personality traits today. Will that description still apply in the future?

11. How is the stability of traits over time studied? What are the general findings?

12. Why does the stability of traits increase after the age of 30? Is personality change still possible after that point? Explain.

Do scores on personality tests actually predict behavior? That is the issue of validity—the extent to which a measure actually reflects what it is purported to reflect.

13. Discuss the ability of personality tests to predict behavior.

14. Are personality differences *more* or *less* apparent in novel situations? Explain.

If you are honest when you detect a bank error in your favor, does that necessarily mean that you will be honest on tests or with your doctor? A point of controversy in trait theories concerns the consistency of traits across situations.

15. In what sense do personality tests describe "the psychology of the stranger"?

16. Summarize Walter Mischel's position on situation specificity.

17. How did the results of a study by Hartshorne and May support Mischel?

18. How did Mischel and Peake study the trait of conscientiousness? What did they conclude? What about results of Mischel's study at a summer camp?

19. Is Mischel right, and are the trait theorists wrong? Is the opposite true? Explain.

Many trait theorists believe that stable behavioral dispositions such as the Big Five arise at least in part from inherited physiological characteristics of the nervous system. Introversion–extroversion has received the greatest attention in terms of physiological bases.

20. Describe Eysenck's view.

21. Summarize evidence consistent with Eysenck's view.

22. How can we most accurately state the conclusions that are now supported by evidence?

How heritable are personality traits? As with the heritability of other characteristics, such as intelligence, twin and adoption studies have been key to answering the question.

23. Describe the most common approach to studying the heritability of personality traits. What is the usual finding? What possible flaw in methodology calls into question the results of such studies?

24. How did David Lykken and his colleagues get around the methodological pitfalls of other twin studies? Were their results consistent with other studies?

25. What are some surprises that have emerged from studies of the heritability of traits and of specific attitudes and beliefs?

26. Discuss the relative lack of effect on personality of sharing the same family environment. Give a well-rounded answer.

Researchers are now only beginning to link behavior genetics and physiological approaches, searching for the actual genes that are responsible for the heritable portion of a given trait and examining its physiological influences.

27. Comment on attempts to find the genetic underpinnings of particular personality traits.

Personality as Adaptation to Life Conditions (pages 585–594)

CONSIDER these questions before you go on. They are designed to help you start thinking about this subject, not to test your knowledge.

Why do people differ so widely in personality? What purpose does such variety serve?

Can knowing whether a person is the first-born in his or her family or the youngest child in the family help to predict anything about personality?

Do men's and women's personalities really differ on average, or are such ideas simply cultural myths?

READ this section of your text lightly. Then go back and read thoroughly, completing the Workout as you proceed.

Personality can also be thought of in terms of adaptation to life conditions. Both proximate and ultimate explanations for personality are sought by theorists. Proximate explanations, as you may recall from Chapter 3, are concerned with the causal mechanisms that operate within the individual's lifetime. Ultimate explanations, in contrast, are concerned with the evolutionary survival value—with the very function—of variation in personality. The fact that sexual reproduction exists, given that there are easier biological means of reproduction, suggests that the diversity it produces confers evolutionary advantages. By extension, it seems unlikely that the particular mechanisms leading to personality differences would have evolved if they produced no survival advantage. (Note that this is true not only for humans but for animal life in general—many nonhuman species have been shown to have variation in behavioral styles.)

1. How is diversification among offspring like owning a diversified investment portfolio?

2. What is meant by the term *niche* in the context of evolution? How might the availability of various niches help to explain the evolution of different traits within a species?

3. Describe two types of research findings about pumpkinseed sunfish adapting to different niches.

4. Choose two of the Big-Five personality dimensions. Then speculate about how extremes on these dimensions might relate to different life strategies and thus to survival and reproductive chances. What evidence did David Buss find to suggest that such correlations exist?

5. How can an evolutionary perspective help to explain both heritable and nonheritable variation in personality dimensions?

Many theorists have assumed a special importance of the early family environment in shaping personality. However, some psychologists now say that the family influence has been greatly overemphasized. They point out that individuals raised in the same home are about as different from one another in personality as people raised in different homes (if we keep the degree of genetic relatedness constant).

6. Explain how children in the same home could have quite different personality-forming experiences.

7. Define the following terms:

   a. sibling contrast

   b. split-parent identification

8. How might sibling contrast and split-parent identification be valuable in reducing sibling rivalry and increasing the diversification of the parental investment in offspring? Provide evidence to support your answer.

Except in cases of multiple births (such as twins or triplets), the children in a family each occupy a different position in terms of birth order.

9. How do birth-order positions provide different niches that could lead to different personality traits?

10. Describe the consistent birth-order differences found by Frank Sulloway. What types of data did he use to reach his conclusions?

11. Has subsequent research by others supported Sulloway's theory? Explain and point out any limitations of the theory.

The psychological differences between men and women—whatever they may be and whatever their extent—may be due to the fact that men and women adapt to different niches. Those niches may stem in part from biological sex, but they are also due to socioculturally defined gender categories.

12. What differences have been found between men and women on the Big-Five traits?

13. What is sensation seeking? How do men and women differ in this tendency?

14. How might gender influence the relationship between personality and life satisfaction?

15. Discuss the possible evolutionary and cultural contributions to gender differences in personality.

16. Is it possible to gauge the relative impact of the two types of influence? How might future trends make such an assessment somewhat more possible?

Personality as Mental Processes
(pages 594–607)

CONSIDER these questions before you go on. They are designed to help you start thinking about this subject, not to test your knowledge.

Are we generally aware of why we do what we do?

Can our dreams tell us anything about ourselves that we don't already know?

What do people mean when they say such things as "I just want to know who the real me is"?

What does a person need in order to fulfill his or her own potential?

Who experiences more anxiety—people who believe that their own efforts determine their rewards or those who believe that rewards are controlled by external factors?

Is positive thinking really beneficial?

READ this section of your text lightly. Then go back and read thoroughly, completing the Workout as you proceed.

Unlike trait theories, some theories focus on the processes and contents of the mind to understand personality and the behaviors that it gives rise to. One such theory is Sigmund Freud's. His theory of personality and his approach to psychotherapy are both referred to as psychoanalysis. It would be difficult to exaggerate the impact of Freud's thought on modern

psychology. Freud's psychoanalysis is the prime example of a psychodynamic theory.

1. What does the term *psychodynamic* mean? What are the guiding principles of psychodynamic theories?

2. What role does the unconscious mind play, according to Freud's theory?

3. Characterize Freud's general approach for revealing the unconscious. What aspects of thought and behavior did he consider to be the best clues?

4. What two drives are central to personality differences in Freud's view? Explain. Be sure to mention the broader sense in which Freud used these terms as his thinking evolved.

Freud believed that people are essentially asocial, being held together in society only because of their needs. Most post-Freudian psychodynamic theorists have instead regarded people as fundamentally social and as motivated by needs that go beyond the sexual and aggressive drives that Freud emphasized.

5. Describe the drives or needs considered essential to personality differences in each of the following psychodynamic theories.

   a. Karen Horney's theory

b. object relations theories

c. Alfred Adler's theory

d. Erik Erikson's theory

Anna Freud, Sigmund Freud's daughter, was also a psychoanalyst. She was most responsible for developing the theory of defense mechanisms.

6. What is a defense mechanism?

7. Define each of the following defense mechanisms, explaining how each defends against anxiety.

a. repression

b. displacement and sublimation

c. reaction formation

d. projection

e. rationalization

8. Indicate which defense mechanism each of the following individuals is using.

_____ **a.** Garth is partying too much to get his studying done. He tells himself that he needs a lot of relaxation in order to handle the pressure of school.

_____ **b.** Yolanda is a sculptor who loves to take a piece of stone and carefully chisel it into a smooth, curving form.

_____ **c.** Eric unconsciously harbors great hostility but instead perceives that his brother Joe is hostile.

9. At present, how well accepted is the concept of defense mechanisms?

10. How can a defense mechanism be adaptive? maladaptive?

A major avenue of personality research inspired by the psychodynamic approach involves the exploration of people's defensive styles.

11. According to George Vaillant, some defenses are more mature than others. Comment on each of the following and list specific examples.

a. immature defenses

b. intermediate defenses

c. mature defenses

12. How is defensive style related to a successful, happy life, according to Vaillant's research?

Social-cognitive theories (also called social-learning or social-cognitive-learning theories) are tied to laboratory research on learning, cognition, and social influence, as well as to the perspective of a clinician.

13. Instead of instinctive, unconscious motives, seen as prime determinants of personality by psychodynamic theorists, _____ and _____ stemming from _____ are the focus of social-cognitive theorists.

The cognitive constructs most often studied in the social-cognitive approach to personality involve beliefs or habits of thought that affect a person's ability to take control of his or her own life.

14. What led Rotter to conclude that people's beliefs about their ability to control rewards affects their behavior?

15. Explain locus of control as a personality trait. In what kinds of situations does this generalized disposition govern behavior?

16. Describe some correlational data consistent with the concept of locus of control. What are your thoughts about the possible causal relationships involved?

Another major construct in social-cognitive theory is Bandura's concept of self-efficacy.

17. Define the term *self-efficacy*, and distinguish it from locus of control. Do the two usually go hand in hand (for example, internal locus of control and high self-efficacy)? Give an example of a case in which they don't.

18. Is self-efficacy positively correlated with performance on tasks? Does it play a causal role? Support your answer.

Many people believe that positive thinking has numerous benefits.

19. Does psychological research support this notion? Be specific.

20. How might positive thinking produce positive effects?

21. Can optimism be maladaptive? Can pessimism be adaptive? Explain.

The founders of humanistic psychology objected to what they saw as the dehumanizing, fragmented conceptions of people inherent in certain other approaches to personality. Theorists from this alternative perspective proposed a different way of viewing personality.

22. Explain each of these aspects of humanistic psychology.

    a. humanistic approach

    b. phenomenological reality

c.   holistic view of the person

The personality theory of Carl Rogers, one of the most influential representatives of humanistic psychology, often is called *self theory* because of its focus on the individual's sense of self.

23. In Rogers's view, one of the most common goals that people have when they enter therapy is to become _____ .

24. Describe research findings on the response to medical advice that is supportive of Rogers's view.

25. Define *self-actualization*. What metaphor did Rogers use to convey his view of self-actualization?

Abraham Maslow proposed a set of five types of needs, all of which must be met in order to achieve self-actualization.

26. Complete the five levels of Maslow's hierarchy of needs.

Highest level _____

_____

_____

_____

Lowest level _____

27. With regard to the hierarchy of needs, what must one do in order to become a self-actualizing person?

28. Discuss Maslow's hierarchy from an evolutionary perspective.

An increasingly accepted means of learning about individuals is to ask them to tell their life stories.

29. How is the life-story approach consistent with humanistic psychology?

30. What common factors has Dan McAdams found in the many life stories he has studied?

31. Why does McAdams refer to the self-told life story as a personal myth? Is the myth generally static? Explain.

32. What does the study of personal transformation conducted by Miller and C'deBaca suggest about the modifiability of personality in adulthood?

33. Why is it important to recognize that the theories described in this chapter were based on and produced by members of a nonrepresentative sample of humanity? What particular biases might this have introduced?

> Be sure to READ the Concluding Thoughts at the end of the chapter. Note important points in your Workout. Then consolidate your learning by answering the focus questions in the margins of the text.

> After you have studied the chapter thoroughly, CHECK your understanding with the Self-Test that follows.

Self-Test 1

Multiple-Choice Questions

1. The Big-Five personality dimension that reflects the largest gender difference is that of:
   a. neuroticism–stability.
   b. extroversion–introversion.
   c. agreeableness–antagonism.
   d. sensation seeking–sensation avoidance.

2. Research has shown that male and female mammals _____ humans differ in response to_____ , with males becoming more aggressive and females more nurturant and motivated to strengthen social ties.
   a. other than; stress
   b. other than; success
   c. including; stress
   d. including; success

3. Freud believed that the best clues to the contents of a person's unconscious are those elements of thought and behavior:
   a. that are least logical.
   b. that are most logical.
   c. for which the person can offer no explanation.
   d. that most clearly signal a lack of self-esteem.

4. Two brothers, Roberto and Silvio, have sought consciously or unconsciously to make themselves different from one another. Whereas Roberto is seen by himself and others as the athletic and friendly one, Silvio projects his personality as being intellectual and artistic but a little withdrawn. This "strategy" most clearly represents the idea of:
   a. birth order.
   b. sibling contrast.
   c. split-parent identification.
   d. self-actualization.

5. According to Alfred Adler, an inferiority complex represents:
   a. an inability to overcome the normal feeling of inferiority that accompanies the dependence of early childhood.
   b. a mask for unacceptable feelings of superiority that arise from sexual and aggressive drives.
   c. a failure to recognize the difference between one's real self and one's ideal self.
   d. an exaggerated tendency to compare ourselves to others and an overreliance on other people's judgments of our worth.

6. Post-Freudian psychodynamic theories are different from Freudian psychoanalysis in their greater emphasis on:
   a. early childhood experiences.
   b. social drives.
   c. the role of the unconscious.
   d. sex and aggression.

7. An emphasis on phenomenology is especially characteristic of _____ theories of personality.
   a. psychoanalytic   c. trait
   b. social-cognitive   d. humanistic

8. According to humanistic psychology, people are powerfully motivated toward:
   a. self-actualization, the direction for which must be environmentally determined.
   b. self-actualization, the direction for which must be determined from within the individual.
   c. self-esteem, which is defended with such mechanisms as rationalization and projection.
   d. self-esteem, which comes from adapting oneself to the norms and judgments of the larger human community.

9. Locus of control and self-efficacy are major constructs in _____ theories of personality.
   a. social-cognitive   c. evolutionary
   b. psychodynamic   d. trait

10. Which of the following statements about birth order is *false*?
    a. Later-borns are more likely than first-borns to challenge the status quo and support new ideas.
    b. First-borns are more likely than later-borns to be competitive.
    c. Later-borns tend to be more agreeable than first-borns.
    d. First-borns score higher on openness to experience than later-borns do.

11. Louise believes that whether she gets into graduate school depends primarily on her own efforts; she also believes that she can succeed in this endeavor. Louise appears to have an _____ locus of control and to be _____ in self-efficacy.
    a. external; high   c. external; low
    b. internal; low   d. internal; high

12. The theorist who has most emphasized the situational specificity of personality variables is:
    a. Cattell.   c. Mischel.
    b. Rotter.   d. Eysenck.

13. Which of the following is true of traits as they are seen from the perspective of trait theory?
    a. A trait is a characteristic that a person either has or doesn't have in all-or-none fashion.
    b. *Trait* and *state* are equivalent terms, but the former is applied to cognitive characteristics, whereas the latter is applied to motivational and emotional characteristics.
    c. Traits are characteristics of the person rather than of the environment.
    d. Traits are temporary, changeable characteristics that can be inferred from current behavior patterns.

14. Which of the following correctly reflects the order of needs (from bottom to top) according to Abraham Maslow's hierarchy?
    a. physiological needs, esteem needs, safety needs, self-actualization needs, attachment needs
    b. safety needs, physiological needs, esteem needs, attachment needs, self-actualization needs
    c. self-actualization needs, esteem needs, physiological needs, safety needs, attachment needs
    d. physiological needs, safety needs, attachment needs, esteem needs, self-actualization needs

15. Research from the trait theory approach generally shows that personality is:
    a. fairly stable over the course of adult life.
    b. not at all stable over the course of adult life.
    c. stable prior to age 40 but relatively unstable thereafter.
    d. relatively unstable prior to age 40 but stable thereafter.

Essay Questions

16. Define the term *defense mechanisms*, and describe two specific defense mechanisms, providing examples for each.

17. Describe the aims of trait theorists. How do the "Big Five" fit in with these aims?

After you have assessed your understanding on the basis of Self-Test 1 and have tried to strengthen your preparation in any areas of weakness, GO ON to Self-Test 2.

Self-Test 2

Multiple-Choice Questions

1. A personality theory that emphasizes the importance of mental forces in shaping personality and determining thought and behavior would, by definition, be a _____ theory.
   a. social-cognitive   c. trait
   b. psychodynamic   d. psychoanalytic

2. In order to gain information about the contents of a patient's unconscious mind, Freud used all of the following as sources of data *except*:
   a. dreams.
   b. questionnaires.
   c. uncensored reporting of patients' thoughts.
   d. slips of the tongue.

3. A psychoanalyst would be most likely to describe working with a patient in terms of:
   a. an advertising campaign in which the patient is the product being endorsed as well as the consumer being targeted by the campaign.
   b. law enforcement, with the patient being warned about various ways in which laws of psychological good health are being violated.
   c. being a mirror for the patient's thoughts and feelings.
   d. a search for clues about the patient's unconscious mind that must then be fitted together.

4. Which of the following is *not* one of the Big-Five personality dimensions?
   a. conscientiousness   c. agreeableness
   b. optimism   d. neuroticism

5. Brian believes that he intensely dislikes Alicia because his real love for her is unacceptable to him. Brian is using a defense mechanism called:
   a. sublimation.   c. reaction formation.
   b. projection.   d. fixation.

6. Dan McAdams's concept of personal myth fits best with:
   a. the Big-Five theory.
   b. Freud's psychoanalytic theory.
   c. humanistic theories.
   d. social-cognitive theories.

7. Carl Rogers emphasized the human drive of:
   a. being one's real self.   c. security.
   b. achievement.   d. safety.

8. Joel is feeling angry about his roommate's loud music on the night before a final exam. Joel's anger is an example of:
   a. a trait.
   b. a state.
   c. a behavioral disposition.
   d. all of the above.

9. The theoretical approach to personality that most emphasizes learned beliefs and habits of thinking is _____ theory.
   a. psychoanalytic   c. social-cognitive
   b. trait   d. humanistic

10. Suppose experimenters give subjects a series of problems that are, unbeknownst to the subjects, unsolvable. Some subjects are led to believe that they are able to solve the problems, but others are not manipulated in this way. The results show that those who are led to believe that they can succeed work longer on the problems. This experiment illustrates the effects of:
    a. locus of control.   c. self-actualization.
    b. self-efficacy.   d. self-esteem.

11. Cattell and Eysenck were pioneers in the development of _____ theories of personality.
    a. humanistic   c. social-cognitive
    b. psychodynamic   d. trait

12. Which of the following statements about traits is correct?
    a. Only central traits are linked directly to specific, observable behaviors.
    b. A number of related surface traits must be identified in order to infer the existence of a given central trait.
    c. Central traits are biological predispositions, whereas surface traits are those traits due primarily to learning.
    d. Central traits are enduring characteristics, whereas surface traits are transitory states.

13. Hans Eysenck proposed that differences in the arousability of higher parts of the brain cause the observed differences in _____ , which he considers one of the basic dimensions of personality.
    a. neuroticism–stability
    b. openness–nonopenness
    c. introversion–extroversion
    d. dominance–submissiveness

14. Hartshorne and May studied dishonesty in children in a variety of situations. They found that children tended to behave:
   a. consistently both within a given type of situation and across situations, a finding that supports the global-trait view.
   b. consistently both within a given type of situation and across situations, a finding that supports the situation-specificity view.
   c. consistently within a given type of situation but not across different situations, a finding that supports the global-trait view.
   d. consistently within a given type of situation but not across different situations, a finding that supports the situation-specificity view.

15. David Lykken and his colleagues have studied _____ and found evidence of high heritability for _____ .
   a. twins raised apart, as well as twins raised together; both groups on virtually every personality trait assessed
   b. twins raised apart, as well as twins raised together; very few of the personality traits assessed in the former but for most traits in the latter group
   c. families that have adopted two children, some twin and some nontwin biological siblings; virtually every personality trait assessed
   d. families that have adopted two children, some twin and some nontwin biological siblings; very few personality traits assessed

Essay Questions

16. Discuss Abraham Maslow's hierarchy of needs.

17. Describe two general characteristics shared by Freudian and post-Freudian psychodynamic theories and one general characteristic that differentiates post-Freudian psychodynamic theories from Freud's psychoanalysis.

Answers

Personality as Mental Processes

8. a. rationalization
   b. sublimation
   c. projection

13. beliefs; habits of thought; one's unique experiences

23. their real selves

26. highest to lowest: self-actualization needs; esteem needs; belongingness and love (attachment) needs; safety needs; physiological needs

Self-Test 1

1. c. Note that d is not even among the Big Five. (p. 591)

2. c. (p. 592)

3. a. Freud wanted to learn what lay behind the consistent, rational explanations so readily offered by the conscious mind. He assumed that what was *least* logical in a person's speech or behavior was most likely to represent the irrational, sometimes troubling contents of that person's unconscious. (p. 595)

4. b. (pp. 588–589)

5. a. Adler suggested that the need to overcome the sense of inadequacy can in some cases lead to a superiority complex. (p. 596)

6. b. (pp. 595–596)

7. d. (p. 603)

8. b. (p. 604)

9. a. (pp. 600–601)

10. d. (p. 590)

11. d.   Louise believes that her success in graduate school admission will be determined by her own efforts; that means she has an internal locus of control. She also believes that those efforts will be enough to gain her admission; that means she has high self-efficacy. (pp. 600–601)

12. c. (p. 579)

13. c. (p. 573)

14. d. (pp. 604–605)

15. a. (p. 578)

16.   Defense mechanisms are one means through which the mind reduces anxiety. A focus on defense mechanisms is one hallmark of psycho-dynamic theories. All defense mechanisms involve some form of self-deception. The most basic defense mechanism is repression, in which the ego exerts pressure to push anxiety-provok-ing material out of consciousness. Reaction for-mation is a defense mechanism in which we per-ceive our true feelings as their opposite. For example, if someone is jealous of his brother's accomplishments, he may behave as if he is excessively proud of or happy about those accomplishments. (pp. 596–598)

17.   Most personality theorists wish to describe human personality in terms of the inner drives, beliefs, and goals that shape it. For them, explain-ing individual differences in these terms is sec-ondary. Trait theorists, in contrast, are primarily interested in individual differences. Their aim is to discover the most basic dimensions along which personality varies, to efficiently describe individual differences in terms of a limited set of characteristics or traits. Traits are assumed to be relatively stable predispositions to behave in a particular way.

The usual method for revealing these traits involves the factor analysis of questionnaire data. Different theorists have collected data in some-what different ways and have identified different numbers and types of basic dimensions. The "Big Five" are a set of five dimensions that have con-sistently turned up in modern factor-analytic studies. Introversion–extroversion is an example of one of the Big Five. There is fairly good con-sensus among trait theorists that individual dif-ferences in personality can be efficiently de-scribed in terms of differences along these five dimensions. (pp. 573–577)

Self-Test 2

1. b.   Freud's psychoanalytic theory is just one example of a psychodynamic theory. (p. 594)

2. b.   Questionnaires are often used by trait theorists however. (p. 595)

3. d. (p. 595)

4. b. (p. 577)

5. c.   In reaction formation, an individual perceives his or her true feelings as their opposites—experi-encing hate where there is love or love where there is hate, for example. In projection, the feel-ing is perceived accurately but is attributed to someone else. Sublimation is a redirection of unacceptable urges into culturally valued chan-nels. (p. 597)

6. c. (p. 605)

7. a. (p. 604)

8. b. (p. 575)

9. c. (p. 599)

10. b.   Studies like this suggest that self-efficacy may have some causal effect on performance. (p. 601)

11. d. (pp. 575–576)

12. b. (p. 575)

13. c. (p. 581)

14. d. (p. 580)

15. a.   By including identical twins reared apart, Lykken and his colleagues avoided the method-ological pitfall of some other studies of identical twins. If identical twins are reared together, they not only are genetically identical but may also be treated more alike than fraternal twins are; thus, it would be hard to separate genetic and environ-mental contributions to their similarities in per-sonality. (p. 582)

16.   Maslow's hierarchy of needs ranks different cate-gories of needs from the lowest to the highest: physiological needs, such as the need for food; needs for safety, such as the need for shelter from rain or snow; attachment (belongingness and love) needs, such as the need for family or friend-ship; esteem needs, such as the need for respect from others; and needs for self-actualization, such as the need for self-expression. Maslow felt that people must essentially meet these needs in order, seeing that lower needs are at least rela-tively satisfied before moving on to other needs.

If we examine the rank ordering from an evolutionary perspective, it makes sense in terms of the survival value of meeting each type of need; for example, food is more directly essential than friends, and so on. (pp. 604–605)

17. The personality theorists who developed post-Freudian psychodynamic theories generally retained some essential elements of Freud's psychoanalysis. One such element was an emphasis on the unconscious. Both Freud and those followers who broke away from his theory held that a person's conscious thought and behavior are determined by unconscious mental forces. The post-Freudians also shared with Freud the view that unconscious mental forces exert their influence through the production of anxiety and that we defend against that anxiety.

Post-Freudian psychodynamic theorists differ from Freud in their emphasis on social needs. Whereas Freud believed that the drives of sex and aggression were at the root of virtually all human thought and behavior, the post-Freudians believed that this emphasis neglected important aspects of personality. They viewed people as inherently social beings and attempted to explain personality in terms of specifically social drives. For example, Karen Horney discussed the need for security, which is fulfilled socially, usually through the influence of the child's parents. (pp. 594–596)

Chapter 16   Mental Disorders

READ the introduction below before you read the chapter in the text.

The concept of a mental disorder is not sharply or clearly defined. Practical guidelines introduced by the American Psychiatric Association help clinicians to decide when a given set of symptoms represents a mental disorder, but they leave "gray" areas. *DSM-III* and *DSM-IV*, the standard diagnostic guides prepared by the American Psychiatric Association, divide disorders into different classes according to their objective symptoms. The labeling involved in receiving a diagnosis can affect a person's self-concept, the way others view him or her, and even the person's chances of recovery.

The biological approach to mental disorders asserts that they are physical diseases of the brain. The psychodynamic perspective suggests that mental disorders occur when mental conflict produces more anxiety than a person can effectively cope with. The cognitive-behavioral view stresses learned behavior and thought patterns. The sociocultural perspective emphasizes the effects of the values, norms, beliefs, and psychological pressures that prevail in a given social and cultural context. Regardless of their perspective, theorists agree that mental disorders have multiple causes, which can be divided into three categories—predisposing, precipitating, and maintaining.

Researchers have investigated the fact that the prevalence of particular mental disorders appears to differ between men and women, identifying several possible reasons. Men are more likely than women to be diagnosed with substance-use disorders and antisocial personality disorder, whereas women are more likely than men to receive a diagnosis of anxiety or mood disorders.

Anxiety disorders have anxiety or fear as their most prominent symptom. They include generalized anxiety disorder, which involves a high degree of relatively unfocused anxiety; phobias, which are intense, irrational fears of specific objects or events; obsessive-compulsive disorder, which involves repetitive thoughts and actions; panic disorder, in which people have unpredictable attacks of overwhelming terror; and posttraumatic stress disorder, which may strike the survivors of extremely traumatic experiences such as plane crashes or wars.

Mood disorders fall into two general categories—depressive disorders (major depression and dysthymia), in which the problem is downward mood swings, and bipolar disorders, in which mood swings both downward and upward. To date, the best-established biological theory about the cause of depressive disorders implicates underactivity at synapses where the neurotransmitters are monoamines, but conflicting evidence makes this theory questionable. Other perspectives suggest that depression involves interpreting a particular style of negative experiences. There is evidence for some genetic basis for depression. Research on bipolar disorder indicates that it is strongly influenced by genes; however, neither the environmental nor the biological factors that may induce the mood swings have been identified.

People with somatoform disorders experience some type of bodily ailment that is not due to a physical disease. In conversion disorders, a person loses some bodily function, such as sight or sensation in the hand. Somatization disorder involves a history of vague medical complaints. Behavior and emotions not only can cause physical symptoms with no physical basis, they can also affect the onset or course of a real physical malady. Research has shown that psychological factors may affect the cardiovascular and immune systems, for example.

Psychoactive substance-use disorders include, as the name indicates, problems of abuse or dependence on drugs that have psychological effects. The most common such disorder involves alcohol abuse and/or dependence. Research indicates that there may be more than one type of alcohol dependence and that heritability is greater for some types than for others. Learning mechanisms, beliefs about the positive value of the drug, and cultural pressures in favor of or against drug use play important roles in these disorders.

Dissociative disorders involve an inability to

recall some period of one's life because it has become separated from the rest of the conscious mind. The simplest form of this disorder is psychologically induced amnesia; the most severe form is dissociative identity disorder. Research indicates that dissociative identity disorder is much more common in women than men and represents an attempt to cope with severe childhood abuse. Some suggest an iatrogenic basis for some cases.

Schizophrenia is a serious mental disorder, the symptoms of which include delusions, hallucinations, disorganized speech and behavior, and the absence of some normal behavior. Schizophrenia is associated with an unusual pattern of activity at synapses where dopamine is the neurotransmitter. A person's predisposition to schizophrenia may be increased by prenatal stress and birth traumas. Sociocultural factors may also play a role in the onset or progression of the disorder as well as the chance for recovery.

LOOK over the table of contents for this chapter in your textbook before you continue with your study.

Notice that there are focus questions in the margins of the text for your use in studying the material. The following chart lists which Study Guide questions relate to which focus questions.

Focus Questions	Study Guide Questions
Basic Concepts	
1–4	1–15
5–7	16–19
8	20
Anxiety Disorders	
9–14	1–24
Mood Disorders	
15–22	1–17
23	18–23
Psychological Influences on Physical Symptoms and Diseases	
24	1–4
25–28	5–9
Psychoactive Substance-Use Disorders	
29–31	1–8
Dissociative Disorders	
32–34	1–6
Schizophrenia	
35–36	1–6
37–40	7–15
41–43	16–18

(handwritten note in left margin) mani- center stage ⊛

The Integrated Study Workout

Complete one section at a time.

Basic Concepts   (pages 611–620)

CONSIDER these questions before you go on. They are designed to help you start thinking about this subject, not to test your knowledge.

What are mental disorders? Are they illnesses with biological causes, learned patterns of maladaptive thought and behavior, or something else altogether?

Is the prevalence of particular mental disorders the same from one culture to another?

Why are men diagnosed more often with some mental disorders, and women more often with others?

How might labeling a person with a mental disorder affect other people's treatment of him or her? Can it affect the judgment of trained clinical observers?

READ this section of your text lightly. Then go back and read thoroughly, completing the Workout as you proceed.

Everyone's psychological processes are subject to disturbances of one kind or another in the normal course of living. We may experience a temporary lack of motivation that makes it difficult to keep up with our work or relationships. Anxiety may seem to tie us in knots, keeping us from sleeping, concentrating, or even enjoying our favorite activities. Confusion may overtake us, making clear, orderly thought seem beyond our grasp. But the disturbances that are a normal part of life differ from those that characterize mental disorders in intensity, duration, and frequency and in the extent to which they disrupt the individual's life.

1. Is *mental disorder* a precisely and unambiguously defined concept? Explain.

(handwritten answer) No – See Q's for #3 in this study guide

2. Complete the following statements.

   a. A(n) _____symptom_____ is any characteristic of a person's actions, thoughts, or feelings that could potentially indicate a mental disorder.

   b. A(n) _____syndrome_____ is the entire pattern of symptoms manifested by a given individual.

3. What three criteria must a syndrome satisfy in order to be classified as a mental disorder, according to the American Psychiatric Association's *DSM-IV*? For each, indicate a question that might arise in its practical application.

   a. clinically significant detriment

   Q- who determines what are the guidelines, whether something is clinically significant or not?

   b. internal source

   c. involuntary manifestation
   Q- anorexia or alcohol abuse involuntary actions?

The scientific study of mental disorders demands that we have some system for assigning them to specific categories. Categorization is important for learning about causes, treatments, and outcomes. From the perspective of the medical model, the assignment of labels to a person's mental disorder is called *diagnosis*.

4. The _____reliability_____ of a diagnostic system is the extent to which different diagnosticians, all trained in the system, reach the same conclusions when independently diagnosing the same individuals.

5. Distinguish between *neuroses* and *psychoses*. What inadequacy in these categories led the American Psychiatric Association to develop the original *DSM*?

   neuroses- anxiety = prevalent underlying cause

   psychosis - out of touch w/reality

6. Specify the overriding goal of the group that developed *DSM-III*. Describe how the creators attempted to reach that goal in *DSM-III* (and *DSM-IV*). Has the goal been achieved? Explain.

   define disorders as objectively as possible to attain high reliability. Remove assumptions about underlying causes or unobservable symptoms

7. The _____validity_____ of a diagnostic system reflects the extent to which the categories it identifies are clinically meaningful.

8. Some have argued that *DSM-III* and *DSM-IV* obtained reliability at the expense of validity. Explain their view.

9. Why do others counter that reliability is a prerequisite to validity?

10. How can further research lead to enhanced validity for *DSM* categories?

11. Can we say with confidence that the diagnostic categories of *DSM-III* (and *DSM-IV*) are valid? Explain. How does Robert Spitzer characterize them?

Of course not.

How common are mental disorders? Two large-scale studies of the prevalence of mental disorders in the United States have been undertaken. More will be said later in the chapter about the issue of sex differences in the prevalence of various disorders.

12. Look at Figure 16.1 (text page 615) to gain an overall sense of the prevalence of mental disorders. Of the disorders listed, which two are most common? Which two are least common?

depression, substance abuse.

Labeling has important clinical and scientific uses, but it also has certain drawbacks.

13. Describe some ways in which labels can have harmful effects.

reduce people's self-esteem, make them feel hopeless, bias people who interact with them.

14. What partial solution to the problem of labeling has been suggested by the American Psychiatric Association?

To label the disorder, not the person

15. What is medical students' disease? How can you protect yourself against developing a case of it?

Finding symptoms that you have in the literature you read & thinking you have that condition. Prevent by knowing it's a tendency & keeping perspective.

Clinicians, researchers, and scholars from various perspectives describe mental disorders differently and think about their causes in different ways. Each perspective has value and none represents absolute truth.

fee for service clinician

16. Characterize each of the following perspectives, and present supporting evidence where available.

a. biological

b. psychodynamic

c. cognitive/behavioral

d. sociocultural

Regardless of their perspective on mental disorders, all theorists acknowledge that disorders have multiple causes. These causes can be divided into three interacting categories.

17. Define each of the following types of causes.

a. predisposing causes

your unborn or acquired tendency to develop a particular condition.

b. precipitating causes

A <stress?> trigger that causes the condition to appear.

c. maintaining causes

factors that favor the continuation of the disorder e.g. isolating yourself in depression leading to further depression.

18. Classify each of the following examples as a predisposing, precipitating, or maintaining cause.

_____ a. Lin has more freedom to behave in socially unacceptable ways because many people think such behavior is due to her disorder and beyond her control.

_____ b. Winona's best friend has committed suicide, which has caused Winona to fall into a deep and long-lasting depression.

_____ c. Because of his bizarre behavior, Jeremy has been treated unkindly by strangers and rejected by friends, which makes his recovery more difficult.

_____ d. Ted has a genetically inherited susceptibility to schizophrenia.

_____ e. From early childhood on, Emma has learned to believe that life is hard and that there is little she can do to affect whatever happens to her.

19. How is the degree of predisposition to a mental disorder related to the amount of stress that will bring on the disorder?

inverse relationship

Though men and women suffer mental illness at similar rates overall, large sex differences exist for specific disorders. Sex differences in the rate of specific diagnoses may be due to biological factors, but may also result from sociocultural factors.

20. Briefly discuss three sociocultural hypotheses offered to explain such sex differences. For each hypothesis, present supporting research evidence.

a. differences in the tendency to report or suppress psychological distress

b. bias in diagnosis

c. differences in the stressfulness of men's and women's experiences

Anxiety Disorders (pages 621–625)

CONSIDER these questions before you go on. They are designed to help you start thinking about this subject, not to test your knowledge.

Anxiety seems to prevail in contemporary Western culture, so where do we draw the line between normal anxiety and anxiety that indicates a disorder?

Do people with irrational fears realize that their fears are irrational?

Are men and women equally likely to be diagnosed with phobias about spiders or snakes? about public speaking or meeting new people?

What is it like to experience a panic attack?

What kinds of obsessions and compulsions do people with obsessive-compulsive disorder experience? Are they fundamentally different from those that most people experience at times?

READ this section of your text lightly. Then go back and read thoroughly, completing the Workout as you proceed.

Evolution has equipped us to experience fear, an emotion with adaptive value. But because we are complex, thinking creatures living in cultural environments that present a variety of real and imagined threats, our fear can be triggered in circumstances in which it is not adaptive. In anxiety disorders, fear or anxiety is the most prominent symptom.

1. Are the terms *fear* and *anxiety* used interchangeably? Explain.

2. In comparison to other disorders, how easy are anxiety disorders to treat and how good are the chances of recovery?

DSM-IV recognizes five subclasses of anxiety disorders. In generalized anxiety disorder, the anxiety is attached to a variety of threats, real and imagined, rather than to one specific threat.

3. What are the symptoms of generalized anxiety disorder?

4. How prevalent is generalized anxiety disorder in North America? How accurate is this estimate likely to be? Explain.

5. Describe the predisposing and precipitating causes of generalized anxiety disorder, along with the typical etiology.

6. What might the sociocultural perspective tell us about the high incidence of generalized anxiety?

A phobia is a type of anxiety disorder in which an intense, irrational fear is clearly associated with a particular category of object or event.

7. Distinguish between *specific* and *social* phobias, and give examples of each.

8. Do people who have phobias fail to realize that their fears are irrational? Explain.

9. Explain the idea that phobias lie on a continuum with normal fears. Which type of phobia is much more common in one gender than the other? Why might this be so?

We do not really know what causes phobias; however, several hypotheses have been offered.

10. Answer the following questions about these hypotheses.

   a. How have behaviorists generally explained the development of phobias? Why is this explanation problematic?

   b. What is Martin Seligman's position on this issue, and what observation does his theory help to explain?

   c. Can phobias take different forms in different cultures? Explain.

Another class of anxiety disorder is obsessive-compulsive disorder.

11. Distinguish between obsessions and compulsions by filling in the blanks below.

   a. A(n) _____ is a disturbing thought that intrudes repeatedly on a person's consciousness even though the person recognizes it as irrational.

   b. A(n) _____ is a repetitive action usually performed in response to an obsession.

12. What is necessary for someone to meet the *DSM-IV* criteria for obsessive-compulsive disorder? How is this disorder both like and unlike phobia?

13. Are the obsessions of people with the disorder similar to those experienced by people who do not have the disorder? Do compulsions always bear a logical relation to the obsessions that trigger them? Explain.

14. What have brain imaging studies of people diagnosed with obsessive-compulsive disorder revealed?

15. How might this finding be interpreted? What are some effective treatments for obsessive-compulsive disorder, and what does this suggest about the role of the caudate nucleus?

People with panic disorder are subject to feelings of helpless terror that strike unpredictably and without any connection to specific environmental threats—which means there is no way to avoid the panic by avoiding the threat!

16. Describe a typical panic attack. Is the individual generally free of anxiety between attacks? Explain. What type of phobia do most panic-attack victims develop?

17. Present evidence suggesting that heredity can predispose individuals to panic disorder.

18. Do environmental events play a role in the onset of the disorder? Explain.

19. How might cognitive factors be involved in panic disorder?

Posttraumatic stress disorder differs from other anxiety disorders in that it is clearly connected to one or more traumatic experiences in the affected person's life.

20. Describe the kinds of traumas that most commonly lead to posttraumatic stress disorder.

21. What are the typical symptoms of the disorder? Do they always occur immediately after the traumatic experience? How can some attempts to alleviate symptoms actually compound the problem?

22. Who is more likely to develop posttraumatic stress disorder—victims of repeated, long-term trauma or victims of a single short-term trauma?

23. The rate of posttraumatic stress disorder has been much higher in U.S. veterans of the Vietnam war than in U.S. veterans of World War II. Why might this be so?

24. Do genes play a predisposing role in posttraumatic stress disorder?

Mood Disorders (pages 626–632)

> CONSIDER these questions before you go on. They are designed to help you start thinking about this subject, not to test your knowledge.

Are biological factors important in determining who suffers from depressive disorders and who doesn't?

Can certain patterns of thinking make people more prone to depression?

Why don't people who experience severe depression just pull themselves out of it?

Is there any truth to the popular notion that moodiness and creativity are associated?

> READ this section of your text lightly. Then go back and read thoroughly, completing the Workout as you proceed.

Some days we seem to experience life through a haze of sadness that affects our view of everything and everyone; at other times, we are full of laughter, warmth, and great expectations, impervious to the frustrations and worries that normally beset us. Moods are a part of normal psychological experience, but if they are too intense or prolonged, as in mood disorders, they can be harmful.

1. The term _____ refers to a prolonged emotional state that colors many, if not all, aspects of a person's behavior.

2. Identify and briefly describe the two main categories of mood disorders.

   a.

b.

Depression can powerfully affect a person's feelings, thoughts, and actions.

3. How is depression related to generalized anxiety?

4. What are the symptoms of depression? When is a diagnosis of a depressive disorder warranted, according to *DSM-IV*?

5. Distinguish between major depression and dysthymia. What is double depression?

Much biologically oriented research on depression has focused on the role of neurotransmitters called monoamines.

6. What is the basic contention of the monoamine theory of depression? What findings led to its being proposed?

7. The three major monoamine transmitters in the brain are _____ , _____ , and _____ .

8. Circle the two transmitters in item 7 that have been the major focus of research on the neurochemistry of depression.

9. How do the drugs used to treat depression work? What does Prozac specifically do?

10. Why is the validity of the monoamine theory still in question?

Depression may also be related to heredity and to stressful experiences.

11. What evidence suggests that genetic predisposition plays a role in depression?

12. Why is it risky to accept cause-effect interpretations of correlations between stressful life events and depression? What is the best evidence in *favor* of a cause-effect relationship?

13. What kinds of experiences are most often associated with depression?

14. What does Randolph Nesse suggest about depression from an evolutionary perspective?

Cognitive theorists suggest that it is not so much what happens to us as how we think about what happens to us that matters in depression.

15. What kind of observation provided a starting point for cognitive theories of depression? Illustrate the cognitive perspective by noting Aaron Beck's conclusions regarding depressed clients.

16. Answer the following questions about Lyn Abramson and Martin Seligman's hopelessness theory of depression.

    a. Describe the attributional style associated with depression in this theory.

    b. Is there evidence to show that this attributional style is *correlated* with depression? that it *causes* depression? Explain.

17. What is the vicious triangle of severe depression? Which therapy is related to which corner of the triangle?

In addition to the unipolar disorders of major depression and dysthymia, *DSM-IV* identifies bipolar disorders (commonly called manic-depression), which involve both upward and downward mood swings.

18. Distinguish between bipolar disorder and cyclothymia.

19. Characterize manic and hypomanic episodes.

20. Cite evidence suggesting that hypomania and mild mania are associated with enhanced creativity. Is the same true of the extreme mania found in bipolar disorder?

21. Describe negative aspects of bipolar disorders.

22. Comment on the heritability of bipolar disorders.

23. Name the drug that can help to control bipolar disorder.

Psychological Influences on Physical Symptoms and Diseases   (pages 632–636)

CONSIDER these questions before you go on. They are designed to help you start thinking about this subject, not to test your knowledge.

Can a person experience a problem as severe as blindness or paralysis for psychological reasons?

Can our minds really affect our vulnerability to physical ailments?

READ this section of your text lightly. Then go back and read thoroughly, completing the Workout as you proceed.

People with somatoform disorders experience physical ailments—even ailments as extreme as blindness or paralysis—that are not due to physical causes.

1. Identify two types of somatoform disorders described in *DSM-IV* by correctly labeling the following descriptions.

   _____ a. A person with this disorder has a long history of dramatic complaints about many different medical conditions, most of which are vague and unverifiable, such as dizziness or nausea.

   _____ b. In this disorder, a person temporarily loses some bodily function—even vision, hearing, or motor functions in more dramatic cases.

2. How did Freud interpret conversion disorders? How does the prevalence of conversion disorders in Western cultures today compare with the prevalence in Freud's day?

3. Where are dramatic cases of conversion disorder most likely to be found now? How is this related to trauma?

4. How has Arthur Kleinman linked somatization and depression? How is the incidence of somatoform disorders related to the Westernization of cultures?

DSM-IV notes that the mind can influence the onset or progress of a disease that has a physical basis. Psychological factors affecting a person's medical condition are not mental disorders but have been the focus of research because of their potentially important health consequences.

5. What relationship has been found between being widowed and developing physical diseases? What are some possible mechanisms for this effect?

6. What was Friedman and Rosenman's original hypothesis about the relationship between behavior and heart disease? Describe their evidence for this hypothesis.

7. Summarize the more recent view of the relationship between psychological factors and heart disease.

8. Describe some evidence that emotional distress can increase our chances of getting a cold. Explain how this effect could be mediated by the immune system.

9. Give a functional explanation of immune suppression during psychological distress.

Psychoactive Substance-Use Disorders
(pages 636–638)

> *CONSIDER these questions before you go on. They are designed to help you start thinking about this subject, not to test your knowledge.*

What is the most commonly abused drug?

Is alcohol abuse really so destructive?

Do some people have a hereditary predisposition to alcoholism?

How can people's beliefs or expectations make them more vulnerable to drug abuse?

> *READ this section of your text lightly. Then go back and read thoroughly, completing the Workout as you proceed.*

A psychoactive substance is a drug that can affect the way we feel, think, perceive, and behave. Psychoactive substance-use disorders involve the abuse of or dependence on such drugs.

1. Distinguish between *drug abuse* and *drug dependence*. Which term is synonymous with *addiction*?

2. Why does this section of the chapter focus on alcohol abuse and dependence?

Psychoactive substances exert their influences on mood, emotion, perception, thought, and behavior by affecting the biological functioning of the brain.

3. Define each of the following types of drug effects, and describe them in terms of the effects of alcohol.

    a. intoxicating effects

    b. withdrawal effects

    c. permanent effects

4. Briefly discuss research findings on the heritability of alcohol dependence.

Behavioral theorists attempt to explain psychoactive substance-use disorders in terms of conditioning.

5. How might operant and classical conditioning each play a part in alcoholism or other drug addictions?

Cognitive theorists focus on the importance of beliefs or expectancies concerning drugs such as alcohol.

6. Describe research evidence that teenagers' beliefs about alcohol can help to predict who will later abuse alcohol.

Other cognitively oriented studies have shown that a change in the way someone uses alcohol may represent a serious step toward alcohol dependence.

7. Explain that change. On the basis of such findings, M. Lynne Cooper and her colleagues have proposed two predisposing causes of alcoholism. What are they?

Some theorists point out that the beliefs that can make people susceptible to addiction arise in a particular social and cultural context.

8. Present some observations that are consistent with the sociocultural view on drug abuse and dependence.

Dissociative Disorders   (pages 639–642)

> *CONSIDER these questions before you go on. They are designed to help you start thinking about this subject, not to test your knowledge.*

What kind of person is most likely to develop multiple personalities (a condition that is now called dissociative identity disorder)?

What kind of life experience may cause the disorder to develop?

> *READ this section of your text lightly. Then go back and read thoroughly, completing the Workout as you proceed.*

Can you imagine losing all memory of your life up to this point and going on to establish a new identity? Can you envision yourself having a different identity within you that sometimes shows up in the outside world without your knowing anything about it? Dissociation is a process in which a person is unable to recall a period (brief or long) of his or her life, or is able to recall it only under special conditions, because it has become separated from the rest of the conscious mind.

1. How might dissociative disorders be related to hypnotic states?

DSM-IV distinguishes dissociative disorders in terms of their complexity. (*Note:* One of the most common errors people make regarding mental disorders is to confuse multiple personality disorder with a very different type of disorder, schizophrenia. Because this error is so often perpetuated by the media and in con-

versation, you may want to take special care to correct it in your own thinking.)

2. Describe the following disorders, listed in order of increasing complexity.

   a. dissociative amnesia

   b. dissociative fugue

   c. dissociative identity disorder (formerly called multiple personality disorder)

3. Briefly comment on the dramatic increase in the number of reported cases of dissociative identity disorder.

4. What profile of the individual with dissociative identity disorder emerged from the long-term study by Philip Coons and his colleagues? Do the results of other large-scale studies confirm Coons's findings?

5. How might repeated abuse during childhood lead to dissociative identity disorder? What may account for the fact that only some victims of severe childhood abuse develop dissociative identity disorder?

6. Some have speculated about other explanations for cases of dissociative identity disorder. What is their alternative viewpoint?

Schizophrenia (pages 642–650)

> CONSIDER *these questions before you go on. They are designed to help you start thinking about this subject, not to test your knowledge.*

Are the hallucinations experienced by some people with schizophrenia related to normal mental imagery in people without the disorder?

How might people with schizophrenia differ biologically from people who do not have schizophrenia?

What kinds of environments may tend to be especially difficult for children with a genetic predisposition to schizophrenia?

Can people recover from this disorder?

> READ *this section of your text lightly. Then go back and read thoroughly, completing the Workout as you proceed.*

The term *schizophrenia* comes from the Greek words for "split mind." Schizophrenia involves a split in the mental processes, such that attention, perception, emotion, motivation, and thought become disorganized and fail to work together. Bizarre thoughts and behaviors can result. The disorder is both serious and relatively common, occurring in about 1 percent of people at some time during their lives. Recovery, partial or full, is sometimes possible.

1. Though schizophrenia is equally prevalent in males and females, it generally strikes earlier and is more severe in _____ . In men the first symptoms tend to appear between ages _____ and _____ , while for women they generally occur between ages _____ and _____ .

2. Specify the two criteria necessary for a diagnosis of schizophrenia, according to *DSM-IV*.

3. Describe each of the following types of symptoms, and identify specific forms that each may take in schizophrenia.

   a. delusions

   b. hallucinations

   c. disorganized speech

   d. grossly disorganized behavior

   e. negative symptoms

Individuals with schizophrenia manifest a wide variety of specific symptoms. There is no single profile that fits all cases. Theorists have attempted to subclassify schizophrenia into different types based on the ways symptoms tend to cluster together, but no system of subcategorization has really been satisfactory.

4. Briefly describe three clusters of symptoms that emerge from factor-analytic studies. Indicate each type of symptom's tendency to go into remission and to respond to antipsychotic drugs.

5. Describe the three subcategories of schizophrenia included in *DSM-IV*.

   a. paranoid type

   b. catatonic type

   c. disorganized type

6. Why are systems of subcategories not very satisfactory?

7. How did a classic study in Denmark use the adoptive method to learn about the heritability of schizophrenia? What did the researchers find? (See Figure 16.10 on text page 645.)

Twin studies have also been used to shed light on the heritability of schizophrenia. (See Table 16.3 on text page 645.)

8. In twin studies, a group of individuals diagnosed as having schizophrenia is identified. These individuals are called _____ cases. Relatives of these individuals are then examined. The percentage of relatives of a particular class (for example, identical twin, nontwin sibling, and so on) who develop the disorder is called the _____ .

9. Table 16.3 shows that over many studies, the average concordance for identical twins is _____ percent, while that for fraternal twins is _____ percent, only a little higher than the concordance for _____ . Since the concordance for identical twins is not _____ percent, these results suggest that there is a strong _____ component as well as a strong genetic component. Reduced concordance could be due to _____ , but this does not account for all discordant identical twins.

10. Do we know anything about the specific genes that predispose people to schizophrenia or contribute to a given symptom?

Because the disorder is both common and very debilitating, the question of causation in schizophrenia has provoked particular interest. Research has not led to definitive answers, however. Biological causes are one area of active investigation. The predisposing role of genes has been very clearly established.

11. How might prenatal factors and birth traumas be implicated in schizophrenia?

12. Explain the dopamine theory of schizophrenia, and describe early evidence consistent with it.

13. How and why has the original theory been modified?

14. Summarize research showing that other brain abnormalities are sometimes manifested among people with a diagnosis of schizophrenia.

No one has yet found a behavioral precursor that can reliably predict whether a given person will develop schizophrenia. However, some average differences have been found among young people who do go on to develop the disorder and those who don't.

15. What average differences exist between children who do and children who do not later receive the diagnosis of schizophrenia?

Both the familial and the cultural environments may play a part in the development of or recovery from schizophrenia.

16. Describe some tentative evidence that factors in the home may promote symptoms in genetically predisposed individuals.

17. What does the concept of expressed emotion refer to? How has it been linked to the prognosis for the diagnosed individual?

18. What have cross-cultural studies of schizophrenia revealed?

> *Be sure to READ the Concluding Thoughts at the end of the chapter. Note important points in your Workout. Then consolidate your learning by answering the focus questions in the margins of the text.*

> *After you have studied the chapter thoroughly, CHECK your understanding with the Self-Test that follows.*

Self-Test 1

Multiple-Choice Questions

1. Which of the following statements is true?
   a. The terms *syndrome* and *symptom* are synonymous.
   b. A syndrome is the same thing as a mental disorder.
   c. A syndrome is the pattern of symptoms a person manifests.
   d. Syndromes are collections of related mental disorders, such as dissociative or anxiety disorders.

2. Research indicates that the susceptibility for schizophrenia involves a strong genetic contribution. Heredity would thus be considered _____ cause of schizophrenia.
   a. a predisposing
   b. a precipitating
   c. a maintaining
   d. both a predisposing and a maintaining

3. Studies show that the diagnostic categories established in *DSM-III* and *DSM-IV* have:
   a. both high reliability and high validity.
   b. low reliability but high validity.
   c. high validity, but the question of reliability is harder to answer.
   d. high reliability, but the question of validity is harder to answer.

4. Labeling people as having a mental disorder:
   a. is essential to our ability to study disorders scientifically.
   b. can affect their self-esteem as well as the way others treat them.
   c. is sufficient to establish the validity of diagnostic categories, provided the scientific community generally agrees with these labels.
   d. involves both a and b.

5. A person with no other mental disorders experiences anxiety that is not attached to any particular threat. The anxiety persists for a prolonged period and disrupts the person's daily functioning. This person appears to be suffering from:
   a. a specific phobia.
   b. obsessive-compulsive disorder.
   c. panic disorder.
   d. generalized anxiety disorder.

6. Behaviorists have suggested that phobias are acquired through:
   a. classical conditioning, which is consistent with the fact that most people with phobias can recall a specific experience that initiated their intense fear.
   b. classical conditioning, which is questioned on the grounds that most people with phobias cannot recall a specific experience that initiated their intense fear.
   c. operant conditioning, which is consistent with the fact that most people with phobias can recall a specific experience that initiated their intense fear.
   d. operant conditioning, which is questioned on the grounds that most people with phobias cannot recall a specific experience that initiated their intense fear.

7. Feelings of worthlessness, hopelessness and a lack of pleasure in life are particularly characteristic of a person with:
   a. anxiety.
   b. depression.
   c. hypomania.
   d. dissociation.

8. Though this theory is now in doubt, biological explanations of depression have centered on the idea that depression involves:
   a. reduced activity at synapses where monoamines are the neurotransmitters.
   b. overactivity at synapses where monoamines are the neurotransmitters.
   c. abnormally small cerebral ventricles.
   d. abnormally large cerebral ventricles.

9. The hopelessness theory of depression most clearly reflects the _____ perspective.
   a. sociocultural
   b. cognitive
   c. biological
   d. psychodynamic

10. A disorder in which the person temporarily loses some bodily function—becoming blind, deaf, or paralyzed, in the most dramatic cases—is:
    a. schizophrenia.
    b. dysthymia.
    c. somatization disorder.
    d. conversion disorder.

11. Research suggests that alcohol dependence is:
    a. heritable.
    b. not heritable.
    c. less severe than addiction.
    d. more severe than addiction.

12. An extensive interview study by Philip Coons and his colleagues suggests that dissociative identity disorder:
    a. develops as a way of coping with severe and repeated childhood abuse.
    b. is not a real disorder but rather a product of the therapist's imagination.
    c. is closely related to obsessive-compulsive disorder and shares a common biochemical basis with it.
    d. is more common in people who are incapable of being hypnotized.

13. Katrina, who has been diagnosed with schizophrenia, reports that she has been sent from a parallel universe to study the people of Earth. Her statement clearly reflects:
    a. a catatonic state.
    b. a delusion.
    c. a hallucination.
    d. negative symptoms.

14. Evidence suggests that the hallucinations associated with schizophrenia are:
    a. not related to the mechanisms of normal imagination.
    b. experienced as coming from inside the person's own head.
    c. much more likely to be visual than auditory.
    d. due to the enhancement of creative ability that occurs during active phases of the disorder.

15. Schizophrenia is found in about _____ percent of people overall.
    a. .2
    b. 1
    c. 4
    d. 11

Essay Questions

16. Describe the symptoms of bipolar disorders and distinguish two forms. Is there any truth to the notion that some people with bipolar disorders experience heightened creativity? Explain.

17. Discuss two different hypotheses concerning the biological causes of schizophrenia.

After you have assessed your understanding on the basis of Self-Test 1 and have tried to strengthen your preparation in any areas of weakness, GO ON to Self-Test 2.

Self-Test 2

Multiple-Choice Questions

1. Anorexia nervosa is an example of a _____ and supports the _____ perspective.
   a. culture-bound syndrome; cognitive
   b. culture-bound syndrome; sociocultural
   c. somatoform disorder; cognitive
   d. somatoform disorder; sociocultural

2. Which of the following does *not* describe a maintaining cause of a mental disorder?
   a. Norman's anxiety has made him unable to work effectively, which has caused him to lose his job.
   b. Camilla's depression came on as she faced the unexpected demands of caring for her infant son.
   c. Bradley's family and friends openly believe it will be impossible for him to recover from schizophrenia.
   d. Burton's phobia has won him a great deal of attention and sympathy from his wife.

3. The major goal of the people who developed *DSM-III* and *DSM-IV* was to:
   a. more clearly distinguish neuroses from psychoses.
   b. define disorders in terms of their causes.
   c. increase the reliability of diagnostic categories.
   d. organize diagnostic categories in terms of the amount of anxiety they involve.

4. According to research evidence, sex differences in the prevalence of anxiety and mood disorders may be due to:
   a. the greater tendency of men to express their anxiety and distress.
   b. gender bias in the diagnosis of mental disorders.
   c. the greater likelihood that males in our society will experience the kinds of stress that contribute to these disorders.
   d. all of the above.

5. The type of anxiety disorder known as a specific phobia:
   a. is more common in males than in females.
   b. is also called a social phobia.
   c. usually involves a fear of something that is feared to some extent by people who do not have a phobic disorder.
   d. tends to disappear once an individual recognizes the irrational nature of the fear.

6. The great majority of panic-attack victims develop _____ at some point after their first panic attack.
   a. bipolar disorder
   b. agoraphobia
   c. obsessive-compulsive disorder
   d. hypomania

7. Posttraumatic stress disorder is an example of a(n) _____ disorder.
   a. dissociative   c. mood
   b. anxiety   d. schizophrenia

8. Research following up on early investigations of Type A personality and heart disease shows:
   a. no relationship between psychological traits and susceptibility to heart disease.
   b. that it is negative emotions such as hostility that promote heart disease.
   c. that it is a rushed, overworked lifestyle that promotes heart disease.
   d. that original interpretations were correct.

9. According to the hopelessness theory of depression, the people most prone to depression are those who attribute their negative experiences to causes that are:
   a. unstable and specific.
   b. stable and global.
   c. unstable and global.
   d. stable and specific.

10. Which of the following is the most severe type of bipolar mood disorder?
    a. dysthymia   c. bipolar disorder
    b. major depression   d. cyclothymia

11. The type of substance abuse and dependence most common in the United States involves:
    a. cocaine.
    b. marijuana.
    c. alcohol.
    d. methamphetamine.

12. Which of the following statements is true?
    a. Psychoactive substance-use disorders include drug abuse but not drug dependence.
    b. Psychoactive substance-use disorders include drug dependence but not drug abuse.
    c. Drug abuse and drug dependence are the same thing.
    d. Drug dependence equals drug addiction.

13. Research has shown that nondrinking teenagers who believe that alcohol has valued effects—such as making a person more sociable—are:
    a. no more likely than other teens to become alcohol abusers within the next 2 years, a finding consistent with the cognitive perspective.
    b. no more likely than other teens to become alcohol abusers within the next 2 years, a finding that does not fit well with the cognitive perspective.
    c. more likely than other teens to become alcohol abusers within the next 2 years, a finding consistent with the cognitive perspective.
    d. more likely than other teens to become alcohol abusers within the next 2 years, a finding that does not fit well with the cognitive perspective.

14. Dissociative identity disorder is the most complex form of:
    a. schizophrenia.
    b. an anxiety disorder.
    c. a dissociative disorder.
    d. a somatoform disorder.

15. In schizophrenia, the term *negative symptoms* refers to:
   a. those symptoms most distressing to the patient.
   b. those symptoms most distressing to other people who come in contact with the patient.
   c. the absence of, or reduction in, expected thoughts, behaviors, feelings, and drives.
   d. the remission of classic symptoms such as delusions or hallucinations.

Essay Questions

16. Discuss the relationship between mental disorders and normal psychological experiences. What are the American Psychiatric Association's criteria for determining that a particular syndrome represents a mental disorder?

17. Describe the sociocultural perspective on mental disorders, and present two kinds of evidence that illustrate its value. Be certain to discuss the issue of labeling.

Answers

Basic Concepts

2. **a.** symptom, **b.** syndrome
4. reliability
7. validity
18. **a.** maintaining, **b.** precipitating, **c.** maintaining, **d.** predisposing, **e.** predisposing

Anxiety Disorders

11. **a.** obsession, **b.** compulsion

Mood Disorders

1. mood
7. dopamine; norepinephrine; serotonin
8. norepinephrine and serotonin
23. lithium

Psychological Influences on Physical Symptoms and Diseases

1. **a.** somatization disorder, **b.** conversion disorder

Schizophrenia

1. males; 18 and 25; 26 and 45
8. index; concordance
9. 48; 17; nontwin siblings; 100; environmental; misdiagnosis

Self-Test 1

1. **c.** A syndrome is considered evidence of a mental disorder by *DSM-IV* standards only if it meets certain criteria. (p. 611)
2. **a.** Although one's genetic endowment remains the same after one has developed a disorder, it is not considered a maintaining cause because the genes are not a *consequence* of the disorder. (p. 618)
3. **d.** (pp. 613–614)
4. **d.** Evidence suggests that labeling can change a person's self-esteem and the judgments of clinically trained observers. However, diagnosis is necessary to better understand and more effectively treat mental disorders. (p. 616)
5. **d.** (p. 621)
6. **b.** (pp. 622–623)
7. **b.** (p. 626)

8. **a.** (p. 627)

9. **b.** (p. 629)

10. **d.** Conversion disorder is a somatoform disorder. Somatization disorder is a less dramatic type of somatoform disorder. (p. 632)

11. **a.** (p. 637)

12. **a.** Other studies are consistent with Coons's results. (p. 640)

13. **b.** Katrina is showing evidence of a delusion, which is a false belief maintained despite compelling evidence against it. She would be reporting a hallucination if she said she heard voices telling her to learn more about Earth people or to come back to her home universe. (p. 643)

14. **b.** (p. 643)

15. **b.** (p. 642)

16. Bipolar disorders are mood disorders in which the individual has both downward mood swings, called depressive episodes, and upward mood swings, called manic episodes. The depressive and manic episodes vary in duration, and the individual may experience relatively normal mood between episodes. Cyclothymia is the less severe form of the disorder, and bipolar disorder is the more severe type.

   Depressive episodes involve the same symptoms found in major depression—sadness, a lack of interest in life, a reduced ability to experience pleasure, feelings of inadequacy and hopelessness, as well as effects on eating and sleeping. Manic episodes are typically characterized by feelings of confidence, energy, and power. Extreme mania may involve bizarre thoughts and potentially dangerous behaviors, while less severe manias may involve spending sprees, sexual adventures, or other behaviors that the person would not normally engage in and may later regret.

   People who experience manic episodes often report feelings of enhanced creativity, and there may actually be some truth to that impression in the case of cyclothymia. Cyclothymia is unusually common in highly creative writers and artists, who appear to do much of their best work during manic phases. People with the more severe bipolar disorder do not appear to enjoy this enhanced creativity, perhaps because the extremity of their mania leads also to disorganized thinking and behavior. (pp. 630–631)

17. A major focus of biological interpretations of the cause of schizophrenia is dopamine, a neurotransmitter in the brain. The dopamine theory of schizophrenia holds that the symptoms of schizophrenia result from overactivity at synapses where dopamine is the neurotransmitter. Supporting evidence comes from drug effects. The antipsychotic drugs that most reduce this neurotransmitter's activity are most effective in controlling the positive symptoms of schizophrenia. Drugs that increase activity at synapses involving dopamine can exaggerate existing schizophrenic symptoms or even bring them on.

   However, not all research findings are clearly supportive of the dopamine hypothesis. For example, *clozapine*, a highly effective antipsychotic drug, tends to affect dopamine to a lesser extent than traditional antipsychotics. Also, antipsychotic drugs that block dopamine are not effective for the negative and disorganized symptoms of schizophrenia. A modified version of the dopamine hypothesis is that schizophrenia involves an unusual form of dopamine activity, one that might include underactivity in some areas and overactivity in others.

   Other biological hypotheses focus on prenatal factors and birth traumas. The hypothesis involving prenatal factors is supported by evidence that, in cases of discordant identical twins, the twin who developed schizophrenia had a less favorable position in the uterus. The hypothesis involving birth traumas is supported by the finding that people with schizophrenia are more likely than others to have undergone a difficult birth, possibly involving oxygen deprivation or other forms of brain trauma. (pp. 644–646)

Self-Test 2

1. **b.** (pp. 617–618)

2. **b.** The unexpected demands of caring for her baby were a precipitating cause of Camilla's disorder. (pp. 618–619)

3. **c.** To accomplish this end, they attempted to define disorders in terms of objective symptoms that could be reported by the client or observed by the clinician. The reliability of most diagnostic categories in *DSM-III* and *DSM-IV* is reasonably high, provided that the diagnostic criteria are carefully followed. (p. 613)

4. **b.** (pp. 619–620)

5. **c.** This illustrates the fact that many symptoms of mental disorders lie on a continuum with psychological experiences that are considered normal. Fears of such things as spiders, blood, or high places are commonplace, but people who have

phobias about such things experience more intense fears that may cause them exceptional distress or may interfere with their lives. (p. 622)

6. **b.** (p. 624)

7. **b.** (p. 625)

8. **b.** (p. 634)

9. **b.** (p. 629)

10. **c.** Of the two bipolar disorders mentioned, cyclothymia is the milder one. (p. 631)

11. **c.** (p. 636)

12. **d.** (p. 636)

13. **c.** (p. 638)

14. **c.** (p. 639)

15. **c.** (p. 644)

16. The difference between "normal" and "abnormal" is largely arbitrary. This is due in part to the fact that many symptoms associated with mental disorders differ from common psychological experiences not in kind but only in degree. For example, most of us feel unattractive, dejected, or unworthy at times. Such feelings are common in depressive disorders but are generally more severe, long-lasting, and disruptive to the affected person's life. As another example, the delusions that distinguish schizophrenia from other mental disorders are false beliefs that persist despite compelling evidence to the contrary. Who among us is not to some degree holding on to a few beliefs that are irrational, that run counter to apparent fact? Our fears, erroneous perceptions, moods, and worries are similar in many cases to the symptoms of mental disorders.

The American Psychiatric Association has established certain criteria to help clinicians determine when that arbitrary line between the normal and the abnormal has been crossed. These criteria are (1) that the syndrome (that is, the person's pattern of symptoms) must involve distress and/or impaired functioning serious enough to warrant professional treatment; (2) that the source of the distress lies within the person, not the environment (such as prejudice, poverty, or other social forces that may lead a person to behave contrary to social norms); and (3) that the syndrome does not represent a deliberate, voluntary decision to behave in a certain way. Even with these guidelines, there is still considerable room for interpretation. We are probably all distressed by our feelings of depression, and we may find it harder than usual to function in our work or relationships, so how do we know when the distress or impaired functioning is serious enough to justify the label of mental disorder? (pp. 611–612)

17. The sociocultural perspective combines insights from various disciplines, including social psychology, sociology, and anthropology. It maintains that we cannot hope to fully understand mental disorders without taking into account the cultural contexts in which people are diagnosed. The culture in which people develop may exert a variety of influences—affecting people's values, their conception of what is normal and expected in society, their experience of certain pressures to act in certain ways or to avoid acting in other ways, even their opinions about what it means to have a mental disorder and whether recovery from that disorder is possible.

Labeling is an issue given considerable attention within this perspective. Sociocultural theorists point out the power of labeling someone as abnormal and as suffering from a given disorder. To label a person as having schizophrenia, for example, is to do more than indicate a diagnostic category for other clinicians to use in treating the individual. Labels can stigmatize. They can make an individual see himself or herself in a negative light, have less hope of recovering, and perhaps make less effort at recovery. They can also affect the way others deal with that person. Even clinicians may fall prey to the power of labels. Cross-cultural studies show that the chances of recovering from schizophrenia are better in societies that do not tend to label sufferers in ways that stigmatize them and foist negative expectations on them.

Another type of evidence for the value of a sociocultural perspective comes from the existence of culture-bound syndromes. These syndromes occur almost exclusively in particular cultural contexts. Koro and anorexia nervosa are examples of culture-bound syndromes found in Southeast Asia and Western cultures, respectively. (pp. 616–617–618, 648–649)

Chapter 17   Treatment

READ *the introduction below before you read the chapter in the text.*

For most of human history, people with serious mental disturbances have not received the care they needed; they have often been the victims of other people's ignorance and fear, as well as of their own disorders. Due in large part to nineteenth-century reformers such as Philippe Pinel and Dorothea Dix, as well as modern views on the needs and rights of people with mental disturbances, the treatment of the mentally ill is immensely better, but certainly not ideal. Although some research demonstrates that institutional treatment can be humane and effective, other research shows that the institutional environment can be dehumanizing. A move to deinstitutionalize people and return them to the community has only partially succeeded and has also created new problems.

People with mental problems may be treated in mental hospitals, general hospitals, nursing homes, halfway houses, community mental health centers, and in the private offices of mental health professionals. Mental health professionals vary in their training and in the kinds of work they do; they include psychiatrists, clinical psychologists, counseling psychologists, counselors, psychiatric social workers, and psychiatric nurses.

Research has shown that most people in the United States who have a mental disorder by *DSM* standards do not obtain care from a mental health professional. Moreover, the chances of obtaining such care differ as a function of sex, education, race, and income. Also, not everyone seeing a mental health professional has a diagnosable mental disorder; many are simply seeking help to deal with a life problem.

Regardless of where treatment is given or who provides it, clinical assessment is necessary to decide what should be done for the patient or client. Assessment, which includes the initial information gathering required for diagnosis, is an ongoing process, and its goal is understanding the person seeking help in order to create an appropriate plan of therapy. The assessment interview is the most common assessment procedure, but objective questionnaires, psychometric personality tests, projective tests, behavioral monitoring, and neuropsychological assessment are often used to supplement the interview.

Biological treatments for mental disorders include drugs, electroconvulsive shock therapy (ECT), and psychosurgery. Drugs are the most common type of biological treatment. These drugs can present problems in the form of harmful side effects and sometimes addiction. ECT is an effective treatment for severe depression; although it can cause some memory loss, a newer form of the technique minimizes this problem. Psychosurgery is the most controversial and least often used of the biological treatments.

Psychotherapy refers to any formal, systematic, theory-based approach in which a trained therapist uses psychological means to treat people with mental problems or disorders. Because there are so many varieties of psychotherapy, the chapter focuses on the most common forms.

Psychoanalysts and other psychodynamically oriented therapists try to help people with neurotic symptoms to recall emotionally charged memories that have been mentally buried, on the assumption that relief of symptoms will follow. Some major tools of psychoanalysis are free association, dream analysis, and the phenomena of resistance and transference.

Humanistic therapies emphasize the person's need to grow toward his or her potential—in other words, to self-actualize. Therapy is intended to help the person gain control of his or her life by becoming conscious of inner feelings and desires, undistorted by external influences. Carl Rogers's client-centered therapy is the most common humanistic therapy.

Whereas psychodynamic and humanistic therapies are oriented toward the whole person, cognitive therapy is more problem-centered. Cognitive therapists assume that much of the mental distress people suffer is due to maladaptive thinking patterns. The cognitive therapist's goal is to help the client replace such thinking patterns with more adaptive ones. Albert Ellis's rational-emotive therapy (RET) and Aaron Beck's cognitive therapy are well-established forms of the cognitive therapeutic approach.

Behavior therapy, rooted in the behaviorist principles of operant and classical conditioning, has close ties to cognitive therapy. In fact, to a considerable degree they have merged to form what is called cognitive-behavior therapy. Behavior therapy has been especially successful in the treatment of specific phobias. Three techniques, all involving exposure to the feared stimulus in order to extinguish the fear, are flooding, systematic desensitization, and exposure homework. Less effective and more controversial is aversion treatment to help clients overcome harmful habits. Other behavioral techniques include token economies, contingency contracts, assertiveness and social skills training, and modeling.

The various clinical approaches described can be used not only for individual therapy but for group, couple, or family therapy, in which the therapist works with more than one client at a time. In some circumstances, these types of therapy offer more benefits than individual therapy.

Does psychotherapy really work? By combining the results of many experiments, researchers have concluded that (1) psychotherapy does work; (2) no one kind of psychotherapy is better overall; (3) some kinds of psychotherapy may work better than others for specific types of problems; and (4) different therapists are effective to different degrees. Nonspecific factors, such as support and hope, which are not unique to any particular psychotherapeutic approach, are important contributors to the effectiveness of therapy.

LOOK over the table of contents for this chapter in your textbook before you continue with your study.

Notice that there are focus questions in the margins of the text for your use in studying the material. The following chart lists which Study Guide questions relate to which focus questions.

Focus Questions	Study Guide Questions
Care as a Social Issue	
1–3	1–5
4–5	6–12
Clinical Assessment	
6–10	1–8
Biological Treatments	
11–12	1–7
13–14	8–14

Varieties of Psychotherapy	
15–20	1–8
21–24	9–12
25–27	13–15
28–33	16–22
34–35	23–25
Evaluating Psychotherapies	
36–39	1–6

The Integrated Study Workout

Complete one section at a time.

Care as a Social Issue   (pages 653–659)

CONSIDER these questions before you go on. They are designed to help you start thinking about this subject, not to test your knowledge.

How were people with mental disorders "treated" in earlier times?

Are mental hospitals today generally doing all that can be done to help those with serious mental disturbances? What kinds of problems persist?

Besides psychiatric hospitals, where can people obtain treatment for mental problems?

What kinds of professionals offer mental health care?

READ this section of your text lightly. Then go back and read thoroughly, completing the Workout as you proceed.

The history of Western society's response to people with mental disorders is largely one of ignorance, prejudice, absence of compassion, and even cruelty. Throughout the Middle Ages and into the seventeenth century, such people were thought to be in league with the devil, and so were tortured and often killed. According to the more secular views of the eighteenth century, mental disorders were due to the unworthiness and degeneracy of those who suffered from them. The places in which these people were shut away were scenes of misery and horror. Only in the nineteenth century did significant reforms begin.

1. Briefly describe the work of Philippe Pinel in Europe and Dorothea Dix in the United States.

2. What inspired the movement toward deinstitutionalization that began in the 1950s in the United States? What alternative approach to care was envisioned by supporters of this movement? Was the dream realized? Explain.

Though some mental hospitals today are genuinely therapeutic environments, problems persist. There is reason to hope, but there are also obstacles to overcome.

3. How did David Rosenhan and his colleagues approach the study of psychiatric hospitals? What conclusions did they reach?

4. Gordon Paul and Robert Lentz compared the effects of different treatment programs for very dysfunctional patients in a state mental hospital system. Describe the treatment programs and indicate their relative success.

   a. standard hospital treatment

   b. milieu therapy

   c. social-learning therapy

5. Describe the approach taken by community intervention programs for the severely disturbed. Does this approach work? Do most people who need such services in the United States receive them?

Not everyone with psychological problems requires treatment in a psychiatric hospital or an intensive community intervention program. In fact, the number of people in psychiatric hospitals dropped from over half a million in 1955 to 62,000 in 1997. Most people have relatively mild problems with anxiety or depression and receive care at other types of treatment facilities.

6. Identify each of the following settings that provide mental health care.

   _____ a. Many older, chronic mental patients who would once have been in a mental hospital live here, but often without benefit of care from mental health personnel.

   _____ b. This facility offers custodial care for patients who require it and brief hospitalization for people experiencing acute psychotic attacks.

   _____ c. This is usually the treatment place of choice for people who can afford it (or have adequate insurance coverage) and who do not need hospitalization. Most mental health patients (72%) are seen in this setting.

   _____ d. The majority of psychiatric inpatients are treated in this type of facility, which is usually associated with less stigma than a psychiatric hospital and is often well located for visits from family and friends.

   _____ e. This place provides transitional living arrangements for people returning to the community after hospitalization. It is also called a group home.

_____   **f.** This offers free or low-cost services such as psychotherapy or
crisis hotlines and may also
hold classes, sponsor legisla-
tion, or do other work aimed at
prevention of mental health
problems.

The people who provide mental health treatment
vary considerably in the nature and extent of their
training and in the kinds of people they tend to treat.

7. List three types of mental health professionals
who hold a doctoral degree, and indicate the
characteristics that differentiate them from one
another.

   a.

   b.

   c.

8. List three types of mental health professionals
who have bachelor's or master's degrees, and
indicate the characteristics that differentiate them
from one another.

   a.

   b.

   c.

9. In what contexts is nonprofessional help for mental health problems sometimes offered?

A large-scale study done in the 1980s examined the
matter of who receives professional mental health
care.

10. Do most people in the United States who have
mental disorders by *DSM* criteria seek and
receive treatment?

11. Does the likelihood of obtaining needed mental
health care from a professional vary with sex,
education, race, or income? Explain.

12. Does everyone seeing a mental health professional have a diagnosable mental disorder? Explain.

Clinical Assessment   (pages 659–663)

> CONSIDER *these questions before you go on. They are
> designed to help you start thinking about this subject, not
> to test your knowledge.*

How do clinicians learn enough about a person to
choose an appropriate therapeutic approach?

Are projective tests such as the Rorschach valid?

How can a person be tested to determine whether
apparent mental problems have physical causes?

> READ *this section of your text lightly. Then go back and
> read thoroughly, completing the Workout as you proceed.*

How does a clinician know what a person with a
mental health problem really needs? How does he or
she know whether the current treatment is working?
Clinical assessment is the process through which the
mental health professional gathers the information

needed to treat a person effectively. Although it generally includes diagnosis, clinical assessment is a much broader enterprise that ideally continues throughout treatment and is designed to help the person providing treatment understand the person seeking it, including that person's current condition and treatment needs. Clinicians with different theoretical perspectives often disagree about the kind of information most useful to them in assessment.

1. By far the most common assessment procedure is the assessment _____ , which is essentially a(n) _____ in which the client may talk about _____ , _____ , _____ , _____ , and other relevant information in a structured or unstructured format. _____ behaviors may also be taken into account.

2. Characterize objective questionnaires and point out some of their advantages. Are they best viewed as substitutes for interviews or as supplements?

Psychometric personality tests, designed to measure a wide range of personality characteristics, are objective questionnaires developed through psychometric methods. The one most often used for clinical assessment is the Minnesota Multiphasic Personality Inventory, or MMPI.

3. How was the MMPI developed? Why was the original version often criticized?

4. Briefly describe the new version of the test (MMPI-2). Be sure to mention clinical and content scales, the L scale and the F scale.

Projective tests are intended to provide information about the client's unconscious wishes and beliefs.

5. What is the rationale for and the general nature of projective tests?

6. Briefly describe two projective tests, and discuss the validity of such assessment techniques.

Behavior therapists are especially likely to use behavioral monitoring, but they are not the only clinicians who do.

7. Define *behavioral monitoring*. Briefly describe a subcategory known as self-monitoring.

In some cases, psychological problems may be symptomatic of brain damage. When a clinician suspects this, neuropsychological assessment may be needed.

8. Name the following neuropsychological assessment techniques.

_____ a. This is a battery of tests that includes assessment of motor control, perception, and cognition.

_____ b. Pictures of brain sections are produced when the brain is subjected to a strong magnetic field.

_____   c.   Multiple brain x-rays are taken from various angles and analyzed by computer to reveal anatomical abnormalities.

_____   d.   Electrodes attached to the scalp indicate patterns of electrical activity in the brain.

_____   e.   This technique produces images that reflect the pattern of blood flow and the rate of oxygen use in different areas of the brain.

Biological Treatments   (pages 663–669)

> CONSIDER *these questions before you go on. They are designed to help you start thinking about this subject, not to test your knowledge.*

Can drugs calm anxiety, lift someone out of depression, or stop hallucinations?

What kinds of harmful side effects are caused by drugs used to treat mental disorders?

In what circumstances are people treated with electroconvulsive shock therapy? Is it safe? Is it painful? Does it work?

Can surgery be used effectively to treat some mental disorders?

> READ *this section of your text lightly. Then go back and read thoroughly, completing the Workout as you proceed.*

Biological treatments are designed to relieve mental disorders by affecting bodily processes. Contemporary biological approaches to mental disorders fall primarily into three categories—drugs, electroconvulsive shock therapy, and psychosurgery. Drugs are the most commonly used biological treatment. Although they may have desirable effects, drugs also commonly involve undesirable side effects and some are also addictive.

1.   Answer the following questions about antipsychotic drugs.

   a.   Comment on the beneficial effects of antipsychotic drugs such as chlorpromazine and other phenothiazines. (See Figure 17.2 on text page 664.)

   b.   Do these drugs effectively treat the negative symptoms of schizophrenia? What does this imply for the patient's quality of life?

   c.   Define *tardive dyskinesia*. List some other unpleasant or potentially harmful side effects of antipsychotic drugs.

   d.   A controversial issue in the use of antipsychotic drugs is that in some patients they might reduce the chances of full recovery from schizophrenia. Explain.

   e.   Comment on the newer antipsychotic drug clozapine.

2. Answer the following questions about anti-anxiety drugs.

   a. What drugs are most commonly prescribed to treat anxiety?

   b. How effective are the benzodiazepines?

   c. How do these drugs produce their tranquilizing effects?

   d. What are some risks of taking these drugs?

3. Answer the following questions about anti-depressant drugs.

   a. Two categories of antidepressant drugs are _____ , such as Tofranil and Elavil, and _____ , such as Prozac.

   b. How are these drugs thought to work?

   c. Cite evidence suggesting that these drugs help people suffering from depression.

   d. Comment on the side effects of antidepressant drugs.

When a drug is developed, we cannot, of course, assume that it will work simply because it is biologically plausible. We subject it to direct testing.

4. How is such testing typically done?

5. What are the overall results of such testing for antianxiety and antidepressant drugs?

6. Why do mere placebos work as well as they do?

7. What is spontaneous remission, and how common is it?

8. Explain the term *active placebo*. Why have some researchers favored their use in studies of drug effectiveness?

Public perceptions of electroconvulsive shock therapy (ECT) often involve images of brutality, even horror, inflicted under the guise of treatment. Such images are no longer consistent with reality. ECT as it is used today is both painless and safe.

9. Describe what happens in ECT today.

10. What disorder is most effectively treated by ECT, and how effective is such treatment?

11. How might ECT produce its antidepressant effect?

12. To what extent does bilateral ECT affect memory?

13. Does unilateral ECT to the right hemisphere reduce or increase such memory effects? Is it as effective as bilateral ECT? What about unilateral ECT in the left hemisphere?

Psychosurgery, still a controversial approach, is the least common of the biological treatments for mental disorders. It involves surgically cutting or producing lesions in parts of the brain in order to alleviate symptoms.

14. Describe the operation called *prefrontal lobotomy*. For which types of disorders was it used and when? Why did this treatment, once held in high regard, become virtually obsolete?

15. Describe the newer psychosurgical procedures, such as the cingulotomy, that involve electrodes. What are these procedures useful for? Are they safe? When are they considered appropriate?

Varieties of Psychotherapy (pages 669–689)

> CONSIDER these questions before you go on. They are designed to help you start thinking about this subject, not to test your knowledge.

How might remembering an emotionally charged experience help to alleviate someone's current psychological symptoms?

In what ways might a person's beliefs contribute to psychological problems such as anxiety or depression? How can a therapist help a person change maladaptive patterns of thinking?

How can therapy help someone unlearn a fear—say, a fear of dogs or of driving a car?

> READ this section of your text lightly. Then go back and read thoroughly, completing the Workout as you proceed.

Psychotherapy refers to any formal, theory-based, systematic approach to treating mental problems or disorders through psychological means. It is carried out by a trained therapist working with individuals, couples, families, or groups of unrelated people. Through talking with the client or clients, the therapist attempts to alter ways of feeling, thinking, or acting.

1. Define the terms *psychoanalysis* and *psychodynamic therapy*.

2. Discuss Freud's views on the role of early childhood experiences in neuroses. Be sure to distinguish between predisposing and precipitating experiences, explaining how the two lead to a diagnosis of mental disorder.

3. Why did Freud include the word *analysis* in the name he gave to his approach? What were Freud's principal techniques for obtaining clues to the unconscious? Briefly describe each.

4. Define the term *resistance*, and give an example of how it might be manifested. How is resistance interpreted by the therapist?

5. What is transference, and why did Freud consider it an important part of psychoanalysis?

6. How are insight and cure thought to be related in psychoanalysis?

7. Briefly summarize the case of the Rat Man as Freud interpreted it.

Most psychodynamic therapists today practice alternatives to classic Freudian psychoanalysis. They share with Freud's original approach the effort to bring problematic feeling into consciousness, the belief that current troubles result from mental conflict over past experience, and the use of the therapist-client relationship to promote understanding of the client's other relationships.

8. Briefly describe three modern psychodynamic approaches, indicating the characteristics that most distinguish them.

a.

b.

c.

Like psychodynamic therapies, humanistic therapies are designed to help people become conscious of their true feelings and desires; but unlike psychodynamic therapies, humanistic therapies expect those feelings and desires to be positive and life promoting. Carl Rogers's client-centered therapy is the most common humanistic therapy.

9. Why does Rogers call his approach *client-centered* therapy?

10. In Rogers's view, what is the origin of psychological problems?

11. In countering the client's maladaptive learning, the Rogerian therapist aims to provide three key elements. Identify each of the following.

    a. _____ reflects the belief that it is impossible to fake empathy and unconditional positive regard, that the therapist must really feel them.

    b. _____ refers to the therapist's attempt to comprehend what the client is saying or feeling at any given moment from the client's point of view rather than as an outside observer.

    c. _____ implies a belief on the therapist's part that the client is worthy and capable even when the client may not feel or act that way.

12. How are empathy, unconditional positive regard, and genuineness achieved and manifested from Rogers's perspective?

Cognitive therapies are based on the notion that people's maladaptive thoughts cause them unnecessary distress, leading to anxiety or depression. These types of therapies focus on conscious thoughts, attempting to replace maladaptive ways of thinking with more productive ones. Albert Ellis and Aaron Beck are pioneers of this approach.

13. What does it mean to say that cognitive therapy is problem-centered? How is the therapist-client relationship characterized? Which therapeutic practice among cognitive therapists is especially consistent with this characterization?

14. Answer the following questions about Albert Ellis's rational-emotive therapy (RET).

    a. What is the basic premise of RET? Illustrate by defining "musturbation" and "awfulizing."

    b. Explain Ellis's ABC theory of emotions. (See Figure 17.6 on text page 679.)

    c. Do irrational beliefs disappear once they are seen to be irrational? Explain.

15. Answer the following questions about Aaron Beck's cognitive therapy.

    a. What observations led Beck to develop his approach?

    b. Beck's cognitive therapy was designed to treat _____ ; it was later expanded to include clients with _____ disorders.

    c. How does Beck's therapeutic style differ from Ellis's?

Underlying behavior therapy are the behaviorist principles of classical and operant conditioning. Although traditional behaviorists would have ignored such mental phenomena as worrying or obsessive thinking, modern behavior therapy has become allied with cognitive therapy in an approach called cognitive-behavior therapy.

16. List several characteristics that behavior and cognitive therapies have in common.

17. How do they differ, according to Chris Brewin?

Behavior therapy is especially effective in treating specific phobias, such as a fear of flying or a fear of spiders.

18. Explain how a behaviorist would interpret a phobia in terms of classical conditioning. Why would extinction be an important phenomenon from the point of view of a behavior therapist?

In exposure treatments, the patient experiences the feared stimulus in a safe context—that is, in a manner that leads to extinction of the fear response.

19. Describe the following forms of exposure treatment.

    a. systematic desensitization

    b. flooding

    c. exposure homework

Behavior therapy is also used to treat maladaptive habits such as smoking, addictive drinking, and compulsive gambling.

20. Explain how maladaptive habits can be interpreted in terms of operant conditioning. What is the basic obstacle to eliminating bad habits, according to a behaviorist analysis?

21. Answer the following questions about aversion treatment.

    a. Describe the technique and provide an example.

    b. Is aversion therapy based on classical or operant conditioning? Explain.

    c. Why has aversion treatment always been controversial?

    d. What problem with the technique is illustrated by the use of the drug *antabuse* to treat alcohol addiction?

A number of other techniques are used by behavior therapists to handle a range of problems.

22. Identify each of the following techniques.

   a. _____ involves direct means to teach the client to be more assertive, effective, and comfortable in social interactions.

   b. _____ is a formal, usually written agreement in which one party promises to provide specific services or rewards if the other party behaves in a specified way.

   c. _____ is an exchange system in which patients earn tokens for performing specific desired activities and trade the tokens for objects or privileges they want.

   d. _____ involves teaching someone to do something, such as dealing with an angry spouse, by having the client watch someone else do it.

Psychotherapy often involves more than one client being treated simultaneously, as in group, couple, and family therapies.

23. What is group therapy? How does it relate to some of the clinical approaches already described for individual therapy?

24. Describe some of the special benefits of group therapy.

25. Explain some basic assumptions and practices underlying couple and family therapies.

Evaluating Psychotherapy (pages 689–692)

> CONSIDER these questions before you go on. They are designed to help you start thinking about this subject, not to test your knowledge.

What elements of the relationship between a therapist and a client are most important for helping the client?

Does psychotherapy really work? Are some forms of psychotherapy more effective than others? Are particular therapies better for certain problems?

How important to the success of therapy are such factors as a supportive therapeutic atmosphere or hope?

> READ this section of your text lightly. Then go back and read thoroughly, completing the Workout as you proceed.

Just as potential drug therapies must be tested, so must psychotherapies be put to the test. In order to evaluate their effectiveness, we must carry out controlled experiments.

1. Why are case studies not sufficient evidence of the value of psychotherapy?

2. The Philadelphia experiment assessed the effectiveness of two forms of psychotherapy for psychiatric outpatients suffering primarily from anxiety disorders. Describe the study and its results. (See Figure 17.10 on text page 690.)

3. List four general conclusions that have been drawn from hundreds of experiments evaluating psychotherapy.

   a.

   b.

c.

d.

The fact that therapeutic effectiveness depends in part on qualities of the therapist has led to further study of how nonspecific factors may play a role in treatment.

4. Explain what is meant by the term *nonspecific factors.*

5. Describe the factor called *support* and cite research evidence demonstrating the importance of this factor.

6. Describe the factor called *hope.* What evidence suggests that hope contributes to the effectiveness of psychotherapy? Why is it difficult to determine the extent to which hope contributes?

Be sure to READ the Concluding Thoughts at the end of the chapter. Note important points in your Workout. Then consolidate your learning by answering the focus questions in the margins of the text.

After you have studied the chapter thoroughly, CHECK your understanding with the Self-Test that follows.

Self-Test 1

Multiple-Choice Questions

1. Nineteenth-century reformers such as Philippe Pinel in Europe and Dorothea Dix in the United States sought to:
   a. release people from mental institutions so that they could be returned to the community.
   b. build institutions to provide humane care for those with mental disorders.
   c. replace psychotherapy with the biological treatments that they considered more effective.
   d. promote scientific research to determine the most effective forms of psychotherapy.

2. In a study of patients in a state hospital system, Gordon Paul and Robert Lentz found that the most effective treatment was:
   a. the standard hospital treatment, which involved both structured routine and drug therapy.
   b. milieu therapy, which involved increased staff-patient interaction, less dependence on drugs, and heightened respect for patients.
   c. social-learning therapy, which involved most of the elements of milieu therapy plus specific training in social skills.
   d. rational-emotive therapy, which involved teaching patients to recognize and alter their irrational thought patterns.

3. Which of the following mental health professionals has a medical degree?
   a. counseling psychologists
   b. clinical psychologists
   c. psychiatrists
   d. both clinical psychologists and psychiatrists

4. The MMPI, which is useful for clinical assessment, is classified as a:
   a. psychometric personality test.
   b. method of neuropsychological assessment.
   c. form of behavioral monitoring.
   d. projective test.

5. A psychodynamic therapist would most likely be characterized as a(n):
   a. teacher showing a student how to think in new ways.
   b. detective piecing together clues.
   c. gardener helping plants to grow in their own way.
   d. friend providing an atmosphere of warmth and concern.

6. Margaret keeps "forgetting" to go to her therapy sessions; when she does go, she refuses to talk about certain issues. Her behavior is characterized as _____ , an important concept in _____ therapy.
   a. transference; psychoanalytic
   b. resistance; psychoanalytic
   c. transference; humanistic
   d. resistance; humanistic

7. The Rat Man, one of Freud's patients, had an unconscious conflict between love and hatred for his father, and a conflict over whether to marry a particular woman. Which of these conflicts represented a precipitating cause of the Rat Man's disorder?
   a. the conflict over whether or not to marry
   b. the conflict over his feelings toward his father
   c. both conflicts
   d. neither conflict

8. Albert Ellis's rational-emotive therapy focuses most directly on the replacement of:
   a. maladaptive thought patterns with more effective ones.
   b. feelings of guilt with feelings of self-acceptance.
   c. rational, thought-based responses with emotional, feeling-based responses.
   d. fear-induced muscle tension with muscle relaxation.

9. Beck's cognitive therapy is most specifically designed to treat:
   a. fears and maladaptive habits such as smoking or gambling.
   b. conversion disorders.
   c. depression and anxiety disorders.
   d. schizophrenia and mood disorders.

10. Antabuse is a drug that reacts with alcohol shortly after alcohol consumption to produce nausea and headaches. Its use illustrates the limitations of _____ in helping people with long-term addictions.
    a. exposure treatments
    b. psychotherapy
    c. antidepressants
    d. aversion treatment

11. Don and Rosemary, a couple with marital problems, have agreed that he will leave the office by 6:00 every workday if she will refrain from complaining about his ambition. This couple has elected to use a behavioral technique known as:
    a. social skills training.
    b. modeling.
    c. a contingency contract.
    d. a token economy.

12. Schizophrenia is often treated with a class of drugs known as:
    a. benzodiazepines.   c. tranquilizers.
    b. phenothiazines.   d. tricyclics.

13. Imagine that you have just read a study testing the effectiveness of a new antidepressant drug. If these results are consistent with previous studies of this type, you might find _____ % improvement in the placebo condition and _____ % in the drug condition.
    a. 5; 80
    b. 25; 75
    c. 45; 65
    d. 50; 50

14. Electroconvulsive shock therapy (ECT) is used as an effective treatment for _____ and is now often applied only to the brain's right hemisphere to minimize the _____ problems that may result.
    a. schizophrenia; motor
    b. schizophrenia; memory
    c. severe depression; motor
    d. severe depression; memory

15. Prefrontal lobotomies, used to treat people with severe cases of schizophrenia and other mental disorders:
    a. have been a common and effective treatment since the 1930s for those who do not respond to drug treatment.
    b. are no longer performed, in part because they permanently damaged the patients' ability to make and follow plans.
    c. are a new, more refined form of psychosurgery that is nevertheless rarely used.
    d. have not been performed since the 1970s because they were shown to have no real effect on the patients' symptoms.

Essay Questions

16. Why is Carl Rogers's client-centered therapy named as it is? From the perspective of this therapeutic approach, describe the causes of mental problems, the aims of therapy, and two critical elements that must be manifested by the therapist.

17. What are exposure treatments used for? Explain the principles of learning on which they are based, and illustrate by describing one type of exposure treatment.

After you have assessed your understanding on the basis of Self-Test 1 and have tried to strengthen your preparation in any areas of weakness, GO ON to Self-Test 2.

Self-Test 2

Multiple-Choice Questions

1. In the United States, from the 1950s to the 1970s, reform was aimed at deinstitutionalizing mental patients and returning them to the community. This movement:
   a. failed to achieve either goal.
   b. succeeded in achieving both goals.
   c. succeeded in deinstitutionalizing many patients but largely failed to reintegrate them into the community.
   d. succeeded in deinstitutionalizing only a small percentage of patients but successfully reintegrated them into the community.

2. David Rosenhan and his colleagues carried out a study of mental hospitals by:
   a. surveying recently released patients; they found that patient-staff interaction in the hospitals was frequent and generally compassionate.
   b. surveying recently released patients; they found that patient-staff interaction in the hospitals was infrequent and often dehumanizing.
   c. posing as patients themselves; they found that patient-staff interaction in the hospitals was frequent and generally compassionate.
   d. posing as patients themselves; they found that patient-staff interaction in the hospitals was infrequent and often dehumanizing.

3. The general term for the process of gathering and compiling information about a patient for the purpose of developing a plan of treatment is:
   a. client-centered therapy.
   b. clinical assessment.
   c. evaluation research.
   d. behavioral monitoring.

4. Which of the following was *not* a technique utilized by Freud in psychoanalysis?
   a. dream analysis
   b. interpretation of patient errors
   c. flooding
   d. free association

5. In _____ therapy, the person seeking help figures out what is wrong, makes plans for improvement, and decides when improvement has taken place.
   a. psychoanalytic   c. rational-emotive
   b. client-centered   d. behavior

6. Carl Rogers believed that the therapist should reflect back the ideas and feelings that the client expresses as a way of achieving and demonstrating:
   a. genuineness.
   b. transference.
   c. unconditional positive regard.
   d. empathy.

7. Humanistic therapy resembles psychodynamic therapy in that it:
   a. is problem-centered.
   b. focuses on inner feelings and wishes.
   c. casts the therapist as the expert on the client's problems.
   d. treats self-actualization as a central concept in therapy.

8. According to Albert Ellis's ABC theory of emotions, the therapist should help the client to directly alter _____ in order to change
   _____ .
   a. activating events (A); beliefs (B)
   b. beliefs (B); activating events (A)
   c. emotional consequences (C); beliefs (B)
   d. beliefs (B); emotional consequences (C)

9. Aaron Beck observed that depressed persons tend to _____ , a pattern of thinking similar to what Albert Ellis labeled _____ .
   a. minimize positive experiences; awfulizing
   b. maximize negative experiences; awfulizing
   c. misattribute negative experiences to their own deficiencies; musturbation
   d. see their lives as the product of an unalterable fate; musturbation

10. The type of therapist most likely to employ homework assignments as a means of helping clients is a _____ therapist.
    a. psychodynamic   c. cognitive or behavior
    b. client-centered   d. biologically oriented

11. Agnes is being treated for fear of flying by learning to relax physically while imagining increasingly fearful scenes related to flying. Her therapist is using a technique called:
    a. modeling.
    b. systematic desensitization.
    c. flooding.
    d. aversion treatment.

12. Acceptance, empathy, encouragement, and guidance are aspects of an important nonspecific factor in therapy called:
    a. support.   c. hope.
    b. warmth.   d. eclecticism.

13. Antipsychotic drugs, such as chlorpromazine, are thought to work by:
    a. increasing dopamine activity in the brain.
    b. decreasing dopamine activity in the brain.
    c. increasing dopamine concentrations in the bloodstream.
    d. decreasing dopamine concentrations in the bloodstream.

14. Tardive dyskinesia, a serious and often irreversible motor disturbance, occurs in many patients who receive long-term treatment with:
    a. antidepressant drugs.
    b. antipsychotic drugs.
    c. placebos.
    d. tranquilizers.

15. The least often used form of biological treatment for mental disorders is:
    a. drug therapy.
    b. electroconvulsive shock therapy.
    c. psychosurgery.
    d. exposure therapy.

Essay Questions

16. Explain the roots of mental problems from the Freudian perspective. What, then, is the job of the psychoanalyst, and what are some means available for carrying out that job?

17. Why is it necessary to perform experiments in order to determine whether therapy is effective? What has analysis of such studies generally shown? Are different therapies equally effective or ineffective? Explain.

Answers

Care as a Social Issue

6. a. nursing home, **b.** mental hospital, **c.** private office, **d.** general hospital, **e.** halfway house, **f.** community mental health center

Clinical Assessment

1. interview; dialogue; immediate symptoms; home and work environment; family history; personal history; Nonverbal

8. a. Halstead-Reitan battery

b. magnetic resonance imaging (MRI)

c. CAT scan (computerized axial tomography)

d. electroencephalogram (EEG)

e. PET scan (positron emission tomography)

Biological Treatments

3. a. tricyclics; selective serotonin reuptake inhibitors (SSRIs)

Varieties of Psychotherapy

11. a. Genuineness, **b.** Empathy, **c.** Unconditional positive regard

15. b. depression; anxiety

22. a. Assertiveness and social skills training

b. Contingency contract

c. Token economy

d. Modeling

Self-Test 1

1. b. Although such asylums were built, they did not receive sufficient amounts of continuing financial support and so reverted to the conditions that had originally horrified reformers. (p. 654)

2. c. (pp. 655–656)

3. c. (p. 657)

4. a. (p. 660)

5. b. The therapist described in **a** sounds most like a cognitive therapist, while the one described in **c** sounds like a humanistic therapist. The description in **d** is nonspecific. (p. 670)

6. b. (p. 672)

7. a. The Rat Man resolved this conflict (linked to the predisposing cause described in **b**) by developing neurotic symptoms, which made it impossible for him to continue his studies and begin a career, and thus impossible for him to marry. (pp. 673–674)

8. a. By altering beliefs, one can also alter emotions, according to cognitive therapists such as Ellis. (pp. 678–679)

9. c. (p. 680)

10. d. Treatment with antabuse does not tend to produce a conditioned aversion to alcohol. When they are no longer taking antabuse, most people suffering from alcoholism resume drinking. (p. 685)

11. c. (p. 686)

12. b. (p. 664)

13. c. (p. 666)

14. d. (pp. 667–668)

15. b. (p. 668)

16. Carl Rogers used the term *client-centered therapy* because the approach focuses on what the *client* knows and what the *client* can do rather than on the therapist's knowledge and abilities. The job of directing therapy, choosing which path to take, deciding how to handle particular issues, assessing progress, and so on, is in the hands of the client. This therapeutic approach is especially consistent with humanistic psychology's respect for the capability and growth potential that lies within each person.

Rogers believed that mental problems stem from people's denial or distortion of the desires and feelings that lie within them. The denial and distortion are thought to result when people learn from parents or other authorities in their lives, such as teachers, that they cannot trust their own feelings or decisions. When this happens, people look outward, to be told by others what to feel or how to behave; but they cannot be satisfied in this fashion and may thus feel resentful, rebellious, or "not real" inside. Therapy is intended to help clients become aware of and accept their own feelings and desires and to learn to trust their ability to make decisions. Letting the client take the lead in directing therapy is fully consistent with this goal and powerfully communicates the message that what is inside the client can be trusted.

Rogers believed that empathy and genuineness were two important elements that the therapist must provide in order to create a climate conducive to the client's learning and growth process. Empathy is the therapist's attempt to understand the client's thoughts and feelings from the client's own viewpoint. Genuineness refers to the reality of the feelings and attitudes that the therapist expresses toward the client, such as empathy; if they are faked, the client will detect this fact and therapy will not succeed. (Unconditional positive regard—the therapist's belief that the client is worthy and capable—is another element you could have discussed here.) (pp. 675–678)

17. Exposure treatments are used by behavior therapists to treat phobias. From the behavioral perspective, fears are considered to be learned responses. A stimulus that can elicit an unconditioned fear response may be paired with another stimulus, which thereby becomes a conditioned stimulus capable of eliciting a conditioned fear response. Of course, what can be learned can also be unlearned, according to the behaviorist. If the conditioned stimulus is repeatedly presented without the unconditioned stimulus, extinction will occur. For example, if an intersection with a four-way stop sign was paired with the frightening and painful experience of a car crash in a person's experience, that person might come to fear such intersections. On the other hand, if the person is repeatedly exposed to such intersections without further harm, then the fear should be unlearned. Systematic desensitization is a type of exposure treatment in which a person relaxes while imagining increasingly frightening forms of the feared stimulus. Through the repeated expo-

sure, even though the exposure is only imagined, the fear is extinguished, or unlearned. (pp. 682–684)

Self-Test 2

1. **c.** (p. 654)
2. **d.** (p. 655)
3. **b.** (p. 659)
4. **c.** (pp. 670–672)
5. **b.** (p. 675)
6. **d.** (p. 675)
7. **b.** (p. 675)
8. **d.** (p. 679)
9. **b.** (pp. 679, 680)
10. **c.** (pp. 678, 684)
11. **b.** Alternative **c**, the other exposure treatment listed, does not involve a gradual increase in the fear level of the stimulus or an imagined presentation of the stimulus. Neither of the other treatments is used for phobias. (p. 683)
12. **a.** (p. 691)
13. **b.** (p. 664)
14. **b.** (p. 664)
15. **c.** (p. 668)
16. Freud believed that mental problems, in the form of neuroses, develop because of an interaction between two types of experiences: (a) predisposing experiences, which take place in early childhood and involve sexual and/or aggressive desires and conflicts; and (b) precipitating experiences, which take place later in life and more immediately bring on the neurotic symptoms. The person's emotions and conflicts are expressed in the form of neurotic symptoms because they are unacceptable and are thus kept from conscious awareness by a variety of means.

    The psychoanalyst's job is to help the individual become aware of the conflict-laden material buried in the unconscious. According to the theory, when the person faces and deals with such information consciously, neurotic symptoms will go away. The psychoanalyst must essentially prospect for and piece together clues about the nature of the underlying memories and conflicts to figure out how the memories and feelings of childhood are meaningfully related to present circumstances and symptoms.

    Two means of gaining such clues are dream analysis and free association, in which an individual talks freely about whatever comes to mind in response to specific cue words or in the natural flow of consciousness. The assumption is that what appear to be illogical and unrelated ideas actually reflect symbolically the unconscious memories and wishes that are at the heart of the problem. (Another means is to analyze transference, ways in which the patient relates to the therapist as a symbolic substitute for a significant person in his or her life. The therapist can also gain information by analyzing signs of resistance, which could include canceling appointments, silence, or efforts to redirect the discussion.) (pp. 670–675)

17. Life is full of ups and downs, and it is generally at the low points rather than the high points that people enter therapy. Therefore, the fact that a person feels better and functions more effectively following therapy is not a clear indication that psychotherapy was responsible for the improvement. After all, the person might have improved anyway, perhaps because of changing social circumstances, or an alteration in body chemistry, or any number of other factors. Only with the control possible through experiments can we tell whether therapy produces some improvement over and above what would have been expected otherwise.

In general, analysis of such studies has shown that psychotherapy is effective overall and that no one form of therapy emerges as clearly superior to others. However, some studies indicate that specific types of problems may be more effectively handled with certain types of therapy. For example, fear may be especially well treated through behavioral or cognitive means, while problems of self-esteem may be most successfully treated through humanistic therapies. (pp. 689–691)

Statistical Appendix

READ *the introduction below before you read the Appendix in the text.*

This appendix supplements the coverage of statistics in Chapter 2. Psychologists use statistical procedures to help them analyze and understand the data they collect. Simple techniques allow us to organize and describe important characteristics of a set of scores. Scores are often organized into a frequency distribution, which shows the number of times scores in particular intervals occurred. For example, a frequency distribution could tell us how many people in a sample earn between $10,000 and $15,000, between $15,000 and $20,000, between $20,000 and $25,000 and so on.

When a frequency distribution is depicted as a graph, the shape of the curve formed by the scores is important. Normal curves, or approximations to normal curves, are bell-shaped curves that are common in psychology. Measures of central tendency represent the center of the distribution, indicating a typical score in that distribution. The mean and median are two measures of central tendency that are based on different definitions of the "center" of a distribution. Measures of variability express the degree to which scores tend to vary from the central tendency. Variance and standard deviation are common measures of variability.

Sometimes we wish to compare scores. In order to do so, we need a language for sensibly describing relationships among scores. A score's percentile rank indicates the percentage of scores in a distribution that fall at or below the score of interest. Thus, if a person earned a score of 64 on a test and that score is at the 88th percentile, then 88 percent of the scores are at 64 or below. Standardized scores, such as z scores, provide another way of converting scores into a form that can be used for purposes of comparison.

Psychologists often ask how two variables are related. How is IQ related to success in college? How are scores on a test of artistic creativity related to later success as an artist? How is age related to perfor-

mance on a memory test? As explained in Chapter 2, a correlation coefficient indicates the strength and direction of such relationships. This appendix illustrates the computation of a product-moment correlation coefficient for a small set of data.

The final section of the appendix does *not* supplement Chapter 2; rather, it supplements the material on psychophysical scaling in Chapter 7. This section is not dealt with in this guide.

LOOK *over the table of contents for this chapter in your textbook before you continue with your study.*

The Integrated Study Workout

CONSIDER *these questions before you go on. They are designed to help you start thinking about this subject, not to test your knowledge.*

If a group of people are tested, how can we describe the performance of the group as a whole?

If people are given two tests—one on ability to speak French and the other on ability to comprehend it—how can their standing as speakers be compared with their standing as comprehenders?

What does it mean to say someone is at the 45th percentile on a particular measure?

How can we determine the degree of relationship between two variables, such as IQ and GPA?

READ *the Appendix lightly. Then go back and read thoroughly, completing the Workout as you proceed.*

Statistics are an important tool for psychologists, helping them to make sense of the data they collect. Descriptive statistics are useful for learning about the shape, central tendency, and variability of a set of measurements.

1. What is a frequency distribution? Describe how it is constructed. (See Table A.1 on text page A-1 and Table A.2 on text page A-2.)

2. Why is a graphical representation of a frequency distribution helpful? (See Figure A.1 on text page A-2.)

The shape of a distribution can be described in a number of ways. (See the four panels shown in Figure A.2 on text page A-3.)

3. Describe the shape of a normal distribution, or normal curve, and produce a rough sketch of one.

4. Why are normal distributions important in psychology? In general, when might we expect a distribution to approximate a normal curve?

5. Define the term *mode* and then distinguish between bimodal and unimodal distributions. Into which of these categories does a normal curve fall? Sketch a bimodal distribution.

6. Describe positively and negatively skewed distributions. Sketch an example of each type of distribution.

A measure of central tendency summarizes a set of scores in terms of a single number. That single number represents the center of the distribution. However, the "center" can be defined in more than one way.

7. Define the following two measures of central tendency.

   a. median

   b. mean

8. Compute the median and mean for the following set of scores: 3 5 6 9 12.

   a. median _____

   b. mean _____

9. Where will the mean be relative to the median in each of the following kinds of distributions?

   a. normal distribution

   _____

   b. positively skewed distribution

   _____

   c. negatively skewed distribution

   _____

10. Which measure of central tendency—the mean or the median—is preferable? Explain.

Variability is another characteristic of a distribution of scores. As with central tendency, there is more than one measure of variability.

11. Explain the concept of variability. Sketch two distributions that have the same mean but different amounts of variability. (See Figure A.3 on text page A-4.)

12. What is the range of a set of scores and why is it inadequate as a measure of variability?

13. Two measures of variability that take into account all the scores in a distribution are _____ and _____ . The measure of variability that is expressed in the original units of measurement rather than in squared units is the _____ .

It is often informative to compare a given score with other scores. For example, we may want to know how a given score stands relative to the other scores in the same distribution. Or we might want to compare score A's standing within its distribution to score B's standing within its distribution. In order to make such comparisons, we must convert scores into a form that permits us to speak of relationships among scores.

14. Define a percentile rank. Look at Table A.1 on text page A-1 and indicate the percentile rank of the score 61.

15. A _____ is one that is expressed in terms of the number of standard deviations that the original score is from the mean of original scores.

16. Answer the following questions about z scores.

a. How is a score converted to the type of standardized score called a z score?

b. In a distribution with a mean of 50 and a standard deviation of 10, the z score of the score 65 is _____ .

c. If a z score is positive, then we know that the original score is _____ (above/below/equal to) the mean.

d. The percentage of scores that lies at or below a z score of +2 is _____ . The percentage of scores at or above a z score of +1 is _____ . (See Figure A.4 on text page A-7.)

Statistical techniques also permit us to describe the relationship between two variables—such as the relationship between age and income, between IQ and creativity, between hours of weekly television viewing and grade point average. A correlation coefficient summarizes in one number the strength of the relationship (how related the two variables are) and the direction of the relationship (whether high scores on one variable tend to go with low scores or high scores on the other variable).

17. Which aspect of the correlation coefficient indicates the strength of the relationship? Which indicates the direction of the relationship?

18. Look at the scatter plot below and indicate whether there appears to be a negative or a positive relationship between variables X and Y. Is the correlation perfect? Support your answer. (See Figure A.5 on text page A-8, along with the corresponding discussion.)

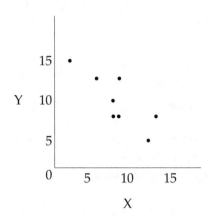

19. In "25 words or less," explain how a correlation coefficient is calculated. In other words, explain where this number comes from.

After you have studied the Appendix thoroughly, CHECK your understanding with the self-test that follows.

Self-Test

Multiple-Choice Questions

1. A normal curve is:
   a. unimodal and asymmetrical.
   b. unimodal and symmetrical.
   c. bimodal and asymmetrical.
   d. bimodal and symmetrical.

2. The scores on a particular test range from 30 to 100. Most scores center around 85, but a number are lower. The frequency of these low scores gradually declines as we approach the lowest score of 30. This distribution sounds as if it is:
   a. positively skewed.
   b. negatively skewed.
   c. normal.
   d. bimodal.

3. In which of the following cases are the mean and median of a distribution necessarily identical?
   a. bimodal distribution
   b. positively skewed distribution
   c. negatively skewed distribution
   d. normal distribution

4. If a distribution is skewed, is one measure of central tendency generally preferred to another?
   a. yes, the median
   b. yes, the mean
   c. yes, the mode
   d. no

5. Which of the following measures of variability take(s) into account all the scores in a distribution?
   a. only the range
   b. the range and the variance
   c. the variance and the standard deviation
   d. only the variance

6. Liz says she scored at the 57th percentile on a test of eye-hand coordination. This means that:
   a. Liz's measured score, out of 100, was 57.
   b. 57 percent of the people tested earned the same score Liz did.
   c. Liz has 57 percent as much coordination as the most coordinated person tested.
   d. 57 percent of the people tested had a measured score equal to or lower than Liz's.

7. If Carmela scores a 70 on a test with a mean of 60 and a standard deviation of 10, her z score is:
   a. +1.00.   **c.** +10.00.
   b. −1.00.   **d.** −10.00.

8. Which of the following statements is true?
   a. If a distribution of scores is normal, one can convert from a percentile rank to a z score, but not vice versa.
   b. If a distribution of scores is normal, one can convert from a z score to a percentile rank, but not vice versa.
   c. If a distribution of scores is normal, one can convert from a percentile rank to a z score, and vice versa.
   d. There is no way to convert between percentile ranks and z scores regardless of the shape of the distribution.

9. The best way to express the direction and degree of relationship between verbal SAT scores and interest in reading is a:
   a. correlation coefficient.
   b. percentile rank.
   c. psychophysical scale.
   d. measure of central tendency.

10. The correspondence between variable X and variable Y is illustrated below.

X:	1	2	3	4	5	6
Y:	4	5	8	10	13	19

Is the relationship between X and Y linear?
   a. yes
   b. no, because each value of Y differs from the corresponding value of X
   c. no, because the increase in Y that corresponds to a unit of increase in X varies
   d. It's not possible to say from the information given.

Answers

The Integrated Study Workout

8. a. 6, b. 7
9. a. identical to it, b. above it, c. below it

13. variance and standard deviation; standard deviation
14. 75th percentile ($\frac{15}{20} = 0.75$))
15. standardized score
16. b. +1.5 [$(65 - 50)/10 = \frac{15}{10}$], c. above, d. 97.72%; 84.13%
18. The scatter plot suggests a negative correlation, which is not perfect because the points do not lie on a straight line.

Self-Test

1. b. (p. A-2)
2. b. On the x axis, negative scores lie toward the left and positive scores toward the right. You can remember that a negatively skewed distribution is one whose tail "points toward" the negative end of the axis; a positively skewed distribution is one whose tail "points toward" the positive end. (p. A-3)
3. d. They could be identical in a bimodal distribution, but they are not necessarily so. (p. A-3)
4. a. (p. A-4)
5. c. (pp. A-4–A-5)
6. d. (p. A-5)
7. a. $(70 - 60)/10 = 1$ (p. A-6)
8. c. (p. A-7)
9. a. (p. A-8)
10. c. (p. A-8)